Building on
Community Bilingualism

Rebecca D. Freeman, Ph.D.

with a foreword by Jim Cummins

Caslon Publishing • Philadelphia

Caslon, Inc.
P. O. box 3248
Philadelphia, Pennsylvania 19130

caslonpublishing.com

ISBN 0-9727507-0-3 pbk
ISBN 0-9727507-1-1 hbk

Library of Congress Cataloging-in-Publication Data

Freeman, Rebecca D. (Rebecca Diane), 1960-
    Building on community bilingualism / Rebecca D. Freeman ; with a foreword by Jim Cummins.
      p. cm.
    Includes bibliographical references and index.
    ISBN 0-9727507-0-3 (pbk.) -- ISBN 0-9727507-1-1 (hard)
      1. Education, Bilingual--Social aspects--United States. 2. Education,
    Bilingual--Pennsylvania--Philadelphia--Case studies. 3. Multilingualism--United States. 4.
    Multiculturalism--United States. I. Title.

    LC3731.F725 2004
    370.117--dc22
                                                                    2003069600

Foreword

This is a radical book. The language policy directions advocated by Rebecca Freeman have the potential to radically transform the educational experience of all students in U.S. schools. The challenge she proposes to policymakers and educators is provocative precisely because few could argue with the goal of promoting a more language-competent society; few could dispute the abundant research highlighting the importance of building on students' prior knowledge—the linguistic and cultural capital they bring to school; and few could claim that we lack program and curriculum models that have repeatedly demonstrated their effectiveness in capitalizing on students' linguistic and academic resources (e.g., Freeman 1998; Oller and Eilers 2002; Thomas and Collier 2002).

It follows that our collective reluctance to implement programs that are pedagogically and linguistically enriching for all students is an ideological choice. This reality is illustrated in the plethora of sociopolitical arguments that have been advanced over the past 25 years against language enrichment programs for bilingual students (e.g., the notion that bilingual education is "un-American").

The radical nature of this book resides in its insistence that, as educators, we are not passively positioned by the societal discourses that swirl around our schools; we actively position ourselves and we define our identities individually and collectively in relation to these discourses. As noted in chapter 4,

> People have choices in how they define themselves, each other, the languages that they speak, and the educational programs and practices that they organize. Although what happens in any given situation may be powerfully influenced by larger historical, sociocultural, political, and economic processes, these processes do not totally determine what happens in the face-to-face interaction.

This applies to educators in the classroom as much as it does to adolescents on the street. Although the fiscal, physical, and ideological conditions under which we work frequently constrict our options, as educators we are never powerless. We have choices in the way we orchestrate the interactions between ourselves and our students in the classroom; we determine for ourselves what social and educational goals we aspire to attain with our students; we have options with respect to the orientation we adopt in relation to the funds of knowledge that students bring from their communities into our schools. In short, in our interactions with students and communities we can choose to create interpersonal spaces in which power is generated collaboratively and shared among participants.

For students, as the author notes, experience leads to expertise. By the same token, expertise does not develop in the absence of experience. If bilingual students are not socialized into communities of practice that use language powerfully to attain academic and personal goals, they are unlikely to develop expertise in these uses of language. If school language policies fail to articulate and support the goal of enabling students to use language powerfully, teachers are unlikely to pursue this objective. In many contexts, too many bilingual students currently are excluded from the educational experiences that lead to expertise in using two or more languages in a range of socially important contexts. Too many are excluded from the educational experiences that lead to more general forms of academic expertise. Too many drop out of school prematurely. The cultural, linguistic, and academic resources that these students bring to school are all too frequently lost to their societies as a result of the constricted interpersonal spaces that we, as educators, tolerate in our schools.

As a society, we reap what we sow. We have allowed one set of priorities related to the need for English language learners (ELL) to acquire proficiency in English to blind us to the importance for individuals, families, communities, and our society as a whole of encouraging these students to maintain and develop proficiency in their home languages. An either-or logic, inconsistent with all of the empirical evidence, has obscured in the public mind the both-and reality that emerges from the positive outcomes of bilingual programs in the United States and in many other parts of the world. As the research reviewed in this volume demonstrates, effectively implemented bilingual programs have the potential to enrich the educational experience of all students. Both ELL students and students already fluent in English can develop proficient bilingual and biliteracy skills at no cost to their academic development in English. As a society, we know how to implement academically effective programs that develop *both* English *and* an additional language. Unfortunately, as a society, we also choose to make these programs available only to a fraction of the students who might benefit from them.

The theme of *choice* runs through this book. The mandarins of educational policy rarely mention *choice* as a central concept of educational reform. Choice undermines control. Teachers are expected to "deliver" the curriculum as handed down, and they are held to account according to their students' performance on standardized tests. In some states, the tests are so high-stakes that virtually all teacher-student interactions are oriented to improving student test performance for several months prior to their administration. The distrust of teachers runs so deep in some curriculum programs that instruction is policed almost to the level of phonemes to ensure that deviations from the script are minimized. This "regime of truth" positions teachers as curricular technicians rather than as professional educators who orchestrate instruction according to the needs and possibilities of their students.

The power of this book lies in its detailed mapping of how educators, both individually and collectively, can choose to create interpersonal spaces that affirm rather than undermine student and community identities. The complexities of bilingual students' language experiences and choices outside of the school mean that there are no simplistic or formulaic solutions to promoting linguistic and academic achievement. However, we can explore with our students the nature of these experiences and the societal discourses that influence their identities and life choices. We can construct with them counter-discourses that challenge the subordinated status that has been imposed on them by the dominant society. We can create spaces where they can begin to articulate their own choices and become aware of the internal power they possess to determine the direction of their lives.

Through detailed ethnographic narratives Rebecca Freeman takes us inside the lives of bilingual students in North Philadelphia. We see the richness of students' cultural and linguistic experiences but also the pressures and contradictions they must negotiate as they explore alternative identity options. We explore with educators how to enable students to "read and write their lives" and to build literacy on the foundation of their out-of-school experience. We see how projects such as documenting family histories can validate, amplify, and extend students' funds of knowledge. We experience the dilemmas of trying to accommodate the mandates of standardized assessment without sacrificing students' education on the altar of accountability. At the school level, the approaches advocated in this volume gain coherence through the development and articulation of school-based language policies. These policies not only provide directions for the promotion of academic expertise, they simultaneously express our collective identity as an educational community and as a learning institution.

Choice implies power and agency. Recent educational policy reforms have diminished power and agency for both educators and students. This book initiates a dialogue on how to reclaim the interpersonal spaces where power and agency are generated. It asks where we stand and it illuminates landscapes where we might choose to travel.

Jim Cummins
University of Toronto

References

Freeman, R. D. 1998. *Bilingual education and social change*. Clevedon: Multilingual Matters.

Oller, D. K. and Eilers, R. E. (eds). 2002. *Language and literacy in bilingual children*. Clevedon: Multilingual Matters.

Thomas, W.P. and Collier, V.P. 2002. *A national study of school effectiveness for language minority students—long-term academic achievement*. Santa Cruz: Center for Research on Education, Diversity and Excellence, University of California-Santa Cruz.

Preface

Much has happened in the United States and internationally to bring questions of language education from the margins to the mainstream in educational policy and practice. The passage of the No Child Left Behind (NCLB) Act in 2002 in the United States means that schools are held accountable for the academic achievement of all students, and mainstream teachers and administrators across the country are actively seeking ways to ensure that their English language learners (ELLs) acquire the academic English and learn the academic content that they need to pass increasingly high-stakes standardized tests. Title III of the NCLB requires that states and school districts develop coherent language policies that outline how schools address the needs of their ELLs and that schools implement theoretically sound, research-based programs that provide evidence of student learning and achievement—now! While bilingual and English as a second language (ESL) researchers and practitioners understand the complexity involved in providing equal educational opportunities to an increasingly linguistically, culturally, socio-economically diverse student population, mainstream educators are just beginning to face these issues. This book is intended for mainstream teachers and administrators as well as for bilingual and ESL researchers and practitioners, who must work together to address this challenge.

Meanwhile, the events of September 11, 2001, focused national attention on the critical need for expertise in languages other than English in the United States. The National Foreign Language Center (NFLC) calls this increased need a "sea change in language" in our global society and has been working to convince the U.S. government of the need for a federal strategy focused on foreign language education similar to what we have seen in math and science education in this country. The Center for Applied Linguistics (CAL) and the NFLC argue that heritage language speakers, or individuals who use a language other than English in their everyday lives, offer an invaluable resource that schools, communities, and the nation overall can and should build on to address U.S. language needs. This book is aligned with the Heritage Languages Initiative that CAL and the NFLC launched in 1998 in the United States. It is intended for world/foreign and heritage language educators, researchers, and community-based activists who are working to promote the development of multilingualism and multilingual literacies on the local level.

One of the main ideas of the book is that states, school districts, and schools in the United States have choices about the ways they organize their programs and practices to address their goals, which, of course, must include all federal educational mandates and accountability requirements. Moreover, the choices that policymakers, program developers, and practitioners make have serious implications for individuals, their families and communities, and the nation overall. This book explains why and demonstrates how school districts and schools can formulate policies and develop programs that enable English language learners AND English speakers to acquire English, achieve academically at school, AND maintain and develop expertise in languages other than English. When schools organize their programs and practices in ways that promote multilingualism on the local level, individuals, families, communities, and the United States all benefit in important ways.

The book also recognizes that policymakers and educators who want to promote multilingualism through schooling in the United States face major ideological challenges. Drawing on anthropological and sociolinguistic studies of language learners at school, the book assumes that most U.S. schools are organized by what Ruiz (1984) has called a language-as-problem ideological orientation. That is, most U.S. schools either implicitly or explicitly see languages other than English, and speakers of languages other than standard English, as problems to be overcome. This deficit orientation is reflected in a wide range of educational policies and mainstream programs and practices, and it contributes to the subordinate status of languages other than English and to the poor performance of speakers of those languages at school.

Schools can, however, choose to see languages other than English, and speakers of languages other than English, as resources to be developed. And they can challenge and transform their programs and practices in ways that provide many more opportunities for ELLs, heritage language speakers, and English speakers than have been traditionally available to them in U.S. schools. Educators can choose to work together to develop policies, programs, and practices that build on community bilingualism, and they can work together to promote educational and social change on the local level. The title of this book, *Building on community bilingualism*, highlights the clear language-as-resource ideological orientation that structures this work.

This book is the culmination of nearly twenty years of research and practice in the interdisciplinary field of language education, including ESL, bilingual education, world languages, sociolinguistics, anthropology of education, and language planning. The question that drives all of my work, *how can U.S. schools organize their programs and practices so that low-income speakers of languages other than English have access to equal educational opportunities?* was stimulated by my first experience in a public school in Brooklyn, New York, in 1986. My research at Oyster Bilingual School, a successful two-way immersion program in Washington D.C. that has been in operation since 1971 (Freeman 1998) convinced me that a school can promote bilingualism, biliteracy development, academic achievement in two languages, and positive intergroup understanding and relations for the students it serves, which at Oyster included a large population of low-income Spanish speakers.

My introduction to schools in the School District of Philadelphia that serve the predominantly Puerto Rican community in North Philadelphia made me question how poor-performing schools in this low-income community could transform their programs and practices in ways that would enable ELLs, heritage language speakers, and English speakers to maintain and develop their expertise in spoken and written Spanish as a vehicle for improving their academic performance in both languages. I spent approximately seven years conducting ethnographic research in schools and homes in the bilingual community in North Philadelphia so that I could identify and document some of the linguistic and cultural resources that educators could expect to find in their students' linguistic repertoires. I also identified and documented examples of teachers who were actively building on this community bilingualism in their classes.

In November 2000, the School District of Philadelphia offered me the opportunity to direct a Title VII project to develop ten dual language programs in five different multilingual communities in Philadelphia, and the schools were to use either Spanish, Chinese, Khmer, Russian, or Vietnamese for instructional purposes. Then in November 2002 the district offered me the opportunity to consult on the formulation of a language policy and implementation plan that promotes bilingualism to the greatest degree possible for students throughout the district. The School District of Philadelphia is the fifth largest school district in the United States. It serves over 200,000 students from a wide range of linguistic, cultural, and socioeconomic backgrounds, and it has been the target of ongoing educational reform. This book pulls together all of my research on bilingual education, ESL, world language education, heritage language education, sociolinguistics, anthropology of education, language policy and planning, and action-research, and it provides concrete examples of language planning, policymaking, program, and professional development projects that are underway in the School District of Philadelphia at the time of this writing. Bilingual schools in the predominantly Puerto Rican community in North Philadelphia are the focus of most of my research and practice, but my audience includes mainstream teachers and administrators, bilingual and ESL teachers, parents and community members, language and education policy makers and program developers, and action-oriented researchers who are working in other multilingual communities in the School District of Philadelphia, across the United States, and internationally.

The book is divided into four parts. Part I is entitled "Promoting multilingualism in the United States," and it argues that schools and school districts that serve students who live in multilingual communities have a responsibility to promote bilingualism to the greatest degree possible for the target populations. Chapter 1 highlights the importance of challenging the assimilation strategy that has been dominant in the United States since the beginning of the twentieth century, and emphasizes that English speakers and English language learners, their families and communities, and the nation overall benefit from programs that encourage the development of bilingualism and biliteracy. Chapter 2 reviews federal and local mandates surrounding the education of language learners, and maintains that there is space in school districts and schools today for policies and programs that comply with all federal, state, and local mandates and accountability requirements AND that support the maintenance and development of languages other than English. Chapter 3 provides an overview of the types of bilingual, ESL, and world language programs that we find in U.S. schools today, and summarizes what research tells us about each of these program types. Chapter 4 offers a series of guiding questions that school-based language planning teams are encouraged to use to examine their local school and sociolinguistic contexts, make decisions about the type(s) of language education that are appropriate for that context, and address the challenges that they face as they develop and implement their programs.

Part II of this book takes us into the predominantly Puerto Rican community in North Philadelphia to investigate and document the ways that spoken and written Spanish and English are used and evaluated by students at home, at school, and in other key contexts in their lives. The rich ethnographic portrait that I present in chapters 5, 6, and 7 describes and interprets the language ideologies that we hear in conversations, read in site documents, and observe in everyday practices, and explains how these ideologies structure the kinds of opportunities that students, their families, and community members have available to them locally and in the larger society. Moreover, the chapters in Part II provide evidence of the kinds of rich linguistic and cultural resources that we can find in what many simply see as a low-income neighborhood that is filled with poorly performing schools.

Part III of the book illustrates how particular teachers who work in particular schools in North Philadelphia build on the linguistic and cultural expertise that their students bring with them to school as they organize their classroom practices. The three classrooms that are featured in chapters 8, 9, and 10 are in many ways atypical of classrooms that serve ELLs in the School District of Philadelphia because of their clear language-as-resource orientations. While the three case studies were located in different types of bilingual and ESL programs, and the teachers were concerned with translating different language and literacy policies into practice, they all highlight the critical role of teachers in the educational project. These teachers, however, are working in isolation and on the margins of the academic mainstream in each of their schools.

The chapters in Part IV demonstrate how educators across the levels of institutional authority in the School District of Philadelphia are working to bring language education from the margins into the academic mainstream in schools that are located in multilingual communities. Chapter 11 describes the recursive nature of language planning, implementation, and policy formulation in the School District of Philadelphia that the Title VII grant stimulated. Chapters 12 and 13 describe dual language planning and implementation projects in schools that serve the predominantly Puerto Rican community in North Philadelphia. Chapter 14 highlights community language programs that move beyond the Spanish-speaking population to address the language education needs of students living in communities with large numbers of Khmer, Mandarin, Russian, or Vietnamese students. Educational researchers, program developers, policy makers, and practitioners working in other multilingual contexts are encouraged to draw on the insider's account of language planning, implementation, and policy development that I share in this part of the book to stimulate creative thinking and action in other contexts.

The concluding chapter summarizes the main ideas that school-based language planners working in other multilingual contexts can consider as they plan programs that they believe are appropriate for their students, school, and community, and it highlights the kinds of challenges that language planners, program developers, and practitioners are likely to encounter as they work their way through the dynamic process of language planning and implementation on the local school and/or school district level. The particular programs that educators are developing in target elementary schools in the School District of Philadelphia are not meant to be uncritically reproduced in other schools. Instead, these detailed examples are meant to stimulate ideas about how educators in other contexts can work together to develop pedagogically sound programs and practices, and to formulate coherent policies, that promote bilingualism, biliteracy development, and improved cultural understanding and intergroup relations in ways that make sense in those contexts.

This work would not have been possible without the support of innumerable individuals and institutions. I would like to thank my colleagues and students at Georgetown University and at the University of Pennsylvania for their encouragement of my work throughout this project. I would like to thank everyone at the National Foreign Language Center for the Carnegie Mellon Fellowship that supported an important part of my writing, and for stimulating my thinking throughout that process. I would like to thank Colin Baker for his invaluable thoughts and Jim Cummins for writing the foreword. Thanks also to the Office of Language, Culture and the Arts of the School District of Philadelphia (formerly the Office of Language Equity Issues) for giving me the opportunity to direct the Title VII project that is featured in Part IV of this book. Special thanks to Cindy Gross-Alvarez, Mary Ramirez, Margaret Chin, and Chiny Ky, dedicated professionals from that office who have worked with me on these projects. Perhaps most importantly, I'd like to thank all of the educators and students that I have learned with and from in the School District of Philadelphia especially Maribelis Alfaro and her family, Maritzabeth Santos and her family, Teresa Alvarez, Melissa Silva, Marjorie Soto, Sol Cotto, José Lebrón, and Lucy Rodriguez for opening their classrooms, schools, and homes to me. I would also like to thank the language planning team members from the target schools in the School District of Philadelphia but there are too many to name here. These educators and students, individually and collectively, have challenged me to make theoretical developments in the field accessible to them so that they could apply them to their programs and practices in ways that make a difference in children's lives.

And, of course, I thank my husband for his (mostly) untiring support.

Contents

Part I

Promoting multilingualism in the United States

Part I of this book provides an important foundation for educators and policymakers who are looking for creative ways to promote multilingualism through schooling, and it draws on the field of language education, broadly defined. By language education, I mean bilingual education, English as a second language (ESL), foreign or world language education, and heritage language education. As this book demonstrates, the interdisciplinary field of language education is full of opportunities and challenges for students and educators who live and work in multilingual communities. When educators build on the linguistic and cultural resources that their students bring with them to school, individual language learners, their families, the communities in which they live, and the nation overall benefit in important ways.

Chapter 3 provides a detailed discussion of the different kinds of language education programs that we find in schools today, and it is informed by research on second language acquisition, biliteracy development, language teaching and learning, and program effectiveness. However, because there is so much confusion and controversy in the field, I will clarify how I use the terms "bilingual education," "ESL," "foreign" or "world language education," and "heritage language education" throughout this book.

- Bilingual education: All bilingual education programs use two
  languages for instructional purposes. However, we find different
  kinds of bilingual education programs in practice that have different
  ideological orientations, different target populations, different goals,
  different program structures, and different outcomes. A critical distinction is made between the transitional and dual language models
  of bilingual education. Transitional bilingual programs exclusively
  target English language learners (ELLs). Their goals are English lan-

guage development and academic achievement in English, and they use the students' native language to facilitate their academic and cognitive development while the ELLs acquire English. In contrast, dual language programs can target ELLs and/or English speakers. They use two languages for instructional purposes throughout the duration of the program, and they aim for bilingualism, biliteracy development, academic achievement in two languages, and positive cultural understanding.[1]

- English as a second language: All ESL programs and/or classes exclusively target ELLs who are living in contexts in which English is used as the language of wider communication (e.g., in the United States, United Kingdom, Australia), and they use English for instructional purposes. We find different types of ESL programs in practice that have different goals, different program structures, and different outcomes.

- Foreign/world language education: "Foreign" or "world" language programs teach the target language as a subject area for students who do not live in contexts (homes, communities, societies) that use that language as a medium of communication (e.g., Spanish as a world language for monolingual English speakers who attend U.S. public schools; English as a foreign language for Koreans who study English at school in Korea). In this book I use the term "world language" to refer to this type of language education program.

- Heritage language education: The term "heritage language" refers to a home language (indigenous, immigrant, colonial) that is part of an individual's linguistic repertoire. Heritage language speakers, as a group, have a wide range of expertise in their heritage language and in the dominant societal language. Some heritage language speakers may be able to speak, understand, read, and write their heritage language as well as the dominant societal language; other heritage language speakers may only understand their heritage language when someone (e.g., a family or community member) speaks to them about a familiar topic. Heritage language programs promote the

---

1. Following Hornberger (1991), I distinguish between bilingual education models and program types. Educational models are broader categories of abstraction than than program types. Models are defined in terms of their language, cultural and social goals. Program types are defined in terms of characteristics relating to student population, teachers, and program structure.

maintenance and development of heritage languages (e.g., Spanish for Spanish speakers; Mandarin for Chinese speakers). There are a wide range of program types and structures but very little research on program outcomes.

As I emphasize throughout the book, when we look across school and community contexts, we find a wide range of variation within and across program types. This kind of variation is to be expected because schools determine the type of language education program that is appropriate for their target populations, school, and community given the resources and constraints they have to work with, and they adapt their programs and practices accordingly.

While the focus of Part I of this book is on schools and school districts in the United States, the chapters are intended to have a wider appeal. Educational practitioners, policymakers, and researchers who work in other national contexts are encouraged to draw on the detail presented about U.S. educational policies, programs, research, and practice to stimulate their thinking about ways to promote multilingualism through schooling in their own contexts. Although the particulars vary tremendously across schools, communities, and nations, the general principles and processes described here are intended to stimulate thinking and action more broadly.

There are four chapters in Part I. Together these chapters provide the foundation for the ethnographic study of bilingualism and education that I conducted in the Puerto Rican community in North Philadelphia from 1996 to 2001, which I present in Parts II and III of the book. The chapters in Part I also provide the framework for the language planning projects that I have directed in the School District of Philadelphia since 2000, which I present in Part IV of the book. The remainder of this introduction provides an overview of the chapters in Part I.

Chapter 1 presents the rationale for the book, and is entitled *Why U.S. schools should promote multilingualism*. I begin this chapter with a summary of the demographic changes that we see throughout the United States, to highlight the tremendous growth in the use of a wide range of languages other than English. I also argue against the assimilation strategy that has dominated the experiences of ELLs in the United States since the beginning of the twentieth century. Then I review the increasing demand for individuals who have expertise in more than one language and who can function in diverse cultural contexts, and I argue that community and heritage languages are important resources that schools can and should build on in effort to meet local community and national language needs. Chapter 1 concludes with an outline of the benefits of bilingualism for ELLs, English speakers, their families, local communities, and the nation overall.

Chapter 2 takes us to the policy level to argue for school language policies that promote multilingualism. I begin this chapter with an overview of language policies that we have seen in the United States on the national and state levels over the last several decades, a period of evolution and change in the educational policies regarding how schools provide equal access to educational opportunities for ELLs. These changes reflect developments in our understanding of effective programs and practices for ELLs as well as competing ideological orientations toward linguistic and cultural diversity in the United States. Title III of the No Child Left Behind Act of 2001 is the most recent national-level language policy in the United States, and it holds states, school districts, and local schools accountable for the English language development and academic achievement in English of all ELLs. However, Title III also leaves room for choices in the ways that states, school districts, and schools organize their programs and practices to meet federal accountability requirements, choices that have important implications for students, families, local communities, and U.S. society overall.

Chapter 3 is intended to help K–12 educators and policy makers make informed decisions about language education based on research on second language acquisition, biliteracy development, language teaching and learning, and program effectiveness. This chapter reviews the literature on bilingual education, ESL, and world language education. The chapter also highlights the effectiveness of bilingual education programs that promote what Lambert and Tucker (1972) call additive bilingualism, or programs that encourage language learners to broaden their linguistic range in their home language while they acquire or add a second language. Clearly, the time is right for educators to work with local communities and build on community bilingualism.

Schools can lead the effort to promote multilingualism on the local level in ways that benefit individual language users, their communities, and the nation overall. Chapter 4 provides an important foundation for schools as they work through this process. This chapter begins with a theoretical orientation that explains how schools can promote educational and social change on the local level by developing more effective language education programs, and then it provides a series of guiding questions that school-based language planning teams can use to facilitate their language planning efforts. This chapter argues that there is no one-size-fits-all type of language education program that can address the language and learning needs of all students. Rather, educators are encouraged to work together and think creatively about theory, research, policy, and practice as they develop programs that they believe are appropriate for their local school and community context.

Language educators face major challenges in their efforts to promote multilingualism in the United States, many of which are ideological. For example, since the beginning of the twentieth century, languages other than English have generally been viewed as problems that speakers of these languages must overcome in order to participate and achieve in mainstream U.S. schools and society (Ruiz 1984). Children who speak languages other than English often resist using their home languages because they are socially stigmatized, and these children tend to become English dominant. Lambert and Tucker (1972) use the term "subtractive bilingualism" to refer to this situation because the new language (e.g., English) takes away from or replaces the home language over time. This language-as-problem orientation has increased in recent years in many parts of the country, and we have seen English-only movements and legislation in a backlash against bilingual education in several states.

English-only language ideologies are not limited to beliefs and practices about language use for ELLs. There is a widespread assumption in the United States that since English functions as an international language, English speakers simply do not need to develop expertise in other languages. This ideological orientation reflects the dominance of English in mainstream U.S. society and the value of English in the international marketplace. This orientation also influences whether and how people learn and use languages other than English. Language educators must listen to local beliefs about language use and language teaching and learning, and we must observe how these beliefs structure opportunities for language learners. When addressing questions from parents, educators, or community members, language educators must also respond with facts about the benefits of multilingualism.

Part I of this book argues that schools that serve multilingual communities in the United States have a responsibility to organize their programs and practices in ways that promote additive bilingualism to the greatest degree possible for all of their students. Together the chapters in Part I provide the foundation that teachers, administrators, and policymakers need to address a myriad of questions that parents and other concerned citizens have about language education, and to begin to develop coherent policies and pedagogically sound programs and practices on the local school and school district levels. These chapters also provide the foundation that readers need to understand Parts II, III, and IV of this book, which illustrate how teachers and administrators are working to build on community bilingualism in the School District of Philadelphia at the time of this writing.

1

Why U.S. schools should promote multilingualism

This chapter argues that schools that serve multilingual communities should promote the maintenance and development of the languages used in the community, and it is divided into three parts. First I describe the changing demographics that we see in the United States to illustrate the scope of the linguistic and cultural diversity that we find within and across communities today, and I critique the assimilation strategy that has been dominant in the United States since the beginning of the twenty first century. Then I review the changing language needs that challenge individuals, families, communities, and the nation overall as we move into the twentieth century. I conclude the chapter with a summary of the benefits of bilingualism for English language learners (ELLs), heritage language speakers, and English speakers. As this chapter makes clear, not only do individual language users have much to gain when U.S. schools promote multilingualism, local communities and the nation overall also benefit.

Contrary to common assumption, bilingualism and bilingual education were actually quite widespread in the United States until the early 1900s. While English had become the dominant language throughout the thirteen colonies by the late seventeenth century, it was still possible to hear, for example, German, Dutch, French, Swedish, and Polish spoken in different communities. During this time, local community-based organizations and schools took responsibility for promoting the maintenance and development of the languages used by community members. However, changing immigration patterns in the 1900s challenged linguistic and cultural tolerance, and monolingualism in English came to be equated with political loyalty to the United States. Since the beginning of the twentieth century immigrants to the United States have tended to abandon their home languages as they assimilate to monolingualism in English, and U.S. public schools have become important instruments in this assimilation process (see Freeman 1998; Heath 1981; McGroarty 1992, Peyton et al. 2001 for further discussions).

Educators in U.S. public schools today are required to provide educational programs and practices that enable all students to reach high standards across the content areas in English, and these educators are held accountable for student performance (see chapter 2 for further discussion). Given the enormity of this task, especially in schools that have too few resources to adequately serve increasing numbers of students who speak languages other than English and/or who have little academic preparation in their native language, many ask why U.S. schools should promote the maintenance and development of languages other than English. For example, in low-income urban areas that have large populations of ELLs, some ask whether instruction in a language other than English takes away from the time that ELLs need to develop basic skills in English. Many question whether low-income English speakers who are struggling to learn to read and write in English, their native language, can handle the demands of learning an additional language.

While the questions we hear demonstrate a genuine concern for the academic achievement and social integration of language learners, they also reflect ideological assumptions about speakers of languages and about what these speakers can and/or cannot, should and/or should not do with languages. Language educators must be prepared to answer these kinds of questions with facts about the benefits of bilingualism for English speakers and for speakers of other languages. When parents, educators, and other concerned citizens clearly understand the negative implications of the assimilation strategy on the one hand and the benefits of bilingualism on the other, they can begin to build on community bilingualism.

Promoting heritage and community language development

The United States is experiencing a period of unprecedented demographic change that has led to an enormous increase in linguistic and cultural diversity throughout the country. This section briefly reviews these changes and highlights the need for educators to build on the linguistic and cultural resources that students bring with them to school. When educators promote the maintenance and development of languages other than English on the local level, schools can begin to reverse the assimilationist trend that has been dominant in the United States since the early twentieth century.

According to Census 2000, the foreign-born population in the United States reached over 30 million, which is slightly over 10 percent of the resident population (Peyton et al. 2001). While the general U.S. population grew at a rate of 17 percent (from 227 million to 275 million) from 1980 to 2000, the rate of growth varied tremendously across the different ethnic/racial groups in the United States. Lindholm-Leary (2000) reviews the trends that we have seen over the past two decades, and she outlines the kinds of changes that we can expect to see across ethnic groups over the next fifty years.

- The Hispanic[1] population is currently the fastest growing population. This population increased by 83 percent from 1980 to 2000. In 2000, Hispanics represented 11.7 percent of the total U.S. population. This population is expected to double to 24.3 percent of the total U.S. population by 2050, which means that in less than fifty years nearly one-quarter of the U.S. population will be Hispanic.

- The Asian-American population increased by 153 percent from 1980 to 2000. In 2000, Asian Americans represented 3.8 percent of the total U.S. population. This population is expected to more than double, to 8.9 percent, by 2050.

- The African-American population has remained more or less stable over the last two decades, and´ population is expected to remain more or less stable over the next fifty years. African Americans represented 12.2 percent of the population in 2000 and are expected to represent 13.2 percent of the U.S. population in 2050.

- The Native-American population has remained more or less stable over the last two decades, and this population is expected to remain more or less stable over the next fifty years. In 2000, Native Americans made up 0.79 percent of the population and are expected to represent 0.8 percent of the total U.S. population in 2050.

- The European-American population decreased from 1980 to 2000 by 9 percent. In 2000, 71.6 percent of the population was European American. This population is expected to decrease to 52 percent of the total population by 2050.

As these data make clear, the "minority" population is growing rapidly, in part owing to continuing immigration and in part owing to the higher birth rates in non-European-American families, and the "majority" population is steadily decreasing. According to these projections, by the year 2050 the "minority" and "majority" populations will be nearly equal.

These demographic changes have been accompanied by dramatic changes in language use throughout the United States. According to Lindholm-Leary (2000), in 2000 nearly 18 percent of U.S. residents age 5 and

---

1. I use the U.S. Census term "Hispanic" when referring to census data. I use the term Latino elsewhere.

older spoke a language other than English at home. Peyton et al. (2001) review data from the 2000 Census to emphasize that both the number of people speaking languages other than English and the number of languages spoken in the United States are increasing. They write,

> Today, more than 50% of the foreign born are Latin Americans, speaking Spanish, Portuguese, French, and various indigenous languages. Another 25% are Asians, speaking a diversity of East, Southeast, and South Asian languages, among them Chinese, Hindi, Khmer, Korean, Lao, Tagalog, Urdu, and Vietnamese. Newcomers from Africa and Oceania, speaking Amharic, Arabic, Fijian, Hausa, Yoruba, Swahili-among other languages-contribute to the cultural and linguistic mix (6-7).

According to Brecht and Ingold (1998), more than 150 languages are used in the United States today.

These demographic changes in the general U.S. population mean that the student population in U.S. schools is considerably more linguistically and culturally diverse today than it has been in the past. What is readily apparent to educators throughout the United States is the increasing number of school-age children who enter the U.S. school system speaking little or no English, because these English language learners (ELLs) need to learn English in order to have access to equal educational opportunities (see chapter 2 for further discussion). What is not so readily apparent to educators is the increasing number of English-speaking students who come from homes in which a language other than English is spoken. According to Lindholm-Leary (2000), an estimated 9.9 million of 45 million school-aged children in the United States live in households in which languages other than English are spoken, which represents a 35 percent increase since 1980. While Spanish continues to be the language of two-thirds (six million) of children who speak a language other than English at home, speakers of languages that are Asian in origin doubled from 1980 to 1990 (Lindholm-Leary, 2000, 9-10).

What kinds of linguistic and cultural resources do students who speak other languages at home bring with them to school? We can begin to think about these students in terms of their linguistic identities, which Rampton (1995) defines as "cultural interpretations of a person's relationship to a language" (340). Following Rampton, we can distinguish students in terms of their "expertise," or skill; proficiency; ability to operate with a language; and their "allegiance" to, or identification with, a language and the values, meanings, and identities it stands for. We can then think about these students in terms of their relationships to their heritage languages, which in the United States include immigrant languages, indigenous languages, and/or colonial languages (Fishman 2001). A student's allegiance to a heritage language may be strongly influenced by the sociolinguistic status of that language relative to the dominant societal language (see Part II for elaboration on this point in the Puerto Rican community in North Philadelphia).

I draw on Rampton's distinction between expertise and allegiance to differentiate "heritage language speakers" and "heritage language learners," because these distinctions have important implications for language teaching and learning. The term "heritage language speaker" is used by foreign language educators in the United States to refer to a student who is raised in a home where a non-English language is spoken, who speaks or at least understands that language, and who is to some degree bilingual in English and the heritage language (Valdés 2000). Heritage language speakers, as a group, have a wide range of linguistic and cultural expertise on which language educators can readily build. The term "heritage language learner" refers to a student who has an ethnic relation to the heritage language but no expertise in that language. A heritage language learner may feel some allegiance to a heritage language and may be more motivated to learn that heritage language than a traditional monolingual English speaker might be. However, because heritage language learners have no expertise in their heritage language to build on, they learn the target language in the same way that English speakers learn a foreign language (Myriam Met, personal communication).

The term "heritage language speaker," although used increasingly in the United States, is not without question or controversy. According to Wiley (2001), the terms "heritage speaker" and "heritage language" originated in Canada, but the term "heritage language" has recently been replaced in Canada and Australia by the term "international language" or "community language" because these latter terms are considered less pejorative. Wiley cites Baker and Jones (1998), who write,

> The danger of the term "heritage language" is that, relative to·
> powerful majority languages, it points more to the past and less
> to the future, to traditions rather than to the contemporary.
> The danger is that the heritage language becomes associated
> with ancient cultures, past traditions and more "primitive
> times." This is also true of the terms "ethnic" (used in the US)
> and "ancestral." These terms may fail to give the impression of
> a modern, international language that is of value in a technolog-
> ical society (509; cited by Wiley 2001, 30).

In this book I distinguish heritage languages and community languages because not all students who live in multilingual communities have a heritage relation to the community language. In North Philadelphia, for example, many African Americans live in the predominantly Puerto Rican community, but they have no heritage relation to the community language. In contrast, the Puerto Rican students in this community are heritage language speakers of the community language. While I use the terms "heritage language speaker" and "heritage language" in this book, I encourage educators to consider local meanings attached to terms like "heritage" in their school and community contexts, and to decide what terms are appropriate on the local level.

Because Latinos are the largest and fastest growing group of heritage language speakers in the United States today, and because the primary focus of Parts II, III, and IV in this book is the Puerto Rican population in North Philadelphia, I turn my discussion here to heritage Spanish speakers. According to the 2000 Census, 35.3 million Hispanics live in the United States (*Philadelphia Inquirer*, September 2001). There is, however, a tremendous amount of diversity within this category. Lewelling and Peyton (1999) divide the category "Spanish speaker" into three groups based on the kinds of expertise a Spanish speaker is likely to have in Spanish. Educators can expect to find the following:

- Third-or fourth-generation U.S.-born Latino students who are dominant in English and understand spoken Spanish. They tend to have a limited range in oral Spanish and they do not read or write in Spanish.

- First-or second-generation bilinguals who have different kinds of expertise in English and Spanish. In most cases, these students have received their education in English and do not read or write in Spanish.

- Recent immigrants to the United States who are Spanish dominant. Their range of expertise in English and the amount of formal education they have had in Spanish vary.

Lewelling and Peyton emphasize that we can expect to see a wide range of variation within each of these groups. Part II of this book illustrates this point in relation to the Puerto Rican community in North Philadelphia.

But what happens to these heritage languages in the United States? Since the early 1900s, immigrants have experienced strong pressure to assimilate to monolingualism in English. Very few families have managed to resist this pressure for more than a generation or two, and there is little evidence to indicate that the process of assimilation for today's immigrants has changed fundamentally. Even within the Latino population, we see clear evidence of an ongoing language shift toward English. One-third of the youngest Latinos, for example, have no expertise in their heritage language, and monolingualism in Spanish among Latinos is weak, encompassing only 16 percent of Puerto Ricans, 12 percent of Mexican Americans, and 1.6 percent of Cuban Americans (Valdés 2000). Although most Latinos in the Unites States today do have some expertise in Spanish, Spanish-speaking immigrants are using more English than Spanish in more domains in their everyday lives. For the majority of immigrants, today as in the past, the native language is generally lost after three generations (Peyton et al. 2001; Wiley 2001).

What are some of the implications of this assimilation strategy for students and their families? When parents who do not speak much English decide to stop speaking their native language at home with their children so that their children can acquire English more quickly, they deprive their children of the language-rich environment that they need to promote first language acquisition. When educators submerse ELLs in the all-English academic mainstream without looking for ways to make the cognitively and academically challenging content comprehensible to those students, they deny children opportunities to develop cognitively and academically at their grade level. When children refuse to speak the language of their home, family, and community because English has more prestige than the home language, they can become alienated from these critical connections that help them understand who they are relative to others in the world. When children believe that they must reject their home language and culture in order to participate and achieve in a monolingual English-speaking world, they deny an important part of their social identity, and they limit the opportunities that are available to them.

Although immigrants do tend to shift to English over time, it is important to recognize the linguistic vitality of languages other than English in multilingual communities in the United States today. Continued immigration of speakers of other languages into areas in which large populations of speakers of these languages live ensures that these languages thrive, at least in private domains. We see this phenomenon clearly in Latino communities. According to Valdés (2000), most Latinos in this country *are* bilingual, and they can function to some degree in *both* English and Spanish. It is quite common to find heritage Spanish-speaking students who have developed an extensive oral vocabulary, but that vocabulary may be restricted to home and community topics. Their speech may deviate considerably from the standard form of the language that is taught in school, and it will reflect the local variety of that language spoken in the community. This kind of expertise in Spanish is to be expected, because most heritage Spanish speakers have developed their expertise in Spanish by participating in informal home and community activities. Because most U.S. schools today do not promote languages other than English, most heritage

Spanish speakers living in the United States today do not broaden their bilingual range through education.

The National Foreign Language Center (NFLC) summarizes the need to challenge the assimilation strategy in a 1995 proposal entitled "Heritage Languages in the National Interest." While they recognize that all residents of the United States need English, they emphasize that

> the United States has critical needs for genuine communicative competency in a range of languages, a level of competency that can rarely be attained by native English speakers in a classroom setting. The ethnic communities constitute a valuable and unique resource in producing true multilingual ability in English and languages that are essential to the national interest (NFLC 1995, 1).

While English-speaking students struggle to develop even limited expertise in another language, many heritage language speakers arrive in our schools with "a level of language proficiency and depth of cultural understanding that would be difficult to replicate in even the most advanced second language learner" (Carreira and Armengol, 2001, 109). Peyton et al. (2001) argue that a national policy that viewed these languages as resources to be preserved and developed rather than as obstacles to be overcome could contribute significantly, and in a relatively short time, to America's expertise in foreign languages. I argue throughout this book that school districts and schools that serve students living in multilingual communities can begin this work in policy and practice on the local level.

Changing language needs

The dramatic demographic changes that we see in the United States mean that language educators who work in multilingual communities should expect to find monolingual English speakers, heritage language speakers, heritage language learners, and English language learners (ELLs) in their classes. This increasingly diverse student population, not surprisingly, has a wide range of short-term and long-term language learning needs. Since students' English language needs are the focus of much research and practice, I focus here on English speakers, heritage language speakers, heritage language learners, and ELLs' needs for languages other than English.

First, all students who live in multilingual communities need community languages for social purposes. Let's start with heritage language speakers. These students need to maintain and develop expertise in their home languages to communicate with monolingual family members. When children cannot speak the language that their parents and grandparents speak, these lines of communication inevitably break down, and the family and community can and do suffer. English speakers also need to develop expertise in community languages so that they can fully participate in institutions throughout their local community. When English speakers and heritage language speakers who live in the same multilingual community learn to communicate with each other, in English and/or in the community languages, intergroup relations are likely to be much more positive.

Second, as many states across the country adopt world language standards, students increasingly need a language other than English for academic purposes. While it is not exactly clear how these new standards will influence promotion and graduation requirements on the state and local levels, it is clear that there is an increasing awareness of English-speaking students' needs to develop spoken and written expertise in languages other than English. In many districts, ELLs and heritage language speakers can use their expertise in their home/heritage language to fulfill the world language requirement.

Third, students in the United States may need languages other than English for professional purposes. There are many jobs available in the local community and in the larger society that demand an educated pool of bilingual and biliterate workers. For example, many schools throughout the United States need bilingual and/or world language educators who have developed spoken and written expertise in other languages in order to teach in those languages. Local businesses need employees who have the necessary expertise to work with their customers through the languages used in the community. We also see increased language demands in U.S. social service institutions, including hospitals, immigration courts, postal services, the Federal Bureau of Investigation, the Social Security Administration, and many other agencies. This suggests the need for schools that serve multilingual communities to "grow their own" locally. Community bilingualism is an important resource on which schools can build to help students, their families, and the local community meet their language and education needs.

Although English has emerged as a major international lingua franca, the need for expertise in languages other than English is actually greater in the United States now than at any other time in U.S. history. The National Foreign Language Center (NFLC) in Washington, D.C., calls this increased need a "sea change in language" in the United States, and their work suggests the scope and complexity of national language needs (Brecht and Rivers 2000). However, as Brecht and Rivers emphasize, a major challenge to U.S. efforts to develop the capacity to meet such unprecedented language needs is ideological. Most Americans at every level of education believe that English is suitable for all individuals, all countries, all occasions, and all tasks. This belief simply does not take into account economic, technological, political, and social developments of the last two decades.

The new global economy has increased the need for workers who can negotiate effectively with business partners, customers, and competitors from diverse cultural backgrounds. According to McGroarty (1997), our present and future national economic security depends on our ability to understand, appreciate, value, and work with foreign cultures, differing sets of social customs, diverse economic contexts, and varied political systems, and this requires expertise in languages other than English. Today the United States accounts for almost one-sixth of worldwide service exports and one-eighth of worldwide exports of merchandise. Mexico is currently the second fastest growing market for U.S. exporters, with a growth rate of 118 percent from 1992 to 1997 (Lindholm-Leary 2000), which means that the demand for expertise in Spanish is rapidly growing. China's recent acceptance into the World Trade Organization also promises to open huge markets, which will require expertise in Chinese.

Increased political and military needs in the United States today are also of unprecedented scope and complexity. According to Brecht and Rivers (2000), expertise in languages other than English is critical to our national security. More than sixty-five federal agencies, from the State Department to the Central Intelligence Agency to the Department of Agriculture, have language requirements, a number that has doubled in the last fifteen years. Since 1991, more than 40,000 U.S. troops are or have been stationed in over 110 nations, including every nation in Latin American and all but two of the fifteen successor states to the USSR, approximately forty nations in Africa, and throughout South and Southeast Asia. More than 140 languages are spoken in these countries. Critical shortages of speakers of Central Eurasian, East Asian, and Middle Eastern languages impact collection, processing, exploitation, and analysis of intelligence data. The events of September 11, 2001 highlighted the need for expertise in Arabic and other Middle Eastern languages. Brecht and Rivers (2000) argue that language competence is as vital to national security as competence in math and science, and they maintain that the NFLC is working to convince the U.S. government of the need for a federal strategy focused on foreign language education similar to what we have seen in math and science education.

The assimilation strategy as currently practiced in the United States denies the development of important national resources. In a publication entitled "Are We Wasting Our Nation's Language Resources?: Heritage Languages in America," Kathleen Marcos emphasizes that

One of our national ironies is that the United States is short on the language expertise needed for national defense, international business, and local government services at the same time that unprecedented numbers of immigrants are arriving in the United States thoroughly fluent in languages other than English (cited in Lindholm-Leary 2000, 6).

Increasing local and national language needs require us to challenge the assimilation strategy that has dominated in the United States throughout the twentieth century. This requires an alternative discourse that promotes additive bilingualism. Let's turn now to what the research tells us about the benefits of bilingualism.

The benefits of bilingualism

There is a wide range of research on bilingualism and education that illustrates the educational, cognitive, sociocultural, and economic benefits of bilingualism for the individual language user. For example, we know that bilinguals tend to perform better than monolinguals on cognitive tasks that call for divergent thinking, pattern recognition, and problem solving, and they tend to demonstrate sophisticated levels of metalinguistic awareness (i.e., knowledge about the structural properties of language). People who can use more than one language can generally communicate across language and cultural boundaries more effectively, and they have generally developed a broader understanding of the world. Bilingual individuals also have a wide range of professional opportunities open to them, especially in our increasingly global economy (see Cloud et al. 2000 for further discussion).

Educators today do not question the value of bilingualism. They do, however, question whether and how their students can develop expertise in more than one language at the same time as they develop academically in English. To answer this question, we need to look separately at the implications for academic achievement that learning a second language has for English speakers and for English language learners.

Let's begin with English speakers, and consider the research about their experiences developing expertise in a second language in immersion programs. Students and teachers in immersion programs use the second language (e.g., French) to study the majority of the academic curriculum (see chapter 3 for further discussion). Immersion programs in Canada have been extensively studied and evaluated (Genesee, 1985, 1987; Lambert and Tucker, 1972; Swain and Lapkin, 1982; cited by Cloud et al. 2000). According to Cloud et al. (2000),

The findings are clear and consistent. Students in immersion programs acquire the same proficiency in English and achieve the same levels of competence in their academic subjects (e.g., mathematics, science, and social studies) as comparable English-speaking students who attend regular all-English programs. At the same time, immersion students acquire advanced levels of functional proficiency in French. They are able to do all of their school work, communicate with their friends and teachers in school and with others outside of school comfortably, effortlessly, and effectively (3).

Cloud et al. emphasize that positive outcomes have been reported not only for middle-class English-speaking students and/or gifted students, but also for low-income English-speaking students and/or English-speaking students who may struggle academically. The fear that English speakers cannot achieve academically through a language other than English is clearly countered by the empirical research evidence from immersion programs.

Although immersion programs are highly effective, they only serve a small percentage of the English-speaking population learning a second language. It is much more common for English speakers to learn a second language by studying it as an academic subject (i.e., as a world language) rather than acquire it by using it as a medium of instruction (i.e., through participation in a dual language program). Marcos (1998) summarizes research that demonstrates the benefits of foreign language study for English speakers. She writes,

Students of foreign languages score statistically higher on standardized tests conducted in English. In its 1992 report, *College Bound Seniors: The 1992 Profile of SAT and Achievement Test Takers*, the College Entrance Examination Board reported that students who averaged 4 or more years of foreign language study scored higher on the verbal section of the Scholastic Aptitude Test (SAT) than those who had studied 4 or more years in any other subject area. In addition, the average mathematics scores for individuals who had taken 4 or more years of foreign language study was identical to the average score of those who had studied 4 years of mathematics.

Although English speakers in foreign language programs cannot be expected to develop the same range of expertise in the target language as English speakers in immersion programs, research clearly demonstrates positive results of foreign language study. If educators want English speakers to develop a broad range of expertise in the target language through a foreign language program, Marcos (1998) and others working in the field of foreign language education (e.g., Gilzow and Branaman 2000) empha-size that schools need to begin offering foreign languages in the early ele-mentary grades. I return to these points in chapter 3.

Let's turn now to English language learners (ELLs) and consider what we know about relationships between first language (L1) and literacy development and the development of oral and written academic English as a second language. First, as Cloud et al. (2000) highlight, one of the great-est predictors of strong second language acquisition (e.g., in English) is a solid foundation in the first language. English language learners who come to U.S. public schools with a strong foundation in their L1 have a far easier time acquiring the academic language and literacies they need in English than do ELLs who have not had the opportunities to develop a strong aca-demic language and literacy foundation in their first language. This find-ing suggests that U.S. public schools should promote L1 literacy programs for ELLs.

This argument is further supported by extensive research on student achievement in well-implemented bilingual programs. Longitudinal research done by Thomas and Collier (2002) and Lindholm-Leary (2001) demonstrates that ELLs who are enrolled in bilingual programs that pro-mote additive bilingualism with an emphasis on biliteracy development (i.e., one-way developmental bilingual programs, two-way immersion pro-grams) are able to reach parity with their English-speaking peers after five to seven years. In general, ELLs who are enrolled in other types of pro-grams (i.e., English as a second language [ESL] programs, early-exit tran-sitional bilingual programs) are not able to close the achievement gap (see chapter 3 for further discussion of different types of bilingual education and ESL programs).

In 2001, the International Reading Association published a position statement on second language literacy instruction that explains why ELLs benefit from time spent learning to read and write in their first language. They write,

> Literacy learning is easiest when schools provide initial literacy instruction in a child's home language. Such instruction is con-sistent with building on children's strengths and with connect-ing unfamiliar material to the familiar to maximize learning effi-ciency. Literacy skills developed in the home language can then be applied to learning to read and write in the second language, which results in students who have become literate and gained proficiency in two (or perhaps more) languages.

This position statement is based on a wide range of reading research con-ducted in the United States and internationally.

We also have a reasonable amount of evidence that supports the hypothesis that literacy transfers across languages. Krashen (1996, 24) summarized the research on literacy transfer and found the following:

1. The underlying process of reading in different languages is similar, even when the languages and writing systems appear to be very different.
2. The process of the development of literacy is similar in different languages.
3. When confounding factors are controlled, there are positive correlations between literacy development in first and second languages.
4. Bilingual programs in which children develop literacy in the primary language are successful in helping children develop literacy in English.

These researchers and others clearly demonstrate that promoting L1 language and literacy development supports language and literacy development in English, the primary goal of all programs for ELLs.

Unfortunately, these important points are missed by English-only advocates who support legislation against bilingual education. And unfortunately, many ELLs across the country suffer the consequences of this confusion and controversy. I return to these points in my discussion of the politics surrounding bilingual education in the United States in chapter 2.

Most bilingual and world language programs in the United States today use Spanish, so let's consider more closely some of the benefits of promoting Spanish. To do this, we need to take a brief look at the history of English. As Jim Cummins has emphasized in recent presentations, modern English derives from Latin and Anglo-Saxon (a Germanic language), and the vocabulary of modern English preserves traces of these ancestral languages. For example, we often find as synonyms in English one word derived from Latin and another from Anglo-Saxon (e.g., observe/see). Furthermore, the Germanic word is generally less formal than the Latinate word. This distribution of vocabulary items has important implications for students' development of academic language proficiency in English. According to Cummins (in press), academic language proficiency

> includes knowledge of the less frequent vocabulary of English as well as the ability to interpret and produce increasingly complex written language. As students progress through the grades, they encounter far more low frequency words (primarily from Greek and Latin sources), complex syntax (e.g., passives), and abstract expressions that are virtually never heard in everyday conversation (2).

Spanish is also a Latinate language, and it is a cognate language with English, which means that there are many words in both languages that derive from the same Latin base (e.g., observar/observe). Students who develop vocabulary in Spanish (or other Latin-based languages), either as a first language or as a second language, have a strong foundation for their development of the heavily Latin-based academic English that they need for success in U.S. schools.

Bilingual individuals may also be able to create new and mixed linguistic identities that allow for many more possibilities than are available to monolinguals. As Rampton (1995) and Romaine (1989) have argued, the measurement of bilingualism and the investigation of bilingual language attitudes have generally both been very slow to acknowledge that the bilingual whole might be more than the sum of two monolingual parts. There has been an overwhelming tendency to treat languages in the bilingual repertoire as if they were separate entities, ignoring the ways in which they can combine to create new forms that are quite distinct from monolingual use in either language. Furthermore, when children learn to communicate through two languages, they develop what may be called intercultural competence. That is, they develop the ability to see the world through two (or more) different lenses, and the flexibility to negotiate meaning across what are traditionally considered linguistic and cultural borders. Although little empirical research has been done on relationships between bilingual expertise and improved intergroup understanding and relations, language educators regularly cite this as a benefit of bilingualism.

Despite the clear research evidence on the benefits of bilingualism, many parents, educators, and other concerned citizens have questions and concerns. Advocacy is therefore an important part of the language educator's job. Language educators need to listen to all questions and concerns, and we need to respond with the facts about the benefits bilingualism for students, families, communities, and the United States overall. Appendix 2 provides a list of useful organizations and websites that advocates can turn to for resources.

Conclusion

This chapter has addressed the question *Why should U.S. schools promote multilingualism?* Demographic changes in the United States have given rise to an increasing number of individuals who speak languages other than English as well as to an increasing number of languages spoken in this country. At the same time, we see unprecedented demand for expertise in languages other than English, as well as a large body of research demonstrating the benefits of bilingualism for English speakers and speakers of other languages. This chapter argues against the assimilation strategy that has dominated the experiences of ELLs in the United States since the early twentieth century, and argues that schools that serve students living in multilingual communities should work to promote bilingualism to the greatest degree possible for their target populations. Educational researchers, policymakers, and practitioners are encouraged to work together in ways that build on the rich linguistic and cultural resources that students bring with them to school. The remainder of the book is intended to consider *how* schools can work toward this goal on the local level.

2

Developing school language policies that promote multilingualism

School language policies are beginning to be seen as an integral part of the administration of school districts and schools, and we see contemporary legislation on the federal, state, and local levels across the United States that mandates the development of well-articulated policies and standards-driven programs for English language learners (ELLs). Although the current national debate is clearly focused on English language development and academic achievement in English, I argue that school district and school language policies and planning should work to promote multilingualism to the greatest degree possible for the students and communities they serve.

This chapter begins by explaining what I mean by school-based language planning and policy development, and I review the larger bilingual education and foreign language policy context in the United States. Next, I introduce the national Heritage Languages Initiative, which aims to counter the assimilationist trend that we see in the United States by promoting the maintenance and development of heritage languages in multilingual communities. I conclude the chapter by moving to the school district and school levels and emphasize that educators working on these levels have choices in the ways that they plan their programs and formulate their language policies to meet the language education needs of the students and communities they serve. This chapter highlights the recursive nature of language planning and policy development on the local level. It is intended to help educators working in schools and school districts develop language policies that comply with all federal, state, and local accountability requirements AND promote multilingualism on the individual and community levels.

Language planning and policy development in the United States

My work on language planning and policy development begins with Cooper's definition of language planning. According to Cooper (1989),

> Language planning refers to deliberate efforts to influence the behavior of others with respect to the acquisition, structure, or functional allocation of their language codes (45).

Cooper (1989) uses the question "Who plans what for whom and how?" to organize his review of the language planning literature. He emphasizes that language planning activities can be undertaken by a wide range of groups (e.g., local, regional, and national governmental agencies, community-based organizations, professional associations, churches, schools, and families). My discussion of language planning and policy development in this part of the chapter focuses on the federal and state language policies in the United States today. These larger planning and policy contexts provide an important foundation for our discussion of school district policy formulation later in this chapter and of school-based language planning in chapter 4.

What is involved in language planning and policy development? When we review the research that has been done since the mid-1970s (e.g., Fishman 1974; Rubin 1977; Cooper 1989; Ruiz 1990; Corson 1999), we find agreement on the kinds of processes that are involved. To develop educational language plans and policies that meet the needs of the target populations, language planners need to do the following:

- Gather information about the sociolinguistic setting, the needs of the target community, and alternative models of education and the research base that informs those models.

- Consider how different language plans would relate to other socio-economic and political processes in the target school and community contexts.

- Define goals, determine outcomes in advance, assess values and attitudes, consider resources and constraints, articulate language plans, and formulate language policies.

- Make provisions for implementation to ensure that the policy is carried out, including plans and strategies for mobilizing human and material resources, motivating and supervising personnel, and sequencing and coordinating different aspects of the policy.

- Determine ways to evaluate the language policy on a regular basis, including ways to monitor, adjust, or change the plan and/or policy if either is not successful.

Although most of the work in the language planning and policy field has focused on the societal level, much of this work is also relevant to our discussion of school district and school-based language planning and policy formulation.

Earlier research on language planning and policy development has been criticized for its focus on upper-level language planning. My work is aligned with that of Bamgbose (1989), Hornberger (1997), and others who see language planning and policy development as complex processes that are neither linear nor unidirectional. According to Bamgbose (1989), drawing on Fishman et al. (1971) and Jernudd (1973),

> Since policy decisions can be taken at any stage in the language-planning process, there is a need to reconsider the unidirectional movement from policy formulation to implementation which is usually presented in models of language planning . . . . This account of the relationship obscures the fact that policy formulation is a dynamic process.

Like Bamgbose, I see language planning and policy development as dynamic, ideological processes that are shaped by multiple levels of institutional authority. This means that language planners and policy makers must identify and work through the relevant levels of institutional authority and/or decision-making structures, which of course vary across schools, school districts, states, and nations over time. This next section briefly outlines what this means on the federal and state levels in the United States in relation to bilingual education and foreign language education in the K–12 system today.

Confusion and controversy surrounding bilingual education

Since the passage of the Civil Rights Act of 1964, U.S. public schools have been required to provide all students with equal access to educational opportunities. There is, however, no unified language policy that mandates exactly how U.S. schools address the language education needs of their students and communities. Instead, policies have been made in response to specific class-action suits (e.g., *Lau v. Nichols, 1974; Castaneda v. Pickard,* 1974) and informed by research on the effectiveness of different educational approaches for ELLs. The federal government attempts to influence local language planning efforts by appropriating funds that support particular approaches to meeting the educational needs of language learners and, more recently, by holding states, school districts, and schools accountable for student outcomes. This part of the chapter presents a brief review of the bilingual education trends over the last several decades and highlights the competing ideological discourses about bilingualism, bilingual education, and schooling that we have seen in the United States throughout this period.

From 1968 to 2001, Title VII (the Bilingual Education Act) of the Elementary and Secondary Education Act provided grants to support districtwide and/or school-based initiatives to address the language learning needs of students defined as "limited English proficient" (LEP). The kinds of language education programs that were financially supported changed depending on the dominant sociopolitical climate of the times. During the 1960s and 1970s, the dominant discourses emphasized tolerance, civil rights, and inclusion. Bilingual education was encouraged, but no particular model or program type was endorsed. During the 1980s, we saw increasing English-only activity across the country, and Title VII supported bilingual and/or English-only programs that emphasized a quick transition to English. In the 1990s, we saw competing discourses about linguistic and cultural diversity on the national level as well as increasing support for dual language programs at school (see Freeman 1998 for further discussion).

In 2001, the U.S. Congress authorized the No Child Left Behind Act (NCLB), which mandates that schools be held accountable for the academic achievement of all students. Title III (the English Language Acquisition, Language Enhancement, and Academic Achievement Act) specifies what this means for "limited English proficient and immigrant students." For the first time in history, the U.S. government has said it will hold State educational agencies, local educational agencies, and schools accountable for increases in English proficiency and core academic content knowledge of limited English proficient children by requiring—

- demonstrated improvements in the English proficiency of limited English proficient children each fiscal year; and

- adequate yearly progress for limited English proficient children, including immigrant children and youth (Section 3102, 8A, B).

Title III emphasizes that state and local educational agencies are to be provided with

> the flexibility to implement language instruction educational
> programs, based on scientifically based research on teaching

limited English proficient children, that the agencies believe to
be the most effective for teaching English (Section 3102, 9).

The decision about whether to implement bilingual education programs or English as a second language (ESL) programs is left up to the state and local educational agencies. These agencies must look to the research to determine which kinds of bilingual education and/or ESL instruction are the most effective for their particular target populations. Chapter 3 provides a review of this research base.

Although Title III does not explicitly advocate for or against bilingual education, the name change of the federal legislation concerning the education of ELLs reflects a change in ideological orientation. Recall that Title VII of the Elementary and Secondary Education Act was also known as the Bilingual Education Act. Title III of the NCLB is the English Language Acquisition, Language Enhancement, and Academic Achievement Act. Although Title III does explicitly endorse development of the native language of ELLs (Section 3202, 3), schools are only held accountable for English language development and academic achievement in English. This exclusive emphasis on accountability in English is sometimes interpreted as endorsing English-only approaches. However, when we consider the findings of research that meets the federal government's criteria for "scientifically based," we see space for well-implemented bilingual programs that promote bilingualism, biliteracy development, and academic achievement in two languages (see chapter 3 for further discussion of this research).

Although we do see "flexibility" on the federal policy level in the United States, we also see increasing efforts at the state level to legislate against languages other than English. For example, in June 1998, California voters passed Proposition 227, which mandates that ELLs be immersed in the English-only academic mainstream after receiving a maximum of one year of ESL instruction. Ron Unz, the billionaire software developer who initiated Proposition 227 in California, labeled this English-only legislation *English for the Children.* Unz has funded a massive media campaign that began in California and then moved to Arizona, Colorado, and Massachusetts. This legislation essentially blames bilingual education for not enabling Spanish speakers to develop proficiency in English. According to Unz, the goal of this campaign is to "teach English to all of America's children and end bilingual education." Arizona passed anti–bilingual education legislation in 1999, and Massachusetts voted for the anti–bilingual education initiative in 2002. Colorado, however, voted against this anti–bilingual education legislation in 2002.

These well-organized and well-funded English-only movements are fueled by stories of Spanish-speaking children who fail to learn English after spending years in bilingual programs. For example, Linda Chavez, President of the Center for Equal Opportunity, included the following account in an article that appeared in the *Philadelphia Inquirer* (June 28, 2001) entitled "Hispanic Parents Leading the Revolt against Congress' Bilingual Boondoggle."

> Just ask Rita Montero, a former member of the Denver school board who is helping lead the effort to replace bilingual education with English immersion.
>
> Montero, a onetime supporter of bilingual education, became disillusioned with the program when her son was placed in a bilingual classroom in first grade. The school put him in the program because Montero answered a survey required of all Hispanic parents, which asked whether a language other than English is ever used in the home. Although Montero and her son are both fluent in English, the family occasionally spoke Spanish, so the school placed her son in the bilingual program.
>
> At first, she thought the bilingual program might give her son the opportunity to learn both languages. Instead, she found that the program taught neither language well, and she worried her son would fall behind in school . . . .
>
> Stories like Montero's occur by the thousands, which is why the Unz initiatives have proved so popular with Hispanic parents themselves. In every state where the initiative has made it on the ballot, the effort has been led by local Hispanic parents, teachers and community activists.

Although the English-only legislation that has been passed in several states seeks to eliminate bilingual education throughout the state and across the country, what Chavez/Montero describes is an implementation problem. Chavez writes that Montero "found a program that taught neither language well, and she worried that her son would fall behind in school."

Unfortunately, there are many cases of poorly implemented bilingual programs in schools across the United States that do not reach their goals, and unfortunately many ELLs are not offered the opportunity to develop the English language necessary to participate and achieve in the English-only academic mainstream. This is why my focus in this book on the local school district and school level—to support the development of bilingual programs that are pedagogically sound and well-implemented. In addition to advocating for language policies that promote bilingualism, our focus as language educators needs to be on implementing programs that most effectively close the achievement gap for ELLs (see chapters 3 and 4 for further discussions of this important point).

Just as we have seen competing discourses over time about the kinds of bilingual programs that the federal government supports, we also see variation from state to state at different moments in time. Although California, Arizona, and Massachusetts passed anti-bilingual education legislation, Colorado voters did not support English-only legislation in their state in November 2001. Furthermore, other states have proposed and/or passed English-plus legislation that advocates the maintenance and development of immigrant and/or indigenous languages. Olsen et al. (2001) provide examples of official position statements, policies, and laws that support multilingualism and cultural pluralism in a wide range of contexts across the United States. Their examples include excerpts from Oregon's English Plus Resolution, an English Plus Declaration in New Mexico, the Louisiana Language Policy, an excerpt from the Hawaiian Constitution, a Tribal Declaration by the Northern Ute Tribe Tribal Business Committee, the Native American Languages Act, and the Navajo Nation Long-Range Navajo Language Goals. Olsen et al. (2001) provide these and other examples of legislation to stimulate policymakers who are working to promote additive bilingualism in other contexts.

The No Child Left Behind Act of 2001 leaves room for language policies and bilingual programs that promote multilingualism. Title III of NCLB mandates accountability for results in developing English language proficiency and academic achievement for all ELLs, and it emphasizes the need for high quality standards for instructional personnel, as well as informed, involved parents who have choices in the education of their children. All schools must implement programs that are based on "rigorous, scientific research," but the burden of responsibility is clearly placed on the state level. States must choose how their school districts respond to federal accountability requirements, and these choices must be understood and supported on the local school and community levels.

I argue throughout this book for policies and action on the local school district and school levels. Since the focus of this book is the School District of Philadelphia, it is important to consider state legislation in the Commonwealth of Pennsylvania. School districts and schools in other states need to consider the implications of their state and local legislation.

Until 2002, Pennsylvania had no specific policies that school districts or local schools had to comply with in order to meet the federally mandated requirement to provide equal educational opportunities to ELLs. In fact, Pennsylvania is one of eleven states that does not require ESL teachers to be certified in TESOL (Teachers of English to Speakers of Other Languages). (See www.ncela.gwu.edu for lists of state certification and endorsement requirements by state.) However, in response to the requirements set forth by NCLB, the Commonwealth of Pennsylvania Department of Education (PDE) now requires all ESL teachers to earn a "Program Specialist Certificate," which ideally provides ESL teachers with opportunities to develop the knowledge and skills in second language acquisition, cross-cultural communication, ESL methods, and assessment that they need to effectively address the needs of their ELLs.

The Pennsylvania requirements for Program Specialist, however, fall short of requirements for ESL and/or bilingual teachers in most other states in the United States. This places a larger burden of responsibility for professional development of ESL and bilingual teachers on the actual teachers, local schools, and school districts in which they work to ensure that all educators (ESL and bilingual teachers, mainstream teachers, administrators, counselors) who work with ELLs have the knowledge and skills they need to provide ELLs access to equal educational opportunities. Parts III and IV of this book illustrate some of the ways that the School District of Philadelphia works to address this challenge.

In May 2002, the PDE also disseminated *A Guidebook for Planning Programs for English Language Learners* to facilitate efforts by Pennsylvania public school districts and charter schools' to develop programs for ELLs that comply with state and federal regulations. The *Guidebook* begins with the Pennsylvania School Code of 1949, Chapter 4, section 4.26, which states,

> Every school district/charter school shall provide a program for
> each student whose dominant language is not English for the
> purpose of facilitating the student's achievement of English
> proficiency and the academic standards under section 4.12
> (relating to academic standards). Programs under this section
> shall include appropriate bilingual-bicultural or English as a
> Second Language (ESL) instruction.

In the Commonwealth of Pennsylvania, there is no mandate for or against a particular kind of bilingual or ESL program. Instead, the state now holds school districts and charter schools accountable for student performance as mandated by the NCLB, and each school district and charter school is required to articulate its own language policy that outlines how its bilingual and/or ESL program(s) enable ELLs to develop content area knowledge and skills and spoken and written academic English.

How are school districts in Pennsylvania to determine what kinds of programs are "appropriate" for ELLs? The PDE 2002 *Guidebook* refers to the three-part test that was formulated by the Fifth Circuit Court of Appeals in 1981 to determine that school districts are in compliance with the Equal Educational Opportunities Act of 1974. This test includes the following criteria:

1. Theory: the school must pursue a program based on an educational theory recognized as sound for ELLs.

2. Practice: the school must actually implement the program with instructional practices, resources, and personnel necessary to transfer theory to reality.

3. Results: the school must not persist in a program that fails to produce results (PDE 2002, 2).

Each school within a school district is expected to develop programs and practices that are aligned with its school district policies, and its plans for ELLs are to be an integral part of the School Improvement Plan. I discuss school district policy development later in this chapter and school-based language planning in chapter 4.

This brief review of the policy context surrounding the education of ELLs in the United States today illustrates confusion, controversy, and competing discourses about the role of languages other than English in U.S. public schools. While the atmosphere on the federal level and in some states today seems increasingly English-only, there is clearly room for school district and school language policies and programs that promote bilingualism for ELLs. The challenge is for schools and school districts to clearly articulate and implement their policies and programs, and to monitor and evaluate those programs on a regular basis to ensure that they enable language learners to reach their goals. Let's now consider the larger policy context surrounding language education for English speakers in the United States today.

World language policies and U.S. schools today

In contrast to the confusion and controversy surrounding bilingual education, world language education has consistently been positively evaluated in the United States. Despite this positive evaluation, most U.S. schools are not provided with the funding they need to develop and implement well-articulated long-sequence world language programs that would provide U.S. students with opportunities to develop communicative competence in languages other than English (see chapter 3 for discussion of world language education in the United States today). Since the early 1990s, however, we have seen federal policy initiatives that aim to increase the national capacity in languages other than English. This section reviews some of those initiatives.

First, the National Security Education Program (NSEP) was established by the National Security Education Act in 1991. The NSEP seeks to lead in the development of the national capacity in languages and cultural understanding in order to strengthen U.S. economic competitiveness and enhance international cooperation and security. Four principal objectives form NSEP's mission.

- To equip Americans with an understanding of less commonly taught languages and cultures and enable them to become integrally involved in global issues.

- To build a critical base of future leaders, both in the marketplace and in government service, who have cultivated international relationships and worked and studied alongside foreign experts.

- To develop a cadre of professionals with more-than-traditional knowledge of language and culture, who can use this ability to help the United States make sound decisions and deal effectively with global issues.

- To enhance institutional capacity and increase the number of faculty who can educate U.S. citizens toward achieving these goals (from www.languagepolicy.org).

To realize these objectives, the NSEP has provided scholarships for undergraduates to study abroad, grants to colleges and universities to improve cultural and language training, and fellowships for graduate students to study in other countries.

Since the attacks of September 11, 2001, numerous committees and subcommittees in Congress have held hearings on national language capabilities, and they have increased funding for government language programs. For example, the 107th Congress increased funding for world languages and international studies in higher education by $20 million. They also passed legislation creating a national language registry and urging the creation of language flagship universities. World languages were also included in the new national Teacher Recruitment Fellowships (see Edwards 2003 for a summary of national language policies and activities in 2002).

The No Child Left Behind Act of 2001 (NCLB) also includes the reauthorization of and appropriations for the Foreign Language Assistance

Program (FLAP), which provides funding for world language education programs in the K–12 system. Although President George W. Bush did not request funding for FLAP, the Senate Appropriations Committee restored the program and increased the budget by $2.1 million in February 2003. Under NCLB, FLAP is no longer included with bilingual education (which is now funded under Title III, the English Language Acquisition, Language Enhancement, and Academic Achievement Act, discussed earlier in this chapter). The Foreign Language Assistance Program is now part of Title V—Promoting Informed Parental Choice and Innovative Programs, Section D.

In addition to the FLAP program, NCLB includes the Foreign Language Incentive Program (FLIP), which was a part of FLAP in the early 1990s but was not included the last time the Elementary and Secondary Education Act was reauthorized. Under the FLIP program,

> The Secretary shall make an incentive payment for each fiscal year to each public elementary school that provides to students attending such school a program designed to lead to communicative competency in a foreign language.

Information about the application process and appropriations for FLIP and FLAP can be found on the webpage of Joint National Committee for Languages and the National Council for Languages and International Studies (www.languagepolicy.org).

States and school districts vary in their world language requirements, and educators who work in different states need to consider how world language instruction is organized in their state. In Pennsylvania, for example, there is currently no graduation requirement for world languages. However, according to the Pennsylvania Department of Education (PDE) webpage (www.pde.state.pa.us/languages), all Pennsylvania school districts are required to provide instruction in at least two languages in addition to English, at least one of which shall be a modern language and at least one of which shall be offered in a minimum four-year sequence in the secondary program, and world language instruction can begin at any grade level. Moreover, a committee of world language teachers, professors, international business representatives, parents, and school directors, guided by the PDE, has created a draft for proposed academic standards for world languages. These standards are aligned with the standards developed by the American Council of Teachers of Foreign Languages (see chapter 3 for discussion). According to the PDE webpage, when the standards are formally adopted, the relationship to graduation requirements for all students in the Commonwealth of Pennsylvania will be specified.

This section has reviewed how federal and state governments currently influence the development of school district and school language policies. As we can see, there is space for schools to develop programs that promote additive bilingualism for their target populations, as long as those programs are based on pedagogically sound research that demonstrates their effectiveness and as long as the educators who work in those programs are held accountable for student performance in English. The next section considers a complementary initiative that promotes the maintenance and development of heritage languages in multilingual communities in the United States. Together these sections provide an important foundation for our discussion of the development of school district language policies that promote multilingualism.

The Heritage Languages Initiative

This section describes the Heritage Languages Initiative, which the National Foreign Language Center (NFLC) and the Center for Applied Linguistics (CAL) launched in 1998 to respond to the national language needs described in chapter 1. According to Brecht and Ingold (1998), the goals of this initiative are to strengthen the ability of the United States to participate effectively in an increasingly interdependent world, to produce a broad cadre of citizens able to function professionally in both English and other languages, and to build an education system that is responsive to national language needs and the heritage language communities in this country. The work of the Heritage Languages Initiative continues through a listserve (heritage-list@glue.umd.edu), a website (www.cal.org/heritage), and regularly held national and research-based conferences.

There are many multilingual communities throughout the country that are rich in linguistic and cultural resources, and we can find many community-based institutions that work to preserve and develop heritage languages (see Peyton et al. 2001 for discussion). For example, in major cities across the United States, we can find after-school programs, Saturday schools, and/or church- or temple-based programs that teach Chinese, Vietnamese, Russian, Khmer, and Korean. While some groups have generally promoted heritage languages through community-based initiatives like these, other groups (most notably Spanish-speaking groups) have worked through the local schools. Most of the heritage language initiatives that we have seen in the United States to date have focused on individual language groups or communities rather than on heritage language planning on the national level. The Heritage Languages Initiative goes beyond the scope of these community-based initiatives to promote the maintenance and development of heritage languages more broadly.

According to Peyton et al. (2001), current efforts to preserve and develop community language resources today differ in at least three ways from efforts in the past. First, past efforts took place mostly in the community. Today public and private K–12 schools and institutions of higher education are involved. Second, we know much more about second language acquisition, and about learning and teaching languages, than we knew in the past, and this research base can help educators make informed decisions about the kinds of programs and practices that can meet the needs of their students and community. Finally, today we see the possibility of public support for the preservation of non-English languages in the United States, as well as increased funding for world language education, especially in the elementary years.

Those involved in the Heritage Languages Initiative emphasize that, to date, we do not have a solid foundation of knowledge and expertise about how to build on the linguistic and cultural resources that heritage speakers in multilingual communities offer. We do, however, know that the instructional needs of heritage language learners are distinct from those of monolingual English speakers (Peyton et al. 2001). We also see an increase in research and practice across the country that is beginning to address this gap.

In October 2002, the NFLC and CAL sponsored the second national Heritage Languages conference in Arlington, Virginia. Nariyo Kono (from the Confederated Tribes of the Warm Springs Reservation of Oregon and Portland State University) and Terrence Wiley (from Arizona State University) chaired a session entitled "A National Policy Statement on Heritage Language Development: Toward an Agenda for Action," and they invited U.S. and international language policy scholars to present statements that could form the basis of a U.S. policy for heritage languages (see the "Forums" page at www.language-policy.org for all of the policy statements and perspectives presented at this conference). Of particular relevance to this discussion is Donna Christian's paper entitled "Heritage Language Education Policy for U.S. Elementary and Secondary Education." Christian is the Director of the Center for Applied Linguistics, and she writes,

> The elementary and secondary education years are critical to
> the maintenance and development of heritage languages. When
> not encouraged, heritage language skills often languish, at best
> remaining static, and at worst being lost totally (the "subtrac-
> tive" result where English is acquired and the native language
> is lost). The individual student loses, and our society loses the

potential contributions from high levels of proficiency in languages.

To address these needs, elementary and secondary education policies at all levels (federal, state, local) should foster the development of heritage language proficiency in all ways possible.

Christian (2002) provides numerous recommendations for what a heritage language education policy could include, which I draw on in the next section in my discussion of what a school language policy might contain.

This section has introduced the Heritage Languages Initiative that the NFLC and CAL spearheaded in 1998, an initiative that is currently being embraced by educators and activists working within and across heritage language communities in the United States. My work in this book is aligned with this initiative, and my focus is on the local school and school district levels. The next part of the chapter brings together the ideas presented to this point in the chapter and outlines how school districts and schools can develop language policies that comply with all federal, state, and local accountability requirements AND promote bilingualism not only for their heritage language speakers but for all of their students.

Language planning and policy development on the local levels

Corson (1999) defines a school language policy as

> a document compiled by the staff of a school, who are often assisted by other members of the school community, to which the staff give their assent and commitment. It identifies areas in the school's scope of operations and programs where language problems exist that need the commonly agreed approach offered by a policy. A language policy sets out what the school intends to do about these areas of concern and includes provisions for follow-up, monitoring, and revision of the policy itself in light of changing circumstances. It is a dynamic action statement that changes along with the dynamic context of a school (ix).

Although Corson (1999) focuses primarily on the local school level, this definition of a school language policy can also be applied to the school district level. My concern here is with the development of school district language policies and plans that support the implementation of those policies.

How does a school district language policy and implementation plan relate to the larger national and state language education policy context on the one hand and to the sociolinguistic situation in the school district on the other? A school district language policy and implementation plan needs to be in compliance with all federal, state, and local mandates and accountability requirements, and it needs to be aligned with all other educational policies and procedures in that school district (e.g., governing curriculum, materials selection, assessments, and promotion and graduation criteria). The school district language policy and implementation plan also needs to be able to accommodate the range of sociolinguistic realities in the school district over time. The variation that we find within and across school districts, both in terms of target populations and language learning needs, presents serious challenges to policymakers and program developers.

What kinds of variation do we see within and across school districts in terms of their target populations? Some school districts are relatively small and may not have large numbers of ELLs in any one school or in the school district overall. Other school districts may have large numbers of ELLs, but they may all come from the same language background. Still other school districts may be quite large, and the target populations and language learning needs across schools may vary within that same district. Large urban school districts like the School District of Philadelphia, for example, serve some communities that have a clearly dominant language group, other communities that include ELLs from a wide range of linguistic and cultural backgrounds, and other communities that include very few ELLs. And, as we saw in chapter 1, the demographics in the United States today are changing, and we see increasing numbers of immigrants who speak a wider range of languages. These changing demographics are not only affecting large urban districts. School districts large and small; rural, suburban and urban; low and middle income are all challenged by these changing demographics and changing language needs.

The language policy that a particular school district develops needs to be able to address these dynamic and variable circumstances. It needs to be broad enough to accommodate the range of sociolinguistic and school realities that are found in the district, detailed enough to provide a blueprint for action on the local school level, flexible enough to drive decision-making in times of demographic and educational change, and endorsed by the school board. The implementation plan should provide the details that educators need to translate the language policy into action within and across schools and communities over time, and it should specify how educators collect and analyze the data they need to guide program development and to provide evidence of the effectiveness of their programs. In order to ensure that the implementation plan is meaningful and relevant, it should be readily available to educators, parents, and other constituents, and it should be reviewed and revised as necessary on a regular basis.

Based on my reading in the field, my conversations with language planners and policymakers across the country, and my own research and practice working with schools and school districts, I suggest that a school district language policy and implementation plan include the following:

- A mission statement that (a) aligns the school district's policies, programs, and practices with all local, state, and federal mandates and (b) promotes bilingualism to the greatest degree possible for the target populations.

- Policies and procedures governing the uses of languages in the school system, including issues of language choice, translators and interpreters, and languages of tests.

- Defining criteria for the kinds of programs (bilingual education, English as a second language, world language education, heritage language education) that are endorsed by the school district with references to the research base that documents their effectiveness.

- Policies and procedures to facilitate program development on the local school level.

- Policies and procedures to enable the identification of the language backgrounds of all students.

- Policies and procedures governing the assessment and placement of students in appropriate bilingual, English as a second language, world language, and/or heritage language programs.

- Policies and procedures governing the recruitment, retention, and professional development of all teachers, administrators and staff who work with language learners.

- Policies and procedures governing all aspects of program implementation, including student movement across levels, testing accommodations, exit criteria, promotion and graduation requirements, and ways to address students' special needs.

- Policies and procedures governing program monitoring and evaluation that comply with all local, state, and federal accountability requirements and that provide data on performance relative to all goals.

- Policies and procedures governing the way that the school district administration uses data gathered through its monitoring and evaluation processes, e.g., to address the professional development of teachers, to improve or change the program implemented at a school, to make decisions about teacher and school rewards or punishments.

- Policies and procedures for involving parents in all aspects of program development, implementation, and evaluation.

- Policies and procedures for articulating with community-based organizations and institutions of higher learning to support all aspects of program development, implementation, and evaluation.

- Policies and procedures governing how components of the language policy are reviewed and revised on a regular basis.

- Policies and procedures for how individual schools and the school district overall can obtain the resources they need to make the language policy a reality.

The particulars of a school district language policy and implementation plan will of course vary across districts across the country and will be shaped in important ways by local demographics and by relevant state policies.

Most schools and school districts in the United States today do not have one explicit, coherent language policy that is endorsed by the school district and supported by explicit policies and procedures guiding implementation and evaluation. However, all schools with language learners have language policies that guide practice on the local school level. In some cases the language policies are not explicitly written, but they are implicit in the practices that we can observe within and across schools in the school district. In other cases the policies are explicitly written, but the practitioners within and across schools are unaware of the existence or meaning of those policies. In many cases we find inconsistencies, confusion, and conflict about policies guiding the education of ELLs. In some cases we find language policies that contradict each other or contradict policies guiding the education of all students in that district.

Like Corson (1999), I argue that school districts need to gather the information that they need to develop a coherent language policy and implementation plan that can and does drive all decisions regarding language in that district. Administrators and teachers are now held accountable for the programs and practices that they develop for their ELLs, and the great majority of those educators do not have the professional development that they need to develop policies for their schools. The school district needs to take responsibility for clearly articulating its language policy; developing an implementation plan that is accessible to all educators who work with language learners; and monitoring and evaluating the effectiveness of its policy, school-based language planning, and program development. The school district also needs to ensure that it has the resources to support the policies and programs that it endorses.

As I mentioned earlier in the chapter, language planning and policy formulation are not linear, unidirectional, neutral processes. Educational language planning and policy development on the local school district and school levels must be understood as dynamic, ideological processes that are informed by multiple levels of institutional authority. Developing school district language policies that (a) comply with all federal, state, and local mandates and accountability requirements, (b) promote bilingualism to the greatest degree possible, and (c) are practicable within the context of the school district organizational structure is indeed a complex, albeit necessary, endeavor.

Conclusion

This chapter reviews language education policies in the United States at the national and state levels, and it highlights the need for school districts and schools to develop language policies that promote bilingualism to the greatest degree possible for their target populations. In the current sociopolitical context in the United States, we see confusion and controversy about bilingual education on the one hand, and endorsement with little financial support for world language education on the other. Educators who believe in the benefits of bilingualism can find space in this contemporary policy context for language education programs that promote bilingualism for their target populations. The burden of responsibility is clearly on school districts and schools to develop language policies and implementation plans that enable their target populations to reach their language education goals, and to monitor and evaluate these programs to ensure that they are effective. The No Child Left Behind Act of 2001 mandates that all schools, school districts, and states be held accountable for the English language development and academic performance in English of all English language learners and it narrowly defines what counts as "rigorous scientific research" on program effectiveness. This mandate presents a challenge to educators and researchers that support bilingual education. Educators must implement standards-based bilingual programs and they need to work with researchers to document the effectiveness of these programs and practices.

3

Reviewing the research
on language education programs

This chapter presents an overview of the research on language education programs that we find in the United States, and it is intended to serve a range of purposes. First, educators can use this review to guide their analysis of their own language education programs and practices so that they can determine whether and how their program is realizing its goals for its target populations. Second, language planners can use this review to determine the type of program that is appropriate for a particular school context, given an assessment of student needs and school requirements. Third, readers can use this review as a foundation for understanding my discussion of language education programs and practices throughout this book. This review is thus intended to provide a basis for working in the field of language education, broadly defined.

Language education in the United States is not generally discussed as one coherent field. Instead, we have seen language education professionals segregated in the fields of bilingual education, English as a second language (ESL), and world language education, and researchers and practitioners in each of these areas have focused on specific parts of the larger language education field. However, as we saw in chapter 1, the United States is experiencing tremendous changes in demographics and language learning needs, and these changes are challenging traditional disciplinary distinctions. Language educators today in the subfields of bilingual education, ESL, and world languages are beginning look to each other to develop programs and practices that can meet the language education needs of all language learners in the United States. We also see increasing interest in the needs of heritage language speakers and we see growing numbers of heritage language programs in secondary schools and universities.

My discussion of language education in this chapter is intended to bring together important developments in bilingual education, ESL, and world language education so that school districts and schools can make informed decisions about how to address the varied and changing language learning needs of all of their students. I use the following questions to structure my discussion of prototypical bilingual, ESL, and world language education programs:

1. Who is the target population?

2. What are the goals of the program for the target population?

3. How is the program structured?

4. How long do students spend in the program?

5. Is the program effective? That is, does the program enable its target populations to reach the stated goals in the allocated time?

Throughout this discussion, I consider research on second language acquisition, biliteracy development, standards-driven instruction, performance-based assessments, and program effectiveness. This review is intended to help educators make decisions about which types of language education programs are appropriate for their schools based on a solid research base, and to determine whether a program is well-implemented on the local school level.

Bilingual education

Bilingual education is a controversial and frequently misunderstood field in the United States. There is considerable confusion and conflict about what bilingual education means, who is served by bilingual programs, what the goals of a bilingual program are for its target populations, and whether bilingual education is or can be effective. General bilingual education policies are often made, amended, and/or abandoned without an understanding of how actual programs function on the local level. California's Proposition 227 and the ensuing local and national debates about bilingual education and English language development highlight some of this confusion and controversy (see chapter 2 for further discussion).

Rather than legislate against bilingual education based on anecdotal evidence about particular programs, we need to consider what research tells us about bilingual education. We need to begin by clearly defining what we mean by bilingual education, and we need to look closely at what the research says about how English language learners (ELLs) develop expertise in academic English and/or in their primary language over time in different kinds of bilingual and English as a second language (ESL) programs. Perhaps most importantly, we need to be clear about our goals. Some argue that one of the reasons that Proposition 227 passed in California was that people simply did not understand that a primary goal of bilingual education is English language development.

This point should not be underemphasized. All well-implemented bilingual education programs should be aligned with the TESOL (Teachers of English to Speakers of Other Languages) standards, which are discussed later in this chapter. Moreover, all bilingual programs must now address all federal and state accountability requirements for ELLs' English language development and academic achievement in English, which means that all bilingual programs must be aligned with all state content-area and English language proficiency standards. As we saw in chapter 2, Title III of the No Child Left Behind Act of 2001 grants states flexibility to develop programs that research demonstrates are effective for ELLs. To comply with federal accountability requirements, states are now required to do the following:

- Articulate concrete, standards-based, observable, and measurable, targets for ELLs' English language development and academic achievement over time.

- Identify and use state-approved standardized assessment tools to measure students' performance relative to those targets.

- Articulate annual yearly progress (AYP) objectives for English language development and academic achievement. These objectives must reflect the annual rate of growth of cohorts of ELLs from one year to the next in learning the English language, attaining English language proficiency, and achieving academically in the content areas according to the state's AYP measures.

- Demonstrate that all students have reached their performance targets in reading, language arts, and mathematics by the 2013-2014 school year (TESOL 2003).

With this understanding of the current accountability criteria that are mandated for all bilingual and ESL programs in mind, I turn to a discussion of the kinds of bilingual education programs that we find in research and practice, and I review the research on program effectiveness.

Part of the confusion about bilingual education is that the same term is actually used to refer to a wide range of programs that may have different ideological orientations toward linguistic and cultural diversity, different target populations, and different goals for those target populations (Hornberger 1991). My review of bilingual education models and program types in this section is organized around a major ideological distinction between the transitional bilingual model on the one hand and the dual language model on the other. As I discuss in more detail below, although transitional bilingual programs use ELLs' first language in the early years of their education, the goal of transitional bilingual education is English language development and academic achievement in English for ELLs. Dual language programs, in contrast, aim for bilingualism, biliteracy, and academic achievement in two languages for their target populations. Transitional bilingual programs tend to lead to subtractive bilingualism, and dual language programs should lead to additive bilingualism. As I stress throughout this book, the choice between these program orientations has serious implications for individual students, for schools, and for society overall.

Transitional bilingual education

The majority of bilingual programs that have been funded in the United States are transitional, and they encourage students' who have been traditionally defined as "limited English proficient" (LEP) to transition to the all-English academic mainstream as quickly as possible. The prototypical transitional bilingual education (TBE) program provides one to three years of content-area instruction through the students' primary language while the ELLs are enrolled in ESL classes. According to Thomas and Collier's (2002) national review of programs for ELLs, some TBE programs may provide as many as five years of bilingual instruction, and some may emphasize first-language literacy instruction as a foundation for literacy development in English.

According to Ruiz (1984), TBE programs are characterized by a "language-as-problem" orientation because the primary language is viewed as a problem to be overcome. The primary language is only used until the student has acquired sufficient English to transition to the mainstream English-only classroom (but see below for research about how long it takes to develop expertise in academic English). Once the "limited English proficient" student is deemed "fully English proficient," he/she is exited to the English-only academic mainstream and, in most cases, not eligible for continued ESL instruction. Because TBE programs provide no continued support for the native language at school, and because they pressure ELLs to acquire English as quickly as possible, ELLs who attend TBE programs tend to assimilate to monolingualism in English.

Although transitional bilingual programs are the most common bilingual programs in the United States, research demonstrates that they are less effective than dual language programs for ELLs (Thomas and Collier 2002; Lindholm-Leary 2001). Cummins' (1987) distinction between "basic interpersonal communication skills," or "BICS," and "cognitive academic language proficiency," or "CALP," is generally forwarded to explain this difference, although Cummins (2001) now uses the terms "conversational fluency" and "academic language proficiency" to refer to these notions. He defines conversational fluency as the ability to carry on a conversation in familiar face-to-face situations, and he defines academic language proficiency as the ability to comprehend and produce the increasingly complex oral and written language used in the content areas (e.g., literature, social studies, science, mathematics). Cummins and others argue that while it only takes second language learners one to two years of exposure to the second language at school and/or in other contexts to develop conversational fluency, it takes ELLs at least five years of exposure to academic English to catch up to native speaker norms. Since prototypical TBE programs only last one to three years, they do not allow sufficient time for ELLs to acquire the academic English they need to participate and achieve as equals in the academic mainstream. As Thomas and Collier's (2002) longitudinal research on program effectiveness for ELLs demonstrates, most ELLs who go through early-exit transitional bilingual programs are not able to reach parity with their English-speaking counterparts by the time they complete the program, or throughout their academic careers in U.S. public schools (see also Ramirez et al. 1991).

Dual language education

Dual language education is another model of bilingual education, and it stands in stark ideological contrast to transitional bilingual education. According to Ruiz (1984), dual language programs are characterized by a "language-as-resource" orientation that sees languages other than English as resources to be developed rather than as problems to be overcome. Three types of dual language education programs are found in the United States: second or foreign language immersion programs for English speakers; one-way developmental bilingual education programs for ELLs; and two-way immersion programs for English speakers and speakers of another language. Before I discuss these program types, I consider how my use of the term "dual language education" in this book relates to other uses of this term in the field.

The term "dual language education" is currently used in two different ways in the field. Consistent with the Center for Applied Linguistics and Cloud et al. (2000), I adopt a broad view of dual language education that includes the following three types of programs:

- Second or foreign language immersion programs for English speakers
- One-way developmental bilingual education programs for ELLs

- Two-way immersion programs for English speakers and speakers of another language

Cloud et al. (2000) use the term "enriched education" to refer collectively to these types of programs because they all use the minority language (e.g., Spanish in the U.S.) for at least 50 percent of the students' content area instruction and they all lead to bilingualism, biliteracy development, and academic achievement in two languages for their target populations. Lindholm-Leary (2001), in contrast, uses the term "dual language education" in a narrower sense to refer exclusively to two-way immersion programs that target English speakers and speakers of another language. With this broader notion of dual language education in mind, let's look more closely at each of the types of programs.

Second/foreign language immersion programs
Dual language programs that exclusively target speakers of the dominant language in society (e.g., English speakers in the United States and Canada) are called second or foreign language immersion programs. Immersion programs use a second/foreign language (e.g., French, Chinese) to teach at least 50 percent of the curriculum, and they last at least five to seven years. Immersion programs can vary in terms of the grade level at which the immersion experience begins and the amount of curriculum taught through the second/foreign language. According to Cloud et al. (2000), *early immersion education* begins in kindergarten and continues through the elementary grades. *Delayed immersion* typically does not begin until the middle elementary grades (around 4th grade). *Early total immersion* teaches 100 percent of the curriculum through the second or foreign language in kindergarten and 1st grade and begins to add English around 2nd or 3rd grade. *Early partial immersion* teaches between 50 and 90 percent of the curriculum through the second or foreign language and the remainder of the curriculum through English.

Extensive research on French immersion programs in Canada clearly demonstrates that second or foreign language immersion programs enable English speakers to become bilingual and biliterate and to achieve academically through two languages with no negative impact on English language and literacy development. English speakers are also reported to develop more positive attitudes toward French and French speakers through their participation in the immersion programs (see Cloud et al. [2000] and Lindholm-Leary [2001] for further discussions and references). Although considerable research evidence demonstrates the effectiveness of second/foreign language immersion education for English speakers, there are only a few such programs in the United States today (see www.cal.org for more information on immersion programs in the United States).

At first glance, many see a parallel between (a) French immersion programs for English speakers in Canada and (b) the all-English academic mainstream in the United States for Spanish-speaking ELLs. Consideration of the larger sociolinguistic contexts in Canada and in the United States, however, makes it clear why these two cases are in fact radically different. In the case of the province of Quebec, both French and English have official status and both have considerable symbolic capital in the linguistic marketplace (Bourdieu 1991; Heller 1994). Because English has such prestige in Canada and in the world, English-speaking children do not resist speaking English while they acquire French. Moreover, because English is the language of wider communication outside of school, English speakers have considerable support for their native language development. English speakers continue to develop expertise in English even as they are immersed in French, and this environment is conducive to additive bilingualism.

In the United States, in contrast, English is the language of power and Spanish does not have nearly as much symbolic capital. As a result, Spanish speakers, especially low-income Spanish speakers, tend to resist speaking Spanish in favor of English. This encourages subtractive bilingualism, and we see that Spanish speakers in the United States, like speakers of other languages in this country, tend to assimilate to English. Although we hear the term "immersion" used (incorrectly) to refer to the educational experience of ELLs who are placed in the all-English academic mainstream, "submersion" is a more appropriate term. English language learners who are submersed in the all-English academic mainstream with no support for their English language development are expected to "sink or swim." Immersion and submersion are very different experiences, and they have very different outcomes.

One-way developmental bilingual education programs

Dual language programs that exclusively target speakers of another language (e.g., Spanish speakers in the United States) are called "developmental" or "maintenance" bilingual programs. These programs are often referred to as "one-way developmental bilingual education (DBE) programs" because they only target one population (see below for discussion of two-way bilingual programs). While DBE programs are more common than immersion programs in the United States, they are not nearly as common as TBE programs.

The majority of the DBE programs in the United States target Spanish speakers. They provide content-area instruction through the native language as well as ESL instruction, and they last for at least five to seven years. The primary distinctions between DBE programs and the TBE programs discussed previously are that DBE programs continue to support the development of the student's primary language once the student has begun to use English for academic purposes, and DBE programs expect students to achieve academically through two languages. Because these programs last for at least five to seven years, ELLs have the time necessary to acquire the academic language and literacies they need in English while they continue to develop expertise in their primary language. And according to Thomas and Collier's (1998; 2002) research, ELLs who graduate from well-implemented DBE programs achieve educational parity with their English-speaking counterparts over time. The key here is implementation. Unfortunately, not all DBE programs are well-implemented.

Two-way immersion programs

Two-way immersion programs (TWI) are dual language programs that target balanced numbers of English speakers and speakers of a language other than English, and they provide content-area instruction through both languages to all students in integrated classes. These programs are sometimes referred to as *bilingual immersion, dual language immersion, two-way immersion, or two-way bilingual programs*, and they combine the best features of immersion education for English speakers and of one-way developmental bilingual programs for ELLs (Lindholm 1990; Lindholm-Leary 2001). The goals of TWI programs are for all students, English speakers and ELLs, to become bilingual and biliterate, achieve academically through both languages, and develop positive intergroup understanding and relations (Christian 1994; Cloud et al. 2000; Lindholm-Leary, 2001).

We find two major variants in TWI programs in the United States, which are referred to as the 90:10 and the 50:50 models. The 90:10 model provides 90 percent of the content-area instruction in the non-English language (e.g., Spanish) and 10 percent in English in the early elementary grades. As students progress through the grade levels the amount of instruction in English increases to 50 percent in Spanish and 50 percent in English in the upper grades. The 50:50 model provides 50 percent of students' content-area in instruction in Spanish and 50 percent in English across all grade levels. According to Thomas and Collier (2002) and Lindholm-Leary (2001), well-implemented TWI programs enable all students to achieve educational parity with their counterparts in English-only programs, and they enable all students to develop oral and written expertise in two languages. But again, the key is implementation.

Two-way immersion programs have attracted considerable attention and funding in the United States since the mid-1990s. Prior to 1990, the Department of Education's Title VII Program primarily funded transitional bilingual programs. However, the Bilingual Education Act (Title VII) was reauthorized in 1994, and the new guidelines specified that up to 25 percent of the grant money could be used for alternative forms of bilingual education. Furthermore, Rita Esquivel, the Director of the Office of Bilingual Education and Minority Language Affairs in 1994, was a strong supporter of dual language education, and federal funds began to be available for dual language programs at that time. Over the past three decades, we have seen the number of TWI programs grow from fewer than five to 261 programs in 24 states. While Spanish is by far the most common language used in TWI programs, we also see TWI programs that use other languages. At the time of this writing six programs use Cantonese, four use Korean, four use French, two use Navajo, two use Japanese, one uses Arabic, one uses Portuguese, and one uses Russian for instructional purposes (Lindholm-Leary 2001, 35; see also the TWI Directory at www.cal.org for updated information).

In March 2000, Richard W. Riley, then Secretary of Education, delivered an address entitled "The Progress of Hispanic Education and the Challenges of the New Century" in which he lauded two-way immersion programs and challenged the United States to increase the number of these programs to at least 1,000 over the next five years. Riley said,

> Right now we have about 260 dual-immersion schools and that
> is only a start. We need to invest in these kinds of programs and
> make sure they are in communities that can most benefit from
> them. In an international economy, knowledge -and knowledge
> of language-is power.

Title VII continued to aggressively fund two-way immersion programs, and at the time of this writing, more and more schools were designing and implementing TWI programs that would ideally meet the language and education needs of their target populations.

In 2003, The Center for Applied Linguistics convened a national dual language standards panel that is developing national standards for dual language programs. According to Hamayan (2003), a member of the national panel, the national dual language standards are inspired by the dual language standards developed in New Mexico, and they are organized around seven strands: program structure, assessment and accountability, staff quality, family and community involvement, curriculum, instructional practices, and resources/support. Each strand includes a number of specific standards that are intended to guide dual language program and professional development efforts. The national standards are to be made public during the fall of 2003.

Valdés (1997) makes a strong cautionary point about TWI programs. She argues that educators need to consider power relations between the target populations at schools, especially between white middle-class standard-English speakers and low-income Spanish speakers. Since white middle-class students tend to outperform their low-income Spanish-speaking counterparts academically in most U.S. schools today, Valdés urges educators to ensure that their TWI programs provide Spanish speakers with the opportunities they need to reach equally high standards in their content-area classes. Otherwise, Valdés argues, Spanish speakers may be exploited for the Spanish resource that they offer to English-speaking students. If teachers do not ensure that their low-income Latinos have equal access to educational opportunities in their TWI programs, middle-class English speakers may continue to outperform Spanish speakers AND they will have developed expertise in two languages. In this case, TWI programs would have the unintended outcome of taking jobs that require bilingual expertise from bilingual Latinos because bilingual whites would now be more prepared to fill those jobs. Valdés maintains that this does not have to be the case if TWI teachers attend to the power relations between languages and speakers of those languages on the local level and provide a high quality content-based program in Spanish as well as English. Again, the key is implementation, and the national dual language standards are intended to support the development of pedagogically sound, well-implemented dual language programs nationally.

International research on bilingual education

There is a solid international research base that supports findings from the research on the effectiveness of different types of bilingual education in the United States. For example, Dutcher (1995) carried out a comprehensive review of research for the World Bank on the use of first and second languages in education. This review examined three different types of countries: (1) those with no (or few) mother-tongue speakers of the language of wider communication (e.g., Haiti, Nigeria, Philippines); (2) those with some mother-tongue speakers of the language of wider communication (e.g., Guatemala); and (3) those with many mother-tongue speakers of the language of wider communication (e.g., Canada, New Zealand, the United States). Tucker (1999) draws the following conclusions from this review of the research:

1. Success in school depends upon the child's mastery of cognitive/academic language, which is very different from the social language used at home.
2. The development of cognitive/academic language requires time (4 to 7 years of formal instruction).
3. Individuals most easily develop literacy skills in a familiar language.
4. Individuals most easily develop cognitive skills and master content material when they are taught in a familiar language.
5. Cognitive/academic language skills, once developed, and content-subject material, once acquired, transfer readily from one language to another.
6. The best predictor of cognitive/academic language development in a second language is the level of development of cognitive/academic language proficiency in the first language.
7. Children learn a second language in different ways depending upon their culture and their individual personality.
8. If the goal is to help the student ultimately develop the highest possible degree of content mastery and second language proficiency, time spent instructing the child in a familiar language is a wise investment.

The cumulative evidence from research conducted over the last three decades at sites around the world demonstrates conclusively that cognitive, social, personal, and economic benefits accrue to the individual who has an opportunity to develop their bilingual repertoire when compared with a monolingual counterpart. Dual language programs that promote bilingualism, biliteracy development, and academic achievement through two languages for their target population(s), when well-implemented, show real promise in our efforts to address our national language needs.

This section has discussed the types of bilingual education program that we find in U.S. schools today. All well-implemented bilingual programs hold students to the same high academic standards as the all-English academic mainstream. Furthermore, all well-implemented bilingual programs provide ESL services to their students that are aligned with the TESOL standards. The next section looks more closely at the kinds of ESL programs and practices that we can find in the United States today.

English as a second language

We can find a wide range of English as a second language (ESL) programs and practices in U.S. schools today. For example, we may see pull-out ESL programs that take ELLs out of the all-English academic mainstream for ESL instruction. We may see push-in ESL programs in which the ESL teacher enters the all-English classroom and works to support the ESL students' needs within the context of that classroom. In schools that have large numbers of ELLs, we may see sheltered ESL programs that segregate ELLs for content-area instruction (see below for further discussion). The organization of the actual ESL program depends on the local context, including the number of ELLs that the school serves, and on the relationship between the ESL teachers and content-area teachers at the school.

Regardless of the program structure, all ESL programs are to use a communicative approach to language teaching and learning (Canale and Swain 1980), and all ESL programs are to address the goals and standards that the professional organization for Teachers of English to Speakers of Other Languages has defined for pre-K–12 students (TESOL 1997). The No Child Left Behind Act now requires each state to develop English language proficiency (ELP) standards that are aligned with state content-area standards, and we see variation across states in the ways that they develop ELP standards that are aligned with the national TESOL standards, their state (English/Spanish) language arts standards, and standards in other content areas. This section begins with a brief discussion of the theoretical notion of communicative competence used in the language teaching and learning field. Then I introduce the TESOL goals and standards and review the range of ESL program types we find in U.S. schools. Future research is necessary to document the range of ELP standards that are developed and how they are translated into programs and practices for ELLs across contexts.

Hymes' (1966) notion of communicative competence is fundamental to most contemporary approaches to language teaching and learning, and it informed the development of the TESOL standards discussed in this section and the ACTFL (American Council for Teachers of Foreign Languages) world language standards discussed later in this chapter. Communicative competence can be broadly defined as what a speaker needs to know to be able to communicate correctly and appropriately within a particular speech community (Saville-Troike 1996). Canale and Swain (1980) extend this notion to the field of language teaching and learning and identify and define the following four aspects of communicative competence:

1. Linguistic competence: the forms, inflections, and sequences used to express the message are grammatically correct.

2. Sociolinguistic competence: the expression of the message is appropriate in terms of the person being addressed and the overall circumstances and purpose of communication.

3. Discourse competence: the selection, sequence, and arrangement of words and structures are clear and effective means of expressing the intended message.

4. Strategic competence: the strategies used to compensate for any weaknesses in the above areas are effective and unobtrusive.

A language learner is considered "communicatively competent" relative to the target speech community when he/she demonstrates competence in each of these areas. Communicative language teaching in U.S. schools is intended to facilitate the learners' acquisition of the spoken and written language they need in order to use language correctly and appropriately in social settings and in all academic content areas.

The three goals that TESOL established for ELLs in pre-K–12 schools reflect this fundamental notion of communicative competence. Each goal is associated with three distinct standards, and ELLs are to meet the standards as a result of the instruction they receive. As they meet the specific standards, ELLs realize the more general social, academic, and personal goals. The ESL goals and standards are as follows (TESOL 1997, 9-10):

Goal 1: To use English to communicate in social settings.
   Standards for goal 1
   Students will:
   1. use English to participate in social interaction.
   2. interact in, through, and with spoken and written English for personal expression and enjoyment
   3. use learning strategies to extend their communicative competence.

Goal 2: To use English to achieve academically in all content areas
   Standards for goal 2
   Students will:
   1. use English to interact in the classroom.
   2. use English to obtain, process, construct, and provide subject matter information in spoken and written form.
   3. use appropriate learning strategies to construct and apply academic knowledge.

Goal 3: To use English in socially and culturally appropriate ways
   Standards for goal 3
   Students will:
   1. use the appropriate language variety, register, and genre according to audience, purpose and setting.
   2. use nonverbal communication appropriate to audience, purpose, and setting.

3. use appropriate learning strategies to extend their sociolinguistic and sociocultural competence.

A framework for ESL language planning and for making use of the standards is also outlined (TESOL 1997). The TESOL standards describe the kinds of English that ELLs need to acquire so that they can attain the same high-level standards within and across content areas, including English language arts, as fully proficient English-speaking students.

Research on effective ESL programs demonstrates that the most effective way to enable ELLs to acquire the academic language and literacies that they need in English to reach the standards across all content areas is through a content-based second-language instruction approach (Brinton et al. 1989). Brinton et al. define content-based second language instruction as

> the integration of particular content with language teaching
> aims. More specifically ... it refers to the concurrent teaching of
> academic subject matter and second language skills. The lan-
> guage curriculum is based directly on the academic needs of
> the students and generally follows the sequence determined by
> particular subject matter in dealing with the language problems
> which students encounter. The focus for students is on acquir-
> ing information via the second language and, in the process,
> developing their academic language skills (1989, 2).

Brinton et al. identify three models of content-based second/foreign language programs that are appropriate for use in different instructional contexts. These are (1) the sheltered model, (2) the adjunct model, and (3) the theme-based model.

Sheltered courses are content-area courses (e.g., math, science, social studies) that are taught by a content-area specialist to a segregated group of language learners, and the primary goal of these courses is content-area mastery. Sheltered ESL courses follow the tradition of second or foreign language immersion education for elementary and secondary school students. Because the content-area teacher employs strategies that make complex content comprehensible to second language learners, language tends to be learned incidentally. Adjunct courses are paired content and language courses that language learners enroll in concurrently. Two teachers are necessary for adjunct courses. The content-area teacher teaches the content area (e.g., math, science, social studies), and the language teacher teaches the content-obligatory and content-compatible language that students need to participate and achieve in the content-area class (Snow et al. 1992). Theme-based classes are taught by language teachers who structure the language course around particular topics or themes. The common feature of all of these types of courses and/or programs is that content material is used as the basis for language learning (see Brinton et al. 1989 for further discussion).

Research on second language teaching and learning highlights several important reasons for integrating language and content for instructional purposes. First, content provides a motivational basis for language learning. When students are interested in the content they are learning about, they tend to learn the language forms and functions they need because those language forms and functions provide access to that content. Content also provides a meaningful context within which learners can connect language forms and functions. Furthermore, students learn language most effectively when they need to use that language in meaningful, purposeful social and academic contexts (see Brinton et al. 1989; Chamot and O'Malley 1994; Cloud et al. 2000; Snow et al. 1992).

The key to an effective ESL program is implementation. The educators who work with ELLs (i.e., ESL teachers, bilingual teachers, mainstream classroom teachers who have ELLs in their classes) must clearly understand their students' content and language strengths and needs, and their programs need to be aligned with the TESOL standards and with state content-area standards. The No Child Left Behind Act holds mainstream teachers accountable for ELLs' academic achievement, and holds ESL teachers accountable for ELLs' English language development. Mainstream classroom teachers and ESL teachers should work together to provide a coherent program that enables all ELLs to acquire the academic language and literacies that they need for access to equal educational opportunities in the all-English academic mainstream. These programs should have clearly articulated objectives for their ELLs' English language development and academic performance, and educators should use multiple forms of assessment to determine how well ELLs are performing relative to those objectives. Educators at these schools must understand that it takes at least five to seven years for ELLs to develop expertise in academic English and to close the gap between their performance and the performance of their English-speaking counterparts across content areas, and exit criteria and promotion and graduation requirements should reflect this understanding (see also Echevarria et al. 2000; NSSE 2002).

World language education

As national recognition of the need for languages other than English grows in the United States, we see exciting new developments in a field that was traditionally called "foreign" language education. In this book, I use the term "world language" to refer to the teaching of a language as a subject area to a student who does not speak that language (e.g., Spanish to English speakers in the United States). This section considers how the changes in language learning goals and the changes in students' language learning strengths and needs (see chapter 1) have influenced the ways that we are beginning to think about world language education in the United States today. First, I review the American Council on the Teaching of Foreign Languages (ACTFL) *Standards for Foreign Language* (1996) and the *ACTFL Performance Guidelines for K–12 Learners* (1999) to suggest realistic and attainable goals and expectations for world language learning at school. Then I describe the prototypical FLES (Foreign Language in the Elementary School) program structure that is recommended for elementary school world language programs, and discuss the increase in elementary and secondary school world language programs that we see nationally. I conclude this section by considering the impact that heritage language speakers have had on a field that traditionally targeted only monolingual English speakers.

In 1995, the ACTFL standards were released to the world language profession at their annual meeting, and they were endorsed by forty-six state, regional, and national language organizations. Like the standards-based projects in other disciplines, the world language standards attempt to outline the focus of instruction with specific reference to 4th, 8th, and 12th grades. The goal of the standards is to clearly articulate what students need to know and what they need to be able to do as a result of their study of world languages.

The standards are arranged into five major goal areas: communication, cultures, connection, comparisons, and communities. Like the TESOL standards, each goal area includes specific standards. These standards do not describe specific course content, they do not provide a recommended scope and sequence, and they do not prescribe an instructional approach or teaching methodology. Instead, the goal areas are intended to be seen as interconnected, and they emphasize using language for communication with other peoples, gaining understanding of other cultures, and accessing information in a wide range of disciplines (Omaggio Hadley 2000). Educators who are familiar with their students' language learning needs and preferences are encouraged to select the content, sequence, and method that are appropriate for their context.

The *Standards for Foreign Language Learning* (1996) outline *what* students need to know, and the *ACTFL Performance Guidelines for K–12 Learners* (1999) provide a framework for assessing *how well* novice, intermediate, and pre-advanced learners can use the world language for communicative purposes. The performance guidelines do not focus on the traditional skills areas of reading, writing, listening, and speaking in isolation. Instead, they define how well students at different levels can use language in what the guidelines refer to as three different communicative modes: the interpersonal, interpretive, and presentational. The interpersonal mode is characterized by active negotiation of meaning among individuals (e.g., in face-to-face communication). The interpretive mode is focused on the appropriate cultural interpretation of meanings that occur in written and spoken form where there is no active negotiation of meaning with another interlocutor (e.g., reading a novel, listening to the radio, watching a film). The presentational mode refers to the creation of spoken and/or written messages in a manner that facilitates interpretation by members of the other culture where no direct opportunity for the active negotiation of meaning between members of the two cultures exists (e.g., writing a report, presenting a speech). The performance guidelines are discussed in more detail in chapter 14.

Both the standards and the performance guidelines are designed to reflect second language learning that begins in kindergarten and that continues in an uninterrupted sequence through 12th grade. These guidelines suggest that English speakers who have been enrolled in a well-articulated, long-sequence foreign language program can demonstrate intermediate to advanced levels of performance in the western languages that are most commonly taught in American schools. The authors of the performance guidelines explain why we can expect different kinds of performances by English speakers studying western languages on the one hand and by English speakers studying less commonly taught languages on the other. They write,

> Students whose native language is English find many similarities between English and the languages of the western world, both in oral and written forms, which aid students in their acquisition of the new language. Conversely, when students encounter the less commonly taught languages such as Arabic, Chinese, Japanese, Korean, and Russian, new hurdles await them: unfamiliar sounds, different writing systems and new grammars. These linguistic features, which oftentimes cannot be linked to anything the students know in their native language, present challenges and generally tend to extend the language acquisition process. It cannot be expected, therefore, that students learning the less commonly taught languages should reach the same levels of performance as those who study the western languages more frequently offered in American schools (3).

Because it may take longer for English speakers to develop expertise in the less commonly taught languages, it is even more important to begin study of these languages earlier. However, since an uninterrupted 13-year sequence of world language study is not commonly found in the United States today, the ACTFL K–12 performance guidelines also account for various entry points that reflect most major language sequences (see American Council of Teachers of Foreign Languages [1999] for further discussion and for performance indicators).

What does a "well-articulated, long-sequence" world language program look like in practice? *Lessons Learned: Model Early Foreign Language Programs* (Gilzow and Branaman 2000) describes seven foreign language programs in the United States that were identified through a selection process informed by the national standards for foreign language education and by research on effective language instruction for elementary and middle school students (Curtain and Pesola 1994; National Standards for Foreign Language Education Project 1996). Each of the programs selected met the following criteria (Gilzow and Branaman 2000, 2):

- Curricula based on the "five Cs" of the national foreign language standards-communication, cultures, connections, comparisons, and communities

- Regular program evaluation

- Outcomes that meet program goals

- Accessibility for all students

- Communication and coordination across content areas

- A student population that reflects the ethnic and socioeconomic diversity of the local population

- Articulation from elementary to middle school and from middle school to high school

- Professional development for teachers

- Support from the community

The seven programs included five content-enriched FLES programs, one partial immersion program, and one middle school immersion program. Because we reviewed the characteristics of second/foreign language immersion programs in our discussion of dual language education earlier in the chapter, the focus here will be on the prototypical FLES program structure.

While secondary world language programs teach the language as a separate subject area, FLES programs integrate language instruction into the students' regular classroom schedule. According to Curtain and Pesola

(1994) and Gilzow and Branaman (2000), elementary school students should have a thirty- to forty-five-minute language class three to five times per week for a minimum of ninety minutes total per week. Of course, when schools allocate more time to target language instruction, students can be expected to develop a broader range of expertise in that language. What is important to emphasize is that the language program be treated as an integral part of the whole school program. Students need to have regular opportunities to participate in language class each week throughout the years of the program if they are to realize the annual and long-term objectives and goals of the program.

Prototypical FLES programs assume that the language teacher and the classroom teacher are two different people, and FLES teachers either travel to the mainstream classroom or the students travel to a separate language classroom for FLES class. Like any pedagogical choice, there are pros and cons to each teaching arrangement. For example, having the FLES teacher travel to the regular classroom can present a wide range of challenges for that teacher (e.g., physical wear and tear, difficulty transporting materials, time to get from one class to the next), but the traveling teacher can help make the target language an integral part of the regular classroom and school. Having a separate classroom for the FLES class can be much easier for the FLES teacher (e.g., to develop libraries full of authentic texts in the target language, display teacher-made materials and student work), but this arrangement could contribute to the marginalization of the world language class in the school.

What is the content of a FLES program? Each of the FLES programs described in Gilzow and Branaman (2000) focused on content, although the ways that they focused on content varied across programs and grade levels. Following Curtain and Pesola (1994), I differentiate between a content-based second language program (like those implemented in English as a second language and foreign/second language immersion programs discussed earlier in the chapter) and a content-related second language program. According to Curtain and Pesola (1994),

> In the typical FLES classroom, in which twenty to thirty minutes per day is devoted to foreign language instruction, it is not realistic to base the curriculum on concepts taken from grade-level curriculum of other content areas, nor is it probable that the foreign language program can take full responsibility for teaching grade-appropriate concepts from the general curriculum in the target language. While many hands-on activities related to content may still be successful, language skills in a second language simply do not develop quickly enough in a

FLES setting to permit the effective initial teaching of increasingly sophisticated and abstract ideas. Through theme-based, integrative teaching, however, the foreign language class can reenter and reinforce important concepts from mathematics, social studies, and other areas, drawing from earlier grade levels as well as from grade-level-appropriate curriculum (151).

According to Gilzow and Branaman (2000), some FLES programs align language curricula with curricula in the subject areas at the district level, and the world language curricula are revised as the district curricula are revised. In other programs, the language class content is closely tied to the content of regular classes, but curriculum development and revision are handled informally by the teachers involved.

What is the state of world language education in the United States today? In 1999, the Center for Applied Linguistics (CAL) published *Foreign Language Instruction in the United States: A National Survey of Elementary and Secondary Schools*. This survey was intended to explore current patterns and shifts in enrollment, languages and programs offered, curriculum, teaching methodologies, teacher qualifications and training, and reactions to national reform issues, and it was designed to replicate CAL's 1987 survey in an effort to show trends during the 1987-1997 decade. According to CAL's executive summary, "foreign language education in the United States is at a unique moment historically." World languages were recognized as part of the core curriculum in the Goals 2000: Educate America Act, and there was evidence of considerable increases in K–12 world language instruction throughout the country (Center for Applied Linguistics 1997).

The CAL survey found that in the past decade, world language instruction in the elementary schools increased significantly. In 1997 one in three elementary schools reported offering world language instruction, and this represented a 10 percent increase since 1987. While most programs offer Spanish, there was some increase in Japanese, Russian, and Italian on the elementary level and in Japanese and Russian on the secondary level. However, CAL's executive summary concludes by saying that there is still reason for concern about the limited number of K–12 long-sequence world language programs that enable students to develop communicative competence in languages other than English. The National Foreign Language Center (NFLC) echoes this concern and highlights the need for well-articulated long-sequence language programs in the less commonly taught languages like Chinese and Russian (Brecht and Rivers 2000). Both CAL and NFLC emphasize that well-articulated elementary and secondary foreign language programs are still the exception rather than the norm. Unfortunately, the increasing interest in world language programs in the United States today is not accompanied by sufficient numbers of well-implemented programs that could dramatically alter the U.S. ability to meet the kinds of language needs outlined in chapter 1.

Heritage language programs

Traditionally, world language classes have targeted monolingual English speakers who generally begin their language study with no expertise in the target language and minimal knowledge about the people who speak it. Until recently, little attention has been paid to developing and coordinating well-designed and carefully articulated language programs for heritage language speakers. However, student populations enrolled in world language programs on the elementary, secondary, and university levels are rapidly changing, and world language teachers see increasing numbers of heritage language speakers in classes with monolingual English-speaking students. As discussed in chapter 1, these students have a wide range of expertise in spoken and/or written languages, and they pose a serious challenge to teachers who are not trained to work with such diversity.

Since the 1990s, we have seen considerable interest in the teaching of heritage Spanish speakers in particular and speakers of other heritage languages more generally. The CAL survey of foreign language programs found a significant increase in Spanish for native speakers (SNS) classes on the elementary and secondary levels. Two major volumes of articles were published that reflected new energy within the Spanish-teaching profession, and we see SNS teachers and researchers looking critically at how they can assess and build on their students' linguistic and cultural strengths (Merino et al. 1993; Colombi and Alarcón, 1997).

Valdés (2000) encourages SNS teachers to draw on the framework of communicative modes (interpersonal, interpretive, presentational) discussed previously in their efforts to understand and expand the bilingual range of students who have grown up in homes where non-English languages are spoken. She offers a wealth of ideas that can help SNS teachers determine what strengths a particular heritage Spanish speaker brings to class (e.g., strong interpersonal abilities) and what needs that student has relative to the framework (e.g., the need to develop interpretive and presentational modes of communication, including reading and writing authentic texts, understanding films, making formal presentations).

Teachers of Spanish to native speakers, Valdés argues, have much to teach, but they must take a different approach from that traditionally taken by world language educators. They need to see heritage Spanish speakers' linguistic and cultural expertise as resources that they can build on. They must not see their students' expertise in nonstandard varieties of Spanish (e.g., vernacular Puerto Rican Spanish) as deficits that they must overcome. Instead SNS teachers need to organize their programs and practices so that heritage Spanish speakers can add standard Spanish and literacies in Spanish to their linguistic repertoires. In the process, teachers can encourage heritage Spanish speakers to think critically about the sociolinguistic variation in Spanish that is a very real part of their everyday lives.

World language programs in the United States face enormous challenges today. National, state, and local education policies are beginning to emphasize the need for U.S. citizens to develop expertise in more than one language in order to participate in the global economy and to ensure national security. High schools are increasingly requiring expertise in world languages to meet graduation criteria, which has encouraged many school districts to offer world language education in the elementary grades. At the same time, student populations enrolled in world language programs on the elementary, secondary, and university levels are rapidly changing, and we see heritage language speakers attending the same language classes as monolingual English speakers. Not only is there a serious shortage of world language teachers available to fill an increasing number of positions in the field, but many world language educators have not been trained to meet the diverse and rapidly changing needs of students today. Some university world language programs, in-service professional development programs, and individual world language teachers are working in creative ways to address these challenges, but much work remains (for further discussion see Peyton 2001).

Conclusion

This chapter has reviewed prototypical bilingual education, English as a second language, and world language programs that we find in the United States today, and it has related these kinds of programs to research on second language acquisition, biliteracy development, content-based second language instruction, and program effectiveness. As we have seen, there are a number of different kinds of language education programs that educators can draw on to promote additive bilingualism on the local school level.

However, language educators face several important challenges as they work to design and implement context-responsive programs and practices. First, program planners need to have a clear understanding of who their students are and they must be able to clearly articulate their language education goals for their target populations. Program planners also need to have a clear understanding about how language education programs are structured to realize those goals so that they can develop and implement programs that are pedagogically sound. Perhaps most importantly, program planners need to understand the ways that languages are taught, learned, used, and evaluated on the local school and community level in order to build on the linguistic and cultural resources that are available. Chapter 4 is intended to help school-based program planners address these challenges.

4

Language planning for educational and social change

This chapter discusses how school-based language planners can challenge the trend toward monolingualism in English for individual students and communities on the local level by developing enriched language education programs that encourage additive bilingualism for their target populations. These bilingual programs stand in opposition to the majority of U.S. educational programs, which generally lead to assimilation to monolingualism in English for English language learners. As we will see in this chapter, enriched language education programs can promote social change from the bottom up.

The chapter is divided into three parts. The first part provides a theoretical orientation that helps us understand how schools function as major socializing agents that can either reflect and reproduce the dominant social order or challenge and potentially transform that social order. The second part of the chapter builds on this theoretical foundation and describes how school-based language planners, by which I mean policymakers, administrators, teachers, parents, and community members, can proceed in their efforts to develop programs and practices that promote bilingualism for their target populations. The third part of the chapter considers how school-based language planning teams can challenge language ideologies that stand in opposition to the language plan they are developing. Together, the parts of this chapter are intended to provide a foundation for educational planners, practitioners, policymakers, and researchers who work to promote this kind of educational and social change in other school contexts.

Schools as socializing agents

In order to understand how language planning can stimulate educational and social change on the local school level, we need to first consider how students develop an understanding of their roles in the social orders at school and in the larger society. The theoretical orientation outlined in this section builds on earlier findings from the ethnography of education, and it is aligned with recent developments in sociolinguistics, linguistic anthropology, literacy studies, and social psychology (see for example Davies and Harré 1990; Fairclough 1989,1993; Gal 1995; Gee 1990; Moll 1995; Rampton 1995; Street 1995). Context is central to the analysis.

My focus in this book is on language, broadly defined. By language I mean social practice, including the actual spoken and written texts that people speak, hear, read, and write as well as the abstract underlying ideological discourses that those texts reflect and shape. One of my primary concerns is to explore how language ideologies, or common-sense assumptions about languages and speakers of those languages, influence the ways that people use and evaluate languages on the local level. Important questions to consider are

- How do we develop our understanding of language ideologies?

- How do language ideologies structure our understanding of who we are in the world and what opportunities are available to us?

As we discuss below, power relations figure prominently in the answers to these questions.

I have divided this part of the chapter into two sections. First, I explain how people learn who they are and what opportunities are available to them through their language use in everyday interactions within particular contexts, and my focus is on students at school. Then I argue that educators have choices in the ways that they structure their educational programs and practices, and the choices educators make have implications for the students they serve. This theoretical orientation highlights the dialectical relationship between knowledge and action.

Social reproduction of "minority" languages and speakers through schooling

According to research on language socialization, people develop their knowledge about the world, negotiate social relations, and construct their social identities through their language use in everyday interactions (Davies and Harré 1990; Freeman and McElhinny 1996; Ochs 1988; Schieffelin and Ochs 1990). For example, girls and boys learn what they can and cannot do and what they should and should not believe through the messages that they hear and read; from their observations of boys, girls, men, and women interacting; and from the activities in which they participate as boys and girls. Likewise, Spanish speakers and English speakers learn how spoken and written Spanish and English should be used by whom under what circumstances through their observations of English speakers and Spanish speakers interacting, as well as through their own everyday inter-actions using spoken and written varieties of Spanish and English. There is, of course, considerable variation across contexts about the possible meanings of particular social identities (e.g., boy, girl, Spanish speaker, English speaker). I return to this below.

The point to highlight here is that the construction of social identity is a dynamic process that takes place in situated activities. According to Davies and Harré (1990), social identity is made up of two interrelated parts: the micro-level position in the face-to-face interaction and the macro-level role in the social order. Davies and Harré's (1990) notion of positioning can help us understand how students construct their social identities at school. They write,

> There can be interactive positioning in which what one person
> says positions another. And there can be reflexive positioning
> in which one positions oneself. However it would be a mistake
> to assume that, in either case, positioning is necessarily inten-
> tional. One lives one's life in terms of one's ongoingly produced
> self, whoever might be responsible for its production (6).

Davies and Harré argue that if an individual is repeatedly positioned in the face-to-face interaction as a particular kind of social being, over time the individual is likely to assume that role with its associated rights and obliga-tions in the macro-level social order. Because schools are one of society's primary socializing agents, this assumption has important implications for educators.

The 1980s yielded a large body of ethnographic research that demon-strates how the micro-level organization of classroom interaction in main-stream U.S. schools can reflect and reproduce macro-level social processes that discriminate against students who speak nonstandard varieties of English (see for example Au 1980; Mohatt and Erickson 1981; Scollon and Scollon 1981; Heath 1983; Philips 1983; Michaels 1986). Although the par-ticulars vary from study to study, what emerges from this literature is an understanding that students who speak nonstandard varieties of English at home and in their local community often communicate in ways that are either not understood and/or not valued at school. The miscommunication that can arise (e.g., from different ways of telling stories, different turn-taking norms, or different participation preferences) can negatively posi-tion these students relative to their Standard English–speaking peers. Such subordinate positioning can restrict students' opportunities to demonstrate what they know and/or can do, which in turn can block their access to equal educational opportunities. In this way U.S. schools have been implicated in the social reproduction of the subordinate role of "minority" groups relative to the white Standard English–speaking, middle-class "majority," albeit unintentionally.

Research on English language learners (ELLs) in mainstream U.S. schools tells a similar story. Ruiz (1984) maintains that the majority of English as a second language (ESL) and bilingual programs in U.S. schools are characterized by a "language-as-problem" ideological orientation because the non-English language is viewed as a problem that ELLs need to overcome in order to participate and achieve in the English-only academic mainstream. These students often experience tremendous pressure to assimilate through their everyday interactions at school, and subtractive bilingualism is a typical outcome (Lambert and Tucker 1972). Study after study demonstrates how mainstream U.S. schools subordinate students who speak languages other than English and who do not behave according to white middle-class Standard English–speaking norms, and this subordination at school is offered as an explanation for their subordinate role in U.S. society. In Bourdieu's (1991) terms, mainstream ESL and transitional bilingual programs reflect and perpetuate the power or symbolic domination of English over other languages in the linguistic marketplace.

Constructing alternatives
to dominant language ideologies at school

Social reproduction through schooling, however, is not the only possibility. People have choices in how they define themselves, each other, the languages that they speak, and the educational programs and practices that they organize. Although what happens in any given situation may be powerfully influenced by larger historical, sociocultural, political, and economic processes, these processes do not totally determine what happens in the face-to-face interaction (Fairclough 1989; 1993). This means that educational policies, programs, and practices in schools that serve students who live in multilingual communities do not have to see students' linguistic and cultural differences as deficits. Educators do not have to define languages other than English as problems that speakers of these languages need to overcome in order to participate and achieve at school. They do not have to (implicitly or explicitly) encourage students who come from homes where languages other than English are used to assimilate to monolingualism in English. Instead, educators can recognize and resist such discriminatory practices, and they can work together to create alternative educational discourses that provide more equitable opportunities to students from diverse backgrounds.

My book *Bilingual Education and Social Change* (Freeman 1998) provides empirical evidence of this transformative process. Drawing on two years of ethnographic and discourse analytic research at Oyster Bilingual School in Washington D.C., Freeman (1998) describes how the Oyster educators collaborated with parents and community members to develop a two-way immersion program that promotes bilingualism and biliteracy for all students. Oyster's program has been in operation since 1971, and it is considered successful because Spanish-speaking students maintain and develop expertise in their native language, English-speaking students acquire Spanish as a second language, all students achieve academically through two languages, and everyone develops positive intergroup understanding and relations. The Oyster educators emphasize the importance of ongoing communication with parents, teachers, and students so that everyone has a coherent understanding of how Spanish and English should be used at school. These educators clearly reject the "language-as-problem" orientation (Ruiz 1984) that is dominant in most U.S. schools. In policy and in practice, Spanish is clearly defined as a resource to be developed by English-speaking and Spanish-speaking students, parents, and the communities in which they live. The Oyster educators, I argued, have constructed an alternative educational discourse for their students, and this alternative provides more options than are traditionally available to English-speaking or Spanish-speaking students in U.S. schools.

The Oyster educators have also developed a shared understanding of the ideological and practical challenges they face in providing equal educational opportunities to their student population. These educators recognize that English has more symbolic capital (Bourdieu 1991) than Spanish in the United States, and they work hard to elevate the status of Spanish at the school. Because these educators believe that mainstream U.S. society discriminates against students who speak languages other than English, they continually work to position their Spanish-speaking and English-speaking students as equals in classes and throughout the school. This is a constant struggle, and the teachers work in creative ways with each other and with the parents to ensure that their low-income Spanish speakers gain access to the same educational opportunities as their middle-income English-speaking counterparts. We can see evidence of efforts to elevate the status of diverse perspectives, contributions, and languages throughout Oyster's policies, curriculum content, organization of classroom interaction, assessment practices, and relations with their parents and communities (see Freeman 1998 for detailed discussion).

In sum, language ideologies at school and in society have important implications for language users as well as for language learners and teachers. On the one hand, established language ideologies can reflect and help perpetuate the symbolic domination of English over other languages at school and throughout immigrant communities, which contributes to the assimilationist trend that has characterized language use in the United States over the last century. This is the case that we see in most mainstream U.S. schools. On the other hand, language ideologies can resist and challenge dominant ideologies in ways that open spaces for alternatives to mainstream language education programs practices. This is the case that I document in my book (Freeman 1998). When language planners (policy-makers, administrators, teachers, parents, community members) work together to construct alternative language ideologies that promote additive bilingualism at school, language planning can stimulate educational and social change on the local level.

Language planning from the bottom up

This part of the chapter is intended to guide language planning efforts on the local school level. It is organized around a series of questions that schools can use to help them organize their programs and practices in ways that comply with all federal, state, and local mandates while they promote additive bilingualism to the greatest degree possible for their target populations. These questions are the following:

1. Who are the language planners, and how should they work together?
2. Who are the target populations?
3. What are the goals for the target populations?
4. How is the school currently addressing the language education needs of the target populations?
5. What type(s) of language education program(s) is/are appropriate for the school and community?

The section concludes with a discussion of how the language planning team can translate the type of language education program that they believe is appropriate for their students, school, and community into a pedagogically sound, well-implemented plan. My focus on school-based language planning processes is aligned with what Hornberger (1997) and others call language planning from the bottom up.

Who are the language planners, and how should they work together

School-based language planning is a complex process, and it is best approached by a team of language planners who are committed to working together over time to develop bilingual, English as a second language (ESL), world language and/or heritage language programs that can meet the needs of their students and community. Members of the language planning team need to understand that language planning is not a linear, unidirectional process. The team needs to be prepared for a dynamic, recursive process of planning, implementation, monitoring, evaluation, and development.

The language planning team should include language educators (e.g., bilingual, ESL, world language), mainstream classroom teachers, the principal and/or another administrator with recognized authority in the school, bilingual coordinators, community liasons, parents, and/or interested community members. While the team should be small enough to work together efficiently and effectively over time, it is important to ensure that the individuals on the team together represent the interests of all of the relevant constituents and that they bring the necessary expertise and/or connections to the group. The language planning team should become an integral and institutionalized part of the school administration. The actual name and configuration of the team, however, will no doubt vary depending on the local school and school district organizational structure. For example, some schools/districts may see the language planning team as an integral part of the school leadership team. Others may consider the team to be an advisory council that meets regularly about all issues regarding language at the school.

The language planning team needs to start by gathering information to guide their decisions about what kind of a language education program is appropriate for their school and community context. According to Corson (1999), the fact-gathering process for school languages policies involves three areas.

> It means coming to grips with the theory (i.e., knowledge) about language and education questions that are relevant to designing language policies in schools; it means thinking seriously about the policymaking process at school level and coming to see it as a vehicle for improving the service to children that an individual school offers; and it means taking steps to understand the unique language situation that prevails in a school and the language needs of its students (28).

Gathering this kind of information takes time and energy, and members of the language planning team will ideally have expertise and/or interest in some of the above areas. For example, the language educators should be familiar with theories about language teaching and learning at school. The mainstream classroom teacher should understand the latest developments and requirements in content-area instruction. The principal should understand how the language policy will interact with other policies, programs, and/or practices at school, and can help the team see the bigger picture of how educational services are provided to students. The bilingual coordinator, parents, community members, and community liasons should bring insight into how languages are used and evaluated by students outside of school in their everyday lives, and they can help the team understand the particular strengths and needs of the students in their community.

Language planning takes time, and the team needs to be prepared to work together and learn from each other over time. The team needs to be committed to developing a language education program that is appropriate for their context and to advocating for that program so that the school and community understand and support it. When the team has developed a plan that is endorsed by the community, they need to continue to work together to support the implementation of that plan, and to monitor and evaluate its effectiveness. The team also needs to use the data that it collects throughout the monitoring process to guide decisions regarding program development. In sum, the language planning team needs to take responsibility for program development, implementation, monitoring, evaluation, and improvement. This is a dynamic, recursive process that often involves conflict and controversy.

Before I move to a discussion of the target populations, I need to emphasize the importance of basing language planning and policy decisions on the facts that the team gathers rather than on *stereotypes* or misconceptions about language education that may be pervasive in their school and/or community. When the language planners encounter misconceptions from any of the constituents (e.g., parents, educators, community members), they need to be prepared to challenge those misconceptions with the facts about the local situation. I return to this point at the end of the chapter.

Who are the target populations

The starting point for all educational planning should always be with the strengths and needs of the target population, and language education is no exception. Consistent with recommendations from the language planning field, my work begins by looking at the sociolinguistic situation of the school. Specifically, the language planning team needs to explore demographic trends, students' language and education backgrounds, and local language ideologies so that they can build on students' strengths as they address their needs. Teams need to seriously consider how the language policies and programs that they are developing interact with the local sociolinguistic context.

Let's start with demographics. Language planners need to know how many monolingual English speakers, heritage speakers of the target language, heritage learners of the target language, and speakers of other languages are enrolled at the school. Language planners also need to determine whether these numbers are relatively stable or whether there are major demographic shifts in progress. School district data, school surveys, observations of local trends, and census data can help educators describe the kinds of demographic changes that a particular school tends to experience. Information about the specific changes that a school is likely to face (e.g., large numbers of new arrivals at upper grades, high attrition rates of certain groups at certain times) is very important because educators need to plan for ways that their programs can accommodate local demographic ebbs and flows.

Educators who work in multilingual communities are likely to have large numbers of heritage language speakers in their classes, and these students are likely to have a wide range of expertise in spoken and/or written English and the community language(s). This means that educators need to find ways to explore how the different categories of students they have (e.g., monolingual English speakers, heritage language speakers, heritage language learners, English language learners [ELLs]) use languages outside of school. This information will help them know how to build on that community bilingualism.

Language planners can conduct large-scale home and/or community language use surveys to gather this kind of information. Corson (1999), drawing on Fishman (1972), maintains that large-scale fact gathering includes the following activities:

- A survey of varieties (languages, dialects) used by speakers, including the domains or functions of those varieties.

- An estimate of the performance level in each domain.

- Some indication of community and staff attitudes toward the varieties and toward their use in various domains.

- An indication of community and staff attitudes toward changing the situation.

In many cases, however, language planners may not have the time or the resources necessary for large-scale fact-gathering. Schools may need to pursue more modest efforts to gather facts about how students use language in their everyday lives.

Much of the work exploring the local language situation can be done by teachers and other educators at school. Moll (1995), for example, encourages educators to look closely at their students' households and in other key contexts in the community for what he calls "cultural funds of knowledge" that they can build on at school. Like Moll (1995) in particular and other linguistic anthropologists more generally, I encourage educators to explore the ways that students and members of their household use spoken and written languages at home and throughout the community (see also Durgunoglu and Verhoeven 1998; Martin-Jones and Jones 2000; Perez et al 1998; Street 1993). Questions like the following are useful starting points for this kind of inquiry:

- Who does the student live with?

- Are the adults at home regularly?

- What kinds of jobs do the adults have?

- What languages do the adults use for professional purposes?

- What language(s) do the students use to communicate with the different people at home (e.g., siblings, parents, grandparents)?

- What kinds of reading and writing occur at home in what languages, and how does the student participate in those literacy practices?

- What other kinds of contexts do students regularly participate in (e.g., church, other homes, community settings, streets)?

- How do students use languages (spoken and written English and/or other languages) within and across these contexts?

We know that experience leads to expertise. When educators know about the kinds of experiences students have outside of school with spoken and written languages, they are more likely to understand the kinds of expertise their students have developed in these languages. For example, when educators know that a student reads the Bible and goes to church regularly in Spanish, they can expect that student to have developed some expertise in oral and written Standard Spanish. When educators know that another student lives in a household with bilingual parents who use both languages at home and a monolingual Spanish-speaking grandmother, they can expect that student to have developed expertise (at least comprehension) in oral vernacular Spanish of home-related topics. As we see in this book, when educators understand the kinds of expertise their students bring with them to school, they can make informed decisions about how they can build on that expertise.

Because students' educational background influences the kinds of expertise they develop, language planners need to know about students' prior experiences at school. Many ELLs, for example, come to the United States with a strong academic foundation in math, science, and social studies and with academic literacies in their primary languages. These students need to focus on English while they continue to build on their solid academic and cognitive foundation in English and/or in the primary language. Some heritage language speakers may have had formal language and/or literacy instruction in their heritage language in a community-based heritage language program, and these students need to build on whatever linguistic and cultural expertise they bring with them to school. Many ELLs, however, do not come to U.S. schools with a strong academic foundation, and many have not learned to read and write in their first language. These students have many more educational needs as they struggle to develop content-area knowledge and academic language and literacies in their primary language and/or English. When language planning teams understand their students' language education backgrounds, they have a solid foundation on which they can build.

Because language ideologies influence both the ways that people use and evaluate languages as well as their motivation to learn other languages, language planners need more than a descriptive account of how students use languages in their everyday lives. They also need to understand local beliefs about the languages, and they need to understand local attitudes toward speakers of those languages. The following kinds of questions can guide this part of the inquiry:

- What are students, parents, community members, and educators' attitudes toward the languages used in the community and toward speakers of these languages?

- Do the different groups believe that students are developing the expertise in spoken and/or written English and other languages that they need to meet their short-term and long-term language education goals?

- What do the students know and/or believe about the histories, cultures, perspectives, and/or contributions of the speakers of the target language? Where and how do they learn this?

- What is the nature of intergroup relations at school and throughout the community? What do the constituents (parents, educators, community members) think about the nature of these relations?

- Are students motivated to maintain and/or develop expertise in the target language? Why or why not?

A word of caution is in order here. While language planners need to explore and understand local assumptions about speakers of the target language and about the target culture, they also need to remember that those assumptions may be based on stereotypes. If groups do not have opportunities to interact with each other in positive ways, their language ideologies are likely to limit their abilities to understand the nature of the actual diversity within the target culture. This suggests areas for education and action that the language planning team should consider. I return to this point at the end of the chapter.

This section has reviewed aspects of the local language situation that language planners need to consider in order to understand their target populations' strengths and needs, and it provides a foundation for determining appropriate short-term and long-term goals for their target populations.

What are the goals for the target populations

This book argues that schools that serve multilingual students and communities have a responsibility to develop language education programs that build on students' linguistic and cultural strengths as they address local and national goals and standards. Moreover, these goals should include promoting bilingualism and biliteracy to the greatest degree possible for their target populations. Of paramount importance is that ELLs develop the content-area knowledge and skills and spoken and written academic English that they need to participate and achieve in the academic mainstream in ways that are compliant with local, state, and federal regulations. At the same time, my work with school-based language planning teams emphasizes the following additional goals:

- To enable ELLs to maintain and develop expertise in their primary language.

- To provide opportunities for heritage language speakers to broaden their linguistic repertoires so that they can use their spoken and written heritage language to communicate across a wider range of topics for both formal and informal purposes.

- To enable English speakers to develop expertise in the community language.

- To improve intergroup understanding and relations at school and in the community.

- To elevate the status of heritage languages and heritage language speakers on the local level.

- To challenge the assimilation strategy.

These goals are general and abstract. To translate these goals into concrete objectives that are observable, measurable, and attainable, school-based language planners need to consider local, state, and federal mandates and accountability requirements, school and community resources and constraints, and the research on second language acquisition, biliteracy development, and models of bilingual education, ESL, world language education (see chapters 2 and 3 for discussion of these areas).

When the language planning team has a clear understanding of its short-term and long-term goals, it is in a position to look at the type of language education program that it implements at school, and to consider whether and how that program enables students to reach all of their goals. It is also in a position to think about creative ways to address those goals if the existing programs and practices fall short of their goals.

How is the school currently addressing students' language education needs

Language planners need to look critically at their language education programs and practices to ensure that they are pedagogically sound and well-implemented. They need to ask themselves about the bilingual, ESL, and/or world language programs they have and determine whether the type of program they have in place allows them to address all of their goals (see chapter 3 for discussion of research on language education programs). Language planners also need to look at the performance of their target populations relative to their annual and longer-term goals and objectives and ask how effective their program is in enabling students to reach those goals and objectives. Throughout this process, language planners need to consider the challenges the existing program faces and the human and material resources and constraints that enhance and/or inhibit the development of their language education program.

Educators may find that their existing program should allow students to reach all of their short-term and long-term social, academic, and professional goals, but that they need to address aspects of program implementation in order for students to realize their goals. Or they may find that the kind of language education program that they have in place at their school does not promote bilingualism, biliteracy development, and improved inter-group understanding and relations. In this case, language planners can turn to the literature discussed in chapter 3 to help them choose the type of language education program that would be appropriate for their context. I return to this point below.

What type of language education program is appropriate for the school and community

As the language planning team works to decide what type of language education program is appropriate for their school and community context, they need to seriously assess their resources and constraints relative to the defining criteria of the program types they are considering. For example, language planning teams need to think about how federal, state, and local mandates and accountability requirements influence educators' and parents' decisions about what the school must, can, cannot, should, or should not do for language learners. Teams also need to consider whether they have the necessary target populations, trained personnel, materials, and ideological support for the types of programs they want to implement in their school. I illustrate each of these points in turn, and I encourage educators to think creatively about ways to reach their goals for the students and community they serve.

First and foremost, language planning teams need to consider how federal, state, and district mandates and accountability requirements influence the kinds of programs and practices they develop for their schools. For example, Title III of the No Child Left Behind Act mandates that all U.S. schools be held accountable for every ELL's English language development and academic performance, and that they provide evidence of how their program enables students to reach academic parity with their peers in the all-English academic mainstream. While Title III clearly articulates that states and local educational agencies have flexibility in determining which type of bilingual education or ESL program they choose to develop, many educators are primarily concerned about performance on standardized tests in English. Educators who do not understand how bilingual education actually promotes academic performance in English, and who do not realize that dual language programs are the most effective means of enabling ELLs to reach academic parity with English-speaking peers who are enrolled in the all-English academic mainstream, may believe that it is better to provide English-only instruction. When educators clearly understand how dual language programs enable ELLs and English speakers to reach the performance requirements that Title III mandates, they see the possibilities that dual language programs can offer their students and community.

Since two-way immersion (TWI) is a type of language education program that research demonstrates enables ELLs, heritage language speakers, and English speakers to become bilingual and biliterate, achieve academically through two languages, and develop positive inter-group understanding and relations, let's continue to consider this type of language education program for a school. Language planning teams need to think carefully about the defining criteria for TWI programs and ensure that their school context meets those criteria. As the Center for Applied Linguistics outlines (www.cal.org), TWI programs need to begin in the early elementary grades, and they require balanced numbers of students from two language backgrounds and trained bilingual personnel who can implement the program. Two-way immersion programs must have the curricular materials necessary to provide at least 50 percent of the content-area instruction through the non-English language, and they must have means of assessing students' performance relative to program goals. Two-way immersion programs must also have the support of parents and the community as well as educators at the school and throughout the larger school district.

Not all schools are able to implement a TWI program. Some schools may not have sufficient numbers of ELLs who come from the same language background. Some schools may not have trained bilingual personnel who can implement a TWI program. Some programs may not have access to curricular materials in the target language. Some programs may not have sufficient educator, parental, or community support. Language planning teams need to take seriously the constraints that they face, and they need to consider how they can draw on the resources (personnel, materials, parental, and community support) that they do have as they work to creatively address their goals.

This book argues that there is no one-size-fits-all type of program that all educators can uncritically implement at their school. Instead, I argue that schools need to consider whether their constraints can be addressed in the short or longer term, and they need to think creatively about how to address them as they develop their school language education plan. The next section provides some suggestions for program planners as they work to translate a generic program type into an actual school plan. Part IV of this book provides concrete examples of school-based planning processes and of language plans that different schools in the

School District of Philadelphia developed that they believed would meet the needs of their students and community, and that could realistically be implemented in their schools.

Translating a program type into a school plan

When a school determines what type of language education program is appropriate for their school (e.g., TWI, ESL, Spanish for native speakers), they need to develop a plan that is realistic for their school. Chapter 3 considered the types of language education programs that we see in schools in the United States. This section explores some of the decisions that program planners must make as they plan their programs and provides suggestions for how they may work through that decision-making process.

Schools that are planning to implement a TWI program in Spanish and English need to decide whether they will offer a whole-school program, or whether they will offer TWI as a strand within their school. Language planning teams need to decide whether they will implement a 90:10 model, in which students receive more content-area instruction in Spanish than in English in the early elementary grades, or a 50:50 model, in which students receive 50 percent of their content-area instruction in Spanish and 50 percent in English at each grade. Teams need to choose an approach to initial literacy instruction, which involves deciding whether they will provide initial literacy instruction to all students in Spanish, to all students in their first language, or to all students in both languages. They need to consider how they will allocate languages for instructional purposes within and across grade levels, and they need to consider how to assess students' performance relative to the goals and objectives that are not mandated by the larger school district and state in which they are working (e.g., how to assess students' development of spoken and written Spanish and their academic competence in Spanish).

Schools that are planning to implement world language programs in the elementary school need to decide what language they want to teach. If the school is located in a multilingual community that has a large number of heritage language speakers of the same language, teachers who are qualified to teach that language, and community support for developing a world language program that uses the community language (e.g., Mandarin, Russian, Spanish, Vietnamese, Khmer) it makes sense to choose the community language for the world language program. Schools that are planning to implement heritage language programs need to find ways to assess the kinds of linguistic expertise their heritage language students bring with them to school, and to assess their performance relative to the language arts standards.

Schools may use other criteria to determine language choice. For example, if there is no clear community language but the school has a teacher who is qualified to teach a particular language (e.g., French, German, Japanese), the choice of language for the world language program may be clear. When there is no clear alternative, Spanish is often considered a good choice. It is relatively easy to find qualified teachers and materials in Spanish, and the increasing numbers of Spanish speakers in the United States today combined with our proximity to Latin America makes Spanish a very useful language for English speakers. Spanish is also considerably easier for English speakers to learn than a linguistically different language like Chinese or Arabic. However, there is a national need to develop expertise in the less commonly taught languages. This means that Chinese or Arabic may be a choice that language planning teams want to consider for their schools. School-based language planning teams are encouraged to consider these and other options as they select a target language.

Once the language planning team has determined which language(s) to offer through the world language program, it needs to determine the amount of time to allocate to language instruction on a daily and weekly basis. It also needs to determine how the world language program will relate to what students are learning in the academic mainstream, and it needs to develop a language curriculum that is aligned with the ACTFL standards. Schools also need to determine how they will assess students' performance relative to those standards, and how they will monitor and evaluate the program.

As I have mentioned repeatedly, there is one-size-fits-all type of language education program that language planning teams can adopt and uncritically translate into their school context. Each decision has numerous possibilities, and must be considered in relation to the resources and constraints at the school. Moreover, there are pros and cons to every choice, which the language planning team must review as it develops its program. I recommend the following strategies to help educators make these decisions.

- Search the Center for Applied Linguistics directories (www.cal.org) to see how other schools with similar profiles implement TWI or world language programs.
- Visit schools and talk to educators about the pros and cons of their dual language and/or world language programs.

- Think critically about how to relate the language education goals and objectives to the existing school district curricula.
- Consider the implications of local, state, and federal accountability requirements.
- Explore local beliefs (of educators, parents, community members) about languages and language teaching and learning.
- Provide ongoing opportunities for open discussion of questions and concerns that parents and educators have throughout the planning stages.

I also emphasize that this is not a neat, linear process. Everyone (bilingual and/or world language teachers and other educators at the school, parents, district administrators, community members) needs to develop a coherent understanding of how the language education program is to function within and across grade levels at the school, and this takes time and energy. Planning teams need to work together over time to think critically about the pros and cons of the decisions they are making as they plan the school's program.

It is important to emphasize that schools can, and in many cases should, have more than one language education program as they organize the whole school to promote additive bilingualism to the greatest degree possible for their target populations. For example, an elementary school that is in a bilingual community that has access to curricular materials in the non-English language, bilingual educators, and community support for a bilingual program (e.g., in a predominantly Latino community or a largely Chinese community) may have a TWI program as one strand in the school for English speakers and speakers of the other language and a world language program that promotes the community language for students enrolled in the all-English mainstream. An elementary school that is in a bilingual community but that does not have the necessary conditions for a dual language program (e.g., not enough materials, personnel, or community support) may have an ESL program for ELLs, a first language (L1) literacy program for ELLs and heritage language speakers, and a world language program that promotes the community language for students enrolled in the all-English mainstream. An elementary school that has a large number of ELLs from a wide number of language backgrounds may have a sheltered ESL program, an extensive library of materials in the languages of the ELLs and creative ways for those students to build on their first language, and a world language program for all students in the language that the school chooses. These are just a few of the possibilities that program planners can consider, several of which are illustrated in Part IV of this book.

Whatever the question that planners are considering, they are encouraged to think critically about the strengths and needs of their target populations, about research on the defining criteria and effectiveness of different program types, and about theories of second language acquisition, biliteracy development, and academic language development. Planners are also strongly encouraged to visit other programs, talk to other educators who are addressing the kinds of questions they have in their own practice, and consider a range of possibilities as they plan their programs. As I discuss in the concluding section to this chapter, planners also need to identify how local language ideologies relate to the goals of the language plan they are developing, and they must challenge those that run counter to their plans.

Challenging language ideologies that do not promote bilingualism

Local language ideologies strongly influence the ease with which a language plan can be effectively developed and implemented. When local beliefs about language use and/or about language teaching and learning are aligned with the beliefs underlying the language education program that the language planners are developing, it is easier to implement the language plan. For example, when parents, teachers, administrators, community members, and students generally agree that bilingualism is an important goal for students who attend the school, it is much easier to develop and implement a dual language program because there is ideological space in that context for additive bilingualism. However, when local language ideologies are in opposition to program ideologies, language planners and program implementers are likely to encounter much more difficulty. For example, some parents and educators may believe that time spent learning in and through the primary language takes away time that ELLs need to spend learning English. When language planners encounter language ideologies that run counter to the ideological orientation of the program they are developing, they must work to address those ideologies.

In the first part of this chapter, we saw that our knowledge and our interactions play an important role in continuously reproducing central features of the social structure. For example, we saw how the nonstandard English–speaking students' ways of speaking and interacting can lead to miscommunication in the classroom, which can in turn lead to limited opportunities for participation at school, which can in turn reproduce their subordinate role in society. We saw how most mainstream U.S. bilingual and ESL programs implicitly define languages other than English as problems to be overcome, which can in turn lead speakers of those languages to abandon those languages and assimilate to monolingualism in English. These kinds of dominant language ideologies are relatively established in many U.S. schools and throughout mainstream U.S. society.

We also saw that it is possible for educators to work together to construct alternative ideologies about languages other than English and about speakers of those languages. Enriched bilingual programs that promote bilingualism, e.g., one-way developmental bilingual programs for ELLs and two-way immersion programs that integrate English speakers and speakers of another language, challenge the assimilationist trend that has been dominant in the United States throughout much of the twentieth century. We have considerable evidence that these kinds of enriched bilingual programs, when well-implemented, enable students to achieve academically through English at or above grade level. Furthermore, these programs enable their target populations to become bilingual and biliterate, and students generally develop improved cultural understanding and intercultural communication skills.

Language ideologies are dynamic, complex, and at times contradictory. This fact has important implications for language planning efforts that aim to challenge established ideologies. According to Gardiner (1992),

> Ideology is not (now) conceived of as a highly systematic or axiomatic "belief system," but as a disparate, contradictory and stratified complex of practices and symbols, which are pitched at different levels of coherence and social effectivity and which are subject to continual contestation and negotiation (66; cited by Rampton 1995, 307).

The real challenge is destabilizing established language ideologies and replacing them with alternative language ideologies. As Bourdieu (1991) maintains, establishing alternative definitions of reality is no simple task. People have come to see the dominant language ideologies not as ideological, but as common sense.

Alternative language ideologies must first break with the dominant ideologies and demonstrate why what has seemed like "common sense" for so long is no longer plausible. Alternative language ideologies must also produce a new "common sense" about languages and about speakers of those languages, and these new understandings must be integrated within the current social practices of the group in a way that makes sense to all of the participants. Furthermore, these alternative language ideologies must be given enduring institutionalized status and they must be publicly sanctioned (see Bourdieu 1991; Rampton 1995 for further discussions).

The complex and contradictory nature of language ideologies can be used to the language planners' advantage. For example, when parents who believe that their children need to spend as much time as they can acquiring English so that they can participate and achieve at school see that their child does not understand what is going on in the all-English content-area classroom, they come to understand the value of teaching content-area knowledge through the primary language. Contradictions like these that language planners identify signal ideological and/or implementational space for alternative language policies. Like Hornberger (2001), I urge school-based language planners to find ways to open up those spaces and make room for multiple languages, literacies, and identities in the classroom, community, and society.

Language planners can use Hornberger's (2001) continua of biliteracy to look closely at how individuals and groups use spoken and written languages in their linguistic repertoires and to address challenges they face in implementing their multilingual language policies. She defines biliteracy as "any and all instances in which communication occurs in two (or more) languages in or around writing" (1990, 213), and describes it in terms of four nested sets of intersecting continua characterizing the contexts, media, content, and development of biliteracy. According to Hornberger (2001),

> The very notion of bi (or multi)-literacy assumes that one language and literacy is developing in relation to one or more other languages and literacies . . .; the model situates biliteracy development (whether in the individual, classroom, community, or society) in relation to the contexts, media, and content in and through which it develops . . .; and it provides a heuristic for addressing the unequal balance of power across languages and literacies (18–19).

Using the continua of biliteracy framework as a guide, language planners can ask questions about the contexts of biliteracy to see if there is ideological space in the community, the school, the classroom, or the home for biliteracy development. They can identify contradictions within particular contexts, for example between beliefs and practices, and they can use those contradictions to open ideological space further. When they identify and/or create contexts that have ideological openings for biliteracy development, they can ask questions about the media and content of biliteracy within and across those contexts. Here they can look for discrepancies between ideal policy and actual implementation, and they can attend to those discrepancies. For example, if they see that the curriculum favors literacies in English over literacies in the other language, they know to pay more attention to literacy development in the other language. If they see that the curriculum is eurocentric and omits the contributions of the target culture, they know to change the curriculum content to make it more inclusive. The continua of biliteracy framework provides a heuristic that allows language planners to decide where they should pay attention, and how they should restructure their programs and practices to promote bilingualism and biliteracy development.

Hornberger's (2001) work helps language planners to focus their language planning attention and resources. However, as research on educational change (e.g., Fullan 2001) makes clear, the language planning team cannot work in isolation. In order for any educational innovation to be effective, everyone involved needs to develop a shared understanding of the goals of the educational innovation, and they need to have a coherent understanding of the best way to achieve those goals. Fullan (2001) provides numerous examples from educational change projects to remind us that coherence does not happen automatically. Instead, educators develop a shared, coherent understanding of the goals of a new program and the best way for them to reach those goals through their involvement and ongoing collaboration in professional learning communities. It is important for language planners to constantly remind themselves, however, that there is no easy recipe that schools can follow as they work toward developing a coherent understanding of what they want to do and how they want to do it. Local beliefs and practices influence this complex process of developing coherence.

Conclusion

This chapter has provided a theoretical basis for understanding that the choices educators make in the ways that they organize their programs and practices have implications for the opportunities that students see available to them at school and in society. For example, schools can reflect and reproduce the mainstream social order, which encourages assimilation to monolingualism in English. Or educators can choose alternative educational programs and practices that can provide more opportunities to students than have been traditionally available. The decision about what kinds of students the school wants to produce needs to be made based on an understanding of the implications of these choices, and through ongoing communication among students, their parents, community members, and educators in the schools that serve them.

Educators must do more than choose to develop dual language or world language programs. Language planning teams must take responsibility for learning about the sociolinguistic situation in which their school is located, and they must assess students' language and learning needs in the short and longer terms. Teams must review the literature on bilingual, ESL, and world language programs to develop an understanding of second language acquisition, biliteracy development, content-based second language instruction, and the effectiveness of different kinds of programs. Once teams choose a particular program type, they must translate that into a concrete plan for their school, and they must clearly articulate objectives for their target populations and means of assessing performance relative to those objectives. Educators must monitor students' performance regularly over time, and they must use the data they gather to guide instructional decisions and program improvement. Ideally, when more schools develop pedagogically sound dual language and world language programs that promote additive bilingualism for their target populations, and when they collect and analyze data on student performance in these programs relative to student performance in all-English programs, we will have solid research with which to counter English-only trends in the future.

Part II

Exploring language ideologies in North Philadelphia

Part II of this book takes us into the predominantly Puerto Rican community in North Philadelphia, and it illustrates how local ideologies about language use and social relations influence the ways that English-speaking and Spanish-speaking students acquire and use spoken and written Spanish and English in this community. It is based on approximately six years of action-oriented ethnographic and discourse analytic research that I conducted in schools, homes, and other key contexts in this part of Philadelphia. The chapters in this part of the book provide an important foundation for my research in classrooms that serve language learners in North Philadelphia in Part III, and for my work facilitating the development of programs and policies that promote bilingualism in Part IV. As I argued in Part I, when educators are equipped with an understanding of how language ideologies structure the ways that students, families, community members, and educators use and evaluate languages in their everyday lives, they have a solid foundation on which they can promote students' bilingual and biliteracy development.

The Puerto Rican community in North Philadelphia provides an outstanding context for researchers and practitioners who are working to reverse the trend toward monolingualism in English, build on community bilingualism, improve the teaching of Spanish, and develop future generations of individuals with a wide range of expertise in spoken and written Spanish and English. Because language ideologies are complex and contradictory at school and throughout the community, there is tremendous potential for social change. When educators clearly understand how local ideologies about spoken and written Spanish and English influence students' opportunities to learn and/or use Spanish and English, they can work with students, parents, and other community members to implement the kinds of policies, programs, and practices that promote the teaching and learning of Spanish. Educators, researchers, and policymakers can also draw on the detailed ethnographic portrait of bilingualism and education in the Puerto Rican community in North Philadelphia to stimulate their research and action in other multilingual communities.

The predominantly Puerto Rican community in North Philadelphia is located in an economically depressed part of the city that is plagued by many of the problems of low-income urban neighborhoods across the United States. According to statistics provided by the School District of Philadelphia (SDP) in 2000, 99 percent of the students who attend schools in this community are considered low-income, and the schools in this area are among the poorest performing. Although Latinos only represent 12 percent of the total student population in the SDP, they are the majority population in many of the schools in North Philadelphia. Latinos make up between 85 and 99 percent of the total student population in this community, and the Latino drop-out rate is disproportionately high in the district. According to a Harvard University report that examined issues of racial justice in the United States, such segregation of Latinos in poorly performing schools in low-income neighborhoods is relatively common across the nation. In fact, it is pervasive in cities in the northeast (Harvard Civil Rights Project, cited in the *Philadelphia Inquirer,* July 20, 2001).

What does the SDP data tell us about the Latino students in this community? According to SDP (2000) data, between 20 and 30 percent of the Latino population in North Philadelphia are designated English language learners (ELLs); the other two-thirds are considered English speakers who are enrolled in the all-English academic mainstream. The overwhelming majority of the Latinos in this community, ELLs and English speakers, are Puerto Rican. Some were born in the United States; others migrated from Puerto Rico. A small but increasing number of Latinos are from other Spanish-speaking contexts, including the Dominican Republic, Central America, and Mexico. Latino students who attend bilingual programs are generally assessed in Spanish, and they generally perform better on standardized tests in Spanish (Aprenda) than their English-speaking counterparts do on standardized tests in English (SAT-9), the standardized tests that the SDP used at the time this data was collected. Most Latino students in North Philadelphia, however, are enrolled in the all-English academic mainstream and they are assessed exclusively in English. The overwhelming majority of students in North Philadelphia, including those who are assessed in Spanish and those who are assessed in English, score at or below basic levels in reading and math. The SDP standardized assessments of English-speaking and Spanish-speaking Latinos highlight student deficits in content-area knowledge and in English. They tell us little about students' strengths in English and even less about their strengths in Spanish.

Although the SDP statistics reveal little about students' expertise in Spanish, the majority of the Latino students living in this bilingual community are heritage Spanish speakers. In a neighborhood that is characterized by widespread poverty and low academic achievement, Spanish is a rich resource that can be developed in ways that benefit individual students, their families, and the community overall. Educators who want to build on this resource must understand the nature of it. The ethnographic and discourse analytic research that I conducted in schools, homes, and throughout the community addresses this gap. The approach can be readily adapted for research in other contexts.

The rest of this introduction describes the research methods that I used to explore language ideologies in North Philadelphia. I begin with the research questions that guided my inquiry. Then I review how I gained access to the contexts in which I conducted research, and I provide a brief chronological description of those contexts with attention to my role as a researcher. Although many of the people and schools that I have worked with in this book encouraged me to use their real names, others requested anonymity. In order to respect these requests, I have used pseudonyms for all of the schools and individuals in this book.

I began my research on bilingualism and education in North Philadelphia in 1996. As I discuss below, I have been a participant-observer in a wide range of school and community contexts and I have taken on many different roles as I work to answer my research questions. The primary research questions are:

1. What are educators, parents, students, and other community members' beliefs about how spoken and written Spanish and English should be used at school, at home, in the local community, and in the greater U.S. society?

2. How are spoken and written Spanish and English actually taught and used at school, home, and in the local community?

3. What kinds of opportunities do these language ideologies make available?

Much of my research has involved traditional ethnographic and discourse analytic methods. However, I also assume an action-oriented stance in my research, and I continually work with educators to apply what I/we learn to the problems they/we are trying to address at school.

My collaborations with educators and students have given me access to contexts and data that would have been inaccessible to traditional ethnographers. This access has strengthened my research in terms of validity and reliability. This reflexive relationship between research and practice has also strengthened my professional development work with administrators and teachers in North Philadelphia who are looking for creative ways to build on community bilingualism. Parts III and IV illustrate some of this work.

Gaining access to do research in schools and throughout the community in North Philadelphia was not a simple matter for me. Rather, gaining access meant that I needed to continually negotiate my role relative to others. I am a white middle-class standard English-speaking woman and an outsider to the low-income, predominantly Puerto Rican community. When I began my research in 1996, I was an assistant professor in the Language in Education Division of the Graduate School of Education at the University of Pennsylvania who wanted to do action-oriented research in bilingual public school programs. In the first year of my research as I began to develop relations, I needed to continually challenge definitions of me as an outsider who would quickly do my research project to further my own professional interests without considering the interests of the educators, students, and their families. My ability to speak Spanish helped me redefine my relationship because the stereotypical white middle-class English-speaking university-based researcher does not speak Spanish. I found that as I demonstrated my commitment to the children, either by volunteering to work on a community-based project, or by offering graduate students who could tutor at school, or by working with a student at home, all doors were open. The key was demonstrating a sincere concern for the interests of the children.

I began my action-oriented research in 1996, and I have worked closely with students and teachers in bilingual and English as a second language (ESL) classrooms in a variety of capacities in different elementary and middle schools throughout North Philadelphia since that time. From 1996 to 1998, I was a participant observer at PS 17 as teachers there struggled to implement a middle school two-way immersion program, and I encouraged graduate students to conduct action-oriented research with me and/or with other teachers at the school. I also began to work on collaborative projects that explored how students use and evaluate spoken and written Spanish and English in key contexts in their everyday lives outside of school. In the fall of 1999, I was an adjunct professor for the Balanced Literacy Initiative in the School District of Philadelphia and I mentored five literacy interns who worked in kindergarten or 1st grade classes at PS 79; four of these interns worked in the all-English mainstream and one of the interns worked in the bilingual program. In the spring of 2000 I worked as a student teacher in an ESL class for 5th grade students who attended the all-English academic mainstream at PS 19. From 2000 to 2001, I was a participant-observer in one 2nd grade class in a one-way developmental bilingual program at PS 11. Since the spring of 2001, I have been working with groups of educators from other elementary schools in North Philadelphia to facilitate their efforts to design, implement, and evaluate one-way and two-way bilingual programs for their schools. In the fall of 2001, I taught a course on dual language education to administrators from the majority of the schools in the community in which they worked together to develop a dual language policy for a new bilingual school that would be opening in the neighborhood the next year. Although I have not been to every school, the range of my research and practice in North Philadelphia has enabled me to understand how spoken and written Spanish and English are used and evaluated by elementary and middle school students and teachers throughout this community. I discuss my role relationships in more detail in the relevant chapters throughout the book.

I began my work in North Philadelphia as an ethnographer/sociolinguist who was interested in identifying and documenting linguistic and cultural resources in the school and community that educators could build on, and I looked for school contexts in which educators were interested in promoting bilingualism for their students. My role has evolved, and now I work primarily as a consultant who works with language planning teams to develop dual language programs, and to help language educators and mainstream educators relate the literature in second language acquisition, biliteracy development, content-based second language instruction, and language education programs and practices to their school in community context. My work with educators, students, and parents has generated a huge database that I analyze to answer my research questions.

Research question 1 asks *What are the educators, parents, students, and other community members' beliefs about how spoken and written Spanish and English should be used at school, at home, in the local community, and in the greater U.S. society?* To answer this question, I conducted ongoing interviews throughout my research with educators, parents, students, and other community members in bilingual schools, in students' homes, and in other community contexts. For example, I interviewed teachers about individual students' histories as we looked over their individual folders. I talked informally with the majority of the students from all of the classes that I worked with about where they were born, how long they have lived in Philadelphia, what kinds of activities they participate in at school, at home, and throughout the community, and what languages they use for what purposes. In several cases, I worked with groups of students in writing workshops that encouraged students to write about themselves, their peers, their families, and their hopes and dreams. I also talked with parents who came for parent-teacher conferences and/or who volunteered at the school. I spent extensive time in the homes of five students, which gave me opportunities to talk informally and at length with students, their friends, and their families. I also worked alongside of sixty students as they explored bilingual discourse practices in their neighborhood, and talked with them about their observations. Many of these interviews were audio- or videotaped and transcribed for analysis, and most were recorded in my field notes. I also reviewed English and Spanish language newspapers to collect media representations of language use at school and throughout the community. Discourse analysis of these texts (interviews, newspaper articles, other site documents) allowed me to identify recurring themes about how spoken and written Spanish and English are used and evaluated within and across school, home, and community contexts. These themes also inform the ways that I look at micro-level social practices.

Research questions 2 and 3 ask *How are spoken and written Spanish and English actually taught and used at school, home, and in the local community? What kinds of opportunities do these language ideologies make available?* To answer these questions, I was a participant-observer in the elementary and middle school classes that I described above. Data collection in these contexts included field notes, audiotaping and videotaping of interaction, and samples of written materials and student work. I identified key contexts in students' lives, and I explored the kinds of experiences students had in these contexts at home, at school, and throughout their local communities (e.g., at church, in the street) here in Philadelphia as well as in other places they had lived (e.g., on the island, in New York or Connecticut). Then I began to explore the range of activities that students participated in within and across these contexts. I analyzed how students use and evaluate spoken and written Spanish and English in these activities with particular attention to print-rich activities and activities in which Spanish figured prominently. My interaction analysis incorporate insights and methods from ethnography of communication, interactional sociolinguistics, and conversation analysis (see Schiffrin 1994 for discussion of these approaches), and the ways that I relate analysis of micro-level spoken and written texts to macro-level sociopolitical processes are informed by recent work on language ideologies (Fairclough 1989, 1993; Gee 1990; Schieffelin et al. 1998).

In sum, my analysis of how educators, students, parents, and other community members' language ideologies structure opportunities for students to learn and use Spanish and English draws on several different approaches to discourse, and it is informed by the ethnographic understanding I have developed over the six-year period of my research. I built a large database, and I related my analysis of beliefs (question 1) to practices (question 2) in a recursive process. I drew on my understanding of the larger social, political, and economic context surrounding bilingualism and education in North Philadelphia to explain the patterns that I identified in the spoken and written texts that I collected, an understanding that I developed through ethnographic research and extensive reading in the field. My research was dynamic and multidirectional as I changed my focus from micro-level interactions to macro-level processes and looked for relationships within and across levels of context. I also looked closely at contradictions between beliefs and practices because they often suggested areas to target for further research and action. I provide more detail about my research methods in the relevant chapters. I have shared my findings with many educators from North Philadelphia as part of my professional development work with them, and they say the patterns that I identify are consistent with what they know about their students and community. In fact, Puerto Rican teachers would often relate the ethnographic detail that I shared or stories that I had collected to their own lives. These insider-group responses provide further support for the analysis.

There are three chapters in Part II. Chapter 5 is entitled *Spanish and English in two students' lives,* and it introduces the reader to language ideologies in this bilingual community by describing the ways that Claudia Gonzalez and Silvia Román use and evaluate spoken and written Spanish and English at home, at school, and in other key contexts in their everyday lives. This chapter demonstrates the importance of exploring students' experiences outside of school to identify strengths that educators can build on. Chapter 6 is entitled *Language and identity in the Puerto Rican community,* and it takes us into the heart of the Latino community in North Philadelphia. This chapter begins with a description of how Spanish and English are used in the Latino business district today, and then provides a brief history of the Puerto Rican community in North Philadelphia to explain the interactional patterns we see throughout the community. Although most outside representations of this community are negative, chapter 6 concludes with evidence of an alternative discourse that represents this bilingual community more favorably. Chapter 7 is entitled *Understanding language ideologies: A basis for action,* and it looks across all of the data I collected to describe the range of expertise we can expect to find within the heritage Spanish-speaking student population, interpret interactions in key contexts that promote students' bilingual and biliteracy development, and explain the complex and contradictory language ideologies that structure relations in this community. This chapter also suggests direction for action.

The chapters in Part II do not provide a quantitative analysis of language attitudes and use in North Philadelphia. Instead, my qualitative analysis are intended to provide a foundation for local educators who want to build on the linguistic and cultural resources that can be identified in this community as they help students work toward their social, academic, and professional goals. It is also intended to inspire other educators and researchers' thinking about how to explore bilingual discourse practices in any multilingual community so that they can build on the linguistic and cultural resources that they identify there.

5

Spanish and English
in two students' lives

Far too often, schools that serve low-income and/or "minority" students operate under the deficit model. Schools assess students on standardized tests, primarily in English. These tests offer evidence of what students lack, and schools struggle to teach "basic skills" and combat "illiteracy." This book rejects the deficit model that is dominant in many contexts in the United States. Instead, I encourage educators who work in multilingual communities to look for students' linguistic and cultural strengths and build on that foundation. Researchers and educators can learn a tremendous amount about students' expertise by going into their homes and listening to the stories students and other household members tell, observing their everyday interactions, and engaging in ongoing conversations about their lives (see also Moll 1995; Street 1993; 1995).

This chapter introduces us to the ways that heritage Spanish speakers in North Philadelphia use and evaluate spoken and written Spanish and English by exploring the everyday lives of two heritage Spanish-speaking students, Claudia Gonzalez and Silvia Román. Claudia is a Puerto Rican student who was born and raised in North Philadelphia, and she has been educated primarily in English. Silvia is a Puerto Rican student who was born in Puerto Rico and migrated to the United States with her family when she was three. She attended bilingual programs in North Philadelphia elementary and middle schools that used Spanish and English for instructional purposes, and she is enrolled in an all-English high school at the time of this writing.

I met Claudia in 1997 and Silvia in 1998 through collaborative projects that I was working on with educators at PS 17 in North Philadelphia. Claudia was in the English program and Silvia was in the bilingual program at the school. In 1998 I asked Claudia, Silvia, and two other students to work with me to write a chapter about their experiences at school for an edited volume entitled *In Our Own Words: Students' Perspectives on School* (Shultz and Cook-Sather 2001). Claudia and Silvia each invited me into their homes, and I spent countless hours with them and their families between 1998 and 1999 as we worked on parts of the chapter. This experience gave me a rich opportunity to observe and document ways that these students use languages in their everyday lives and to talk with them about the meanings of their practices.

My analysis of how Claudia and Silvia use and evaluate languages provides examples of ways that language ideologies structure relations on the local level. This descriptive account is not exhaustive, and it is not generalizable to all heritage Spanish speakers in North Philadelphia. It is, however, intended to stimulate educators' thinking about how their students' experiences at school and in other key contexts in their lives lead to the development of a range of linguistic and cultural expertise. As this chapter demonstrates, when educators understand the nature of that expertise, they have a solid foundation on which they can build to help students broaden their linguistic range.

Claudia's life

This section begins with an excerpt from Claudia Gonzalez's writing about her family history, and we explore the language ideologies that we see in her story. Then I describe the ways that Claudia and her family members use and evaluate spoken and written Spanish and English in their everyday lives. As this section demonstrates, although Claudia uses English much more than Spanish at school, at home and with her friends, she sees an important role for Spanish in her life.

This piece of Claudia's writing was part of the chapter that she wrote about her experiences at school (Alfaro et al. 2001). Claudia's story explains why her family came to the United States. Her story also highlights how her family members have struggled with language issues as they work to participate in mainstream U.S. society on the one hand while they try to maintain close family ties on the other.

> *I'm fourteen years old and I'm in the eighth grade. I have two sisters and one brother, and we have never lived anywhere outside of Philadelphia. Both of my parents were born in Puerto Rico (PR) and they were both brought to the United States (US) as teenagers.*
>
> *My mother was born in Guayama. My grandparents brought my mother and their other children to the US because my grandpa had accepted a job here as a construction worker. He made a good decision to move his family to the US because it's not easy to find work in PR. My grandpa dropped out of school when he was in the fifth grade because his family was very poor and they couldn't pay his way to continue his studies. Since my grandpa couldn't attend school*

anymore, he worked in the fields with his father and he learned how to grow crops. As my grandpa got older he learned how to build houses out of concrete, he learned how to repair electric wires and he learned other things. But the payment for good work like my grandpa's wasn't enough to support a wife and ten kids. Until one day he was lucky and someone in the US wanted to hire him. He thought that raising his kids in the land of opportunity would be the best place for them. That's why he accepted the job in the US.

My father is from Utuado, PR. My grandma brought my father to the US because my grandpa had died. She was left alone to take care of her children so she used my grandpa's insurance money to bring the family to the US because she had other married children living there. She thought that it would be a good decision to live in the US because her older sons and daughters could help her take care of their brothers and sisters.

My mom was 16 years old when she was brought to the US and my dad was 13 years old when he was brought to the US. My dad was brought to the US at a younger age than my mother so he is able to speak English well. But at first when he was brought to the US he didn't know English at all. As a teenager, my dad was a fighter so he didn't learn English at school all the time. He would learn it by watching TV in English, listening to English music, and to how people spoke. By the time he went to . . . High School he spoke proper English but he was still a fighter, a fighter who is real good with math, speech, and technology. My mom was 16 when she was flown in from PR, so she went to ... high school. She learned English in school, but at that time there were a lot of PR teenagers so she didn't worry about learning English fast to make friends because she was put in a bilingual classroom. She did learn to understand English but her writing, reading, and speech weren't so good.

My parents got married in their 20s and they had three daughters. My dad wanted the three of us to learn English as our first language because he didn't want us to go through what he went through when he first came here. My mother wanted the three of us to learn Spanish because Spanish was her family language. The three of us are a big deal to my mom's side of the family because we're my grandparent's first grandchildren. And my grandparents can only speak Spanish.

So my parents made an agreement—the three of us were taught English as our first language and then when we had finally made English as our first language we would begin to learn Spanish. Our English was really good because when we would go to school the three of us would learn as much as we could about the alphabet, the sound a letter makes, and the English rules of writing because when we got home my dad would take any book and teach us how to read.

Then five years later my parents had my little brother. At that time my dad had to work two jobs to support four kids and a wife. So when my sisters and I came home my dad couldn't teach us how to read English or help us with our homework because he wasn't home. My mom couldn't teach us English because we felt so uncomfortable being taught by her. And most of the time she didn't understand what we were saying. So while my dad was working, my brother would sleep in his crib, my little sister would play with her dolls while my twin sister and I would watch TV. Whenever my dad wasn't around to teach us or talk to us we would just sit on the rocking chair and watch the Thunder Cats cartoon, the Ninja Turtles or some other cartoon. We used to watch TV a lot so we learned English a lot faster that way because we would repeat every word that was mentioned in the cartoon and we would watch how they used the words to express their emotion.

We spoke English very well but our Spanish wasn't yet taught to us. In our family every Sunday after church the whole family would meet at my grandparents' house. Everyone would be so happy to see us but sometimes we weren't happy to see them because they all spoke Spanish and we didn't. At first it didn't bother us because all we did at my grandparents' house was watch TV. But when we got a little bit older and a little wiser we felt out of place because everyone else could speak a whole different language and we couldn't.

It was hard and embarrassing to be a part of a family that a person can't even talk to because that person can't speak their family language. I never wanted Sunday to come because every time we went to visit the family they would laugh at me, tease me, or just ask me the question that I never liked, "What are you —an American or a Puerto Rican?" Of course it was hard for me because what do I know, I was just a kid. What was I going to tell them? But imagine how my mom felt. Everyone used to tease her because sometimes when we talked to her she didn't understand

*a word we said. It must be sad to have kids and not be able to
understand what they're saying.*

*All those negative things that both sides of the family gave us
we put to good use. Every weekend my mom would sit us down
in the kitchen table and teach us the alphabet in Spanish. We
never liked it because not only that we took a lot of time learning but on the weekends our favorite cartoons would be on and
we could never watch them. The more and more practice we had
and the better we got to understanding it. But my mom thought
that we needed to learn some words so she noticed that we
learned more when we were watching TV. So every night from 7
pm to 9 pm we would all go up to my mom's room and watch the
"novelas" (soap operas).*

*My Spanish was getting better but it wasn't enough to talk to
my family correctly because we would mix the two languages
together and they used to wonder "which language are you
speaking-English or Spanish?". Years later we moved out of our
second home into our third home. My mom arranged it so that
my sisters, brother and I would go to school at . . . elementary.
She understood that in that elementary school it had a Spanish
class so my mom wanted us to go there.*

*To get in the Spanish class a woman had to test me to judge
the Spanish that I already knew. My sisters and I passed the test
and were put in the class. We studied Spanish in that class for
four years and it turned out to be good for me. The more and
more we studied and the more that we watched TV, the better we
made Spanish our second language. But our only problem was
that we have an accent when we speak Spanish. Yet all is well.
We learned both languages and we are the smartest teenagers in
our family because we are the only ones that can speak, read,
write and understand both languages.*

Let's now look more closely at some of the assumptions about how Spanish
and English should be taught, learned, and used that Claudia expresses
through her story. We'll build on this discussion as we look at language ideologies in North Philadelphia more broadly in chapter 7.

First, we see a belief that languages should be acquired sequentially
and that English should be the first language of a child growing up in the
United States. This emphasis on English first suggests that English has
more symbolic capital (Bourdieu 1991) than Spanish in the Gonzalez

household. Claudia's story also highlights a widespread yet mistaken assumption that maintaining and developing Spanish threaten a student's ability to acquire English. This assumption encourages many parents, including Claudia's, to speak English instead of Spanish to their children at home.

The belief that languages should be acquired sequentially actually runs counter to the experiences of many people who grow up in bilingual or multilingual communities in the United States, including many who live in the predominantly Puerto Rican community in North Philadelphia and other parts of the world. For example, one day I was talking to Marisa, a nonteaching assistant (NTA) at one of the middle schools about the term "second language acquisition." Marisa is a bilingual Puerto Rican who was born and raised in Philadelphia. She told me that she was taking a graduate course at Temple University on second language acquisition and she was trying to figure out whether Spanish or English was her "first" language. She said, "You know, I just kind of grew up speaking both languages at the same time." The term "second language acquisition" reflects an assumption of sequential language acquisition, which does not accurately represent the language acquisition process in many real-world contexts.

When we look at domains that Claudia associates with Spanish and domains that she associates with English, we see that Spanish is clearly associated with private domains, for example, at home with her mother, at family functions with her grandparents, and at church. Although she attended a bilingual school that she credits for enabling her to learn Spanish, most of her education has been through English. This private/public distinction also gives English greater symbolic capital than Spanish, and contributes to the symbolic domination of English over Spanish.

We also see a close relationship between language and identity in Claudia's story. She tells us about how difficult it was for her to go to her grandparents' house when she couldn't speak the "family language." She involves us in her story with the question "What are you, Puerto Rican or American?" We see here that Spanish is an undeniable part of ethnic identity for Puerto Ricans growing up in the United States. Claudia positively evaluates Spanish as a symbol of ethnic identity as well as a means of connecting herself to her family and to other monolingual Spanish speakers that she encounters.

Claudia's assumptions about language use and language learning reflect her experiences growing up in North Philadelphia. Let's now visit Claudia's neighborhood and Claudia's household so that we can better understand those experiences.

Claudia lives with her mom, her twin sister, Clarissa, her younger sister, María, and her younger brother, Hector. Her father and her mother have been divorced for many years, and with the exception of about one year when Claudia lived with her father, she has lived in the same house since I have known her. Claudia's dad lives nearby in the neighborhood (but not within walking distance), and Claudia sees him frequently. He does not work now because he hurt his back. Until recently, Claudia's mom had worked at a meat-packing factory. She was in an automobile accident recently, and at the time of this writing she had not yet returned to work.

Claudia's house is located on a relatively narrow street that is one block long, and although the two-story row houses on the block are painted in different colors and are in various states of repair, the houses look similar to each other from the outside. When the weather is nice, many of the doors to the houses are open and there are always people outside on the street or sitting on stoops.

The first day that I went to visit Claudia, I was not sure which house was hers so, speaking Spanish, I asked a lady who was standing on a stoop talking to someone at their door if she knew where Claudia Gonzalez lived. She told me that she did and to follow her, so I went with her into her house. She offered me coffee and asked me all about who I was and what I was doing. After we talked about 15 minutes I asked again if she knew where Claudia was, and she told me that Claudia lived next door. When we finished our coffee, she took me next door, knocked on the door, and presented me to Claudia. When I told Claudia what had just happened, she laughed and said that was just like that neighbor—she always needed to know what was going on and that she was just checking me out.

When you visit Claudia's street on any given day that the weather is good, you might find a group of mothers on one stoop while their children are playing nearby. A group of adolescent boys who are close friends of Claudia's might be outside of her house, and they might come in and out while you visit. María, Claudia's younger sister, might run across the street to talk to one person on one stoop, and then to another on another stoop. The sounds of music—salsa, hip-hop, merengue, and rap—mix in the air and you can always hear people talking in Spanish and in English, sometimes laughing, sometimes arguing, sometimes fighting, but always interacting.

For example, one day when I was at Claudia's house, we heard some fighting outside and we ran to the door to check out what was going on. There was a fight between a Puerto Rican family who lived on one end of the block and a Mexican family that had just moved in on the other end of the block, and according to Claudia, it was all about respect and about how people should treat each other on the block. I mention the national backgrounds because they were important to the people on the block, reflecting larger tensions that we often see between Puerto Ricans and Mexicans in North Philadelphia. Apparently, when an eight-year-old Puerto Rican boy went down the block to ask the Mexican boys if they wanted to play, they got into an argument. The Puerto Rican kids went back to tell their families while the Mexican kids told their families about what had happened. The fight escalated so that it involved in turn adolescents, a baseball bat, a grandfather, Mexican adults, Puerto Rican adults, and guns. Someone called the police, and according to Claudia everyone talked through the problem without anyone getting hurt (I left when the police came). Claudia said that this kind of interaction is part of life in her neighborhood. Sometimes it's violent as people look for ways to take care of themselves and those they care for.

There is considerable cross-generational interaction on the block. According to Claudia, it all starts with the kids. They first meet each other when they are looking for playmates, and then the parents and other family members become acquainted with each other and continue to interact. Sometimes these interactions are friendly and sometimes they involve conflict. When Claudia and I were reading through this part of my writing, I asked her if there was anything else that she thought was important to include in my description of her neighborhood and she said, "it's kind of corny, but you know how they say 'It takes a village to raise a child' . . . that's like our street . . . it gets annoying but it's true."

Compared to my experience growing up in a white middle-class suburban neighborhood, Claudia's street seems really lively. In fact, when I took Claudia to my house, about 15 minutes away in Fairmount, she commented on how quiet my street was. There was no music and no one was outside on the block. I explained to Claudia that it was quieter during work hours because most people weren't home at that time. Claudia was especially surprised to learn that I didn't know all about all of my neighbors and that they didn't know all about me.

Let's move now into Claudia's house. This is where Claudia, her brother, her sisters, and her mom spend most of their time when they are not at work or at school. When you go into the house, you enter one long room that is divided into a living room area, and beyond that is the dining area, and beyond that is the kitchen. I have spent most of my time either in the living room area or at the dining room table when I visit. In the living room, there is a sofa and some chairs and an entertainment center, and recently they bought a computer that sits on a table. Whenever I have visited, the TV has always been on (although people may or may not be attending to the program), and the programs are always in English. There are pictures of family members around, and a few religious messages in Spanish on the wall. Sometimes there may be magazines (e.g., *Latina Girls*, written in English but about Latinas), or storybooks, or novels in English lying around.

There are stairs on the right side of the house leading to the second floor, which has three bedrooms and one bathroom. One bedroom is Claudia's mom's, one is Hector's (her little brother), and Claudia shares a bedroom with her twin sister, Clarissa, and her younger sister, María. I have never been in any of the rooms on the second floor except for Claudia's and the bathroom.

Claudia's room is really full of things: furniture, clothes, a TV, phone, lots of books, toys etc. On the shelves are photo albums, a dictionary, a Bible, assorted books (e.g., *The Monica Lewinsky Story, Eden Burning, Of Mice and Men*), and the journals Claudia writes. Of those books, only the Bible is written in Spanish. The girls tend to spend a lot of time upstairs in their room when they are at home either watching TV, talking on the phone to their friends and boyfriends, doing their homework, reading and/or writing for pleasure, or just hanging out alone or together.

When I first went to Claudia's house, her mom would only speak with me in Spanish, and she asked me if I would teach her English (although she never had time to schedule any classes because she worked such long hours). She always speaks Spanish to her children, and they speak either English or Spanish back to her. Claudia, Clarissa, María, and Hector all choose to speak English with each other and with their peers. Claudia only seems to speak Spanish with monolingual Spanish speakers, and when she does, she almost always begins by saying "perdona mi español . . . no sé hablar en español muy bien" (pardon my Spanish . . . I don't know how to speak Spanish very well).

As Claudia told us in the story that opened this chapter, she attended Spanish class in elementary school because her mom wanted her to learn Spanish and be able to communicate with her family members. Although Claudia did develop an increasing amount of expertise in Spanish as she progressed through elementary school, at the time of this writing she did not seem to be very comfortable reading or writing in Spanish. For example, one of the student authors who joined the *In Our Own Words: Students' Perspectives on School* project was a monolingual Spanish speaker who had recently migrated from the island to Philadelphia. She wrote about her experiences for the chapter in Spanish, and Silvia translated her writing to English. All four of the student authors decided that they would write their entries in Spanish and English so that all of their family members and friends, regardless of what language they knew, could read what they had written. However, Claudia had a difficult time translating what she had written, and Silvia offered her a tremendous amount of support as she struggled with the translation.

Claudia had the opportunity to visit Puerto Rico for the first time in 1999 when she and her family went to visit her grandparents. When I asked her what she thought of the island, she said it was "small and kind of boring, nothing like Philadelphia." She said that she had to speak Spanish all of the time because no one there could speak English. This led us into a conversation about relationships between being Puerto Rican and speaking Spanish. She said that Puerto Ricans on the island don't consider Puerto Ricans who live in the United States to be Puerto Rican-they consider them "wannabes." For example, she told me a story about how her cousin couldn't understand her when she said "parquear el carro" when she meant "park the car." The cousin said that she couldn't understand what Claudia was saying so Claudia told her aunt in English that she just wanted to say "park the car." Her aunt translated this as "estacionar el vehículo." Claudia couldn't see the difference, and her aunt explained that in Puerto Rico they use "correct Spanish from Spain" and in the Unites States they use "broken Spanish" like she was using. For this reason, Claudia said, Puerto Ricans from the island consider her and others like her as either American or as wannabes. When I asked her what she considered herself, Puerto Rican or American, she said that she considers herself "American with Puerto Rican blood."

Claudia's family is relatively religious. They go to a Pentecostal church one to four times every week, and Claudia takes a Bible study class with other kids her age. Although I never went to church with Claudia, she told me that the adult church services are conducted in Spanish. She said the youth study class is conducted in English because most of the kids are more comfortable in English, but because the Bible is written in Spanish, students learn to read this text in Spanish.

When I first met Claudia at PS 17, she told me that she wanted to be a writer when she grew up. She said that she had been writing stories for as long as she could remember, and she showed me a number of journals that she filled with her writing. Many of the stories that she wrote early in her middle school years were science fiction, and she was beginning to write romance stories around eighth grade. Her twin sister, Clarissa, said she was Claudia's greatest fan, and that she had been reading Claudia's stories forever. Clarissa emphasized that Claudia's science fiction stories were better than her romance stories because she didn't have enough experience with romance yet.

At the time of this writing, Claudia has just completed 10th grade at PS 87. She says it is hard and not very interesting. She is also taking a course on robotics through Temple University, which gives her college credit and a small stipend. Claudia says she is not all that interested in the robotics course; she thinks she would rather study psychology. She also says that she is not writing much on her own anymore or at school. She seems to have lost interest in writing, at least for now.

In sum, Claudia is a heritage Spanish speaker who has developed much more expertise in English than in Spanish because she uses much more English in her everyday life. She is an avid storyteller, a strong writer in English, and a good student at school. She is also able to communicate about a wide range of topics in the variety of Puerto Rican Spanish spoken by adolescents in North Philadelphia. Although she regularly tells me stories about conflicts she has over language and identity issues, she believes that it is important to know Spanish so that she can communicate with her family members. She is aware of the stigma associated with Puerto Ricans who speak "bad" Spanish, and she often apologizes for her Spanish when she speaks.

Silvia's life

This section introduces us to Silvia Román's world. I begin with the excerpt that Silvia wrote about her family for the *In Our Own Words: Students' Perspectives on School* project. Then I describe the ways that Silvia and the members of her household use and evaluate spoken and written Spanish and English in their lives. We see that Silvia, like many other students who were raised in bilingual households, is using more English in more domains of her life as she grows up.

Silvia's introduction to herself and her family highlights the fact that she and her family members move around a lot.

> *I'm 12 years old and I'm in the seventh grade at . . . Bilingual School. My mom and my dad were born in Coamo, Puerto Rico, and they had two children in Puerto Rico.*
>
> *My mother and my father came to the United States to start a new life with their family. When they first came to the US, they lived in Perth Amboy, NJ where they had two more children. Then they moved to New Haven, Connecticut where they had me. After I was born, my mom, my dad, my brothers and I moved to Puerto Rico and lived there for a year. After Puerto Rico we moved to Perth Amboy, New Jersey. One of my brothers moved to Connecticut to live with my aunt, and three of my brothers, my mom, and my dad and I moved to Philadelphia where I have lived for ten years. I have moved four times since I've been in Philadelphia because of housing problems* (Alfaro et al. 2001).

One of Silvia's brothers died of a drug overdose in 1992, and her father died in an automobile accident in 1996. When I met Silvia, she was living with her mother and her stepfather on 8th Street in North Philadelphia. One of her brothers also lives in North Philadelphia, another lives in Perth Amboy, and another has been in jail in western Pennsylvania most of the time that I have known Silvia.

The student authors and I worked on the *In Our Own Words: Students' Perspectives on School* project when Silvia was living on 8th Street, and she invited us to spend afternoons writing at her house. At that time, her stepfather was working as a construction worker in South Philadelphia, and her mother babysat in the house everyday for a friend's children. Silvia's mom and the children she babysat would stay in the living room with us while we worked on the chapter. Her mom would get involved in lively conversations with us about language use and life in the neighborhood as we talked about the students' perspectives on their experiences at PS 17.

Spanish is the language used most often at Silvia's house. Her mom only speaks Spanish, and her stepfather understands English but always spoke Spanish whenever we talked. Silvia always talked to her mom and her stepfather in Spanish, and if her friends were visiting and her mom was in the room, she generally used Spanish (that is, if her friends spoke Spanish). The TV was always on when I visited, and it was always turned to the Spanish language programs. I have never met Silvia's brothers, but she said that the oldest one speaks more Spanish than English, and the two younger ones who are in their twenties both speak more English than Spanish.

When Silvia began elementary school, she was a monolingual Spanish-speaking English language learner (ELL). She was educated in a one-way developmental bilingual program for ELLs for five years, and she learned to read and write in Spanish and English. When she began middle school, Silvia was considered a bilingual student, and she was placed on the "two-way bilingual communication" team where she continued to receive her education through Spanish and English. At the time of this writing, Silvia had just completed her second year of high school, being educated entirely through English. She was not taking any Spanish classes, and with the exception of her interactions with her mom, Silvia said that these days she mostly uses English.

Silvia has moved four times in the three years that I have known her. About two years ago, Silvia, her mom, and her stepfather moved into her grandfather's house on 6th Street, and they lived there for about one and one half years. During this time, her stepfather moved back to Puerto Rico to take care of family matters, and shortly thereafter Silvia and her mom moved into their own house on Potter and Clearfield. After about seven months, Silvia's stepfather came back to Philadelphia, and Silvia, her mom, and her stepfather moved into a house on Reach Street. Her grandfather recently moved in with them. When I asked Silvia what she thought about all these moves, she said it was just difficult moving all of her stuff around.

These moves have disrupted Silvia's schooling. Last year, for example, Silvia began high school in one school but transferred to another when her family moved to Potter and Clearfield. However, Silvia did not like the second high school so she transferred back to her first school. She says that she likes this high school better, but it's difficult. In fact, she failed 10th grade this year and has to repeat this grade. This kind of mobility around the neighborhood is relatively common in North Philadelphia, and many students' education suffers because of repeated interruptions.

Although Silvia does not do very well in school, she has developed an excellent ability to translate oral and written Spanish to English or English to Spanish. Like many children whose parents do not speak English, Silvia serves as a mediator and translator for her mother and stepfather. She is responsible for translating all of their written correspondence from English to Spanish so that her family can understand, and then she is responsible for responding as necessary in spoken and/or written English. I have observed her work with her mother as they go through the mail together. Silvia generally reads a sentence to herself in English and then points to that sentence as she translates for her mom. They talk about the text as Silvia translates the words and sentences to the best of her abilities, and her mom draws on her understanding of the particular social institution (e.g., the gas company) to help her make sense of the text. When I asked Silvia and her mom what happens if she doesn't understand something, for example a legal document or an official letter, they said that they seek help from a local agency on 5th Street. Or, Silvia said, when she really messes up, someone always contacts her family again.

Silvia also demonstrated her ability to translate oral and/or written Spanish to oral and/or written English and oral and/or written English to oral and/or written Spanish as we worked on the *In Our Own Words: Students' Perspectives on School* project. As I mentioned earlier, one of the student writers, Leticia, was a monolingual Spanish speaker and she wrote her contribution for the chapter in Spanish. Silvia enthusiastically offered to translate what Leticia had written to English. To do this, she asked Leticia to slowly read out loud what she had written. Silvia would first translate orally to English, perhaps to confirm her translation with me and Isabel, another one of the writers. Sometimes Isabel and I would help with particular words, and sometimes we would involve Silvia's mom in the conversation about an idea that Leticia was writing about. Once we had confirmed the meaning of the Spanish text orally in English, Silvia would write it in English. When Silvia saw that we were including Leticia's Spanish text in the chapter, she said that she wanted her contribution to be in both Spanish and English so that her family members could read it. She effortlessly translated her contribution and worked closely with Claudia to translate what she had written (although they decided not to include the Spanish version of Claudia's writing because they decided it was too long). These translations were much easier for Silvia than some of the legal document translations that she does with her mother because she was familiar with the topics that the students were writing about. Translation from Spanish to English and from English to Spanish in speech as well as in writing is an activity that many of these students must perform for their families, and they develop an impressive ability. However, because the schools do not encourage translation, teachers rarely have the opportunity to see students' expertise in this area.

When I asked Silvia what else she read and/or wrote in either Spanish or English, she said that she didn't read too much, mostly just magazines like *Cosmopolitan* and *Mademoiselle*. She also really liked *Winnie-the-Pooh*. At the time of this writing, however, Silvia loved to write letters. She wrote letters to her girlfriends all of the time at school, and she shared many of them with me. Mostly they wrote about various romances, and they switched from Spanish to English with ease. Silvia traveled to Puerto Rico most summers with her mom, and she would write to family members and friends on the island in Spanish. Silvia also wrote often to her brother who was in jail, and he regularly wrote to Silvia and to their mom. I was there one day when Silvia and her mom each received one of his letters. The one that he wrote to Silvia's mom was in Spanish, and the one that he wrote to Silvia was in English. This language use pattern in writing is consistent with Silvia's account of how different members use Spanish and English with each other at home.

In sum, Silvia is a heritage Spanish speaker who can read and write, speak about, and understand a wide range of topics in Spanish and/or English. As she gets older and receives less support for Spanish at school, Silvia is beginning to use English in more domains in her life. Like many children who live in low-income neighborhoods, Silvia has moved around a lot and these moves have disrupted her schooling. Although she is not a strong student, she has developed an impressive ability to translate, simultaneously, from Spanish to English and English to Spanish in speech and in writing.

Building on Claudia's and Silvia's strengths

The descriptive accounts of the ways that Claudia and Silvia use and evaluate spoken and written Spanish and English in their everyday lives are not exhaustive, and they are not directly generalizable to other heritage Spanish speakers in North Philadelphia and/or in other Latino communities. However, these accounts do reveal different kinds of linguistic expertise that educators can readily build on. This concluding section summarizes some of this expertise, and provides ideas for educators who are working to expand heritage Spanish-speaking students' bilingual range. Following Valdés (2000), I turn to the foreign language field's work on the interpersonal, interpretive, and presentational modes of communication to structure my discussion. I supplement this discussion with references to Hornberger and Skilton-Sylvester's (2000) work on the continua of biliteracy framework.

Claudia demonstrates considerable expertise in the interpersonal mode of communication in Spanish. Recall from chapter 3 that the interpersonal mode is characterized by the active negotiation of meaning among individuals in face-to-face communication. Although she apologizes for her accent, Claudia can readily talk about a wide range of familiar topics using the variety of Puerto Rican Spanish spoken in North Philadelphia. This variety of Spanish shows considerable influence of nonstandard varieties of English spoken in North Philadelphia (e.g., African-American English, Puerto Rican English) in terms of phonology and vocabulary (see Zentella 1997 for detailed discussion of the multidialectal, bilingual repertories of New York Puerto Ricans). It makes sense that Claudia would have developed expertise in this variety of Spanish because her experiences using Spanish have been in interactions with monolingual family members and/or friends in North Philadelphia. Since she has not had much exposure to other varieties of Spanish (e.g., Standard Spanish, informal Puerto Rican Spanish spoken on the island) or other modes of communication (e.g., formal oral and written presentations), Claudia has developed less expertise in these varieties and/or modes in Spanish.

Understanding the nature of Claudia's expertise in Spanish gives educators ideas about how to build on her strengths. In order to broaden her linguistic range, Claudia needs opportunities to develop the interpretive and presentational modes of communication in Spanish. Recall from chapter 3 that the interpretive mode is focused on the appropriate cultural interpretation of meanings that occur in spoken and written form where there is no active negotiation of meaning (e.g., reading a novel, listening to the radio, watching a film). The presentational mode refers to the creation of spoken and/or written messages in a manner that facilitates interpretation by members of the other culture where no direct opportunity for active negotiation of meaning exists (e.g., writing a report, presenting a speech). Claudia is an avid storyteller and a strong reader and writer in English. Educators could begin their work with a student like Claudia with informal, oral communication in Spanish about topics that Claudia knows and/or cares about. Educators could then build on that foundation by providing Claudia with opportunities to read, write, listen, and speak about that topic in different varieties and registers of Spanish. Claudia also demonstrates her interest in looking critically at Spanish. Educators could help Claudia develop this strength by encouraging her to look critically at the social implications of using one variety and/or register over another in particular times and places. Since the variety of Puerto Rican Spanish spoken in North Philadelphia is already stigmatized, educators would need to be sure that they did not further devalue this variety. Instead, they would want to challenge the social stigmatization of that variety and help students like Claudia understand that this is one important variety within their multidialectal, bilingual repertoire. The goal is to add other varieties to that repertoire, not replace one (stigmatized) variety with another (more valued) variety.

Silvia's experiences as a Puerto Rican in North Philadelphia have been very different from Claudia's, and she has developed different kinds of expertise as a result. Perhaps because her schooling has been interrupted, Silvia is not as strong of a student as Claudia. However, Silvia has developed expertise that educators could readily build on that would benefit her academically, socially, and professionally. Like Claudia, Silvia has developed considerable expertise in the interpersonal mode in Spanish. Because Silvia is in regular contact with monolingual Spanish speakers from the island and in North Philadelphia, she also speaks and understands different varieties of conversational Spanish with ease. Furthermore, since Silvia was educated in bilingual programs throughout her elementary and middle school years, she has learned to read and write in Spanish. She also has a regular need for spoken and written Spanish in her life so that she can perform the complex translation and mediation tasks that are required of her as she helps her monolingual Spanish-speaking mother interact with institutions in the English-speaking/writing United States. Educators could readily build on this foundation and this motivation and draw on the ways that Silvia uses Spanish outside of school as the basis for her Spanish instruction. Silvia needs more opportunities to use oral and written Spanish at school so that she does not lose the expertise that she has developed through her schooling to date. With such support, Silvia could develop considerable expertise in Standard Spanish and she could readily develop the literacies she would need for academic and business purposes in Spanish. Without further support, Silvia is likely to continue her shift to English.

Hornberger and Skilton-Sylvester's (2000) work on the continua of biliteracy suggests ways that educators can direct their efforts to promote biliteracy on the individual, classroom, community, and societal levels, and it helps explain how micro-level language teaching and learning processes can challenge macro-level sociopolitical relations. Here our attention is on the micro-level of the individual student. According to Hornberger and Skilton-Sylvester, the continua of biliteracy framework allows us to situate an individual's development of biliteracy along three intersecting continua (first language-second language, oral-written, and receptive-productive). Furthermore, they argue that one end of each continuum is typically associated with more power than the other, with society valuing receptive, oral, first language skills less than productive, written, second language skills.

Although Spanish is not always the "first language" and English is not always the "second language" in my discussion of heritage Spanish speakers in North Philadelphia, Spanish is attributed less power than English in the United States. I have therefore indicated that Spanish, the less powerful language, is on the left side of the continuum and English, the more powerful language, is on the right side of the continuum in my discussion of biliteracy development in the Puerto Rican community in North Philadelphia.

Receptive <---> Productive

Oral <---> Written

Spanish <---> English

Educators can situate their observations of the ways that a student understands (receptive) and produces (productive) oral and written Spanish and English in relation to the contexts, media, and content in and through which biliteracy develops, and they can think about balancing power relations.

In this chapter, for example, we see an imbalance in the ways that Claudia produces written languages, with the English end of the continuum much more heavily weighted than the Spanish end. In fact, she is a strong writer in English who produces very little written Spanish in any context. Educators can direct their attention to this imbalance in Claudia's biliteracy development and emphasize development of expertise in written Spanish across topics, genres, and registers (i.e., the content of biliteracy). We also see an imbalance in the ways that both Claudia and Silvia use Spanish, with the oral, nonstandard ends of the continua much more heavily weighted than the written standard ends. In these cases, educators can address these imbalances by emphasizing Standard Spanish especially written Spanish across topics, genres, and registers. Hornberger and Skilton-Sylvester (2000) see this kind of work promoting biliteracy development as a way that educators can challenge power relations on the local level. By emphasizing the less powerful ends of the continua (e.g., Spanish) and by giving students access to the more powerful varieties (e.g., Standard Spanish, literacies in Spanish), educators broaden students' linguistic repertoires in ways that give them access to opportunities not traditionally available.

Valdés' (2000) work in the foreign language field and Hornberger and Skilton-Sylvester's (2000) work in the bilingual education field use different frameworks for thinking about biliteracy development. However, both highlight the need to identify the particular nature of students' expertise in relation to broader, clearly defined notions of and goals for biliteracy development. Both also emphasize the need to give students language-rich, print-rich opportunities to develop the expertise they have not had the chance to develop. Since experience leads to expertise, educators can explore the kinds of experiences that particular students have had with spoken and written Spanish and English in their everyday lives through the stories that students tell and/or write as well as with observations of their practices, and they can identify the kinds of expertise students have developed. Educators can then make informed, pedagogically sound decisions about ways to build on those strengths.

6

Language and identity in the Puerto Rican community

This chapter takes us from the homes of particular students into the larger community to explore issues of language and identity, and it is divided into three parts. The chapter begins in El Bloque de Oro (The Golden Block), the center of the Latino business district, and we look closely at how Spanish and English are used and evaluated in the community. Then I give a brief history of the Puerto Rican community in North Philadelphia, which provides an important lens for looking at some of the complex and contradictory language ideologies in El Barrio (the neighborhood). While English tends to be the prestige language and Spanish-especially informal Puerto Rican Spanish-tends to be socially stigmatized in North Philadelphia, we do see evidence of alternatives to dominant discourses about the community and the people who live there. The last part of the chapter provides an example of one such alternative that rejects the negative representation of North Philadelphia as "the Badlands," and offers a more positive discourse about hope, possibility, and change.

Exploring El Bloque de Oro

This section takes us to the center of the Latino business district to explore "El Bloque de Oro," or The Golden Block, in North Philadelphia. El Bloque is actually three blocks on 5th Street between Lehigh and Indiana, and it is a key context in the bilingual community. Although we do see evidence of the kinds of problems that are associated with low-income urban neighborhoods across the country, we also see that there are many more linguistic and cultural resources available in the neighborhood than the mainstream media generally acknowledges. When you walk down the street along the faded golden path that was painted on the sidewalk years ago, you can hear Spanish and English and read signs on the shop windows in Spanish and English. Salsa and merengue emanate from shops, restaurants, passing cars, and boom boxes, and they mix with the sounds of rap and hip-hop. Murals that evoke images of the island and of Puerto Rican culture abound, and the Puerto Rican flag is proudly displayed on T-shirts, in windows, on car mirrors, and on jewelry. Puerto Rican food can be bought in local bodegas and on the corner from a vendor. This business district is a vital linguistic and cultural resource in this bilingual community that I wanted to explore with local educators and their students.

In June and July of 1997, I worked with ten teachers and approximately sixty middle school students from PS 17, which is a bilingual middle school in North Philadelphia, to explore and document the role of El Bloque de Oro in the Latino community today. El Bloque is about three blocks away from the school and, in many of the people's words that we met there, El Bloque is "the heart and soul of the Latino community" (*"el corazon, el alma"*). Our goal was to develop a student-directed project that would encourage the students to explore their own community and to develop the oral, written, and technical expertise they needed to share what they learned with a wider audience. This section describes the project and shares what we learned about bilingual discourse practices in the community.

Title VII funded a TV/communications lab for PS 17, and one of the educators' goals was to have the students develop video literacies in Spanish and English. The educators that I worked with and I decided that the students should make videos about what they learned about El Bloque. We decided that we should organize the students into four teams. Each team of fifteen students was led by two teachers, and each team took responsibility for doing research on one part of El Bloque and for making a video about what the team found in that section. Each of the teams was equipped with matching baseball caps (which the kids quickly personalized), school T-shirts, notebooks and clipboards, cassette recorders, and cameras and given access to a video recorder. Each team also included at least one graduate student and several parents and community volunteers working with them on El Bloque every day.

The teachers divided the students on their team into cooperative learning groups so they could share responsibility for collecting the necessary data for the project. Each team assigned its groups to (a) diagram the social space, (b) interview shop owners, employees, customers, and anyone else they met on El Bloque, (c) observe interactions on El Bloque, or (d) videotape key interactions for a culminating video. The teachers assigned students to particular parts of the project depending on student strengths and interests. At the end of each day, the small groups of students would share what they had learned so that they could focus their interview questions and observations and prepare to get the video clips they needed for their video.

I worked as an ethnographer alongside the students and demonstrated my own interest in exploring and documenting the role of El Bloque in the Latino community. Rosa Fuentes, one of the parents who volunteered to work on the project, worked by my side every day. At the time of this project, Rosa had lived in the neighborhood for 25 years. Although she could speak and understand English, she was passionate about the need to maintain Spanish and she was proud of her community. As we moved from establishment to establishment, Rosa would tell me what she knew about local history and she would introduce me to people along the way. Rosa and I would regularly reflect on our conversations and observations on El Bloque. My collaboration with Rosa was invaluable as I was learning about language use and social relations in the neighborhood.

In addition to my goal of exploring and documenting how Spanish and English were used and evaluated in the community, I wanted to involve the students in the research process. I regularly shared my questions and observations with the students and I asked them to reflect on those questions and observations with me. For example, I shared my preliminary observations of relationships among language, gender, and age. I found that older men seemed to use more Spanish than younger men, and older men seemed to spend a lot of time reading Spanish newspapers. Teenage boys on the street seemed to speak almost exclusively in English. The girls and women who I observed used more Spanish than the boys and younger men did. Our discussions about these kinds of gendered language use patterns would often lead to conversations about how boys and girls and men and women in their families used Spanish and English. At the end of a conversation, I would encourage the students to follow up on whatever we had talked about in their research on El Bloque, and I asked them to meet with me to share our field notes. When we met, those who had taken up my challenge to observe language use would talk some more about what they had seen. These kinds of interactions with the students allowed me to model the research process and to focus their observations. At the same time, this approach yielded an enormous amount of data about how the students interpret the patterns of language use that they observe. I summarize those language use patterns in chapter 7.

Through our research on El Bloque, we learned a lot about a wide range of establishments that serve the Latino community. There were food stores, health care establishments, travel agencies, clothing and jewelry stores, book stores, botánicas, music stores, bodegas, clubs, furniture stores, party supply stores, and establishments providing legal advice or help with income tax or immigration. Almost all of the stores had signs that were written in Spanish and English, and most of the employees that we talked with and/or observed were able to use Spanish and/or English in their transactions. There were a few exceptions. For example, an audio store that had been on El Bloque for about nine years was owned by Israelis who do not speak Spanish. All of the advertising on the beer distributor was in English. One of the food markets was owned by a Chinese family, and the Chinese woman that I talked with spoke a little bit of English and was learning Spanish through her experience on El Bloque. While most of the buildings were occupied and open for business, a few were closed or preparing to open again. Some of the establishments had only been there for a year or two, others had been there for five or more years, and some had been there for more than thirty years.

Most of the establishments provide services to the Latino community and many of the employees that we talked with are Puerto Rican. However, we learned that most of the establishments that have been on El Bloque for a long time were not owned by Puerto Ricans. For example, Bill is a white European American who owns a ladies' fashion store. Bill told us that his family has lived in the neighborhood for over seventy years, and his family has had a clothing store on 5th Street since before it became a Puerto Rican neighborhood. According to Bill, he and his brother are the only proprietors who have remained in the area since the demographics changed. They both now own businesses on El Bloque (his brother owns a discount store, which sells clothing for infants, boys, girls, and men), and although neither of them speaks much Spanish, they say they sell clothing that they believe caters to Puerto Rican tastes. The carnicería (butchershop), mueblería (furniture store), and joyería (jewelry store) have also been on El Bloque for over thirty years, and their owners are all Cuban. The owners of these three businesses have been very active in the local business association, and they told us that Cubans were responsible for establishing El Bloque as a Latino business district in the 1970s. We were told that many of the original Cuban proprietors have also left over the years.

Both the students and I observed a prevailing sentiment that El Bloque has deteriorated. The owner of the carnicería talked fondly about Inauguration Day of El Bloque de Oro when they painted the golden swirling line along the sidewalk on both sides of the street. People reminisced that in those days everyone was united and they all worked together. Today, many say, *todo ha cambiado mucho* (everything has changed a lot). Bill of the ladies' fashion store said that if the people in the neighborhood would care more about it (e.g., stop throwing trash, stop writing graffiti, stop using drugs, stop criminal activity), then the merchants would go back to being united and everything would work well again.

One day, for example, we heard a gunshot and an adolescent boy stumbled from a sidestreet to El Bloque. Several of the parent volunteers who were working with us tried to stop the boy's bleeding leg with a T-shirt, and someone called the police. We gathered all of the students who were on El Bloque at the time into one of the medical centers to make sure no one would get hurt, and we learned that the shooting was related to the drug-dealing activity on the corner down the street. When the police came, we hurried all of the students back to the school (knowing that the streets were safer at this moment because there were police all around), and we talked about what happened when we were all safely in the school lunchroom.

The shooting was an extreme example of the violence that people said was tearing apart the neighborhood. When we asked about ways that the neighborhood had changed, they would point to trash and graffiti as evidence of how El Bloque had deteriorated. Many, however, expressed a strong desire to see a revitalized El Bloque. Some told us about local projects that were working toward this end. For example, Jesus from a local restaurant told me that he was a politician who believes that kids need safe places for recreation. He is very involved in the community, and he walks door to door trying to get people to vote. Another person told me about an organization of professional Latinas who mentor girls at local schools. Others had messages for the kids in particular and for the video more generally that they expressed either to me or to the kids. The people at the local Puerto Rican arts and culture center talked at length with the students about activities they organized for kids in the community. When the owner of the carnicería talked to the kids about the future of the neighborhood, she addressed the kids directly and said, "It's all up to you-you control the future here." As the project progressed, the students became very interested in learning about the changes that people thought were necessary to revitalize El Bloque. The students' stories had a strong emphasis on change. One of the videos that one team made was entitled "It starts with us," and another was entitled "El Bloque then and now."

In summary, El Bloque is a vital business center that functions as the "heart and soul" of the bilingual community. It is easy to find many examples of people who are working together for positive change in the neighborhood, despite the many setbacks they encounter that can be tremendously frustrating. Moreover, spoken and written Spanish are pervasive, and they coexist easily with English in the neighborhood. One can hear Spanish (and English) being used for business as well as for everyday social interactions. There are several different newspapers, some exclusively in Spanish and others in Spanish and English, that are available in the neighborhood (*Al Día*, for example, is free in North Philadelphia but costs fifty cents in other parts of the city). These papers connect those who read in Spanish to each other in Philadelphia as well as to life in other parts of the Spanish-speaking world. Several of the teachers who worked on the project had never been to El Bloque before. These white middle-class teachers who were not from the neighborhood were fascinated to discover this part of the community.

A brief history of the Puerto Rican community in North Philadelphia

When I began my research in North Philadelphia in 1996, one of the bilingual coordinators that I first worked with said to me, "You can't understand Puerto Ricans at school without understanding the colonial relationship between the United States and Puerto Rico." Although Puerto Rico is technically no longer a U.S. colony, many still characterize the relationship as one of colonialism. This section presents a brief discussion that allows us to understand the development of the Puerto Rican community in Philadelphia (see Morales Carrión 1983 and Whalen 1994 for detailed discussions). This political and economic context in turn allows us to explain the language ideologies that we find throughout the community, ideologies that strongly influence the ways that Puerto Ricans use and evaluate languages in their everyday lives.

Puerto Rico has been economically dependent on the United States for over 100 years, and the status of the relationship between the island and the United States has been and continues to be vigorously debated. The relationship between the United States and Puerto Rico formally began in 1898 when Puerto Rico was transferred from Spain to the United States as one of the spoils of the Spanish-American War. Since that time, Puerto Rico has been subjected to U.S. policies, and Puerto Ricans have received considerable U.S. aid. In 1917, Puerto Ricans were granted U.S. citizenship-some say just in time to fight in World War I. Since 1952, Puerto Rico has been a self-governing "Commonwealth" or "Freely Associated State" under U.S. jurisdiction. According to this political arrangement, Puerto Ricans are subject to all federal laws, yet they are not permitted to vote in U.S. elections or to influence the political decisions that affect most aspects of their lives. These policies have had far-reaching consequences for all aspects of Puerto Rican life, and they play an important role in contemporary debates about the status of the island.

Three options for Puerto Rico's status are currently debated: become the 51st state of the United States, maintain the status quo, or declare independence. Passionate arguments are presented for and against each of the status positions, all of which reflect a general concern for economic security and linguistic and cultural integrity. For example, the statehood position claims that Puerto Rico will be the first Spanish-speaking state in the United States, and that all other options not only maintain the subordinate position of Puerto Ricans relative to other U.S. citizens but also threaten Puerto Rican claims to U.S. citizenship. The commonwealth (or status quo) position argues against statehood because they believe that statehood would threaten the sovereignty of Spanish, especially in the increasingly English-only, antibilingual atmosphere that we find in many parts of mainstream U.S. society today. Proponents of this position maintain that a continued commonwealth status does not threaten U.S. citizenship for Puerto Ricans. The *independentistas* argue that anything but independence ensures Puerto Ricans' status as second-class citizens of the United States. Independentistas living in the United States maintain that they have experienced the subordinate position of Puerto Ricans in the United States firsthand. According to recent polls, Puerto Ricans on the island favor statehood and the status quo options almost equally, and only about 5 percent favor independence. The independence position receives stronger support among Puerto Ricans living in the United States than among Puerto Ricans living on the island.

Although all of the political parties in Puerto Rico have given ideological support to the supremacy of Spanish, Zentella (1981) describes ambivalent attitudes toward English and Spanish among island Puerto Ricans. She writes,

> On the one hand, the colonial language, in this case English, enjoys greater prestige, many parents are eager for their children to acquire it, and many more students want more and better instruction in it. It is seen as the language of the wealthy, the most educated, the most powerful . . . . The local language enjoys less prestige: the poor speak it, less powerful countries speak it, the USA does not speak it. On the other hand, the colonial language is in many quarters bitterly resented, and school failures and high drop-out rates are attributed to the role of the colonial language in the schools (221-222).

Puerto Ricans living in Philadelphia also have complex and contradictory feelings about the role of Spanish and English in their lives. These language ideologies have important implications for language teaching and learning at school.

Let's briefly consider how the political and economic relationship between Puerto Rico and the United States led to the development of the Puerto Rican community in North Philadelphia. After World War II, the United States needed laborers for their agricultural programs, and the U.S. government was opposed to recruiting foreign laborers. The U.S. government therefore recruited African Americans from the rural south and Puerto Ricans from the island to work as seasonal farm laborers. Puerto Rican women were also brought to the Philadelphia area on domestic-labor contracts. Many of these Puerto Ricans, however, were attracted to the abundant number of manufacturing jobs that were available in Philadelphia at the time, and many chose to stay in Philadelphia rather than return to the island. Since Puerto Ricans are U.S. citizens who are entitled to live and/or work anywhere in the United States, this choice was clearly a viable option. The Puerto Rican migrants drew on their informal social networks (e.g., family members and/or friends) that were already established in the Philadelphia area to help them secure manufacturing jobs and get settled. According to Whalen (1994), labor contracts and informal networks enabled the "Great Migration" of Puerto Ricans from the island to Philadelphia that took place from 1945 to 1965, and to the development of the Puerto Rican community in North Philadelphia today.

The Puerto Rican migrants originally settled in the Spring Garden area on and around Green Street. At that time, the people living in North Philadelphia were primarily African American or European American, and their neighborhoods were very segregated. Fifth Street was then a predominantly white-owned business district that bordered the black and white communities. According to Goode and Schneider (1994), there were racial riots in the neighborhood in the 1970s, and the overwhelming majority of the white business owners left Fifth Street (recall, however, that Bill's clothing stores remained). At the same time, real estate in the Spring Garden area was becoming much more expensive, and many Puerto Ricans began to move in along the recently abandoned Fifth Street corridor. The Puerto Rican community began to serve as a kind of a buffer zone between black and white spaces in North Philadelphia.

Racial relations in Philadelphia, as in many other parts of the United States, have largely been understood in terms of black and white. Puerto Ricans, however, do not fit neatly into this binary opposition, and one hears many stories of how Puerto Ricans have experienced racism in the United States. For example, one Puerto Rican educator told me a story about a Puerto Rican mother who tried to enroll her two children in a predominantly black school in the 1970s. According to desegregation policies that were in effect at that time, the school was obliged to have a certain quota of white students. Since there were no racial categories other than black or white at that time, the office administrator said that she would accept the child who appeared white but not the child who appeared black. Other Puerto Rican educators that I know who lived in North Philadelphia during this time period told me stories of being harassed by whites in the white neighborhood where they went to school. As children, they would have to run through Fishtown, the predominantly white neighborhood where they went to school, until they safely crossed Front Street back into their newly adopted home near 5th Street. While racial boundaries in the neighborhood and policies and practices regarding race relations have changed in Philadelphia, as in the rest of the country, local ideologies about race and identity play an important role in Puerto Rican lives.

Migration patterns have changed since 1965, largely because of economic changes that have taken place in Philadelphia. Most of the factories that initially attracted Puerto Ricans to North Philadelphia have closed, and there are few jobs available to relatively unskilled laborers. Today, many men work in construction and/or as mechanics. Many women work in retail stores outside of the neighborhood, or work locally providing child care services. There is also chronic unemployment in the area. Since 1965, we have seen what scholars call "revolving door" migration as Puerto Ricans move back and forth between the island and the continental United States in search of economic opportunities, and they draw on informal social networks to help them meet the demands of their everyday lives. This revolving door migration has important implications for the vitality of Spanish in North Philadelphia today.

Puerto Ricans living in North Philadelphia today express complex and at times contradictory ideologies about the languages that they speak and the community in which they live. The larger historical political and economic context explains much of this complexity. On the one hand, Spanish is associated with the local community in Philadelphia, ethnic identity, family traditions on the island, unemployment, and poverty. English is associated with economic opportunities in the United States, technology, and prosperity. As we see in chapter 7, these patterns dominate in interactions throughout schools and the community. However, as the next section highlights, we also see evidence of alternative discourses that position Puerto Ricans in North Philadelphia and the languages that they speak more favorably.

Resisting dominant discourses

This section provides a brief look at an act of resistance by educators and students from one bilingual middle school as well as by others in the Latino community. Here I focus on the mass media, which exerts a powerful influence over local definitions of identity groups relative to each other. The example presented here explores how the label "the Badlands" was being actively contested, and it illustrates how Puerto Rican identity is a site of struggle. As we see in this section, multiple representations of groups and communities offer more choices to the individual about his/her roles, rights, and obligations in society, and they offer more options for everyone.

In the mid-1990s, it was relatively common for North Philadelphia to be referred to as "the Badlands" by the mainstream media. One angry response to this label was published in the December 5, 1996 issue of the bilingual newspaper *Community Focus/Enfoque Comunal*. La Cotorra (the parrot) has a regular feature in each issue, and this one was entitled *'Bad' qué?*. La Cotorra begins the article by writing,

> *Señores, estoy ya fastidiado del mote ese que nos tienen los gringos a quienes residimos decentemente en este barrio nuestro al norte del Fildelfia.*

> Gentlemen/ladies, I am fed up with this nickname that the gringos have for those of us who live decently in our neighborhood in North Philadelphia.

The author offers a series of names for the neighborhood that he does not see as objectionable, for example, *North Philly, Kensington, El Barrio* (the neighborhood). He continues,

> *Pero mencionar uno de esos nombres a los gringos y no saben una vianda de qué rayos estamos hablando. Ahora, diga usted "Badlands" e inmediatemente las antenas se les paran y te dicen, "usted viven allí. Ay que cosa tan mala!*

> But mention one of these names to the gringos and they don't have any idea what you are talking about. Now, say "Badlands" and immediately the antennas go up and they say to you, "You live there. Oh what a bad thing!"

As this author points out, the majority of the people who live in Philadelphia have no idea what North Philadelphia is like outside of the dominant representation of it as "the Badlands."

La Cotorra expresses outrage because people from the neighborhood have begun to adopt the term "the Badlands" to refer to their own neighborhood, which he maintains is a sign of self-hate, loss of identity, and lack of self-respect. Such negative feelings about one's community, La Cotorra argues, aggravate so many of the problems that exist in this low-income neighborhood. He implores the readers, especially *nuestros líderes* (our leaders), *gente de la cultura* (cultured people), *educadores* (educators), *politicos* (politicians) to stop using the term "the Badlands." He concludes by asking the local representative to introduce legislation *que cese el fuego a nuestro orgullo, ese asedio a nuestra dignidad en disfraz lingüístico* (that stops the attack on our pride, this assassination on our dignity in a linguistic disguise).

Carmen Alvarez, the director of the PS 17 bilingual program from 1995 to 1997, also opposed the use of the term "the Badlands" by the mass media to refer to the Puerto Rican neighborhood in which she worked. Like many of the other bilingual educators that we meet in this book, Alvarez is Puerto Rican. She was born in Puerto Rico, came to the northeast coast of the United States as an adult, and has worked in the field of bilingual education throughout her professional life. According to Alvarez, when she heard Ted Koppel use the term "the Badlands" to refer to North Philadelphia, she decided to take action on the local school level. Alvarez brought local artists to the school to work with 30 of her mentally gifted students (all Puerto Rican), and they created a musical, *The Children of the Badlands*. This case provides an example of how the mass media can be used to resist dominant representations of Puerto Ricans and their community.

Although I did not witness the process of creating the musical "Children of the Badlands," Alvarez provided me with the following account. When she heard the Koppel report about problems in North Philadelphia, she wondered how her students felt about the ways in which the mainstream media represents their community. Alvarez decided to organize a project in which her students would reflect on their experiences, first coming to the United States from the island full of hope for a better life and then confronting the poverty and associated challenges in North Philadelphia. Alvarez wanted this project to enable her students to see themselves as agents of change in their own lives and in the life of the community. To this end, she envisioned a musical, and she generated the names of eight songs: ""This is my culture," "Puerto Rico, NO!," "Prejudicial ways," "Some day," "And after that school starts," "Children of 'The Badlands," "PORTAL," and "My place in this world." She called a composer whom she had collaborated with on another project, told him about the project she wanted her students to create, and gave him the titles of the songs.

Alvarez said that she had a strong idea of the final project in her mind from the outset, and she asked local artists to guide her students through the production of *The Children of the Badlands*. The students began by working with a poet. The poet gave the students Alvarez's list of song titles, and they brainstormed about their experiences before they came to the United States, when they arrived, what they found, and what they hoped for the future. The poet worked with the students for about one and a half months to write poems that would provide the lyrics for the songs of the musical. According to Alvarez, the students took up the opportunity to write poems about these themes in different ways. Some students wrote poems about all of the themes, others concentrated on four or five of the titles, and others focused on one theme that was meaningful to them. Next Alvarez invited the composer to come and work with the students to put their poems to music. The composer asked the students what radio stations they listened to, and he began to listen to those stations so that he could capture the sounds. The composer took the lines from the students' poems and combined them into what he referred to as a collage. He put the lyrics to music-rap, salsa, hip-hop, and reggae-and brought the finished songs back to the students. According to Alvarez, the students loved the collage that the composer had created from their work because they could see the ways that they had expressed themselves individually put together in new and powerful ways. Once the music was finished, the students worked with a choreographer to develop the dances they would perform. They also began to make the sets that they would take with them in their performances; these sets included island scenes with palm trees, a Puerto Rican flag, and city scenes with buildings covered with graffiti and trash all around. Alvarez maintains that although the idea for the project was hers, and although students were guided by adults throughout the process, the students really took ownership of the project and developed it far beyond her original vision.

According to Alvarez, the students performed *The Children of the Badlands* more than fifty times from 1996 to 1999 in a wide range of venues. For example, the students performed for the School District of Philadelphia Board of Education, for the City Council, in Washington D.C. for a national conference for Puerto Rican women, and for a variety of local community-based organizations, including Aspira, Congreso de Latinos Unidos, Concilio, Norris Square Center, and the Kensington Neighborhood Association. They also performed at other schools across the city. I saw *The Children of the Badlands* performed at Abington Friends School, which serves a primarily white middle-class student population.

At each performance, the students handed out a program that listed the names of the songs: "This is my culture," "Puerto Rico, NO!," "Prejudicial ways," "Some day," "And after that school starts," "Children of 'The Badlands,'" "PORTAL," and "My place in this world." The program also listed the names of the participating students and a text describing the production that is written first in Spanish and then in English. I include the entire English text here because it presents the storyline of the musical. I underline the words that were underlined in the original texts because these underlined words index the main ideas of the songs and allow the reader to see the storyline at a glance.

This musical production is embedded with a vision. Our children have gone through a reflection on their past and their cultural heritage and then are confronted with the present reality of the inner city, El Barrio and what the media calls "The Badlands." Finally, they project themselves to the future and its possibilities. This is a lesson for all about the reality of the struggles of an ethnic group that is trying to rise and overcome the social ailments that they must endure.

Puerto Ricans celebrate their <u>culture</u> and arrive to the mainland (the land of opportunities) with expectations of a better future. But they confront cultural shock when they reach El Barrio

<u>Racial discrimination</u>, closed doors, the need to conform to the dominant culture to be accepted: To be accepted forces them to <u>deny who they are</u>. Their beloved language and culture turns into a curse. Life conditions make you <u>deny yourself</u>.

But there is hope: "Someday we will reach our dreams." <u>Someday</u> we will be somebody and then we will come back and reach out for those who stayed behind. The harsh reality of the poverty and the environment that wants to swallow our youth is a great challenge. Day after day our children need to battle and conquer the challenges of <u>the badlands</u>, the land of the "have-nots."

<u>Before they get to school</u> everyday the devastation of the city screams at their faces: "you can't; this is what is here for you: drugs, garbage, poverty, killings and abandonment." But the children of the badlands, full of courage, respond with a strong and angry scream: "you don't know us, you don't understand us. We are not what you say we are. We have the power within ourselves to conquer these living conditions and transform this society. We, the underestimated, are the power of the future."

There is <u>a door</u> that leads to the future. We will enter through it because we know where to find the key. We will open the path and we are getting ready to take what is ours. We will have <u>our place in</u> this society and in this world.

The Children of the Badlands is one example of a local effort to challenge negative representations of Puerto Ricans and of North Philadelphia. The text that the students and educators created rejects dominant representations of Puerto Ricans as criminals, drug dealers, unemployed, untrustworthy, or lazy. It rejects the notion of Puerto Ricans as either monolingual Spanish speakers who are backward and unable to fit into urban America, or monolingual English speakers who have abandoned their Puerto Rican identity and any sense of who they are or where they come from (see Urcuioli, 1996 for extensive discussion of New York Puerto Rican experiences of language prejudice). Instead, *The Children of the Badlands* and some of the media surrounding it provide evidence of the struggle to define Puerto Ricans as bilingual, sophisticated, employed and respected, confident in their Puerto Rican identities, and committed to helping their community.

This school-based effort to challenge dominant media representations was taken up by the local media. For example, the January 16, 1997 edition of *Al Día,* one of the major bilingual newspapers in Philadelphia, featured *The Children of the Badlands* project as its cover story. On the cover page was a full-page color photograph of the children who performed the musical and a caption that read

> *No todo es malo en las "Badlands" de Filadelfia. En la*
> *Escuela Media . . . este grupo de muchachos se están*
> *convirtiendo en embajadores de la comunidad hispano del*
> *Norte de Filadelfia a través del Coro del Portal, cuyas*
> *canciones intentan, partiendo de la aceptación de su*
> *etorno, acabar con los estereotipos y prejuicios que de su*
> *barrio tiene el resto de la ciudad.*
>
> Not all is bad in the "Badlands" of Philadelphia. In . . .
> Middle School this group of children is converting itself into
> ambassadors of the hispanic community of North Philadelphia
> through the Portal Choir, whose songs intend, through the
> acceptance of their environment, to end the stereotypes and
> prejudices that the rest of the city has about this neighborhood.

This caption provides evidence of the dominant discourse it opposes: a construction of the *"Badlands"* where all is bad, with *stereotypes and prejudices that the rest of the city has about this neighborhood.* The caption also constructs the children as agents of change: they are represented as *angels of the Badlands* and *ambassadors of the hispanic community of North Philadelphia.* Their songs tell a story different from the story one usually hears about the Puerto Rican community in North Philadelphia.

That same issue of *Al Día* also includes an editorial entitled "Tierras inhóspitas" or "Badlands." Although the newspaper published the editorial in both Spanish and Engish, I include only the English version here. The editorial begins with the Webster's Dictionary definition of the term "badlands":

lands with intricate erosional sculptures, scarce vegetation and fantastically formed hills. The author also makes reference to the original Badlands in South Dakota as well as to science fiction features that use this term to describe moonlike, *desertlike, lifeless landscapes.* The author goes on to explain that

> The North of Philadelphia, in particular the area in which most of the Hispanic population lives, was renamed years ago by the mass media as "the Badlands." People, even Hispanics themselves who live there, have a perception of the neighborhood as "Bad Lands," instead of the appropriate one, described above.

The article continues by listing some of the problems facing this impoverished community. It concludes by arguing that the area's image is negative and community members have to change it. The editorial explains that *The Children of the Badlands* production is an example of one such effort to change that image.

Conclusion

This chapter built on the description in chapter 5 of how two heritage Spanish-speaking students use and evaluate Spanish and English in their lives to describe, interpret, and explain issues of language and identity more broadly in the community. First I identified some of the linguistic and cultural resources that educators can find in the heart of this bilingual community and provided an example of how one group of educators worked with their students to build on these resources. Then I gave a brief political and economic history of the Puerto Rican community in North Philadelphia and explained some of the competing language ideologies we see in the community. I concluded the chapter with a discussion of one alternative representation of language and identity in the Puerto Rican community. This act of resistance reflects local community and school efforts to challenge dominant discourses that discriminate against Puerto Ricans, and contributes to local efforts to transform those discourses so that Puerto Ricans are positioned more favorably.

7

Understanding language ideologies: A basis for action

The last two chapters have introduced us to some of the variation we can expect to find in bilingual discourse practices in the Puerto Rican community in North Philadelphia. This chapter looks across data collected from a large group of heritage Spanish speakers, and it describes, interprets, and explains how students use and evaluate languages. These language ideologies are important to understand because they help structure the everyday lives of the people who live in this community today. The contradictions are also important to understand because they provide a basis for action.

My analysis is based on close examination of data collected from four different groups of students (total 187) at three different schools in North Philadelphia. One group of students was in the 5th grade in a Reading/English Language Arts class for English language learners (ELLs) that was conducted almost exclusively in English (see chapter 8). Another group was in the 2nd grade in a self-contained classroom that was conducted nearly entirely in Spanish in a one-way developmental bilingual program (see chapter 9). The third and fourth groups were middle school 7th and 8th grade students in a dual language program that provided instruction through Spanish and English (see chapter 10). As I discussed in the introduction to Part II, I observed these students as they interacted with each other in a wide range of activities at school, and I collected samples of their writing. I observed some of these students as they interacted in different contexts outside of school, for example, in their homes and in the neighborhood. I also interviewed many students and their parents and teachers to explore local beliefs about how spoken and written Spanish and English should be used at home, at school, and throughout the community. Although the patterns that I identify are not supported statistically in this book, they resonate with educators from these and other schools that I have worked with in North Philadelphia. The qualitative analysis presented in this chapter also provides a foundation for quantitative research to determine the significance of the patterns of language use identified here.

I have divided the chapter into three parts. First, I describe the students who attend North Philadelphia schools in terms of their expertise in spoken and/or written Spanish and English. Second, I identify key language and literacy-rich activities at home, throughout the community, and at school, and I draw on teachers', parents', and students' interpretations of how these experiences influence language and literacy development and use. Finally, I summarize the language ideologies that we have reviewed throughout Part II of the book and explain how migration, socioeconomic class, age, and gender interact with students' personal histories to structure bilingual discourse practices in the community.

Who are the students

In North Philadelphia, there is a tremendous amount of variation in the category heritage Spanish speaker. As we saw in chapter 5, Hornberger and Skilton-Sylvester's (2000) continua of biliteracy framework allows us to describe an individual's biliteracy development in relation to the intersecting continua of Spanish-English, receptive-productive, and oral-written language. Furthermore, these intersecting continua can be represented in relation to the contexts, content, and media of biliteracy. Here our focus is on biliteracy development on the school and community levels.

On one end of the continuum are monolingual Spanish speakers; these students are identified by the School District of Philadelphia (SDP) as English language learners (ELLs), and they receive support for their English language development. Although some monolingual Spanish-speaking Puerto Ricans were born in Philadelphia, most of these students were born in Puerto Rico. A small but increasing number of the monolingual Spanish speakers in North Philadelphia come from other Spanish-speaking countries, primarily the Dominican Republic. There are also a few students on this end of the continuum from other Central and South American countries. Depending on their prior experiences with literacy (e.g., at school on the island and/or in Philadelphia, at church), these students may or may not have been offered opportunities to learn to understand and produce written Spanish. These students are all learning English at school in some kind of English as a second language (ESL) or bilingual program. Ideally these students will acquire academic English and literacies in English across the content areas. Actually, most of these students begin to shift to English over time, and they quickly acquire conversational fluency in non-standard varieties of Puerto Rican and African American English. Although many of the ELLs who are enrolled in bilingual programs do better than their English-speaking counterparts on content-area standardized tests in

Spanish, they still tend to perform at "below basic" levels, and they are not often offered opportunities to acquire academic literacies in English through their experiences at school.

On the other end of the continuum are monolingual English speakers. Between 1 and 20 percent of the students at any given school in North Philadelphia are not Latino, and most of these non-Latino students are African American. Theoretically, we could also find Latinos in North Philadelphia who are monolingual in English. According to the literature on language shift, this group would more than likely be third generation (Peyton 2001). These students would live in households where English was the primary language of communication. Although these Latino children might have some contact with Spanish-speaking grandparents, they would rarely use Spanish in their daily lives.

My research in North Philadelphia, however, did not offer evidence of the theoretically possible category of monolingual English-speaking Latinos. First, the revolving door migration that characterizes the lives of many Puerto Ricans makes the notion of "generation" problematic. Second, Puerto Ricans living in North Philadelphia are in regular contact with monolingual Spanish speakers, and they tend to at least be exposed to Spanish in their lives in the barrio.

This is not to say, however, that there are no monolingual English-speaking Puerto Ricans in Philadelphia. As Puerto Ricans in Philadelphia become upwardly mobile, they tend to move north along 5th Street into the Greater Northeast of Philadelphia, which is a predominantly white lower-middle to middle class part of the city where monolingualism in English dominates. This is the experience of some of the bilingual educators I have met as well as of some of the bilingual educators' children. Middle-class Puerto Ricans, the majority of whom do not live in North Philadelphia, tend to speak more Standard English than the low-income Puerto Ricans who live in North Philadelphia.

Between the extremes of monolingual English speaker on one end of the continuum and monolingual Spanish speaker on the other (shifting toward the English end), we find the majority of the students in this community. In the middle of the continuum we find heritage Spanish speakers who have a wide range of expertise in spoken and written Spanish and English, and these students can use either Spanish or English for a wide range of purposes. We can also find heritage Spanish speakers who may know how to speak and understand their heritage language in some domains but not know how to read and/or write in Spanish. Others may be English dominant and only understand the Spanish spoken to them by their grandparents. An individual's expertise in spoken and/or written Spanish will, of course, depend on how he or she has used spoken and/or written Spanish in his or her everyday life. As we discussed in chapter 5, an understanding of an individual's everyday life can provide considerable insight into the kinds of expertise that individual may have.

Although I have no quantitative data to support this assertion, my experience working in North Philadelphia leads me to believe that the majority of the English-dominant Puerto Rican students in North Philadelphia can speak and understand Spanish. These students were born in the United States (generally in Philadelphia or in New York) and/or have lived in the United States for years. They may use Spanish at home with monolingual Spanish-speaking parents, grandparents, and/or pre-school children. They may use Spanish at church and/or at family reunions in the neighborhood and/or when they visit relatives in Puerto Rico. They may watch *telenovelas* in Spanish and listen to music in Spanish. They may use Spanish when they translate for monolingual Spanish-speaking family members. Some of these students have participated in bilingual programs in elementary school (either in Puerto Rico or in Philadelphia), where they may or may not have had the opportunity to develop literacies in Spanish. Others have been educated primarily through English, although they may have had a Spanish course here or there. Most of the Spanish courses, however, use traditional foreign language teaching approaches, which generally are not appropriate for heritage Spanish speakers. In fact, many heritage Spanish speakers fail Spanish class, and they learn that the varieties of Spanish that they speak do not count as "good Spanish." Most of the English-dominant Puerto Ricans who live in North Philadelphia speak nonstandard varieties of English (Puerto Rican English, African American Vernacular English) and Spanish (Puerto Rican Spanish). Some people use the term "Spanglish" to describe the ways Puerto Ricans use Spanish; this term can be used both negatively (generally by educators) and positively (sometimes by adolescents).

Many bilingual educators describe students in terms of their "dominance," but they generally use this label in a binary, static way. We hear students in two-way immersion programs, for example, categorized as either "English dominant" or "Spanish dominant" because they come from homes that the school identifies as either English speaking or Spanish speaking. In North Philadelphia, students who are enrolled in ESL or bilingual programs are often generally described as "bilingual," even if they are monolingual Spanish speakers. Despite the fact that schools have no official record of the kinds of expertise heritage Spanish speaking students have in Spanish, students who are enrolled in the all-English academic mainstream are generally considered "English dominant."

However, heritage Spanish speakers who are enrolled in the all-English academic mainstream actually have a wide range of expertise in spoken and written, oral and productive Spanish across the context, content, and media continua of biliteracy. Furthermore, a student's expertise in Spanish or English may change over time depending on the language(s) used in their social networks, and on their attitude toward the two languages and toward speakers of those languages. Although there is no clear compartmentalization of languages by domains (e.g., we tend to find some English in traditionally "Spanish" domains like church), it is possible to make several generalizations about factors that influence expertise in spoken and written Spanish. In order to do this, we need to consider the contexts in which this expertise develops.

How do students use languages in their everyday lives

My research investigated some of the key contexts in which students learn and use languages. The continua of biliteracy framework (Hornberger and Skilton-Sylvester, 2000) explains how the English end of the continua is more heavily weighted, and we see a general shift toward English across contexts. To address this imbalance, this section explores Spanish-rich and/or literacy-rich activities, first at home, then throughout the community, and finally at unofficial interactions at school. This account describes the kinds of opportunities that heritage Spanish speakers may have participated in to develop their expertise in spoken and/or written Spanish, expertise on which educators can readily build.

Spanish-rich and/or literacy-rich activities at home

The theoretical orientation presented in chapter 4 explained how students develop their understandings of the world as well as their ways of interacting with that world through their language socialization in key contexts in their lives (Heath 1983; Schieffelin and Ochs 1990; Philips 1983). Home is an important context for language socialization, especially for younger children who spend much of their time at home. This section looks at Spanish-rich and/or literacy-rich activities that heritage Spanish speakers may have participated in at home to determine the kinds of expertise educators may find within their heritage Spanish speaker linguistic repertoires.

Family composition is likely to influence the ways that children use language at home. Students whose parent(s) and/or older siblings are monolingual Spanish speakers generally speak more Spanish, and these students are likely to have developed more expertise in the Spanish that they use for family purposes. It is common for the first child of monolingual Spanish-speaking parents to have developed more expertise in Spanish than subsequent children. The principal of one of the middle schools that I worked with, for example, is a Puerto Rican woman who was raised in North Philadelphia. As the oldest child in her family, she said that she was required to help raise her younger siblings. Since she spoke more English with these younger siblings than her parents did with her, and since the younger siblings spoke with the parents less frequently than the older children did, the younger children had fewer opportunities to develop their expertise in Spanish. Because the older child generally has more expertise in Spanish, this is the child who is generally responsible for translation in her family.

We can find exceptions to this pattern. For example, Silvia (see chapter 5) is the youngest child in her family, and she has developed more expertise in Spanish than two of her older brothers. Part of this can be explained by the fact that she currently lives at home alone with her monolingual Spanish-speaking mother and stepfather, and her brothers no longer live at home. Although she is the youngest child, as the only child at home she is the one responsible for translation within the family.

Translation is a complex social practice that bilingual children regularly perform for their monolingual parents. As we saw in chapter 5, Silvia is often asked to read official documents in English that are mailed to their house. She then translates the written formal English to oral Spanish so that her mother understands the nature of the official correspondence. Then, when her mother has decided how to respond, she tells Silvia in informal, oral Spanish. Silvia must then translate the oral Spanish either to oral English (in a follow-up phone call or visit to an agency) or to written English to mail a response. Thus, translation requires bilingual children to move across languages, across registers, and across genres to accomplish their interactional goals. Although there are services available to assist families in their negotiations with official agencies, it is common for parents to turn to their bilingual children or to other bilingual family members.

Storytelling in Spanish was a very common activity at Claudia's house, and the stories served a variety of functions. Sometimes Claudia's mom would tell the children stories about her own experiences or about the experiences of other family members, and these stories seemed to be intended as models for appropriate behavior or warnings about inappropriate behavior. Sometimes Claudia's mom would tell me stories about the latest adventures in the family. Since Claudia and Clarissa are teenagers now, the stories often focused on recent boyfriends. These stories entertained and they highlighted a mother's concerns about adolescents in North Philadelphia today. When I met Claudia's father to ask his permission for her to work on the *In Our Own Words: Students Perspectives on Schools* project, he told me stories about ways that he has protected his children that seemed to be intended as warnings to me not to take advantage of his child. Later, he told me stories about his own experiences growing up on the island and the challenges he faced when he came to North Philadelphia. The topics of the stories that everyone told were familiar (in fact, many of the stories were told and retold as part of the family lore over time). The language used was Puerto Rican Spanish that was generally informal and often formulaic. Claudia has become an avid storyteller and writer, perhaps because she has been immersed in storytelling activities at home. While Claudia can understand all of her parents' stories and participate in the interactions surrounding their production, most of the stories that Claudia tells are in English.

A very important home literacy practice that I have been told about repeatedly (but have never observed) is reading the Bible. When I ask Puerto Rican educators who were raised in North Philadelphia how they learned to read in Spanish, they often respond that they read the Bible everyday with their mothers when they were growing up. One teacher told me that she was never allowed to go outside after dinner, and that every night after dinner her mother would read excerpts from the Bible to her. As she got older, she said that she began to read the Bible out loud to her mother, and they would talk about the meaning of the passages they read at length.

Teachers regularly told me that their best readers and writers read the Bible, either at home with their family or at church in Bible Study class. For example, Gloria was a 2nd grade student in a developmental bilingual class, and her mom was a bilingual teaching assistant in that class. Gloria was very shy at school, and she never read in front of the class. However, according to her mom, Gloria read and wrote extensively at home. Although Gloria's mom said that she read the Bible to her children everyday, Gloria preferred to write alone. Gloria's mom designated one section of her living room as the library, and she collected all kinds of books for the children to read. Gloria's mom said that Gloria wanted to be a writer when she grew up, so she also put a writing desk in the library to support her writing at home.

Another common literacy practice that I have observed at home is "school." Almost all of the girls that I have talked to either play school (if they are in elementary school) or said that they played school when they were younger. The older child is usually, but not always, the teacher of the younger siblings, cousins, or neighbors. There is generally a special place in the house that is reserved for school-at one student's house it was in the basement, and two other girls said that house school took place in their bedrooms. There is always a desk or a table and places for children to gather; sometimes there are chairs for the "students" but not always. Sometimes the child has a blackboard, and there are always books, paper, and pencils or markers available for the children to work with. The books may have been bought by family members or borrowed from school. Recently, since many children are encouraged to take books home to read to an adult as part of the "100 Book Challenge," more literature is available from school. The books may be in Spanish or in English depending on what the language of the household is and on what the language used at school is.

Older children imitate what they understand school to be, which is of course based on their experiences at school. Sometimes the older children read the younger children stories, or sometimes they have the "students" read stories out loud. Sometimes the "teacher" asks the "students" to write, for example "sobre lo que hiciste en el fin de semana" (about what you did over the weekend). Sometimes the "teacher" will have the "students" work on the work the "teacher" is doing as a student at school. For example, one of the 2nd grade students in Ms. Santiago's class liked to use her math book as a text for her school. She and her older brother organized school at their house so that her older brother, a "student" in the class, provided regular help for her with her math homework. Sometimes a "student" misbehaves and is punished-he or she might have to go and sit in the corner or do extra work.

We can see the important role that bilingual children play in the community. Sometimes parents are not able to help children with their homework. They may be working or they may not understand the language of instruction. In this case, older siblings often help younger siblings with homework. For example, the 2nd grader mentioned above talked extensively about her older brother and about how much he helped her. In addition to helping with her homework through their school playing activity, her older brother regularly went to Ms. Santiago's class to pick up his sister's report card and have parent conferences when their mom had to work.

Mass media is another important source of language in students' everyday lives. Music and television are pervasive in this community. Whenever you are in the streets, you hear music-salsa, merengue, rap, reggae. Making music and dancing are important parts of many of the students' lives. When you go to a street festival (e.g., the Puerto Rican Parade), everyone is moving to the sounds of the music, and no party would be acceptable without dancing. Whenever you go to someone's house, the television is on, although people may or may not be directly attending to it. In some households, the television is always turned to the Spanish station; in other households, it is always turned to the English station; and in other households family members watch television programs in both Spanish and English. One important genre is the *telenovela* (soap opera), which is generally on in the evenings. Everyone seems to watch the novelas-in fact one person told me it was impolite to call someone on the phone or to visit someone's house in the middle of a novela. As Claudia mentions in the story that opened chapter 5, the television was an important source for second language acquisition—both in English and in Spanish. Videotaping is also common. Many families have a video recorder, and they record important events in their family and community lives (e.g., quinceañera, weddings, parties). As we see in chapter 10, students are very interested in developing expertise in video production.

Letter writing also figures prominently in many of the students' lives. Some students write letters to family members and/or friends who are living in Puerto Rico, and that correspondence is generally in Spanish. Some students write letters to family members who are in jail, and they use whatever language their addressee uses for that correspondence. For example, Natalie was a 5th grade student in an all-English program, and she struggled whenever she wrote in Spanish. However, her father is in jail and he is a monolingual Spanish speaker, so she challenged herself to write regularly in Spanish to keep in touch. As we saw in chapter 5, Silvia's brother is in jail and, according to Silvia, he is more comfortable in English than in Spanish. However, when he wrote to his monolingual Spanish-speaking mom, his letter writing was in Spanish. Several middle school students that I worked with asked me if I could help them write Mother's Day cards to their mothers in Spanish—they wanted to be able to express their feelings in writing, and their mothers were monolingual Spanish speakers.

This section has introduced some of the key activities that many students regularly participate in at home that provide them opportunities to use Spanish and to acquire and use literacies in Spanish and English. This review is not exhaustive, and there is considerable variation from one household to the next. For example, in many households, the adults are out working long hours. In this case, the children have fewer opportunities to interact with the adults, and they may not have been exposed to a range of language-rich activities with them. Not all families are religious, and so not all children have the experience of reading the Bible at home with their mothers. Most children have considerable contact with other children—either siblings or cousins or friends—but as we discuss below, most of those interactions are conducted primarily in English. The key for educators is to learn about what languages are used at home, the kinds of activities that their particular students participate in at home, and to learn which activities are really motivating to those students. Such an understanding provides educators a foundation on which they can build as they work to broaden students' linguistic repertoires at school.

Spanish-rich and/or literacy-rich activities in the community

Educators need to go beyond the household and explore other key contexts to understand the role of Spanish in students' lives. The discussion of El Bloque de Oro presented in chapter 6 suggests some of the ways that spoken and written Spanish and English are used in the center of the Latino business district. This section presents an overview of other places that offer students the opportunity to use and develop their Spanish. Since I spent the majority of my time with students at school or in their homes, this section simply gives an introduction to the kinds of expertise educators are likely to find when they look more closely at any of these contexts and more broadly throughout the community.

Almost all of the public schools and many of the community-based organizations offer some kind of summer school program or camp for interested students. The public school offerings are varied, and they change from year to year. For example, PS 31 offers a dual language kinder camp for the young children who will be entering their dual language program in the fall. The local arts and cultural education center offers a Youth Artists Program that promotes the development of local Latino artists, and it offers many other cultural and educational programs for children of all ages. Congreso de Latinos Unidos and ASPIRA, as well as many other smaller organizations, offer programs for students of all ages. Some programs are offered in English, some are in Spanish, and some are in both languages. Some programs are more academic, others may be more recreational and emphasize sports or other activities to enrich the students' lives.

Religion is an important aspect of many students' lives and, as we have seen, many students read the Bible at home with their mothers. Most of the students who go to church (generally either Catholic or Pentecostal) attend a church where Spanish is used as a dominant language. According to several teachers I have spoken with, students who read the Bible at church (in Spanish) are generally better readers at school (in Spanish and/or in English). Claudia, for example is Pentecostal, and her family goes to church between four and six times a week. One of the Puerto Rican teachers that I worked closely with migrated to Philadelphia when she was thirteen. She said that she maintained her Spanish through church because she assimilated to English everywhere else. She said,

> Puerto Ricans have a way of maintaining their language
> through different avenues . . . in my case it was church . . . I
> had to read the Bible and if you read the Bible it's quite difficult
> . . . that's how I maintained my Spanish.

She went on to describe how this influences the students she works with.

> "It makes the biggest difference . . . I can pinpoint to you all my
> Pentecostal children . . . they're the best readers . . . the best
> comprehension . . . the best students . . . the best grades . . .
> why? . . . obviously that they've been reading.

Not all students participate in these kinds of organized activities. As students grow older, they tend to spend more and more time outside of the house in the streets. While this is especially the case for boys, it also applies to girls (see below for further discussion of gendered language use patterns). In some cases, as we saw with Claudia, this means time spent on the block outside of her house. On Claudia's block, the extensive cross-generational interaction is closely supervised, and the block is really more an extension of the household. In other cases, adolescents choose to hang out "on the corner" or "in the streets." For example, as Silvia grows older, she prefers to hang out with her friends, especially on the street where she last lived. The corners and streets are primarily populated by adolescents, and they are generally not closely monitored by adults. Although I haven't spent much time just hanging out in these contexts with adolescents (I'm sure that my presence would dramatically change the quality of the inter-action), I have been told that the dominant language among peers in this kind of space, as in other public spaces, is English.

While some students have the opportunity to travel beyond their neighborhood (for example to visit extended family in New Jersey, New York, or Puerto Rico), the majority of the students I have met spend most of their time in the neighborhood. Their knowledge of the world and their expertise in communicating with others in the world are tied closely to the contexts that we have visited.

Spanish and English at school: A look at unofficial interactions

Part III of this book is concerned with official classroom interactions and demonstrates what educators can do to build on their students' strengths as they help them work toward their goals. However, students learn much of what they learn at school through peer-group interactions that are not officially sanctioned by their teachers or their school. This section explores some of the ways that students construct and perform their identities through unofficial practices at school.

Writing notes is one such literacy practice. Students, especially girls, write and pass notes to each other all of the time. These notes may be in Spanish, they may be in English, or students may switch from one language to another for expressive purposes. Silvia, for example, writes notes to her best friend three or four times a day. There were note-writing networks among the girls in the 5th grade class that I taught that reflected the primary friendship groups, and these networks contributed to the construction of social relations and identities at school. Many of the notes that I have seen are written primarily in Spanish, with expressions in English here and there. For example, one note begins:

> *Beba* [the name that Silvia's family and friends call her]
>
> Well, what's up girl? Well *yo aqui aburrida Bueno que vamos hacer entonces?*
>
> (I'm here bored. Well what are we going to do then?)

The note continues in Spanish, although there are a few other expressions in English (e.g., curse words) throughout the text. This written note, like the phone conversations that these best friends have daily, move between Spanish and English freely (see below for further discussion of codeswitching practices).

The term "jíbaro" names an important social category in students' lives, and it indexes a wide range of related social practices. According to Zentella (1997), "jíbaro" legends and stories are an important part of Puerto Rican heritage. These legends are usually referred to in family storytelling with nostalgia. However, the middle school students that I talked with often used the term pejoratively.

The following excerpt from the *In Our Own Words: Students' Perspectives on School* chapter illustrates how Claudia uses the term "jíbaro" to refer to Spanish-speaking students who are in the bilingual program on the second floor of the school. As part of the chapter, I asked Silvia and Lizette to read and respond to what Claudia had written since she was essentially writing about them. After I present the excerpt that Claudia wrote, I include Silvia and Lizette's written response. Claudia writes:

> Now, the rest of the students in the school know the second
> floor as the "hick" floor. Last year, the second floor had blacks
> and Spanish and it wasn't a hick floor. There were hick classes

but mostly all of the kids on the second floor talked English and not Spanish. Now everyone considers the second floor as the hick floor, and considers the Spanish-speaking students as *jíbaros*, which means people that live in the countryside of Puerto Rico. They don't understand a word we say because they all speak Spanish. And when they speak English it sounds funny.

What makes the hick floor different from the other floors is the way the students conduct themselves. They speak loud, they're always making a joke of things, and the way they dress makes a big difference in our school. I mean, have you ever seen an American guy wearing a shirt with flowers on it? Some were born in America but they are being taught Spanish a whole lot and English would be their second language.

The rest of us call them *jíbaros* no matter where they come from because they have a strong accent, they conduct themselves like *jíbaros,* they dress like *jíbaros.* Some of them are born in the United States and some of them were born in Puerto Rico. It's how you look and how you talk that makes you a *jíbaro* or not. Sometimes I talk to the students on the second floor in Spanish but it's hard to communicate with them because they speak Spanish so well and I don't and it makes it difficult to continue a conversation (from Alfaro et. al. 2001).

Lizette and Silvia responded to Claudia's writing with the following excerpt:

The people on the first floor and the third floor call the people on the second floor "hicks" because we know more Spanish and we speak both languages. They think that we speak only Spanish. I don't think they should call us hicks because I think that they should be proud that we know both languages, both Spanish and English. In the world, we'll have more opportunities because we know both languages and we probably could learn more languages if we wanted to study them. Like . . ., our sixth grade teacher, he taught us French. He knows a lot of languages and has visited a lot of places.

Not all of the people on the second floor are *jíbaros.* I . . . am not a *jíbara* even though I was born in Puerto Rico. I consider myself both Puerto Rican and American because in Puerto Rico they taught me Spanish and in Philadelphia they taught me

English. I'm from both worlds. I . . . don't consider myself
jíbara. I don't get embarrassed when students call me *jíbara*
because I'm proud of my culture (Alfaro et. al. 2001).

Although in this excerpt Silvia and Lizette positively evaluate their use of
both languages at school and they reject the label "jíbaro/a," I repeatedly
heard teachers talk about students' resistance to being placed in the bilingual program on the second floor at PS 17 because kids refer to it as "the
hick floor."

One of the graduate students who was working with me at PS 17 during the 1998-1999 academic year became interested in how the term
"jíbaro" was used and evaluated among students in the bilingual program.
According to Hernandez (1999), if a student used too much Spanish at
school, for example, in a response that was deemed too lengthy to a
teacher during official class time (in Spanish), that student risked being
categorized as "jíbaro." But as both Claudia (above) and Hernandez (1999)
point out, being a "jíbaro" also involves nonverbal communication, for
example, the clothing that students wear, body movement, and the social
networks in which they participate. A "hick" boy may wear tight-fitting
high-water ("brinca charcos") pants, which are pulled up to his waist,
instead of loose-fitting pants that are worn low on the hips, and he may
wear shoes or sandals instead of the more fashionable boots. His shirts
may be brightly colored with bold designs instead of the oversized plain or
plaid shirts worn by "cool" students. Girls risk being categorized as
"jíbaras" if they wear too much make-up or gel, or if they wear flat shoes
instead of heels or boots. "Payless" shoes instead of Nike or Reebok shoes
also can mark boys and/or girls as "hicks." Body movement can reveal a
"jibaro" because "jíbaros" tend to leave less space between people and
touch each other more during communication than African Americans do,
patterns that are associated with Latinos. Social networks also matter. If a
student is popular, and/or if he/she has many African-American friends,
this student is less likely to be called a "jibaro" (Hernandez 1999).

My own experience confirms Hernandez's (1999) observations. One
day the Communications Team at PS 17 was having a holiday party and
there was music, food, and dancing. At that time, the Communications
Team was trying to develop a two-way immersion program; they had integrated African-American students and English-dominant Latinos with
their Spanish-dominant ELLs, and everyone was studying through both
Spanish and English. In one room students were listening to salsa and
merengue, and in another room students were listening to rap and hip
hop. One of the teachers and I were talking about which students chose to
listen and/or dance to which music. More of the bilingual students (those

who were comfortable with Spanish and English and who used both in their everyday lives) and the few African Americans who had been placed on the bilingual team and who were trying to learn Spanish were listening to salsa and merengue. The others, i.e., most of the English-dominant Puerto Ricans who tended to resist Spanish and the Spanish-dominant new arrivals, were listening to rap and hip hop.

Puerto Rican adults also signal who they are relative to each other through their nonverbal communication. For example, one day I went to one of the local bodegas with one of the nonteaching assistants who is an English-dominant bilingual Puerto Rican who grew up in North Philadelphia (she sometimes refers to herself as a "Filariquen," or a Puerto Rican from Philadelphia). When we walked into the bodega, she began a conversation in Spanish with one person she didn't know, and later she began a conversation in English with another person that she didn't know. When I asked her how she knew which language to use, she said, you just look at the person, at what they are wearing, at the way they move, and you know. My observation of Puerto Rican interaction in North Philadelphia is that they read each others' nonverbal cues with great accuracy.

Another way that Puerto Rican students, like other bilinguals, signal who they are relative to each other is through their codeswitching practices. Codeswitching can be understood as the systematic alternation of languages (see, for example, Gumperz 1982). Although codeswitching is often maligned by many Puerto Ricans as well as by much of the literature on bilingualism and bilingual education, Puerto Rican children regularly develop their expertise in Spanish and English in speech communities that are characterized by widespread codeswitching (Zentella 1997). In fact, codeswitching is part of most bilingual/multidialectal Puerto Rican students' linguistic repertoire.

The fact that bilinguals alternate between Spanish and English does not mean that they are unable to distinguish between Spanish and English. Evidence that students can separate the two languages is readily apparent. For example, when bilingual students address a monolingual Spanish or English speaker, they do not codeswitch, and they rarely codeswitch in writing (see Edelsky 1989 for a related discussion of Mexican students' emergent literacy in a bilingual program). As Zentella (1997) illustrates, Puerto Ricans living in the United States draw on the numerous varieties in their linguistic repertoires in creative ways depending on the demands of the situation.

Racial identity also informs individual's assumptions about language use. One day, when I was sitting in a small group in class with Lizette and several other students, one of the students asked me if I was white or if I was Spanish, reflecting the assumption that white people do not speak

Spanish. This was a question that I have been asked repeatedly, presumably because I speak Spanish but I do not look or act like a Puerto Rican. I said that I was white, but that I could speak Spanish because I had studied it at school and I had lived in Spain for a year and had traveled extensively in Mexico and Puerto Rico. After we talked about how and why I had learned Spanish one of the boys looked at Lizette, a student who preferred English and who generally only spoke Spanish to monolingual Spanish speakers. He said "she thinks she's white—she always speaks English."

This section has illustrated how students use and evaluate spoken and written Spanish and English in key contexts at home, throughout the community, and in unofficial interactions at school. These interactions are structured by language ideologies that dominate in the community. The following section looks more closely at these ideologies.

Contradictions as a basis for action

The language ideologies that we hear in conversations and see reflected in everyday interactions are structured by power relations. This section explores how macro-level sociopolitical processes (e.g., migration, age, gender and socioeconomic class) influence the ways that heritage Spanish speakers use and evaluate spoken and written Spanish and English on the micro level of person-to-person communication. I begin with a brief summary of the kinds of language ideologies that we find throughout the Puerto Rican community. Then I present a series of assertions about language use that have emerged through my qualitative analysis, assertions that could provide the basis for hypotheses about language use that could be tested quantitatively. As this part of the book makes clear, language ideologies in North Philadelphia are complex and in some ways contradictory. As I argue in the conclusion to this section, when educators understand the location and nature of contradictions, they can direct their efforts in ways that promote bilingualism on the local level.

First, we see many ways in which Spanish is positively evaluated. Spanish is an undeniable part of ethnic identity for Puerto Ricans living in North Philadelphia. Puerto Rican students want to speak Spanish to family members and visitors who do not speak English, and they want to be able to speak Spanish when they visit the island. Parents want children to maintain Spanish so they can maintain close family ties and values. Spanish is spoken extensively in private domains like home and church. Even if heritage Spanish speakers do not produce Spanish in many of their interactions, most of the Latino students that educators find in their classes understand nonstandard varieties of Spanish about familiar topics. Many of these students need to use Spanish, and some are motivated to learn to read and write in Spanish.

At the same time, however, we see evidence of ways that Spanish, especially Puerto Rican Spanish, is often stigmatized. Many students, especially English-dominant Puerto Ricans who have spent the majority of their lives in the United States and Spanish-dominant new arrivals, see Spanish as the "hick" language that they associate with "jíbaros." These students resist speaking Spanish and/or associating with Spanish-speaking peers because they do not want to be categorized as "hicks." Many teachers believe that Puerto Rican Spanish is not "good Spanish," and speakers of Puerto Rican Spanish are often told that they do not speak Spanish. Uriciuoli (1996) explores similar kinds of language prejudice in a Puerto Rican community in New York.

Although Spanish is a vital language in this community, it often does not find space relative to English. Some parents of English language learners believe that using Spanish takes away time that their children need to acquire English. Since English is the language of opportunity, parents and educators want students to learn (Standard) English so they can do well in school and get good jobs in the United States. Some parents stop speaking Spanish to their children at home for fear that their language use may interfere with their children's opportunities. Some parents and educators worry that time spent learning through Spanish at school may threaten struggling students' development of English, and with the exception of students in well-implemented bilingual programs, heritage Spanish speakers in North Philadelphia have few opportunities to learn to read and write in Spanish. English is the language of wider society, mass media, the streets, and schools, and children want to learn (local varieties of Puerto Rican and/or African American) English so that they fit in with their peers.

Although educators can expect to find a wide range of variation in the kinds of expertise in Spanish that their students bring with them to school, they can also find patterns in language use. Migration, age, gender, socioeconomic class interact with each other and they structure many of the patterns that we can identify. The micro-level interactions that we observe at home, in schools, and throughout the community can be explained when we consider these macro-level processes.

Migration plays an important role in the Puerto Rican community in North Philadelphia. A student's migration history influences his/her expertise in and allegiance to Spanish. Students who migrate back and forth between the island and the continental United States and/or whose families migrate back and forth have generally developed more expertise in Spanish. These students generally more positively evaluate Spanish because they see a real need for this language in their everyday lives. For example, Leticia (one of the authors of the *In Our Own Voices: Students Perspectives on School* piece) recently migrated to North Philadelphia from New York, and prior to New York, she had lived in Puerto Rico. According to Leticia,

> *Yo pienso que el ingles y el español se tiene que aprender*
> *porque si uno sale al cualquier lado en los Estados Unidos*
> *y no sabe ingles, no puede hablar y no puede entender lo*
> *que te dicen. Y si yo vuelvo para Puerto Rico y no sé*
> *español, me bajan de grado.* (I think that everyone has to
> learn English and Spanish because if you don't know English in
> the United States, you can't speak and you can't understand
> what they say to you. And if I return to PR and I don't know
> Spanish, they will fail me.) Translated by Silvia Román in Alfaro
> et. al. 2001.

A student's age when he or she migrates to North Philadelphia also influences his or her expertise in Spanish. Older students have had many more experiences using Spanish for a wide range of purposes on the island, and they have developed more expertise than students who migrate at a younger age. I return to the importance of age as a social construct below.

Migration also influences the vitality of Spanish in the neighborhood. The continual influx of monolingual Spanish speakers gives many Puerto Ricans who live in North Philadelphia an important reason to maintain and develop their expertise in Spanish. Puerto Ricans in North Philadelphia, like Puerto Ricans in other continental contexts, thus challenge the traditional pattern of assimilation to monolingualism in English that has been characteristic of most other (im)migrant groups in the United States (see Zentella 1997 for parallel discussion of Puerto Rican language use in New York).

A second factor that influences a student's attitude toward Spanish and Spanish speakers is age. Pre-school students, for example, generally use whatever language is used in the household. Elementary school students generally use whatever language is used in the household and at school. They generally begin to use more English than Spanish in their everyday lives over time, even when they are enrolled in bilingual programs that encourage the maintenance and development of their Spanish. Middle school students generally use more English than Spanish. As the "jíbaros" discussion above suggested, these adolescent students often begin to resist speaking Spanish and associating with Spanish speakers at school. Some high school students begin to use more Spanish again if they begin to explore their "Puerto Rican identities." For example, one bilingual educator told me that she grew up as a third-generation Puerto Rican who was a monolingual English speaker. As she went through high school, she said that she wanted to explore her roots, and she wanted to be able to talk to her grandmother (a need commonly expressed by many English-dominant Puerto Ricans). She sought out ways to access Spanish, including a move to the island for a few years so that she could attend college. She said that it was challenging to go to school in Spanish, but that this experience provided the opportunity to develop the academic Spanish that she needed to become a bilingual educator.

Third, language use patterns in North Philadelphia are gendered in many ways. For example, with the exception of men who migrated from Puerto Rico at an older age, women tend to speak more Spanish than men. This fact reflects and helps perpetuate the distribution of language, social space, and labor in the community. Spanish tends to be associated with private domains like the home, and women tend to spend more time at home as caretakers. Furthermore, part of a woman's caretaking responsibilities includes passing on the "mother tongue" and maintaining family connections, both of which require Spanish. In contrast, English tends to be associated with public spaces like the streets and work, although the varieties of English used in these domains may differ (it is more likely to hear nonstandard African American English or Puerto Rican English in the streets and Standard English in the workplace). Males tend to spend more time outside of the home in these public domains, and they tend to speak less Spanish than the women.

Socioeconomic class also plays an important role in the structuring of bilingual discourse practices. Middle-class Puerto Ricans are much more likely to have developed expertise in spoken and written standard varieties of Spanish and English than low-income Puerto Ricans. Part of this can be explained by the experiences they have had available to them—which lead them to see Spanish as a resource to be developed. Their expertise in Spanish give them access to many more opportunities on the island and in the United States, and they are comfortable using both languages in their lives. Low-income Puerto Ricans, in contrast, often see Spanish as a problem that they need to overcome in order to have access to opportunities in the United States, and those opportunities are largely available in English. We are much more likely to see the either/or attitude about Spanish and English in a low-income family than in a middle-income family.

These structuring influences do not operate in isolation from each other. So, for example, we can see that gender interacts with age in important ways. Adolescent girls generally use more Spanish than adolescent boys, and girls also generally spend more time at home (where Spanish is more likely to be spoken) and less time on the streets (where English is more likely to be spoken) than boys do. Socioeconomic class is perhaps the most important factor influencing language ideologies. Since we see middle class women occupying roles at work that were traditionally held by men, more women are using English for more activities in their every-day lives. The binary opposition that links women and Spanish to the home and men and English to work is becoming increasingly blurred. Further-more, as Spanish gains status as a legitimate business language in the glob-al economy and at school, we can expect to see more educated profession-al men and women developing more expertise in a wider range of varieties of spoken and written Spanish and English. Individuals simply have to develop more areas of expertise in an increasingly complex society.

Teachers, program designers, curriculum developers, and policymak-ers who are working to promote bilingualism all benefit from an under-standing of how language ideologies structure language use patterns on the local level. Teachers, for example, who understand the kinds of exper-tise their students bring with them to school do not see Spanish as a prob-lem. They see Spanish as a resource to be developed, and they know how to build on this foundation. Program designers can address language ide-ologies that reflect the symbolic domination of English, and they can orga-nize programs in ways that emphasize students' biliteracy development in balanced ways throughout the day. Curriculum developers can encourage the development of a wider range of topics, genres, and registers in Span-ish, and they can emphasize Standard Spanish as an additional, not alter-nate, variety of Spanish. And policymakers can ensure that schools open ideological space for the development of programs, curricular materials, and practices that give students opportunities to broaden their linguistic range. The chapters in Part III and Part IV of the book illustrate a range of ways that educators in North Philadelphia have been organizing their pro-grams, practices, and policies to build on this community bilingualism.

Part III

Translating policies and programs into practice

Part III of this book builds on our understanding of how students living in the predominantly Puerto Rican community in North Philadelphia use and evaluate spoken and written Spanish and English in their everyday lives, and it takes us into schools that serve these students. These chapters explore and document how particular teachers in North Philadelphia build on their students' linguistic and cultural expertise in order to facilitate students' acquisition of the academic language and literacies that they need to participate and achieve at school. The research question that these chapters address is: *How do teachers translate language and literacy policies and programs into classroom practices that build on community bilingualism?* Each chapter explores how the teacher mediates among (a) her interpretation of the policy or program that is handed down to her to implement, (b) her understanding of relevant theories of language, literacy, and learning, (c) her knowledge of the local sociolinguistic and school context, and (d) her ongoing assessment of her students' strengths and needs, as she organizes her classroom practices. Together the chapters demonstrate how teachers can create communities of practice (Wenger 1998) within their classrooms that provide more opportunities for language learners than have traditionally been available to them.

This introduction provides important background information for the three chapters that are included in this part of the book. First I give a brief theoretical orientation about academic language and literacy that is intended to help teachers promote students' acquisition of the academic languages and literacies that they need to participate and achieve at school and in the community. Then I introduce the three teachers who are featured in these chapters, and I describe the nature of my relationship to the teachers, students, and the data that I collected to address my research question. Finally, I preview each of the chapters and highlight the fundamental role that the teacher plays in educational initiatives. Since any educational policy or program is only as good as its implementation, and since teachers are responsible for implementing policies and programs on the classroom level, understanding how teachers translate policies and programs into classroom practices is key to understanding the outcomes of any educational initiative.

As I mentioned in chapter 4, my work is aligned with recent research in sociolinguistics and literacy studies that sees language and literacy as social practices that are situated within particular sociocultural contexts and structured by power relations (see, for example, Gee 1990; Martin-Jones and Jones 2000; Street 1993, 1995 for further discussions). My focus in this part of the book is on academic languages and literacies, which can be understood as the range of languages and literacies that are considered correct and appropriate within the target academic discourse communities. The use of the plural "literacies" highlights the fact that we find a multiplicity of literacies that are used by different social groups, at different times, in different places, for different purposes. The languages and literacies associated with the different academic disciplines vary, and so researchers and practitioners may focus on the languages of science, the genres associated with history, the literacies of math, and so on.

Researchers who adopt a social view of language and literacy are fundamentally concerned with the ideological dimension of literacy practices. Their detailed ethnographic accounts of literacy practices within and across a wide range of home, school, and community contexts throughout the world clearly demonstrate that not all literacies are equally valued in all contexts. So, for example, we see evidence of ways that mainstream schools value academic languages and literacies in the dominant societal language more than the range of local languages and literacies that students acquire through their interactions at home and/or throughout the local community. Educators who view languages and literacies as social practices reject the notion that nonstandard varieties of the societal languages (e.g., African American Vernacular English, or "ebonics," Puerto Rican English in North Philadelphia) or languages other than the dominant societal language (e.g., Spanish in the United States) are seen as deficits or problems to be overcome. These researchers and practitioners see the range of languages and literacies that students use in their everyday lives as important resources that schools can draw on as they promote the acquisition and use of additional varieties, including oral and written academic English.

The social view of language and literacies that informs my work can be contrasted with what Street (1995) calls the traditional, or "autonomous," view of literacy. Under the traditional view, reading and writing are seen as a set of skills that are independent of social context, and learning to read and write means the same thing for all individuals in all contexts. When reading and writing are thought of as discrete skills, they can be taught separately from each other and separately from the larger social context in which reading and writing occur. Traditional literacy educators and policymakers advocate the adoption of standardized curricula for the early elementary grades that focus on the discrete set of reading and writing skills that students need to decode and encode meaning in print, and students' mastery of these skills is assessed by standardized tests. Under this view, if the individual learns these reading and writing skills, they are considered "literate." If not, they are considered "illiterate."

Consider briefly some implications of the skills-based approach to literacy instruction that is becoming more widespread in the United States and other national contexts today. In this era of accountability, standardized test scores have become increasingly high stakes. Educators and policy makers describe a "literacy crisis," and we see evidence from across the country of what is often referred to as the *4th grade slump,* with low-income students beginning to fall behind grade level norms starting at 4th grade and the gap between middle-income and low-income students widening with each successive grade (Chall, Jacobs and Baldwin 1990; Cummins, in press; Rand Reading Study Group 2002). An enormous amount of attention and money has been directed to literacy programs for the early elementary years, and we see an increasing focus on a standardized curriculum that privileges phonics over other important aspects of literacy instruction. This trend is criticized by many researchers and educators for a variety of reasons, including its failure to understand the nature of academic language and of how students develop expertise in the range of academic languages and literacies that they need for success at school.

For example, Jim Cummins explains the 4th grade slump by distinguishing between what he calls "discrete language skills" on the one hand and "academic language proficiency" on the other. He reviews the literature and argues that drill-based early literacy programs can effectively teach discrete language skills (e.g., knowledge of the letters of the alphabet, the sounds represented by individual letters and combinations of letters, and the ability to decode written words into appropriate sounds) to both second language learners and low-income students, and we do see increases in the test scores of students who participate in these kinds of skills-based programs in the early elementary grades. However, Cummins argues that in the later elementary years the standardized tests focus less on discrete language skills and more on "academic language proficiency," or the ability to comprehend the meaning of increasingly complex academic texts within and across content areas.

What do we know about how students develop expertise in academic languages and literacies? When we synthesize research on second language acquisition, biliteracy development, language teaching and learning, and effective literacy instruction (e.g., Cummins 2001; Edelsky 1989; Fountas and Pinnell 1996; Gee 2003; Genesee 1987; Hornberger 2003; Martin-Jones and Jones 2000; Peregoy and Boyle 1997; Snow, Burns and Griffin 1998), we see that students acquire the range of academic languages and literacies they need (e.g., in language arts, social studies, mathematics, science) when they have opportunities to make sense of and produce the kinds of texts that are considered correct and appropriate within the target academic discourse communities (e.g., within communities of writers, historians, mathematicians, scientists). One critical feature of effective first and second language and literacy instructional programs is that students are immersed in language-rich, print-rich environments in which students and teachers, working together and independently, read and write and talk about a wide range of topics for authentic purposes across content areas.

However, simply immersing students in language-rich, print-rich classrooms is not enough for many readers and writers to develop expertise in the range of spoken and written academic English that they need to participate and achieve at school, especially for those students who come from homes in which standard spoken and/or written English is not used. Teachers need to build on the ways that students use and evaluate spoken and written languages in their everyday lives, and they need to help students make connections between their local languages and literacies and the languages and literacies used at school and in the larger society. Teachers need to provide students with opportunities to transact with academic texts in different genres across content areas so that students develop an understanding of the underlying values and beliefs that structure relations in the target discourse communities (e.g., that are implicit in the scientific method, mathematical reasoning, logical argumentation, and/or in cultural assumptions about the individual relative to the group in the mainstream United States), because these values and beliefs may be different from the values and beliefs that they have come to understand through their everyday experiences at home, at school, and/or in their local community up to that point in their lives. Teachers also need to give students regular opportunities to investigate the language used in the academic texts that they read and hear so that they can learn how speakers and writers from the target discourse communities use that language (vocabulary, grammar, discourse form) to communicate their meanings within those communities.

As the chapters in this part of the book demonstrate, when teachers adopt a social view of languages and literacies, they can promote students' development of academic language and literacies without encouraging assimilation to dominant, monolingual Standard English speaking norms. Teachers must begin with a clear understanding of their short-term and long-term goals as articulated in the local, state, and national standards within and across content areas, policy statements, program descriptions, and curriculum frameworks, and they must think critically about those goals relative to their understanding of theories of language, literacy, and learning on the one hand and their knowledge of the local school and community context on the other. Teachers also need to look for creative ways to build on the linguistic and cultural expertise that students learn and value at home and in other contexts in their everyday lives as they work toward their goals and objectives. With this broader theoretical orientation in mind, let's turn now to the actual teachers who are featured in this part of the book.

The lead teacher in each of the chapters is a Puerto Rican woman who has a long history in North Philadelphia. I met these teachers when I was working as an assistant professor in the Educational Linguistics Program at the Graduate School of Education of the University of Pennsylvania in 1995. The Educational Linguistics program had been awarded a three-year Title VII personnel training program grant known as Project TEAM (an acronym for Teachers of English in the Academic Mainstream), and the grant supported ten School District of Philadelphia (SDP) teachers as they earned their M.S.Ed. in TESOL (teaching English to speakers of other languages). I taught two graduate courses (Content-based Second Language Instruction and Teaching Writing to ELLs) to the TEAM cohort, and Andrea Rodriguez, María Santiago, and Carmen Muñoz (pseudonyms) were graduate students in my classes. These teachers shared my enthusiasm for promoting bilingualism and biliteracy development through schooling, and they each invited me to do research and/or work with them on an aspect of their programs and practices at different points in time.

My relationship to the teachers and students described in these chapters varied from class to class and school to school. In one case, I was a team teacher who was conducting research on her own classroom practice (chapter 8). In another case I was a traditional classroom ethnographer who was working to describe, interpret, and explain the classroom culture without trying to change that culture in any fundamental way (chapter 9). In the third case, I was an action-oriented microethnographer who was analyzing classroom discourse in order to inform the development of the struggling two-way immersion program (chapter 10). As I describe in more detail in each chapter, the way that I defined my role relative to the teachers, students, classrooms, and programs influenced the questions that I asked, the data that I collected, and the ways that I analyzed that data. However, in every case my goal was to explore and document how teachers translate particular language or literacy policies and programs into classroom practices that build on the linguistic and cultural resources that students learn outside of school and bring with them to school.

The classrooms featured in this part of the book are located in different kinds of bilingual and English as a second language (ESL) programs. Although they represent a range of program types that we can find in schools in North Philadelphia today, the classrooms that I have chosen to work in and write about are not necessarily typical of ESL and/or bilingual programs in the SDP or in the United States. While we do see efforts to promote bilingualism and biliteracy development through schooling in other multilingual communities in Philadelphia and in other parts of the United States today, transitional bilingual education and/or ESL programs that see languages other than English as problems to be overcome are still the norm at schools locally and nationally. In contrast, the classrooms described in these chapters provide concrete examples of a language-as-resource orientation (Ruiz 1984) and a sociocultural approach to instruction.

It is important to mention that I did not select these classrooms as examples because I consider them to be perfect; in fact, readers will find areas for improvement in each case. Rather, I selected these examples because each of the educators in these classrooms looks for linguistic and cultural funds of knowledge (Moll 1992) to build on as she works to address the language education policy or program mandate that is handed down to her to implement. As Moll (1992) writes,

> A sociocultural approach to instruction presents new possibilities in bilingual education, where the emphasis is not solely on remediating students' English language limitations, but on utilizing available resources, including the children's or the parents' language and knowledge, in creating new, advanced instructional circumstances for the students' academic development (Moll 1992, 23).

The focus of each chapter is different, and together the chapters suggest a wide range of ways that educators who work with linguistically and culturally diverse student populations can identify and build on the kinds of expertise that their students bring with them to school as they address the standards, goals, and objectives of the target academic discourse communities.

There are three chapters in this part of the book. Chapter 8 explores how two teachers draw on their 5th grade students' knowledge of their families' migration histories to promote their ELLs' development of academic literacies in English within the context of a middle school ESL program. Chapter 9 documents how one teacher builds on her 2nd grade students' knowledge of oral Spanish to promote their literacy development, first in Spanish and then in English, within the context of a one-way developmental bilingual elementary school program. Chapter 10 illustrates how one teacher draws on the ways that her 8th grade students use spoken and written Spanish and English outside of school to elevate the status of Spanish and Spanish speakers within the context of a struggling two-way immersion middle school program. Each chapter highlights the importance of the teacher as she mediates among her interpretation of the language education policies and programs that are handed down to her to implement in her classroom; her understanding of relevant theories of language, literacy and learning; the local sociolinguistic and school contexts; and her ongoing assessment of her students' strengths and needs. Each chapter also documents the serious challenges that these teachers face as they work in relative isolation to meet their students' needs. I address this important point in detail in Part IV of the book.

Each chapter begins with a description of how larger contexts influence the classroom practices that are illustrated in detail in the body of the chapter. Although the particulars of these descriptions vary across the chapters, each discussion of the larger context includes an introduction to the following:

- the students, with attention to their language and education histories and expertise

- the school, with attention to the kinds of language education services that the school provides to its language learners

- the policy mandate and/or educational program that was handed down to the teacher to interpret and implement, with attention to critical features of that policy mandate or program

- the classroom, with attention to the ways that the teacher organizes instruction

These chapters highlight the fundamental role of teaching in educational reform initiatives. Those concerned with the outcomes of educational reform initiatives must understand that learning and teaching are situated, dynamic, negotiated, and negotiable processes. Teachers are not blank slates who uncritically embrace and implement a policy that is handed down to them from the top without interacting with that policy in important ways. The student population matters, the local school and community context matter, teachers' beliefs and histories matter, and the ways that teachers organize interactions with students in their classrooms and programs matter. If we want to change educational practices through educational reform initiatives, we must pay serious attention to how students and teachers work together in situated practice.

8

Promoting academic literacy development in English

This chapter explores how two teachers worked together to provide opportunities for one class of 5th grade English language learners (ELLs) to develop academic literacies in English in a middle school that provided little coherent support for these students. During the spring 2000 semester, I worked as a student teacher in Andrea Rodriguez's 5th grade class at PS 19, which is a public middle school that serves grades 5 through 8 in North Philadelphia. Ms. Rodriguez had been a graduate student in a content-based second language instruction course that I taught in 1996, and she expressed an interest in concentrating our work during the spring 2000 semester on improving writing instruction in her English as a second language (ESL) class. Rodriguez and I saw the School District of Philadelphia (SDP) English language arts (ELA) writing standards as explicit statements of the expectations of the target academic discourse community for writing in English, so we worked together to develop a readers and writers workshop that would build on our students' linguistic and cultural strengths and address their diverse language and learning needs relative to the SDP ELA writing standards within the context of PS 19's ESL program.

This chapter illustrates how Rodriguez and I organized our readers and writers workshop so that we could draw on students' knowledge of the world and on their expertise in spoken and/or written Spanish and/or English as a means of promoting their development of academic literacies in English. We viewed students' experiences with migration and bilingualism as important "funds of knowledge" (Moll 1992, 1995), so they became the foci of the family history project that we developed for our class. This chapter highlights how our ongoing assessment of our students' strengths and needs informed the ways in which we organized instruction throughout the family history project.

The chapter begins with an introduction to the context surrounding our 5th grade ESL class. The majority of the chapter describes the readers and writers workshop that Rodriguez and I implemented in our classroom and briefly considers how this kind of a project could be integrated with and/or adapted to other types of language education programs. The chapter concludes by returning to the school level and emphasizes the need for schools to develop coherent, well-articulated policies, programs, and practices that ensure that all language learners develop the academic literacies they need in English and in other languages over time.

The context

My discussion of context in this section first reviews the kinds of language education services that PS 19 made available to its students at the time of this project (spring 2000). Then I offer some important background about Rodriguez's class, including an introduction to the students and an overview of the ways that Rodriguez organized interaction in her classroom in order to promote student learning. This description of the language and learning context in Rodriguez's class at PS 19 provides a foundation for understanding the design and implementation of our readers and writers workshop.

When I use the present tense in this section, it is to describe the general student population and school context at the time of my involvement in the spring of 2000. This use is not intended to suggest that no changes have taken place in the student population, language education programs at the school, or student performance since that time. In fact, given the dynamic nature of educational policy, programs, and practices in the School District of Philadelphia (SDP), the Commonwealth of Pennsylvania, and in the United States overall throughout this period, it is hard to imagine that the context has not changed in important ways (see chapter 2 and the introduction to Part IV for further discussion of these contextual changes).

Language education services at PS 19

PS 19 is a large middle school in North Philadelphia that serves grades 5 to 8, and it provides a variety of language education services to address the needs of its student population. Like the student population in other schools in the neighborhood, the majority of the students who attend PS 19 are Latino. While most of the Latino population is Puerto Rican, there are a few students with other Spanish-speaking backgrounds (e.g., Dominican Republic, Mexico, Columbia). There is also a sizable African-American population at the school. All of the students are considered low-income, and the majority of students are performing at "below basic" levels on standardized tests in reading and math.

Approximately one-quarter of the students at PS 19 are considered English language learners (ELLs). All but a few of these ELLs are Spanish speakers, and there is a bilingual class at each grade level to serve these students. English language learners in the bilingual program are instructed primarily through Spanish while they ideally acquire English as a second language (ESL). When ELLs are exited from the bilingual program, PS 19 provides little additional support for their development of academic English. The other three-quarters of the PS 19 students are enrolled in the all-English academic mainstream. All of these students are supposed to take Spanish as an academic subject, i.e., as a world language. The majority of the students in the Spanish class are heritage Spanish speakers.

Although there are many experienced and dedicated teachers at PS 19, the bilingual, ESL, and Spanish programs at the school lack coherence. None of these programs has a clearly articulated language policy, and there is considerable confusion about program goals and structures. For example, some educators believe that ELLs should maintain and develop their expertise in spoken and written Spanish while they acquire English (as in a one-way developmental bilingual program), and others believe that the exclusive goal of the bilingual program is for students to acquire English (as in a transitional bilingual program). Most of the educators believe that it is important for the students in this community to maintain and/or develop expertise in Spanish, but many believe that this is not the responsibility of the school. Many educators are not sure when or how students are exited from the bilingual program; many are not sure what kinds of academic language support ELLs might need when they enter the all-English academic mainstream; and few could express the goals of the Spanish program. While the principal of PS 19 expressed her support for well-implemented language education programs that promote bilingualism and biliteracy development for all students, she recognized that the bilingual, ESL, and Spanish programs at PS 19 needed considerable work to reach those goals. I return to this point at the end of the chapter.

Andrea Rodriguez's 5th grade
Reading English language arts class

When Ms. Rodriguez, my former TESOL graduate student, learned that I was being certified in elementary education, she invited me to do my student teaching in her self-contained 5th grade class. She explained that part of her job included teaching Reading English language arts (RELA) to the group of students that the 5th grade teachers described as "ESL students who are not in the bilingual class." Rodriguez was concerned that these students were not developing the academic literacies that they needed to participate and achieve in the all-English academic mainstream. This section introduces the students in this class, articulates our goals, and outlines the organizational structure that Rodriguez and her students had created in her classroom to promote student learning.

All of the students in our RELA class were Puerto Rican. These students all came from homes in which Spanish is spoken at least part of the time, and they had a wide range of language and education experiences. Some of the students were born in Puerto Rico, others were born in Philadelphia or New York, and many had experienced "revolving door migration" between the island and the mainland that characterizes so many families' lives in this community. Some students had been educated primarily through Spanish either on the island and/or in a bilingual program in North Philadelphia, and others had been educated primarily through English. All of the students in our class were receiving all of their content-area instruction that year through English (except for an occasional world language class in Spanish), and they were tested exclusively in English. According to Rodriguez's records, their reading levels in English ranged from grade 1.1 to 3.9 at the beginning of 5th grade.

Although these students were still learning English, the majority chose to use English instead of Spanish at school, especially for reading and/or writing. In fact, I was initially surprised to learn that only three of the twenty-nine students in our class demonstrated any expertise in written Spanish. Of those three, two had been educated primarily through Spanish, first on the island and then in North Philadelphia, and this was their first year in an all-English program. The third said that she had learned how to read and write in Spanish by reading the Bible with her mother every day. Outside of these exceptions, however, the students in our RELA class were all heritage Spanish speakers who were not developing their expertise in spoken or written Spanish. Furthermore, although these students were rapidly assimilating to monolingualism in English, they were not acquiring Standard English or literacies in English according to grade-level norms. This population is considered at-risk in the SDP, and it poses a tremendous challenge to teachers, who struggle to meet its language and learning needs.

My preliminary observations of Rodriguez's classroom practice suggested that there was a very narrow definition of writing in this class. Like many other classes in U.S. public schools that I have observed, "writing" seemed to mean copying from the blackboard or from a textbook, spelling or punctuation exercises, jotting down short journal entries in response to teachers' prompts, or providing answers to simple questions about a reading, which often could be copied directly from the text. I could find no examples of what Edelsky (1989, 18) referred to as "authentic writing," or "cases where the *child's* intentions (rather than the teacher's) were what was being graphically displayed" as part of the official classroom interaction (note-writing, however, was common and was a more authentic form of writing). Furthermore, the writing tasks assigned in this class gave students few opportunities to address the English language arts (ELA) writing standards. These standards require students to do the following:

1. plan, draft, revise, and publish writing using correct grammar, sentence structure, punctuation, spelling, and effective vocabulary appropriate to the purpose, context, and audience

2. write for academic, personal, social, civic, and school-to-career purposes

3. conduct and document inquiry-based research using oral, print, and communications systems

Rodriguez was aware of the need to develop her writing program, and she asked me to help her focus on this aspect of her classroom practice while I worked as a student teacher in her classroom.

Rodriguez and I decided to turn her RELA class into a theme-based writers workshop that would enable us to build on students' language and literacy strengths, and we decided to base our instruction on the ELA writing standards outlined above. Our primary goals included having each student conduct research on his or her family's migration history and write a book about that family history (I motivate the choice of this theme later in the chapter). Because of our focus on language and literacy, an important aspect of this project was to have the students explore how the members of their families used and evaluated spoken and written Spanish and English in their everyday lives. Following Atwell (1987), Calkins (1986), and Graves (1983), we decided to organize the RELA class so that students would have regular and predictable blocks of time to write as well as periods of time dedicated to drafting, conferencing and sharing, revising, redrafting, editing, publishing, and celebrating. The organizational structure described below, which Rodriguez had already implemented in her classroom, provided an excellent foundation for our work.

To address the diverse learning needs of her students, Rodriguez had implemented what she called the "adaptive learning environment model" (ALEM) developed by the Laboratory for Student Success (LSS) at the Temple University Center for Research in Human Development and Education. According to the LSS workshop materials that Rodriguez shared with me, teachers who implement ALEM in their classrooms can expect maximized success in learning through individualized instruction, the development of student self-responsibility for learning, and the development of positive attitudes toward learning. To achieve these outcomes, teachers plan a well-organized and efficient classroom management system that provides students with opportunities to work in a variety of instructional groupings on purposeful tasks.

According to this organizational structure, sometimes students work in groups with or without the teacher and sometimes students work alone. Different students work simultaneously on different tasks and use different materials depending on their expertise, learning styles, and interests. Implementation of this structure requires that students clearly understand the learning objectives, the tasks that they are to perform, the groups they are to work with, and how their work in the range of activities that the teacher organizes enable them to reach their learning objectives. Teachers continuously assess their students' performance as they are working on different tasks in different groupings, and they structure activities that address students' diverse learning needs relative to the standards-based learning objectives the teacher has identified. Students in Rodriguez's class were comfortable working with this organizational structure, so we built on it for our readers and writers workshop.

Prior to my working in the class, Rodriguez had posted the following class rotation schedule for her class on Tuesdays, Wednesdays, and Thursdays when they had RELA. As this rotation schedule illustrates, Rodriguez had organized her RELA class so that she could offer short whole-group mini-lessons on whatever skill the students were addressing. This structure also enabled her to work closely with a small group (8–10) of students during reading time while the other two groups were either reading independently or working at centers on a student-directed task.

Since there were now two teachers in the classroom, Rodriguez and I decided to divide up our responsibilities and work as team teachers to implement the readers and writers workshop. During the group time (2:05–2:55), Rodriguez worked with one group of students on the readers workshop, I worked with another group of students on the writers workshop, and a third group of students worked on centers that supported their work in the readers and/or writers workshop. Together, we worked to facilitate our students' writing development by providing a language-rich, print-rich environment, mini-lessons to address needs as they arose, and authentic responses to their writing. We also decided to provide opportunities for the students to publish and share their writing. With this understanding of the context surrounding our RELA class in mind, I turn to a discussion of the actual readers and writers workshop.

RELA Rotation Schedule

	Tuesday	Wednesday	Thursday
1:40–1:50	Journals	Journals	Journals
1:50–2:05	Skills Mini-Lesson	Skills Mini-Lesson	Skills Mini-Lesson
2:05–2:55	Groups Rotation Schedule		
Group 1	2:05–2:30 Independent Practice 2:30–2:55 Reading	2:05–2:55 Centers	2:05–2:30 Reading 2:30–2:55 Independent Practice
Group 2	2:05–2:30 Reading 2:30–2:55 Independent Practice	2:05–2:30 Independent Practice 2:30–2:55 Reading	2:05–2:55 Centers
Group 3	2:05–2:55 Centers	2:05–2:30 Reading 2:30–2:55 Independent Practice	2:05–2:30 Independent Practice 2:30–2:55 Reading
2:55–3:00	Clean Up and Prepare for Dismissal		

Reading and writing our lives

This section describes the writers and readers workshop that Rodriguez and I organized and highlights how our ongoing assessment of students' strengths and needs informed our decisions about how to proceed in our teaching. First I provide an overview of the approach to teaching, learning, and assessment that guided our work. Then I describe a small writing project that we used to begin to assess our students' needs and clarify our objectives. Next I move to a discussion of the migration history writers workshop that was the primary goal of our class, and then I focus on the readers workshop that we developed to support our writing objectives. I conclude this part of the chapter by highlighting the role of Spanish in our ESL class project.

An integrated approach
to teaching, learning, and assessment

The readers and writers workshop that Rodriguez and I implemented in our RELA class for ESL students is an example of a theme-based sheltered content-area course (see chapter 3 for further discussion). Although writers workshops often encourage students to choose their own topics, Rodriguez and I decided that we would choose the topic of family history for our writers workshop. This topic would be familiar to all of the students and would allow them to draw on their background knowledge and prior histories as a vehicle for learning how migration influences social life and for acquiring academic literacies in English.

The idea for our family history project was inspired by an oral history project that Temple University students conducted with first-generation Puerto Ricans living in Philadelphia in 1976, the product of which is now housed in the archives at *Taller Puertorriqueño,* which is a local arts and cultural education center located in North Philadelphia. Rodriguez and I hoped that a family history project would connect students and their families, their lives today with their families' histories, and their work in school with their lives outside of school. We also wanted to create an opportunity for the students to have their experiences in the world and the varieties of language that they use positively evaluated by the school.

We wanted students explore to their families' migration histories and patterns of language use and then write and publish books based on that research about themselves, their families, and their community. We believed that students would develop and demonstrate an understanding of the writing process through this project, and we planned to build on their developing understanding of related themes and genres for future projects in our RELA class. The projects that students worked on throughout the writers workshop would address both the ELA standards and local student, family, and community needs. Although we drew on social studies themes in this project (and addressed social studies standards), our primary focus was on English language arts.

Rodriguez and I took an integrated approach to teaching, learning, and assessment in our RELA class. To assess our students' needs relative to our goals and objectives for the family history project, we continually asked ourselves three basic questions:

1. What do our students need to know and be able to do in order to write books about their family histories?
2. What what kinds of expertise do students already have that we can build on?
3. What evidence can we find to demonstrate students' performance and development relative to our short-term objectives and long-term goals?

Our needs assessment was ongoing and continually informed our instruction.

What do students need to know and be able to do in order to write books about their family histories? They need to know how to collect data and write up their findings. They need to interview people about their migration histories and about how they use spoken and written Spanish and English in their lives. They need to listen to and record stories that people tell them, and they need to organize the data they collect into a coherent piece of academic writing that is rich in ideas and presented according to the norms of the academic discourse community. Unfortunately, the students in our RELA class had had few opportunities to develop this kind of expertise in research and writing through their experiences at school. Rodriguez and I had a lot of work to do to "close the gap" between what our students could do with written English and what they were expected to do at this grade level. The needs that we identified were the basis for the specific language and literacy objectives that organized our short-term and longer-term planning.

What kinds of expertise did our students already have that we could build on? All of our students were Puerto Rican, and their families had all migrated from the island to Philadelphia either in the students' lifetime or in their parent's lifetime. All of the families used Spanish and English, although we expected that there would be considerable variation in the ways that individuals and families used and evaluated these languages. We expected that the topics of migration and bilingualism would be important to these students and their families and that they would provide content that we could work with to to help them acquire academic literacies in English (if we had been working in a dual language program, we could have easily adapted this project to promote academic literacy development in both languages).

What evidence could we find to demonstrate students' performance and development relative to the objectives and goals? We decided that we would use a variety of performance-based assessments in this class. For example, we observed students as they participated in the range of activities that we organized in the class, and we identified their language, literacy, and learning strengths and needs. We also created portfolios that provided evidence of the process as well as the product of the readers and writers workshops. We used these portfolios in our conferences with our students about their work so that the students would take responsibility for and direct their own learning, and we shared these portfolios with parents and other teachers to demonstrate what students knew and were able to do with language. I discuss assessment in more detail throughout the remainder of the chapter.

Friends writing about friends

With a clear idea of our goals in mind, Rodriguez and I began to plan backwards. We decided that it was important to break the family history project down into more manageable pieces in order to help students develop the research and writing expertise they would need. In Peregoy and Boyle's (1997) terms, we needed to provide literacy scaffolds to support the students as they worked toward their writing goals. Since these students had never had any experience interviewing or writing books, we decided that they needed concrete experiences in these areas right away. We assumed that if students gained experience working together to write a simple first book, they would develop a foundation to support their independent work writing a book about their family history later. We decided to have the students work together to write a book about their class. This section tells the story of this preliminary book writing project.

Because Rodriguez and I wanted to create a context in which students would see each other as resources in their writing, we first thought about how to group the students to write their class book. We decided to organize students into pairs, and we told them that they would work with this partner throughout the remainder of the readers and writers workshop. This was important because we often had problems with social relations among group members, and some students refused to work with other students. By addressing this challenge at the beginning of the workshop, we hoped to avoid having social problems become an ongoing issue. For the most part this approach worked. Furthermore, since absenteeism is often a problem in schools in this neighborhood, students knew that if their partner was missing one day they would work with someone else whose partner was also missing that day.

Since our objectives for the family history book included having students interview someone and write about that person based on the interview data they had collected, we decided to have students interview and write about their partner for their contribution to the first book. We brainstormed interview questions, and students interviewed each other. Each student asked their partner where they were born, where they lived now, how long they had lived in Philadelphia, who they lived with, what languages they used in their interactions with different people and in different places in their lives, what they liked best about school, and what they liked to do in their spare time. We also encouraged the students to share stories about important events in their lives in their interviews. We hoped that this interviewing activity would give students experiences with the structure of interviews and would provide a foundation for our family history project.

Prior to our class, students had had few opportunities to give and receive authentic responses to their writing, and we wanted this kind of interaction to become an integral part of our workshop. We assumed that a student would respond to another student's writing if he/she was the topic of that writing, and in most cases this approach led to students' involvement in each other's writing processes. For example, sometimes a student would get some information about his/her partner incorrect and the partner would become actively involved in the revision process to correct that information.

This first writing project helped demonstrate that writing is a process, which is one of the ELA writing standards. Students collected information from their partners, and they wrote a draft based on the data they had collected. They shared their drafts with their partners and received feedback on content, for example, about what was correct or incorrect or what they thought of how their partners had represented them. Then they revised their drafts based on their partners' feedback. For this first book we did not worry too much about style, sentence structure, or spelling because our goal was to introduce students to the overall process of book publishing. Rodriguez and I did, however, take a lot of notes about language issues that we would need to address as we planned and implemented the process for the second book publication.

We developed a good understanding of our students' strengths and needs through this preliminary phase of our family history writers workshop. First, we learned that although the students were able to write down and copy answers to information questions, they generally were reluctant to ask each other open-ended interview questions that generated lots of data that they could use in their writing. We also learned that the students did not generate much writing about each other. We decided that if we wanted these students to write stories about their families' histories, we would need to immerse them in a language-rich, print-rich environment in which they were reading stories that would be relevant to our theme. Since we knew that this would take more time, we decided to quickly finish the first book project about our class. We needed to broaden the scope of the second book project about family histories to address these emergent needs by incorporating a strong reading component.

Since we were pressed for time to complete the first book, we spent less time on the content, structure, and form of each student's contribution. I quickly typed up what each student had written about his or her partner on one page and we attached a photograph of the student to that student's page. Since the students had not generated much text about each other, we asked each student to write something that he/she remembered—a funny or scary or embarrassing story—about themselves that they wanted to share. We were ready to pull the students' individual contributions together to produce our first book.

Although we were pressed for time, Rodriguez and I decided to pay attention to the publication and celebration part of the writers workshop. A very important goal of our writers workshop was to position the students as book authors. I had already shown them a copy of my first book, *Bilingual Education and Social Change* (Freeman 1998), and we talked about titles for their book. Since it was a collective book, the students needed to decide on a title that they could all agree on. They submitted choices, we voted, and the title *Friends Writing About Friends* easily won. The students decided that since many of their family members could only read in Spanish, the book should be written in Spanish and English. Although everyone agreed with this idea, it turned out that only three of the twenty-three students were able to translate their stories into Spanish, so only three were translated in the final copy of the book. The students did, however, translate the title to *Amigos escribiendo de amigos*. One student (a girl) looked at the title and complained that the word "amigos" did not include girls. At first, I tried to explain that in Spanish "amigos" can mean "boys and girls," but she said that the title should be *Amigos y amigas escribiendo de amigos y amigas*. We put this new title to a vote, and the students agreed unanimously.

Writing this first book took about two weeks, and the students seemed excited as they worked through the process. We celebrated the publication of their first book by inviting the principal, other teachers, and parents to our official "book signing" and each of the students signed his/her page for all of the other students. Everyone expressed their excitement about writing a second book, and the students seemed to really enjoy writing and publishing the first one. In fact, many of the students carried *Friends Writing About Friends/Amigos y Amigas Escribiendo de Amigos y Amigas* around with them in their backpacks everyday, and several of the parents that I talked with expressed their enthusiasm for the work we were doing in the writing workshop.

Writing our lives

Through the first book project, our students had begun to demonstrate their developing understanding of the writing process, and some had begun to present themselves as authors. For the second book, we wanted our students to research their family's history and write a book about what they had learned. This project would address all three of the ELA writing standards that I mentioned earlier in the chapter: (1) to plan, draft, revise and publish using correct grammar, sentence structure, punctuation, spelling, and effective vocabulary appropriate to the purpose, context and audience; (2) to write for academic, personal, social, civic, and school-to-career purposes; and (3) to conduct and document inquiry-based research using oral, print, and communications systems. Rodriguez and I continued to assess each student's strengths and needs relative to our standards-based goals, and we continued to build on our ongoing assessments. This section tells the story of how we worked to support our students' efforts to write independent books about their family histories. The detail is intended to provide concrete suggestions about ways that teachers can organize such a writing project in other contexts.

First, we needed to demonstrate to the students what a family history text might look like so the students would clearly understand what was expected of them. We began our work on the family history project with an oral and written retelling activity. I simulated the role of the interviewer in the front of the class, and Ms. Rodriguez told me a story about when her parents came to the United States from Puerto Rico, what her family had hoped to find, and what they actually found when they got here. The students were asked to talk to their partners about Ms. Rodriguez's family history and fill in any gaps in their understanding either through their conversation with their partner or by asking Ms. Rodriguez follow-up questions. Then the students each wrote down Ms. Rodriguez's story. Next, we gave the students a copy of Claudia's story (see chapter 5) and told them this was an example of a family history written by another Puerto Rican middle school student who lived in North Philadelphia. After the students read Claudia's story independently, pairs of students were asked to retell specific parts of what she had written. We came together as a group, and each pair retold their part of Claudia's story in their own words. These two activities, the oral and written retelling of Ms. Rodriguez's oral family history and the oral retelling of Claudia's written family history, were intended to give students concrete examples of family histories of Puerto Ricans who had migrated to Philadelphia from the island. We recommended that the students use these concrete examples as models for their own work.

We also needed to demonstrate how the interview process could lead to a written family history. After the students had retold Claudia's story, we showed them a series of questions that Claudia might have used if she had interviewed her family members to collect the information that she included in her story. We asked the students to look at Claudia's story to see where she had provided the information that answered the interview questions. We also encouraged the students to work together to generate interview questions that they could use when they interviewed their own family members. We wanted to help the students understand that we did not want to just collect short answers to questions in their interviews, which is what they had done for the first book project. Instead, we wanted them to see concrete examples of how they could elicit stories through their interviews, and how they could use those stories to tell and write their family history. This proved to be a difficult challenge that we continued to address in different ways throughout the project.

After the class looked at the example of Claudia's family history, Rodriguez and I encouraged the students to begin work on their own books with a brainstorming activity. Each day during the journal writing time at the beginning of class, we listed a series of questions about a different family member (Day 1: brothers and/or sisters; Day 2: mother; Day 3: father; Day 4: mother's parents; Day 5: father's parents). We asked the students to free-write about their family members so they could get an idea of what they already knew about their family history, which would help them identify what else they needed to learn. We tried to emphasize that our questions were just intended to stimulate their thinking, and I showed them examples about how I used the questions to stimulate my writing about my family members. We repeated that the students did not have to answer every question that we wrote, and we encouraged them to write about anything else that was important to know about that family member.

Despite our efforts, we found that many of the students seemed to interpret this journal writing activity as just another school assignment. Some students copied our questions into their journal and then answered each question. Others simply answered the questions in the order that we had written them. Few used this activity as an opportunity to write freely about their family members. Few of the students seemed to embrace this project as an opportunity for authentic writing at this point.

About the second day that the students were working on the family history project, one of the students asked me if I was going to write a book about my family. I told her that I thought it would be really hard for me to write about my family history in the United States because my family had come in the 1700s and their families had come much more recently. One of the students said to me, "Oh missy, that'll be cool," and others got so excited about my writing a book with them that I could not say no. Interestingly, at first I did not see my writing a book about my family as an authentic task, even though that is what I had hoped it would become for the students. I simply saw this task as a requirement that the students had imposed on me, much like the task that I had imposed on them. What happened over time, however, is that I embraced this project as an opportunity to learn about my family history with my sister, and I wrote a children's book that I gave to each of my sisters and my mom for Christmas. In other words, writing the children's book alongside of the 5th graders moved from being just a school assignment for me to an authentic task.

And my writing a book about my family history alongside of the students had consequences for the students' work. More and more of them seemed to be changing the way that they were working, demonstrating that many of them (not all of them) came to see writing the family history book as an authentic task. For example, as I shared aspects of my research process and product with them-the kinds of questions I asked my mom and my sister; pictures of my family and my family tree-or when I would ask a group of students to help me with something I was stuck on, more and more of them became involved in my work. Several of the students began to do the same kinds of things that I was doing in their work. Many of them brought pictures of their family, and one student, Juanito, gave me short stories about his family every day. He told me one day, "Missy, I don't know what's happening but I can't stop writing." Several of the kids would not wait until RELA class in the afternoon to share their work with me—they would enthusiastically give me pieces they had written when the day began.

Students developed portfolios of their work in the writers workshop that allowed us to assess their performance relative to our objectives and that enabled students to take responsibility for and direct their own and each others' learning. The family history portfolios each had a cover sheet that said "History of the _____ Family" on the front. Rodriguez and I had broken the family history project down into a series of concrete tasks that students had to accomplish as they worked through the writing process, and each portfolio included a checklist of those tasks. For example, students were required to generate interview questions, make a family tree, make a list of family members to interview, interview each of those family members, and summarize each of those interviews in writing. Students were then required to write a first draft of a family history based on their interviews. Next students were required to read and respond to their partners' family history draft using a peer response form that focused their attention on ideas. Then students were required to write a second draft, and they were expected to consider their peers' responses in their revisions. The next step in the writing process required the partners to read each other's second draft but this time use a peer response form that focused their attention on grammar, spelling, and punctuation. Finally students were expected to write a final draft that included photographs and/or drawings. Once the students had completed the final draft, they were required to reflect on the project and write about what they had learned.

I had regular conferences with each pair of students several times throughout the course of the project, and we would assess what they had done and what they needed to do next. Students kept samples of their work at each stage in the process, and they knew what was expected of them at any time. I drew on my observations of common problems across the students' work and developed mini-lessons to help students address those areas in their work. I also had many opportunities to learn about how the students drew on the ways that Spanish and English were used at home as they worked to interview their families and write their books. I discuss this in more detail later in the chapter.

Rodriguez and I realized that if we expected students to write detailed stories about their family histories, we needed to immerse them in a print-rich, language-rich environment. We needed to create opportunities for them to read, write, and talk about their families' experiences, with attention to their migration histories and the ways they use Spanish and English in their everyday lives. Since good writers are almost always good readers and poor readers rarely are strong writers, we decided to strengthen our writers workshop by developing a content-related readers workshop. Stories about other children's migration histories provided an important source of input for their second language acquisition and an important model for their writing.

Reading about other children's lives

Rodriguez and I realized the importance of reading for our writers workshop. However, we wanted our 5th grade students to read grade-level texts, and none of the students in our class was reading at grade level (recall that the students' reading levels ranged between 1.1 and 3.9 at the beginning of 5th grade). We needed to provide students with authentic texts that were related to our topic, and we needed to provide literacy scaffolds so that our students could access those texts. This section describes the kinds of activities we organized in our readers workshop to support our students' reading development.

Most of the books that we selected for the readers workshop were about children and their families' migration experiences. Reflecting our goal of positively evaluating and possibly building on students' expertise in Spanish, I looked for grade-level books that were written in Spanish and English. In some cases I found the same book written in Spanish and English (e.g., *Friends from the Other Side, Amigos del Otro Lado* by Gloria Anzaldua; *Family, Familia* by Diane Gonzales Bertrand). In other cases, I found the same story in Spanish in one book and in English in another book (e.g., *Amelia's Road/El Camino de Amelia* by Linda Jacobs Altman; *The Keeping Quilt/ La Colcha de Recuerdos* by Patricia Polacco). Since our class was an ESL class, and the explicit goal was to promote academic literacy development in English, students were not required to complete any tasks using the Spanish texts or in Spanish. However, they were encouraged to read in both languages, to write in both languages, and to think about the role of spoken and written Spanish and English in their lives.

Immersing students in texts on the same topic that they were writing about gave the students opportunities to develop vocabulary that was relevant to the topic. Students who chose to read in both Spanish and English were learning vocabulary related to the topic in both languages. Immersing students in the storytelling genre gave the students opportunities to develop expertise in this genre. As Rodriguez and I saw that students needed literacy scaffolds to support, for example, vocabulary development and/or development of expertise in the storytelling genre, we developed activities to meet those needs. For example, we introduced a short story retelling activity that took place at the beginning of each class. Every day, either Rodriguez or I read aloud a very short story that was related in some way to our family history project. Then we asked the students to work with their partners to retell the story orally. Once the students confirmed that they understood all of the details of the story, they would each retell the story in their own words in writing. Like many of the activities that we developed in this class, at first the retelling activity was met with resistance. However, once the students learned the process, they embraced these story retellings, and over time many of them began to demonstrate more complex understanding of narrative structure in their own writing.

Their written retellings also increased in length as students included more details about the stories they had been told.

We organized one section of the room for the readers workshop where we laid out the books that students were to read. We also organized a variety of literacy scaffolds to support the students' independent reading. For example, we hung up posters that we generated with the students during the mini-lessons that outlined strategies that good readers use or that outlined exactly what we expected students to do during the readers workshop. We provided vocabulary development activities and a variety of graphic organizers that students could use to map the stories that they read. Each student had an individual folder for his/her work that included a checklist of all of the activities that students were required to complete. These portfolios helped students organize their own work, and they helped teachers structure their conferences with students and their parents about the students' reading development. We organized listening centers where students could listen to the books as they were read aloud. If the students did not finish all of their readers workshop activities during the allocated time, they could return to an activity during center time.

Each student was required to read at least four of the books that Rodriguez and I had selected and then complete a series of story retelling activities. The activities were increasingly complex. The first two activities were shared retellings that required students to work in pairs, and the second two activities required students to work independently. For each story retelling activity, pairs of students would begin by reading one of the stories. Some pairs chose to read silently and other pairs chose to read aloud to each other for this first step. Once the pair finished reading the story, they would discuss it and use a graphic organizer to map the story. When the pair finished their story mapping, they would collaborate to write a summary of the story. Finally, each student would write his/her own response to the story. The third and fourth retelling required more independent work. In these cases, each student would read a book on his/her own, map the story, summarize the book, and write a response to the story. Each student was to present his/her summary and response of the third book orally to the class, and the fourth summary/response was to be handed in to the teacher in writing.

Our RELA class became a lively community of readers and writers in which students, working in pairs and/or independently, directed their learning. Team teaching and a predictable rotation schedule allowed Rodriguez and me to structure many different yet complementary activities during the RELA class. Since Rodriguez and I each worked with a relatively small group of students each day, we were able to closely monitor their strengths and needs, and we worked together to design and implement activities to support their literacy development. Rodriguez and I saw evidence of students' English language and literacy development over the course of the semester. For example, most of our students were becoming more involved with reading and writing. Many of the students were beginning to write longer texts that were richer in linguistic detail; some were beginning to talk about what they had read outside of the structure of the readers workshop activity, and others were talking and writing about the ways that they used languages at home. One semester, however, is not enough time to close the gap between our students' performance and the grade-level norm. I return to this point at the end of the chapter.

The role of Spanish

Because our class at PS 19 was an ESL class, we had no explicit goal of promoting Spanish literacy development, and Spanish was not used in any official way in the class. However, Rodriguez and I did not want our work teaching English at school to further stigmatize the varieties of vernacular Spanish and English that students used at home and throughout the community. We did not want our work to suggest that students replace those varieties with Standard English. Instead, we wanted our work at school to help students extend their linguistic range by promoting the acquisition of Standard English as an additional variety that is critical for success in school and in mainstream U.S. society. Rodriguez and I worked to create an environment that encouraged these students and their families to draw on their expertise in spoken and/or written Spanish and/or English as a vehicle for their work toward our academic goals in English.

For example, Rodriguez and I originally planned that the books that students wrote in our class would be published in English and Spanish. Since the majority of the students' family members use Spanish as their primary language, bilingual books would be more accessible to more of the students' family members. We imagined that since the students all spoke Spanish at home, they would be able to translate what they wrote in English to Spanish. This assumption, however, turned out to be incorrect. Although the students unanimously agreed that their class book *Friends Writing About Friends* should be published in Spanish and English, only three of the students volunteered to translate their contributions for the class book. The others said that although they understood Spanish and used more Spanish than English at home, they could not write in Spanish. I originally thought of having the three students who had translated their contributions to Spanish work as what I called "the Spanish translation team," and I asked these students to work with the other students to translate all of their contributions so that we could publish a bilingual book. I believed that this translation activity would provide a good opportunity for these three students to demonstrate and develop this expertise. I also believed that the other students who were reluctant to translate to Spanish would benefit from the opportunity to see and hopefully read their writing in Spanish themselves and with their Spanish-speaking family members. However, it quickly became obvious that it would take too much time for these three students to translate everyone's work, and in the end only those three contributions appeared in the class book in both languages.

Despite the fact that most of the students were not able to write in Spanish in our class, Spanish was an important resource that several of the students drew on to complete their interviews with their family members. When the students and I were working together to generate their interview questions, one of the students (Isabel) asked me to write her questions for her in Spanish because she could not write in Spanish and her mother could not understand English. Isabel and I worked together to translate the interview questions, and the next day she gave me the paper with the answers written in Spanish. She explained that she had given the questions to her mother and her mother had written the answers. Isabel wanted me to translate the answers for her to English so that she could write her story.

At first I was a little bit annoyed because I assumed that Isabel had not done her homework. I assumed that she had persuaded her mother to do her work for her instead of doing it herself. When I asked Isabel why she had not written the answers to the interview questions herself, it became obvious that my assumption was wrong. At first Isabel seemed offended that I had suggested that she had not done her work. As we continued to talk, she explained that she could talk to her mom in Spanish, but she could not write the answers to the questions because she could not write in Spanish. When I asked Isabel why she did not write the answers in English, she explained that she could not listen to her mom in Spanish and write in English at the same time. This makes sense because simultaneous translation from oral Spanish to written English is a very demanding task, especially for someone who is just learning how to interview and who is relatively reluctant to write in English.

This incident made me think a lot about what it means to involve parents in students' education. Isabel's mom wrote a note in Spanish on the bottom of the paper that said, "Thank you very much for this assignment. It's so important for me to have the chance to talk to my daughter about how difficult it is to be a single mother. If you have any more questions, please call me at . . ." (and she left her phone number). What was obvious was that Isabel's mom knew that I would be reading the paper and that I would know she had written the answers. What was also obvious was that this mother wants to be involved in her daughter's education, and that this can be very challenging if the education is only in English.

This interaction with Isabel also stimulated several of the other students to work with me in Spanish and English to help them complete their assignment. At first I thought that Carla and Jesus simply had not done their interviews, and I assumed that they either forgot or were not interested. However, after Carla saw me working with Isabel on her mother's questions in Spanish, she asked me if I would translate her questions into Spanish. She did the exact same thing—she gave her mother the questions, her mother wrote the answers in Spanish, and she asked me to translate the answers to English so that she could continue to do her work in English. Because both Isabel and Carla were able to talk with me about the answers to the questions that were written in Spanish, I assumed that they talked to their moms in Spanish as their moms wrote the answers. The breakdown seemed to happen when they tried to move from written Spanish to written English. Jesus showed me what his mom had written in Spanish, but he told me that he was going to get his sister to help him translate what his mom had written.

My ability to use spoken and written Spanish allowed me to provide a literacy scaffold for several of the students as they collected data in Spanish at home about their family history in order to complete their books in English at school. An important goal of this project was for students to look to their families as important funds of knowledge that they can draw on to do their work at school. The students and I believed that they should be able to share the fruits of their labor with their family members in the languages they could understand. The students, their family members, and I worked in different ways to make this happen.

Making connections

This chapter has provided an example of how two teachers worked together to promote their students' acquisition of academic literacies in English. The readers and writers workshop that Ms. Rodriguez and I developed provides an example of an integrated approach to teaching, learning, and assessment, where ongoing assessment of students' strengths and needs relative to the goals for the class guided our efforts to differentiate instruction to address the needs of our students as they arose. The project that we chose to work on with the students not only addressed academic writing standards in English language arts, it also helped connect students to their families, their community, and to each other. This concluding section takes us beyond the actual readers and writers workshop that Rodriguez and I developed for our RELA class to discuss ways that the project could be adapted and/or extended to address other educational goals within this type of all-English program and/or to other kinds of language education (bilingual, world language) programs.

The classroom described in this chapter was a pull-out ESL class for intermediate-level English language learners (ELLs) who come from homes in which Spanish is spoken as the primary if not exclusive language of communication between children and their parents and grandparents (siblings and friends tend to use English with each other, unless they are new arrivals). This kind of a writing project could easily be integrated with instruction in other content areas. For example, students could use their family history projects as a basis for work in social studies and math as they consider relationships between migration and social life. Students could be encouraged to look across each of their families and identify patterns in migration histories and language use. They could use their identification of these patterns as the basis for a community-based inquiry into the history of the Puerto Rican community in North Philadelphia, and they could do quantitative and/or qualitative research to explore the role of spoken and written Spanish and English throughout the community.

This kind of a project could also be readily adapted to another language education context. Teachers who work in one-way developmental bilingual programs, two-way immersion programs, or Spanish as a second language programs could distribute languages for instructional purposes in ways that are aligned with the specific goals and structure of their programs. For example, teachers working in a one-way developmental bilingual program could implement this kind of a readers and writers workshop entirely in Spanish, and/or they could encourage the students to begin to read, write, listen, and speak about their family history in English over time. Teachers who work in two-way immersion programs could spend half of the workshop time in Spanish and half in English, requiring that students read and write through both languages. Regardless of the way that teachers allocate languages for instructional purposes, teachers need to begin with what students know and help students make connections between what they know and what they are learning. Teachers can help students move from their primary language to their second language orally and/or in writing, and/or they can help their students move from oral communication in either of their languages to written communication in both of their languages. Teachers can also help students build on their expertise in one genre as they work to develop expertise in additional genres. And students can be encouraged to look critically at the ways that spoken and written languages are used and evaluated in their everyday lives at school, at home, and in other key contexts in their lives. I develop each of these points throughout the remaining chapters in the book.

Articulation is critical to the success of any type of language education program. Our primary concern in this chapter has been with ELLs who are enrolled in a pull-out ESL program. In order for ELLs to acquire the academic literacies that they need to participate and achieve within and across content areas in English at school, ESL teachers cannot work in isolation. Schools must offer well-articulated programs that provide language learners structured opportunities to acquire the academic language and literacies they need in English within and across content areas (e.g., social studies, math, science, language arts) within and across grade levels (K–12). All of the educators that serve these students (mainstream teachers, ESL teachers, bilingual teachers, world language teachers, administrators, counselors) need to develop a coherent understanding of their program goals and the best means to reach those goals, and each of the educators needs to understand how their individual part fits into the larger educational whole. When the whole school takes responsibility for ELLs' academic literacy development, these language learners will have opportunities to acquire the academic literacies in English and other languages that they need to participate and achieve in all content areas at school over time. I return to these important points in Part IV.

9

Providing initial literacy instruction in Spanish

This chapter explores how one teacher organizes her 2nd grade classroom to promote her English language learners' (ELLs) development of initial literacies in Spanish within the context of a one-way developmental bilingual elementary school program at PS 11 in North Philadelphia. It is based on ethnographic research that I conducted in María Santiago's classroom during the 2000–2001 academic year to investigate how Ms. Santiago interprets what the district-mandated approach to literacy instruction means in a bilingual setting, and to document how she implements this literacy program on the classroom level. I first met Santiago in 1995 when she was a graduate student in the TESOL (teaching English to speakers of other languages) program in which I was working at that time, and her classroom was recommended by many educators in the School District of Philadelphia (SDP) as an outstanding context to study the implementation of the Balanced Literacy Framework that was mandated throughout the SDP from 1999 to 2002. My goal in this chapter is not to advocate this particular literacy program but to make explicit how Santiago translates her understanding of the Balanced Literacy Framework into classroom practices that she believes are appropriate for her students, school, and community.

The chapter is divided into three parts. First I describe the context in which this 2nd grade class is situated with attention to ways that this context structures Santiago's interpretation of how she should provide initial literacy instruction for her students in Spanish. Next I illustrate how Santiago implements the Early Balanced Literacy Framework on the classroom level so that her students learn to read and write first in Spanish and then in English, and I discuss how the students read and write to learn in both languages in Santiago's classroom. The chapter concludes by emphasizing the importance of first language literacy instruction for ELLs in other contexts.

The context

Ensuring that all students acquire the literacies that they need to participate and achieve at school and in society is one of the primary goals of
schooling. In recent years, national and local attention has turned to the
preschool and early elementary school years because these years ideally
provide students with an essential foundation for acquiring the wide range
of literacies they need to realize their short-term and long-term academic,
professional, and social goals. Like school districts across the country, the
School District of Philadelphia (SDP) has been working to address this
challenge on the local level. In 1999 the SDP began a systemwide reform
effort known as the Balanced Literacy Initiative (BLI) that began by targeting all K-3 classrooms. The Balanced Literacy Framework structured
literacy instruction in the early elementary grades throughout the SDP
from 1999–2002, and it is an important place to begin our discussion of the
context surrounding Santiago's class. The next level of context that is relevant to our discussion is the one-way developmental bilingual program at
PS 11. Finally I introduce the students in Santiago's 2nd grade class.
Together, the parts of this section provide a foundation for understanding
how Santiago translates the district-wide Balanced Literacy Initiative into
practice in her 2nd grade bilingual classroom.

Early Balanced Literacy
in the School District of Philadelphia

My discussion here of the SDP Reduced Class Size/ Balanced Literacy Initiative (BLI) policy and of the Early Balanced Literacy (EBL) framework is
intended to make explicit the theory of literacy instruction that is implicit
in this systemwide initiative. Teachers like Santiago who are asked to
implement this (or any other) literacy program in their classroom must
mediate their understanding of that literacy program with their understanding of relevant theories of language and literacy development, the
sociolinguistic and school context in which they work, and the strengths
and needs of their particular students. In this way teachers can translate
the literacy program into classroom practices that they believe make pedagogical sense within their local program and school structure and which
meet the developmental and social needs of the students and community
they serve.

The SDP BLI began by targeting all kindergarten and 1st grade
classes throughout the district, and all pre-service and in-service K–3
educators ideally participated in professional development in EBL (see

below for discussion of the EBL framework). Each year pre-service and in-service teachers of successive grades were to participate in professional development in EBL so that they would understand how to implement a balanced literacy program in their classroom. Class size in the early elementary grades was to be reduced because each class would ideally have a literacy intern (LI) who would work full-time with the class in addition to the regular classroom teacher. In this way, every early elementary class in the district would have two teachers who were to share responsibility for up to 33 students.

The first year of the BLI only addressed the all-English academic mainstream. The SDP began to pay attention to the needs of ELLs in the second year of the initiative, and the district's professional development offered opportunities for English as a second language (ESL) and bilingual teachers to adapt the prototypical balanced literacy classroom to meet the needs of their ELLs. For example, the SDP's Office of Language Equity Issues (OLEI) coordinated a graduate course at the University of Pennsylvania entitled Balanced Literacy for English Language Learners that targeted bilingual and ESL teachers. In the spring of 2000, Santiago and her colleague Sonia Barinov began to co-teach this graduate course. The Office of Language Equity Issues also had an educational video made about bilingual balanced literacy in the spring of 2002 that features Santiago and one of her colleagues who worked in another one-way developmental bilingual program in North Philadelphia.

The Balanced Literacy Framework that SDP teachers implement in their classes is based on The Ohio State University Early Literacy Learning Initiative (see also Fountas and Pinnell 1996). This framework includes eight major elements that can be distinguished by the nature of the interaction between teacher, student(s), and text. These elements are referred to as *Read Aloud, Shared Reading, Guided Reading, Independent Reading, Shared Writing, Interactive Writing, Guided Writing or Writing Workshop,* and *Independent Writing,* and these terms are increasingly used by SDP teachers as they talk about their practice. During *Read Aloud* time, the teacher reads to the students as a whole class as she introduces the students to a text, provides a language and literacy-rich environment, and models a love of reading. During *Shared Reading* time, the teacher reads with the students either as a whole class or in a small group as they work together on a particular skill or strategy. During *Guided Reading* time, the teacher reads to small groups of students who have been identified as reading at the same level, and she focuses on a particular skill or strategy that the group needs. During *Independent Reading* time, the children read on their own or with another student. During *Shared Writing* time, teachers and children compose messages together, and during *Guided Writing* and *Independent Writing* time, students write with other students or independently.

The approach to early literacy development advocated by the SDP is to be *balanced*. That is, teachers ideally balance their attention to reading and writing, and they ideally balance their focus on the meaning of the whole text and on the parts of language in which students may need more practice (e.g., concepts of print, phonics, mechanics). Teachers ideally move students' literacy instruction from teacher demonstrations and modeling to cooperative group work to students' independent production. Students ideally learn to read and write for a variety of purposes, and they ideally read and write to learn across the curriculum. The Balanced Literacy Framework is intended to provide structure for teachers who are working to enable their students to acquire the academic literacies they need to meet the English language arts (ELA) standards and to use reading and writing to learn in the other content areas.

At the time of my research in Santiago's classroom, the BLI had been underway for three years in the SDP and the majority of K–3 classroom teachers across the district had participated in ongoing professional development in this area. Although all K–3 teachers across the district were originally mandated to implement a more or less standardized EBL program in their classes, there actually has been a wide range of variation in how teachers interpret what balanced literacy means and how they translate that interpretation into practice. Teachers draw on their beliefs about and prior experiences with literacy instruction to inform their implementation of the program, and many schools continue to struggle to enable their students to read at grade level.

With the recent state takeover of the schools in the SDP and increasing local, state, and federal accountability requirements, many low-performing schools are abandoning the Balanced Literacy Framework. We see an ideological struggle within and across schools about what kind of literacy instruction is best for low-performing students, and we see schools increasingly mandate more phonics-based literacy programs that focus primarily on phonemic awareness and other discrete language skills and that promise to raise test scores. We see as well a very structured scope and sequence that is to guide instruction in all schools. For example, the SDP now mandates that all teachers implement a "Comprehensive Literacy Framework" that includes the same components of the "Balanced Literacy Framework" but highlights the central role of phonics in literacy instruction. In the fall of 2003 the SDP also will begin to mandate a core curriculum with a strict scope and sequence that all schools must follow. As state, district, and program mandates continue to change, teachers must continue to interpret the new mandates in ways that make sense to them in their classrooms.

In order to understand how Santiago translates the Balanced Literacy Framework into practice, we need to look beyond the Balanced Literacy Framework. The next section introduces the bilingual program at PS 11, which structures the allocation of languages used within the EBL program within and across grade levels at the school. This discussion of the program level of context provides an important foundation for understanding how students acquire literacies, first in Spanish and then in English, through their participation in Santiago's 2nd grade classroom practices.

One-way developmental bilingual program at PS 11

PS 11 is located in North Philadelphia, and it is a Title I K–4 school that serves 720 children. Approximately 80 percent of the students are Latino and 20 percent are African American. About one-third of the Latino students are designated ELLs, and PS 11 offers a one-way developmental bilingual education (DBE) program for these students. The goals of the DBE program are for the ELLs to maintain and develop their expertise in oral and written Spanish while they acquire academic language and literacies in English.

The developmental bilingual program at PS 11 is structured so that students in grades K–2 receive the majority of their instruction through Spanish, including initial literacy instruction in Spanish. During time devoted to English in the early years teachers place an emphasis on oral communication, and ELLs begin formal literacy instruction in English in 3rd grade. As they progress through the grade levels, ELLs receive an increasing amount of content-area instruction in English, and they continue to receive content-area instruction through Spanish. By 4th grade students in the bilingual program receive approximately 50 percent of their instruction through Spanish and 50 percent through English. Ideally, these students develop expertise in oral and written in Spanish and English, and they meet the academic standards in both languages.

PS 11's bilingual program is considered one of the better bilingual programs in the SDP, especially in North Philadelphia. The Office of Language Equity Issues designated Santiago's class a "demonstration" classroom for bilingual balanced literacy in the district. Let's turn now to the classroom level of context.

Maria Santiago's 2nd grade class

Ms. Santiago's classroom offers an outstanding context for research on how teachers can provide initial literacy instruction in Spanish for a variety of reasons. Santiago grew up in a bilingual family in North Philadelphia, and she has been teaching in bilingual classrooms in this neighborhood for more than 20 years. She is also considered a local expert in literacy instruction. She was a participant in the Philadelphia Writing Project (PhilWP) at the University of Pennsylvania, a site of the National Writing Project that is nationally recognized for its teacher research and teacher leadership. She also co-taught the graduate course on Balanced Literacy for English Language Learners at the University of Pennsylvania that I mentioned earlier. Santiago recently won the Rose Lindenbaum Improvement of Education Teacher of the Year Award, and she opens her classroom to educators who want to observe how she implements the bilingual balanced literacy program.

Santiago had 29 students in her classroom during the 2000–2001 academic year, which is the year that I conducted my research. Three of the students were Dominican, and 26 were Puerto Rican. All of the students were Spanish dominant and spoke Spanish most or all of the time at home. Although several of the students were born in Philadelphia, most of them had moved to Philadelphia from either Puerto Rico or the Dominican Republic within the last few years. Santiago believed that it was essential to know her students and their families, and she had visited all of their homes over time. Mothers and/or other family members talked with Santiago regularly, and there was always at least one mother working in the classroom.

The year that I observed Santiago's class was the second year that she had worked with this group of students. Santiago had been their 1st grade teacher the year before and she "looped" with them to 2nd grade. Looping is a relatively common practice in the SDP in the early elementary years because it allows teachers time to develop relationships with students and their families, and to observe and direct their social and academic language and literacy development over time.

In many ways, Santiago's class looks similar to other well-implemented balanced literacy classrooms in the school district. The class is filled with print, and observers can see commercial materials, teacher-made materials, and student work everywhere. The class has a library of big books, regular-sized books, and little books that are classified by level. The different levels are identified by color and letter, and the classification scheme is standardized across the school district. Like all early elementary classrooms in the SDP, Santiago's class has a brightly colored rug with shapes and colors for the students to sit on, and the rug is a focal point of many literacy activities. For example, Santiago does her *Read Aloud* and *Shared Reading* with her students everyday in this part of the classroom. When students are not sitting on the rug, they are encouraged to sit in small groups around tables or in desks, and there are centers lining the periphery of the classroom. There is a computer center, a writing center, a listening center, and other theme-based and/or skills-based centers that change over time. Like other teachers in the SDP, Santiago aligns the centers in her classroom with her instruction. The primary difference between Santiago's class and other balanced literacy classrooms is that the majority of instruction at this grade level is in Spanish. As we see in the remainder of this chapter, students learn to read and write in Spanish, and they read and write across the content areas in Spanish as they work to reach the same high standards as their English-speaking counterparts do in English.

The 100 Book Challenge *(Reto de Cien Libros)* is also an important part of Santiago's class, and it is becoming a part of an increasing number of schools in the SDP. Through the 100 Book Challenge, students are encouraged to take books home every day and read to their family members. The goal is for each student to read at least 100 books at their independent reading level, and they are to involve their family members in the reading activity. At the time of this writing, a group of teachers was working to ensure that the 100 Book Challenge would become available in Spanish for bilingual teachers across the district.

Santiago organizes her classroom instruction around themes or topics, and she uses a variety of formative and summative assessments to provide evidence of her students' actual performance and development over time. Since the national and local standards do not specify all of the themes or topics that teachers must include in their curriculum (at least not at the time of this writing), SDP teachers have been relatively free to choose the content of their work in language arts. Santiago often draws on social studies concepts, themes, and topics because she believes that social studies is currently being overlooked in the SDP. She argues that since social studies is not a "tested" subject (i.e., there are no high-stakes standardized tests in social studies like there are in reading and in math), teachers tend to pay less attention to this content area. Furthermore, social studies is a language-rich content area, and social studies concepts, themes, and topics provide a context for Santiago to facilitate students' development of a wide range of vocabulary and genres. Some of the thematic units she chooses to develop are based on her students' interests, and some are based on her own interests. As Santiago selects themes and topics, she also considers the standards in social studies and in the other content areas.

Santiago encourages students to take responsibility for their own and each other's learning. She clearly demonstrates what she wants students to do before she asks them to work cooperatively or independently, and students always know exactly what is expected of them. Santiago posts the daily schedule and the center/guided reading rotations every day so that students can read what they are expected to do, with whom, where, and when. Sometimes students work together as a whole class with the teacher facilitating their whole group learning, sometimes they work cooperatively in small groups or in pairs on tasks that the teacher has organized, and sometimes students work independently. This organizational structure encourages students to use each other as resources in their own learning, and it allows the teacher to assess students' performance as they participate in a wide range of activities.

A typical day in Santiago's class is structured as follows. The schedule is written below in Spanish as it appears on the bulletin board at the back of the classroom, and the English term used in the Balanced Literacy Framework is provided in parentheses.

8:45-9:45	Matemáticas (Math)
9:45-10:05	Mensaje Escrito (Morning Message)
10:05-10:20	Leer Ms. Santiago (Read aloud)
10:20-11:15	Grupos de Lectura (Centers/Guided Reading)
11:15-11:45	Escribir (Writing Workshop)
11:45-12:00	Lectura Compartida (Shared Reading)
12:00-12:45	Almuerzo y Recreo (Lunch and Recess)
12:45-1:20	Reto de 100 Libros (100 Book Challenge)
1:20-2:15	Estudios Sociales (Social Studies)
2:15-3:00	Ciencia (Science)

In the morning, during math time and during the literacy block, instructional time is organized so that students learn to read and write and do math. In the afternoon, during social studies and science time, students use their math, reading, and writing skills to learn within these content areas. English language learners also build their oral language skills in English on the concepts and skills they develop across content areas in Spanish. With this understanding of the instructional context in Santiago's bilingual 2nd grade class in mind, let's look more closely at how she organizes instruction so that students learn to read and write, first in Spanish and then in English.

Learning to read and write in Spanish

This section illustrates how Santiago draws on concepts, themes, and topics from the content areas and on the Balanced Literacy Framework to facilitate students' development of literacies in Spanish. While my focus here is not on content-area instruction, I use an example of a thematic unit on animals to illustrate how content and the standards drive language and literacy instruction in this 2nd grade class. Then I show how Santiago draws on the components of the Balanced Literacy Framework to ensure that her students develop the literacy strategies and skills that they need to achieve academically in her classroom. Santiago's integrated approach to teaching and learning enables her to continually assess her students' literacy development, first in Spanish and then in English, and to address their language and literacy needs based on this ongoing assessment over time.

A theme-based approach to literacy instruction

First Santiago decides on a particular theme, and then she begins to organize a thematic unit for instruction with goals and objectives that are aligned with the School District of Philadelphia (SDP) standards. Early in her development of a thematic unit, Santiago decides on culminating projects that her students will work on throughout the unit. Santiago then defines content and language objectives that structure students' work on their projects. Students' performance relative to the content and language objectives provides Santiago with evidence of what each student knows and/or can do relative to those objectives. This kind of classroom-based assessment informs instruction because teachers build on what students already know as they address their needs.

For example, once Santiago chose animals as the focus of a thematic unit, she decided on two projects that would provide students with opportunities to develop their expertise in expository and narrative reading and writing. For the expository reading and writing project, each student picked an animal, did research to learn facts about that animal, made a poster, and wrote a paper. For the narrative writing project, students worked in groups to write a fictional story about an animal of their choice. Both of these projects are illustrated in my discussion of how Santiago translates the Balanced Literacy Framework into practice in the next section.

Since Santiago wants her instruction to build on students' prior knowledge, she needs to know what students already know about the topic relative to her short-term and long-term objectives. She therefore begins implementing every unit with some type of K-W-L activity to see what the students KNOW and what they WONDER about the theme they will be studying. At the end of the unit students return to their original questions and add what they LEARNED throughout their studies.

For example, when the students were beginning their work on the unit on animals, Santiago asked them to work in groups at their tables and she gave each group a piece of chart paper. She asked the groups to brainstorm what they knew about animals in general, and they wrote those ideas down on their chart paper. Santiago then invited each group to bring its chart paper to the front of the room and orally share with the whole class what the group had written down about animals. During this part of the activity, Santiago worked as a scribe. As each group of students shared what it knew about animals, Santiago recorded the contribution on another piece of chart paper, and she synthesized what the whole class knew about animals.

Next, Santiago led the whole class in a brainstorming activity and they generated a series of questions about animals. Some students expressed an interest in learning about where certain animals lived, others wondered where certain animals were born, and others asked what kinds of food different animals ate. Santiago kept these questions posted on chart paper in the front of the room, and these questions guided the class inquiry throughout the unit. Students addressed a range of content-area standards in the context of their inquiry. For example, as students learned about where animals live and what they eat, they considered big ideas about ways that the environment influences animal behavior, and they developed map-reading skills through the process. As students asked how far particular animals could jump, they developed measuring skills, and they made comparisons and contrasts, which they represented in different ways. As they learned about the life cycle of animals, they made observations, documented those observations, predicted behavior, and generated hypotheses. Throughout this theme-based approach, students read and wrote expository and narrative texts, and as we see in the next section, they used those texts as vehicles for their ongoing analysis of different genres.

Santiago regularly asked students to make connections between the new concepts and skills that they were learning and what they had already learned, and she encouraged the students to look back at the questions that they had earlier asked and to assess for themselves what they had learned. This process often led the students to generate new questions about the unit they were working on and to relate what they were learning across content areas. Santiago also asked the students to connect what they were learning about their focal theme with their everyday lives outside of school. For example, she encouraged students to talk and/or write about the animals that they knew about in this country and in their home countries, first in Spanish and later in English. This kind of talk enriched the students' understanding of the world and provided access to important vocabulary across content areas and across languages. Students would often bring videotapes or books or some other realia from home, which demonstrated that they were making connections outside of school with what they were learning in Santiago's class.

Translating the Balanced Literacy Framework into practice

The K-W-L activity had activated students' prior knowledge and stimulated students' questions about animals. As we see in this section, Santiago uses this content as a foundation for the different components of her literacy program. I have italicized the terms that refer to the Balanced Literacy Framework in my discussion.

After the introductory K-W-L activity on animals, Santiago organized students into small groups for a *Guided Writing* activity. The goal of this activity was for each small group to focus on a particular animal and write a descriptive paragraph about that animal. Santiago began this guiding writing activity with a demonstration of the task that students would later be asked to complete in their small groups. She held up a picture of an owl, and she and the students discussed what they saw in the picture. Santiago emphasized that they were to describe only what they could see in the picture; they could not include any details that they knew about owls if they could not observe those details in the picture. Santiago worked with the students to generate sentences based on their observations. They pulled their sentences together into one descriptive paragraph that Santiago wrote on poster paper and hung in the front of the room for easy reference.

The *Guided Writing* activity led to a *Shared Writing* activity. Using the descriptive paragraph about the owl that the class had just generated, the small groups were asked to work together to complete a similar writing task. Santiago gave each table of students a picture of an animal and a big piece of chart paper, and she asked the members of the group to write down everything they observed about that animal. Again, they were told that they could only write what they could see in the picture. After they worked together to generate a series of observations, each student wrote one sentence describing the picture of the animal and that student wrote his/her name in little letters next to the sentence that he/she had contributed on the poster paper. Each group of students later brought their descriptive paragraph of their animal to the front of the room to share what they had written. Santiago hung all of the students' posters around the room.

This series of writing activities provided many literacy scaffolds for Santiago's students as they learned how to write to share information, which is one of the SDP writing standards. Santiago modeled the kind of writing she expected in front of the whole class, and she structured a collaborative activity for the students to complete at their desks. These activities provided students with opportunities to write more than one sentence, and they organized their observations into a series of sentences describing their animal. Santiago returned to these descriptive paragraphs in a later writing activity when she wanted the students to focus more on paragraph form, detailed description, sentence structure, spelling, and punctuation.

Reading and writing are integrated in Santiago's class. In order to support students' efforts to learn about animals, Santiago needed to provide considerable oral and written input about the topic. To this end, Santiago read to the students at least once every day, and many of the books that she selected were about animals. Since she wanted to introduce her students to a wide range of genres, some of the books that Santiago chose were fiction and some were nonfiction. When Santiago read to her students, she addressed many of her literacy goals. She demonstrated reading for a purpose, and she involved children in the reading activity in a variety of ways. Sometimes she invited the students to tell the story based on the pictures in the text, sometimes she encouraged them to recite the choral parts or rhyming parts of the texts with her, and sometimes she asked the students to make predictions about what was going to happen next. When Santiago immersed her students in the texts that she read aloud, the students learned how texts were structured and they developed a sense of story, knowledge of written language syntax, an increased vocabulary, and an expanded linguistic repertoire. Since Santiago read the same content-related books (e.g., about animals) to all of the students in a large group, the *Read Aloud* activity helped create a community of readers who worked together to jointly construct knowledge about their theme. I observed students regularly making intertextual connections between texts that Santiago read aloud to them. They also regularly shared experiences that they had outside of school that connected in some way to their readings.

Although the daily schedule only designated a certain time in the morning for Santiago to read aloud to the students, it was common for her to read aloud during social studies or science time in the afternoon. Most of the books that Santiago selected to read aloud were in Spanish. However, as she progressed through the thematic unit and students were developing knowledge about animals, Santiago would begin to read to them in English. The goal of English language instruction at this grade level in the one-way developmental bilingual program was to foster oral language development, and they used the themes they worked on in Spanish as scaffolds for their English language development. As they progressed through the year, it was common for Santiago and her students to use more and more English.

Santiago returns to many of the books that she read aloud to the students more than once during a thematic unit so that she could focus on a particular reading skill or strategy with the whole class. For example, during the animal unit Santiago read *La Gallinita Roja* (the red chicken) aloud to her class on several consecutive days so that they could focus their attention on narrative structure. On the second day, the class discussed who the characters were, and they used a story map to outline where the story took place, what the problem was, and what the solution was. Then they rewrote the story in a book that had the pictures from the original text but no text. During center time later in the day they colored the pictures in their book. This story connected with work they were doing in science on the growth cycle of chickens. It also connected to work they were doing in math as they measured how far they could jump and hypothesized how far different animals could jump.

Since students learn in different ways, Santiago continually assesses and regroups her students for instruction. *Running record* is a form of assessment that all Balanced Literacy teachers are required to use to identify their students' literacy strengths and needs and to determine their independent reading level. One day I observed Santiago as she did a running record with a new student who had just arrived from Puerto Rico. She began the running record by giving a quick background on a story that Marco had not read before. She asked him to look through all of the pictures and tell her what he thought the story would be about. After Marco responded, Santiago asked him to read the first paragraph. As he read, Santiago used a checklist to check off each word that Marco got right and to mark the errors in the margin. She noted when he self-corrected, and she marked his pronunciation errors. Santiago noted that "he needs fluency" because Marco pronounced each separate syllable slowly, seemingly with little attention to meaning. After he read the first page aloud, Santiago asked him to make a prediction about what was going to happen next in the story. After he made his prediction, Santiago determined that he needed to continue reading at the level of this book. Because he had made five errors, Santiago could not move him up to the next level. At the end of the running record activity, Santiago asked Marco to read aloud to his family members every night so he could become a more fluent reader. Santiago also asked his older sister María to have Marco read aloud to her at home.

Students are organized into *Guided Reading* groups based on Santiago's assessment of their independent reading level. During *Guided Reading* time, Santiago worked with a small group of students, generally no more than five or six, who she had determined have similar reading processes. Santiago would select a new book that was at the students' instructional level, which was slightly above the students' independent reading level, and she would introduce the book to the group. She worked with the small groups of students in different ways to guide their understanding of the novel text, and the strategies that she chose depended on the students' needs and the challenge that the particular text offered. For example, sometimes she encouraged the group to engage in problem solving while reading for meaning, sometimes she demonstrated the use of particular strategies to support their reading of extended texts, and sometimes she focused their attention on particular words or structures that were causing difficulties for this group of students. Guided reading by the teacher provides an important literacy scaffold for students, and this structure is intended to help students develop the particular strategies and skills they need to continually read more varied and demanding texts.

While Santiago was working with her *Guided Reading* Group, the rest of the students would be working on different *Centers* throughout the classroom. In general these centers were in some way related to the class theme and/or to a skill that the students needed to practice in order to complete a culminating project. Some students would be working at the listening center where they listened to a big book on tape that Santiago had already read aloud to them as a whole group. These students would be asked to do some kind of activity that gave them practice with the text they had just heard. For example, they might be asked to put the sentences of the story in the order in which they were presented in the original text. Other students might be working at an art center, for example, drawing pictures for a book that they were writing or making something for a math, science, or social studies project. Other students would be reading a book that they had selected with a partner or by themselves.

During center time, one group of students would go to the library and select books that related to their theme. Although most of the books in the library at PS 11 are in English, there is a sizable Spanish collection. The students would often ask me to go with them to the library, and they would regularly show me the books that they picked out. Most of the students selected books in Spanish. However, some students would choose to read together or independently in English as the year progressed, especially as they developed more knowledge of the theme and began to be able to access content-related texts in English. Although I can speak Spanish, the students all know that English is my stronger language. Whenever they picked books in English, they would ask me if they could read aloud to me to show me how they were acquiring English.

While Santiago's first concern in reading and writing instruction is always with meaning, she is also committed to teaching her students the skills and strategies that they need. *Morning Message,* or *Mensaje Escrito,* provided a daily highly predictable format for skills practice. Santiago, like many teachers throughout the SDP, begins the day with this activity. The morning message is generally very formulaic across classes, especially in kindergarten and the early part of 1st grade. It provides a simple example of a *Shared Writing* activity, in which the teacher and students work together to compose the message, and the teacher supports the process as a scribe. When students are first learning how to do the morning message, teachers generally guide the students as they write something like: "Good morning boys and girls. Today is (month, day, year)." The class usually works together to compose a sentence or two about the weather or about what they are doing in school or what they did at home. For example, sometimes Santiago would encourage them to reflect on or plan an activity that was related to their theme. Their first concern was always with meaning.

The students quickly learn the structure of the morning message. This structure facilitates the teacher's efforts to demonstrate concepts of print and how words work, and it allows teachers to draw students' attention to letters, words, and sounds within the context of a meaningful message. Santiago made a poster with a key that tells students how to work with the texts that they created during the morning message activity. For example, students were asked to put a green triangle around punctuation marks, an orange rectangle around capital letters, a purple rectangle around a whole word, a squiggly-lined rectangle around the silent h, and a blue circle around vowels; they underlined whole sentences in yellow. Because their initial literacy instruction was in Spanish, Santiago directed students' attention to vowels and to the silent h in Spanish. This structured learning opportunity provided a context for Santiago to encourage her students to focus on different aspects of language and literacy that the SDP regularly assessed.

As the year progressed, Santiago would change the structure of the morning message activity to accommodate the students' developing needs and interests. For example, one day Santiago asked María, a new student who had just migrated to Philadelphia from Puerto Rico, to come to the front of the class. Santiago guided the class's efforts to use the morning message as a way to get to know more about their new classmate. The students asked María a few questions, and they collaborated in making sentences about what they learned. One student was invited to the front of the class to write *María es una estudiante nueva en nuestro salon*

(María is a new student in our class), and another student came up and wrote the next sentence *Ella estraña mucho a Puerto Rico* (she misses Puerto Rico very much). Santiago asked more questions to guide the students' joint construction of meaning and then writing. She asked *qué más podemos escribir de María* (what else can we write about María), and they talked about whether she had any pets. Another student came up and wrote *Eya tiene dos perritos* (she has two dogs). Then the students asked María whether she had any brothers or sisters. Following that short conversation, one student wrote *María tiene dos hermanitos* (María has two little brothers) and another wrote *Se llaman Marco y Carlos* (they are called Marco and Carlos). This activity got everyone involved in using listening, speaking, reading, and writing to learn more about María. To this point, the students had been directed to concentrate on the meaning of their message, and they had not been asked to focus on the form.

Once the students had finished constructing the meaning of their morning message text, Santiago asked them to check for areas that they might need to correct. In this way, the teacher guided the students' efforts to learn to edit, and she asked them to focus on the skills areas that they had been focussing on through the morning message activity for the past year and a half. For example, Santiago asked them to tell her rules about capitalization, spelling, and punctuation, and students volunteered to come up to the front of the room to identify these concepts of print and edit the text. In the example above, Santiago guided their attention to spelling errors. One student changed the *s* to an *x* in *estraña*, and another changed the spelling of *eya to ella.*

Morning Message began as a teacher-led activity. Over time, however, students learned to do the morning message as a small group at their table, and they would generally work on some message that was related to their thematic unit. When students generated their own morning messages at their tables without the guidance of the teacher, Santiago would often select different messages to work on as particular mini-lessons during their *Guided Writing* time. She would often put the morning messages that were related to their theme around in the classroom, and these posters would function as language resources for the students to use in their work.

Students in Santiago's class were encouraged to learn to read and write for authentic purposes. For the last several years, for example, one class of high school Spanish (as a world language) students from one of the local public high schools have come to Santiago's class to make books with her students. This year Santiago wanted her students to make books about animals, and she structured the classroom so that the high school students would guide the 2nd grade students through the project. The first day that the high school students came, Santiago organized her students into seven small mixed-ability groups and placed one high school student with each group. Each group included at least one strong reader and one strong writer, and the students were encouraged to draw on each other's strengths in order to complete their collaborative book project. Each group brainstormed ideas for stories that they would write, and they talked about characters, plots, and settings. Each of the 2nd graders took responsibility for drawing one of the pictures from the story that they had brainstormed, and each wrote a few words about his/her picture. Each of the high school students went back to their Spanish class and wrote their group's story on the computer. The high school students brought the stories back to Santiago's class so that the students could confirm and/or revise the story. The high school students then brought the stories back to their class, revised them, and translated them into English. The next week, the high school students came back and shared the stories that they had written in Spanish and English with the PS 11 students, and the PS 11 students finished illustrating their books.

This *Guided Writing* activity benefited the PS 11 students who were learning to read and write in Spanish and who were also acquiring their oral language and a basis for literacy development in English. This activity also benefited the high school students who were learning Spanish because they had an authentic purpose for using spoken and written Spanish. The high school students provided models of adults who could read and write in Spanish and English and they offered scaffolds to support the 2nd grade students' writing development. The PS 11 students were proud of the books that they had co-authored and produced with the high school students. All of the groups enthusiastically showed their books to me, and most of the groups asked if they could read their stories to me.

One of the culminating activities of the animal unit was an *Independent Writing* project. Each student was to make a poster about an animal that they had selected and researched. Students worked together to brainstorm the kinds of information that they needed to include in their poster, and this information addressed the questions that they had brainstormed during the introductory K-W-L activity. For example, students asked questions about where their animals lived, what they ate, and how they were born. Santiago encouraged her students to read for information to find answers to their questions. She brought books into the classroom and encouraged the students to go to the school library to check out books on animals. Students gathered the information that they needed, and each made an individual poster with sentences or paragraphs describing, for example, where their animals lived, what they ate, and how they were born. Many of the parents got involved in this activity with their children at home, and the students shared their posters orally with the class once they had completed the assignment. Santiago encouraged the students to look across their examples of specific animals to consider big ideas about animals in their environments. Santiago also hung the posters throughout the room and into the hall to celebrate the hard work that they had all done.

In summary, Santiago's thematic instruction in her balanced literacy classroom is aligned with her content-area instruction, and it enables her to teach her students to read and write, first in Spanish and then in English. She begins every thematic unit with a K-W-L to activate the students' prior knowledge, to generate student questions to guide the unit, and as a basis for assessing what students learned throughout the unit. Santiago draws on the components of the Balanced Literacy Framework to structure her classroom, and she organizes the children into a variety of groupings throughout the unit to facilitate their joint construction of knowledge about animals. The components of the Balanced Literacy Framework are integrated, and Santiago structures and sequences the activities so that they move from teacher demonstration and guidance to collaborative group work to independent work. Students move from a focus on meaning to a focus on form, and they develop skills and strategies within the context of meaningful communication. Before students are expected to read and write about a particular topic, in this case animals, they are encouraged to talk about the topic so that they develop knowledge of important concepts like animal habitats, reproduction, and sources of food. Once students understand the concepts and can talk about them in Spanish, they are guided in their efforts to write about them in Spanish and to talk about them in English. Some students begin to experiment with writing in English, but they will not begin formal literacy instruction in English until 3rd grade. At that time, the students are expected to have developed a solid foundation for literacy through their first language, which readily transfers to English.

Talking, reading and writing to learn in two languages

The last section illustrated how Santiago organizes instruction to teach students how to read and write. By 3rd grade, however, students are expected to know how to read and write. At this point, they are expected to be able to read a wide range of texts to learn within and across the content areas, and they expected to be able to write a wide range of texts as evidence of what they have learned. This section looks at how Santiago uses math instruction as a time to read and write to learn in her 2nd grade class.

Santiago uses *Everyday Math,* a math program developed by the University of Chicago and Everyday Learning, to structure her math instruction. The math program takes a spiral approach, which means that the students are introduced to a variety of concepts but are not expected to master those concepts right away. The goal during the initial stages of instruction is exposure, and the concepts are repeated several times over each year. This spiraling continues throughout the early elementary grades of the program as students develop their knowledge of math concepts and math literacies over time. This approach stands in opposition to traditional approaches to teaching math that are organized around worksheets, mastery of one concept at a time, and moving on to the next concept in a predetermined order from simplest to more complex. Here, the students connect what they are working on in the math unit to their work in other content areas (e.g., science, social studies, language arts), and they are encouraged to relate what they learn within and across these content areas to their developing understandings of the world around them. This approach reflects the assumption that not all students will master a concept at the same time or in the same way, and it offers students a wide range of opportunities to develop their understandings of core concepts of the curriculum.

Students in Santiago's class worked on the weather unit during the month of January, and they drew on their developing expertise in reading, writing, and math to learn about temperature change. This unit built on the work the class had done during the temperature unit in December when students began to take the temperature daily. During the weather unit, students used the data that they collected each day to make charts and graphs to document temperature change. On one chart that they were making, Santiago had written the numbers that corresponded to their recordings of the temperature by 2s: 2, 4, 6, 8, 10 . . . .. One day one of the students, Manuel, took the temperature and found that it was 35 degrees. Santiago asked him to record the temperature on the temperature chart, but Manuel could not find the number 35 because odd numbers were not written.

Santiago used this as an opportunity to teach Manuel a strategy to solve this problem, and to model this learning strategy for the other students. Santiago sent Manuel to a number chart on another wall in the room and asked him to find the number 35 (he was "reading the room," a language arts routine that Santiago encourages throughout the day). When Manuel found the number 35 on the number chart, Santiago instructed him to look at the number before and the number after it. She asked him to come back to the temperature chart they were making and point to 35. Manuel followed these directions, marked a red dot at 35 on the temperature chart and stamped the date at that point. Santiago instructed him to connect this red dot to the dot at the end of the graph they had been generating over the past few weeks, and Manuel drew a line to connect the temperatures. Santiago and the students read the graph together and talked about their observations of temperature changes since they had begun this project in December, which led to a discussion about weather changes in the different seasons more broadly. Students were encouraged to write and draw about their observations in their journals in Spanish. They later used their journal writings as a foundation for writing more formal expository texts on the weather and on seasonal change.

Activities like these illustrate how Santiago, using the *Everyday Math* curriculum that her school requires, integrates math, science, and Spanish language arts. Students in Santiago's class are using Spanish to study the curriculum, and they are addressing the same content-area standards in Spanish that the English speakers address in the all-English academic mainstream at PS 11. They are also applying their developing number sense to solve problems. When a student like Manuel has difficulty with a particular skill in math or language arts, Santiago stops and addresses that skill either within the context of the larger lesson and/or later during focused math or language arts time. Students are acquiring academic literacies in Spanish, and they are using various symbol systems to observe and record temperature change on graphs, on charts, and in writing. Students in this class use their stronger language, Spanish, as a vehicle to develop this content-area knowledge. Later, during English time, Santiago and the students talk and read about the content-area concepts that they are studying in math, science, and/or social studies, which provides a foundation for their development of expertise in English. Santiago works with students to move from what they know (e.g., a concept, language, or skill) to what they do not know, and they build on their strengths.

This spiral approach to content-area concept development also provides an environment that is conducive to (second) language acquisition and (bi)literacy development. Santiago's students are immersed in a language-rich, print-rich environment, they have many opportunities to negotiate meaning about any incomprehensible input, and they are encouraged to produce lots of oral and written output which provides evidence of what they have learned. When Santiago sees that students are having difficulties with a particular skill or form, she focuses students' attention on that form either within the context of the content class or later during more focused language arts instruction. These conditions are considered necessary conditions for second language acquisition, and they can be summarized as follows: (1) comprehensible input at a level slightly above their current level of comprehension, (2) opportunities to negotiate the meaning of incomprehensible input to make that input comprehensible, (3) opportunities to produce a wide range of oral and written output, and (4) focus on form within the context of meaningful communication (see, for example, Krashen 1982; Long 2001; Peregoy and Boyle 1997; Pica, Young and Doughty 1987; Swain 1985 for discussions of second language acquisition research).

This chapter has taken us into María Santiago's 2nd grade classroom, and we have seen how she organizes instruction so that her students learn to read and write in Spanish, and how they use oral and written Spanish and English to learn within and across the content areas. We have also seen how Santiago and the students regularly talk about their problem-solving processes and strategies. Sometimes Santiago talks about her learning strategies in the context of demonstrations, and sometimes she asks the students to think aloud as they work through a writing or math activity or project. When students hear the wide range of strategies that can be drawn on to solve any problem, they broaden their own repertoire of learning strategies. Furthermore, when students talk and/or write about their problem-solving strategies, Santiago can expand her understanding of how to address their specific learning needs.

The importance of first language literacy instruction

Maria Santiago's class is part of a one-way developmental bilingual program that provides initial literacy instruction for its Spanish-speaking English language learners (ELLs) in Spanish first. English language learners are encouraged to build on their stronger language, Spanish, to develop content-area knowledge in that language. Then they are encouraged to build on their oral and written Spanish and their knowledge of content-area concepts to develop their expertise in English. When ELLs begin to develop expertise in oral and written English, they are encouraged to maintain and develop their expertise in oral and written Spanish. According to Santiago, the overwhelming majority of her students are reading at grade level by the time they leave her class in 2nd grade (in the spring of 2002 two students were below grade level; one was a new arrival that year and the other was absent repeatedly). This is a notable accomplishment in North Philadelphia, given that so many low-income Latinos in North Philadelphia schools are performing below grade level.

This accomplishment provides further evidence of the importance of strong first language literacy instruction for ELLs. This position is widely advocated in the bilingual education field and is increasingly advocated in the mainstream language arts field (see chapter 1 for further discussion). The students who leave Santiago's class have a strong foundation in their primary language on which to build. The challenge for educators in this one-way developmental bilingual education program is for the upper elementary grade teachers to support these students' development of the academic language and literacies they need to participate and achieve in both English and Spanish as they progress through the grades. This challenge becomes greater as the language and literacy demands become increasingly complex.

10

Elevating the status of Spanish and Spanish speakers

One of the primary challenges facing U.S. schools that aim to promote bilingualism is ideological. English has more symbolic capital than Spanish in the United States, and Spanish tends to be socially stigmatized. This social stratification of languages has important implications for language choice patterns in bilingual communities. Many English-speaking Latinos do not see a need for Spanish beyond familiar domains, and they tend to only develop expertise in oral, local (nonstandard) varieties of Spanish. Many English language learners (ELLs) begin to resist using Spanish as they acquire English, and they tend to shift to English over time. Unless individuals and their families see a need to use and continue to develop expertise in spoken and written Spanish, they tend to assimilate to monolingualism in English, generally within two to three generations. If schools want students to develop expertise in spoken and written Spanish, they must ensure that there is ideological space for bilingualism and biliteracy development.

This chapter explores how one teacher worked to address this ideological challenge within the context of a developing two-way immersion (TWI) middle school program in North Philadelphia. In 1996, PS 17 began to implement a TWI program that would ideally enable English-speaking and Spanish-speaking students to develop academic literacies in Spanish and English and achieve academically through both languages. I began to conduct ethnographic research at the school at that time in order to document how the program and practices at PS 17 challenged the symbolic domination of English and English speakers on the local level.

Most ethnographic research documents the range of typical activities in a particular cultural context so that an outsider can understand the norms of interaction and interpretation that guide behavior in that cultural context. However, what was more typical at this stage of development of the TWI program was language prejudice (Urciuoli 1996) against Spanish and Spanish speakers, and the social reproduction of the subordinate status of Spanish-speaking students at school. I therefore chose to focus my research on atypical activities that I identified at the school, those in which Spanish was positively evaluated as a resource to be developed rather than as a problem to be overcome.

This chapter illustrates how one bilingual teacher opened ideological space for Spanish literacy development at PS 17, and it is divided into four parts. First I introduce the context surrounding the development of the TWI program at PS 17, and I highlight some of the challenges that the bilingual educators faced in their efforts to implement a middle school TWI program. Next I describe a project that Carmen Muñoz developed to address language prejudice at school. Then I present an analysis of Ms. Muñoz's classroom interaction to illustrate how she builds on the varied linguistic repertoires of all of her students and elevates the status of Spanish and Spanish speakers in the class. The chapter concludes by considering how the bilingual educators' experiences working to implement their middle school TWI program informed their dual language program development.

The context

This section introduces the PS 17 students and describes the ideal two-way immersion (TWI) policy that was to be implemented throughout the school. Although the policy created ideological space for additive bilingualism at school, language ideologies on the local level challenged the TWI teachers' efforts to implement their program. As this chapter emphasizes, teachers' awareness of these kinds of contextual challenges can direct their work at school.

At the time of this writing PS 17 was a relatively large middle school located in North Philadelphia. According to 1994–1995 School District data, approximately 1100 students were enrolled at the school; 81 percent of those students were Latino and 19 percent were African American. A large number of English language learners (ELLs) attended the school. During the 1994–1995 school year 342 students were enrolled in the bilingual/ ESL (English as a second language) program, and 99 percent of these students were Spanish speakers. Nearly all of the students (98 percent) who attended PS 17 were considered low-income. Like many other schools in low-income urban areas, student performance was low. Under 10 percent of the students scored above the 50 percent in reading and math achievement on the Comprehensive Test of Basic Skills in 1994, and the school's comparative achievement score was 42nd out of 45 middle schools in the district.

In 1995, the School District of Philadelphia was awarded a five-year Title VII: Bilingual Education Comprehensive School Grant, and part of the grant funds were intended to support the development of a TWI program at PS 17. The development of the TWI program was to be one part of an integrated, systemic reform effort known as the Program Organizing Resources for Teaching, Achieving, and Learning: Into the Future, or the PORTAL program. The PORTAL proposal emphasized its goal of additive bilingualism for all students:

> PS 17 LEP (limited English proficient) students must be able
> to communicate in English while maintaining and growing in
> ability to read, write, and speak in Spanish. We expect students
> to be able to transfer knowledge learned in one language to
> their general knowledge base and use that information in the
> other language. English dominant students need to understand
> the importance of being bilingual in an interdependent world
> and in the Americas where Spanish is the majority language
> (SDP 1995b, II-2).

PS 17's TWI program was to begin in one small learning community and then spread to other small learning communities throughout the school over the five-year period of the Title VII grant.

Each of the small learning communities at the school was made up of a team of four content-area teachers (one science, one social studies, one math, and one language arts) who worked with a small group (approximately 100) of 6th, 7th, and 8th grade students throughout their middle school years. The content-area instruction in each small learning community was organized around a theme chosen by the team, and students on that team were to work on interdisciplinary projects that would prepare them for future educational and professional opportunities related to that theme. The TV/Communications Team was the team that initiated the TWI program, and students on this team were to use the TV/Communications Lab that the grant funded to develop expertise in the area of TV/Communications using both Spanish and English.

The TWI policy was developed by school administrators and an outside consultant. According to the ideal plan,

> The concentration in one of the teams will be a two-way bilin-
> gual educational program in which half or more of the students
> are LEP. Two teachers will teach their content areas (math and
> science) in Spanish for all of the students. Two teachers will
> teach their content areas (social studies and communications
> skills) in English. All reading classes will be taught in English
> and students will be instructed at their individual reading lev-
> els. Also, reading classes will have a maximum of 20 students.
> In other teams all children will have Spanish classes and will be
> instructed at their levels in Spanish (SDP 1995b, II-11).

Although the teachers on the TV/Communications team had no input in the development of the TWI plan, they were expected to implement this policy.

The competing language ideologies at PS 17 challenged the bilingual educators' efforts to implement their TWI program. On the one hand, the dual language policy, TWI teachers, and many of the students positively evaluated bilingualism and/or the use of two languages for instructional purposes. At the same time, however, there was also widespread language prejudice against Spanish and Spanish speakers among students at school, which led some students to resist using Spanish in favor of English. Since Spanish is often referred to as the "hick" language, which is negatively associated with "jíbaros" on the island, PS 17 students who could speak English often chose not to be associated with the TWI program because Spanish, the "hick" language, was used.

The teachers at PS 17 understood the ideological challenges their TWI program faced, and they looked for creative ways to encourage their middle school students to positively evaluate Spanish. They realized that unless the status of Spanish and Spanish speakers was elevated at school, English speakers simply would not be interested in using and/or developing their expertise in Spanish, and Spanish speakers would continue to shift to English.

The teachers at PS 17 also understood the practical challenges their TWI program faced. Although the policy made ideological space at school for bilingualism and biliteracy development, the educators had not made implementation space for a TWI program. After the first year of the POR-TAL program, the PS 17 educators realized that a successful TWI program should begin in the early elementary years and that three years of middle school did not allow students enough time to develop academic language and literacies in a second language. They also realized that English-speaking students who had not learned to read and write in Spanish in the elementary grades had a difficult time reading and and writing texts in Spanish on the middle school level. The next section illustrates one project that a TWI teacher developed to address the ideological challenge. I return to the practical challenge of initiating a TWI program in middle school in the conclusion to this chapter.

Redefining what it means to be a Spanish speaker at school

Carmen Muñoz was one of the bilingual teachers struggling to implement the TWI program at PS 17 in 1996, and her personal experience as a Puerto Rican who migrated to the United States when she was thirteen informed her work with her students. Ms. Muñoz said that she had felt pressure to use only English and to hide her Puerto Rican identity when she was in middle school, and she was determined to alleviate this kind of pressure for her middle school students. Muñoz wanted her students to maintain and develop their expertise in spoken and written Spanish, and she wanted them to see the wide range of opportunities that are available to bilingual individuals.

To this end, Muñoz worked with the other TWI educators to link bilingualism to technology and redefine what it means to be a Spanish speaker at school. The Title VII grant funded a TV/Communications Lab to be used for video production, and the TWI teachers were working to make the lab an integral part of their program. Their goal was to challenge the local assumption that students in the bilingual program were monolingual Spanish-speaking "hicks." Instead, these educators worked to position students in the bilingual program as bilingual and technologically sophisticated individuals who could work through two languages in the high-tech, high-profile field of TV/Communications. Since video production was attractive to all of the students, English-speaking and Spanish-speaking students ideally would choose to develop their expertise in Spanish. The status of the TWI program, of the Spanish language, and of Spanish speakers ideally would be elevated.

The *telenovela* (Spanish soap opera) project that Muñoz produced throughout the 1997–1998 academic year with her students was evidence of Muñoz's work toward this goal. She saw the telenovela as a "cultural fund of knowledge" (Moll 1992) that she identified in the community. Although the telenovela is not generally considered a legitimate genre in academic settings, telenovelas are very popular in the Puerto Rican community and throughout the Latino world. This cultural fund of knowledge is a resource that educators can build on as they promote the acquisition and use of academic literacies in both Spanish and English.

The telenovela project began quite accidentally. One day there was some confusion in the students' schedules, and Muñoz had a group that was supposed to have gone to an assembly during that class period. Since Muñoz had not prepared anything for this group, she asked the class to write a premise for a novela. The students' response to this request was incredible. Students who generally resisted writing at school and who barely produced more than one or two sentences in response to any assignment that I had seen were writing furiously. At the end of the period, when Muñoz asked the students to hand in their papers, several asked if they could take them home, finish them, and hand them in during the next class. Others took great care to white out (correct) errors that they found in their drafts before they handed in their papers.

The quantity of writing that the students produced and their concern for form encouraged Muñoz to draw on her students' interest in telenovelas and on their knowledge of the genre as a resource to help her develop their video literacies. She decided to have her class collaborate in the development of their own novela, which they entitled *Amor Imposible* (Impossible Love). Through their production of the novela, students were learning to write, storyboard, build sets, act, direct, and produce. And as we see in the next section, Muñoz drew on her students' diverse linguistic repertoires to help them all expand their linguistic repertoires in Spanish and English.

There was evidence that the telenovela was elevating the status of Spanish and Spanish speakers at school during the time period that it was produced and broadcast. For example, the principal organized a special event to celebrate the filming of the first episode of *Amor Imposible*. She invited parents and community members (including the deputy mayor) to participate in the filming of the first scene, and these VIPs were assigned roles as "extras." The school broadcast a new episode of *Amor Imposible* in every classroom several mornings a week (part of the Title VII grant that funded the TV/Communications Lab also funded TVs and VCRs in each classroom). This regular broadcasting reflected the telenovela's legitimacy as an official part of the school day. In order to address the concern that monolingual English speakers be included, Muñoz's bilingual students provided students in every class with a written English translation of each scene the day that it was broadcast. The teachers noticed that the telenovela broadcast was also addressing another chronic problem at the school, which was student tardiness. Since the telenovela was featured at the very beginning of the day, students began to arrive at school on time because they were motivated to see the latest episode.

The telenovela was very popular at PS 17. Students talked about it, the actors acquired celebrity status at school, and English-speaking students often requested the opportunity to assist in its production. Since English speakers had to use Spanish to participate, we saw English speakers choosing to use Spanish at school.

The telenovela project is just one example of how a teacher can organize a project that will encourage middle school students to use and develop Spanish. Muñoz drew on her understanding of how languages are used and evaluated naturally in the community as she worked with her students to redefine what it means to be a Spanish speaker at school and to facilitate their production of their own Spanish language telenovela. But exactly how did Muñoz organize her classroom interaction in ways that enabled all of her students to draw on their own expertise in spoken and/or written

Spanish and/or English as they each broadened their linguistic repertoires in both languages and developed video literacies? The next section provides a close analysis of this process.

Negotiating language, negotiating participant role

This section presents a microethnographic look at how Muñoz and her students negotiated an interactional order in her classroom that elevated the status of Spanish and Spanish speakers and that positioned students as agents who direct their own learning. The activity that I videotaped, transcribed, and analyzed took place in February 1997 at a relatively early stage in the telenovela project's development. To date, each of the students had written his/her own premise for a telenovela, which all of the students read. The students selected the premise that Aida had written for *Amor Imposible* as the best, and they organized into groups to collaborate in the writing of individual scenes. At this stage, Aida and Muñoz were co-directors, and the members of the working groups were sitting together as they wrote and storyboarded their scenes. If anyone had questions or needed assistance, they were encouraged to ask either Aida or Muñoz for help.

Although the finished telenovela was to be in Spanish, students were allowed to work through either Spanish or English or both in whatever ways worked best for their group. In this way, the norms of interaction that guided language use within the classroom were distinct from the ideal TWI policy that maintained that Spanish and English should be separated for instructional purposes. The use of either or both languages, however, was consistent with the norms of interaction that guide how languages are used naturally in this bilingual community, and they allowed students to draw on their strengths as they worked together to reach their goals. These norms also enabled the English-speaking students in the class who had previously been educated entirely in English to participate more actively in the production of the telenovela.

I have divided my presentation here into three major parts. First I introduce the students. Then I demonstrate how the students worked with Muñoz to negotiate their understanding of their participant roles relative to each other. I conclude my analysis by focusing on one of the "Spanish-dominant" students to illustrate how the group's switch from English to Spanish functioned to position this student as a legitimate participant and Spanish as a legitimate language in this classroom.

Who are the students

My analysis focuses on Muñoz's interaction with one group of four 8th grade students-Clarisa, María, Miguel, and Eduardo. Although this group was more linguistically heterogeneous than others, I selected them because the variation in their migration histories and language expertise was representative of the kinds of diversity that I found throughout the school and community.

Clarisa is Puerto Rican, was born in Philadelphia, and her teachers describe her as "English dominant." According to Muñoz, Clarisa "refused" to speak Spanish at the beginning of the year but began to speak much more Spanish as the year progressed because she realized a need and a desire to communicate with the "Spanish-dominant" students in her class. At the beginning of the school year, Clarisa told me that she could not speak Spanish very well and that although she did not really like to speak Spanish, she could understand some Spanish. While she said that English was the language that was used most often at home, sometimes her mom or other relatives spoke to her in Spanish.

María is also Puerto Rican and was born in Philadelphia. María was considered bilingual by the teachers, and although she had considerable expertise in spoken Spanish and English, her writing in Spanish was much weaker than her writing in English. María told me that she spoke both Spanish and English at home and was equally comfortable speaking in either language.

Miguel is also Puerto Rican, but he was born in Puerto Rico and migrated to Philadelphia from the island at the beginning of the school year. Miguel was described by the teachers as "Spanish dominant," and he could read and write in Spanish. Although Miguel seemed to be motivated to learn English, he used Spanish almost all of the time at school. At the time of the classroom activity analyzed here, neither he nor the teachers believed that he could understand or speak very much English.

Eduardo is Dominican. He was born and raised in the Dominican Republic and at the time of this activity, Eduardo had only lived in Philadelphia for about three weeks. Eduardo was described by the teachers as a monolingual Spanish speaker at this point in time, and he told me (in Spanish) that he could not understand any English at all. In fact, from the time that Eduardo arrived at school until the time of this activity, I never heard him speak any English and I rarely observed him interacting with the other students in the class in Spanish. However, I did hear him begin to speak English and interact with other students in both languages more and more as the year progressed.

Redefining participant roles in the classroom

This section presents an analysis of four consecutive speech events to illustrate the students' efforts to negotiate their participant roles relative to each other, to the assignment, and to Muñoz (see Hymes 1974 for discussion of speech events). The first speech event demonstrates how the students initiate interaction with the teacher to request her help; the second speech event demonstrates the teacher's response to the students' request for help; and the third speech event demonstrates how the students negatively evaluate the teacher's response to their request for help. It is important to emphasize that these three speech actions, INITIATE-RESPOND-EVALUATE, are the three basic units of the sequence that is most commonly found in mainstream U.S. classes (see, for example, Cazden 1988). However, in the case presented here, it is the students and not the teacher who have the right to initiate interaction with the teacher and to evaluate the teacher's response. These participant roles reflect an alternative to the power arrangement that is found in mainstream U.S. classes, one in which the students have been allocated more power. The fourth speech event then demonstrates how the students and teacher determine what kind of help the students need, which then enables them to continue to work independently of the teacher to accomplish their goals.

Initiating interaction with the teacher

In the following excerpt (lines 1–27 on the original transcript), the students are working together to write their scene for the telenovela, they realize they are stuck, and they request the teacher's assistance. My analysis focuses on the ways that they use Spanish and English among themselves and on the participant roles that they construct for themselves and each other. Through their interactional moves in the beginning stages of this classroom activity, students construct a hierarchical role relationship among themselves and the languages used, with María positioned as the clear leader and English as the dominant language. Clarisa and Miguel both play subordinate roles, although in very different ways, and Eduardo is noticeably silent. I use bold face in the transcript to highlight the use of Spanish, and translate the Spanish to English in parentheses. I also use a series of dots (. . .) to indicate pauses.

1	María:	**dale dale dale dale** (go go go go)
2	Clarisa:	**pero que escribo** (but what do I write)
3	María:	ok we first have
4		one day . . . Mateo . . . went to . . . Maritza . . . Azucena (laugh)

5	Clarisa:	Azucena (laugh)
6	María:	Marisol
7	Clarisa:	to make another plan (reading)
8	María:	to make another plan
9		to break up Ana and Pablo
10	Clarisa:	mmm
11		(LONG PAUSE)
12	María:	uh uh uh uh I . . . I did this one
13		now you do another one
14		I'm the one that made that one up
15		(LONG PAUSE)
16		I said . . . that Mateo went to the . . . uh
17	Miguel:	(to María) **mira** (look)
18	María:	(to Clarisa) see I got you
19		(to Miguel as she looks at his drawing) yeah . . . a close up
20	Clarisa:	(to Miguel) really nice . . . really funny
21		(PAUSE)
22		(to Miguel) now the window's not going to show so
23	María:	no she didn't go there (laugh)
24	Miguel:	what
25		(PAUSE)
26	Clarisa:	**ay dios** . . . what are we doing
27	María:	miss (calls Muñoz)

I begin my discussion with the students' participant roles relative to each other, and I continue with a few comments about their use of Spanish and English.

We can see in this activity how María takes on the role of leader and how that speaking position is ratified in a variety of ways by the other students. For example, María initiates their work on their scene with her utterance **dale dale dale dale** (go, go, go, go) in line 1. The language that she uses is Spanish, which is the language that the finished telenovela is to be broadcast in. Consistent with the "follow-the-leader" type of codeswitching that Zentella (1997) documents as prevalent in New York Puerto Rican (NYPR) language use, Clarisa follows María's use of Spanish (although she claims to speak very little Spanish and not to like speaking in Spanish) with her utterance **pero que escribo** (but what do I write) in line 2. Clarisa takes up María's positioning of herself as leader with the authority to tell Clarisa what she should write next. María continues to take on the role of leader in the interaction by initiating their joint reading aloud of what they have written so far (lines 3-9). Then after Clarisa pauses in lines 10 and 11, María changes her footing (Goffman 1981) toward Clarisa and toward the text they had been creating through her utterance *uh uh uh uh I. ...I did this one now you do another one* (lines 12-13). María has changed from what we are writing, as reflected in her pronominal reference in line 3, to what *I* and *you* are writing in lines 12-16. She is no longer aligned with Clarisa in this activity. I return to the subject of Clarisa and María's alignment below.

Miguel also ratifies María's role as leader as he draws her attention to the storyboard that he has been drawing for their scene with his utterance *mira* (look) in line 17. He uses Spanish, which is his dominant language and is consistent with the language that he generally uses in class. María ratifies Miguel's contribution with her utterance yeah . . . *a close up* in line 18, and Clarisa follows María's lead in line 20 *really nice . . . really funny.* After a brief pause, first Clarisa (line 20) and then María (line 23) suggest that the window that he had drawn would not be visible on film. Notice that although Miguel initiated their interaction in Spanish, both María and Clarisa use English in their response, the language that they had been speaking for the majority of this activity. Given that it is much more common for Puerto Rican students to switch languages according to their understanding of participants' expertise in each language, it is somewhat surprising that neither María nor Clarisa responds to Miguel in Spanish.

Not only has Miguel attempted to include himself in the group's interaction, this brief exchange with Miguel has also functioned to reposition Clarisa and María in alignment with each other, and both as legitimate evaluators of Miguel's work. For example, Clarisa in line 22 tells Miguel *now the window's not going to show,* which María ratifies with her utterance *no she didn't go there* in line 23. Both María and Clarisa talk to Miguel in English, demonstrating either their assumption that he understands English or their lack of concern for whether he understands or not. Miguel's utterance in line 24 *what* suggests that he may not have understood what Clarisa and María have said to him about his drawing. However, none of them discuss this point any further at this time. We can see that at this point in the activity, Clarisa and María have authority over Miguel, writing has authority over drawing or storyboarding, and English is the dominant language of communication in this group.

Clarisa expresses her confusion about their work in her utterance *ay díos* (oh god) *what are we doing* (line 26). María again demonstrates her role as leader in the small group interaction by calling Muñoz to help them.

Notice, however, how the participation framework (Goffman 1981) changes as a result of María's request:

27   María: miss (calls Muñoz)

28   we need your help . . . look

29   this is what we got written

30   we don't got . . . we don't know what to do

María continues to use English to request the teacher's help, despite the fact that it is not the language that is being used most often throughout the classroom as the other groups work together on their scenes, nor is it the language that the finished telenovela is to be written in. María represents the students as a collective with the pronoun *we* (line 28), although it is not exactly clear who is included in this reference (i.e., is Miguel or Eduardo included?). Notice, however, that this is an exclusive we, and that Muñoz is not included in this pronominal reference. Through her interactional work, María positions the students' as in *need* of the teacher's *help* in order for them to continue with their work, which in turn positions the teacher as the expert, or the one who can provide the help that the students need. The norms of interaction that constitute this activity are consistent with those of cooperative learning classrooms in which students are encouraged to initiate interactions with the teacher, but they are less common in traditional teacher-centered classrooms in which the teacher more often initiates the interactional routines. This kind of interaction was typical in many of the activities that Muñoz organized in her classes, especially in the telenovela project.

Responding to the students' request

The preferred response to a request for help is help (see Sacks, Schegloff, and Jefferson 1974 for discussion of preference relations and turn-taking). The next excerpt (lines 31-65 of the original transcript), in which Muñoz moves to the group's table and begins to look at their written work (as María had directed her to do-line 29 above), can be understood at this point as "help." In a student-centered classroom activity like this, the teacher's goal is not to tell the students exactly what to do but rather to facilitate their efforts to understand what they need to do next and to provide them with the tools necessary to accomplish the task. In this way, the teacher's "help" ideally enables the students to take responsibility for and direct their own learning. As we see below, Muñoz has assessed the students' strengths in this activity (they know how to TELL a story), and she has assessed what they need to understand in order to accomplish the task without her guidance (they need to know how to SHOW a story to make a video). I begin by focusing on Miguel, in particular on the ways that he bids for the right to be a legitimate participant in this activity as well as the ways in which his participation is not ratified by the teacher. I then briefly discuss the teacher's interactional work to involve all of the students in their own learning.

31	Muñoz:	ok
32		(reading their script)
33		ok this sounds really *go:od* (her emphasis)
34		if I was writing a *bo:ok* (her emphasis)
35	Clarisa:	(LAUGH)
36	María:	(LAUGH)
37	Miguel:	(LAUGH)
38	Muñoz:	but since it's a *movie* (her emphasis)
39		how're we going to *show* that (her emphasis)
40		how're we going to show that on video
41	Clarisa:	it will look like . . . just the way
42	Muñoz:	well see you don't want
43		I don't want you to tell me that one day Mateo went to Maritza
44		ok . . . to make another match
45		no no no
46		I want you to *show* me . . . . . . where (her emphasis)
47	Clarisa:	well . . . we are writing first . . . what is going to happen
48	Miguel:	the house (holds up storyboard)
49	Muñoz:	well yeah . . . but you have to have an . . . ok and and and
50		exactly *how* is it going to happen (her emphasis)
51		what is your scene exactly
52		what is it that you're supposed to be writing
53	Clarisa:	**el bochinche** (the gossip)
54	Muñoz:	**el bochinche**
55		see that's the juicy part
56	Miguel:	(LAUGH)
57	María:	(SMILE)
58	Muñoz:	yeah this should be fun
59		ok how are you going to make this **bochinche** happen

60	exactly how are we going to
61	what are they going to say
62	what is he going to say
63	I mean
64	you know what I mean?
65	how are they going to accomplish this **bochinche**

Now that Muñoz has joined the group, the role relationships within the group change. Muñoz is clearly the leader in this speech activity. Notice that although María initiated the interaction with her, Muñoz directs all of her interactional work toward Clarisa. In fact, Muñoz's back is to María as she leans over the text that Clarisa has in front of her. Clarisa takes on the role of negotiator with the teacher, perhaps because of the authority attributed to the written text in this activity (as in many school activities) and the fact that Clarisa is acting as "scribe" for the group.

Consistent with the follow-the-leader code choice that is prevalent in this classroom and throughout the school and community, Muñoz follows María's lead and uses English at this point in her interaction with Clarisa (English is also Clarisa's preferred language). In line 37, Miguel demonstrates his involvement in the activity by laughing at Muñoz's humorous evaluation of their written work. While it is not clear whether he understands what Muñoz has said, he has clearly aligned himself with Clarisa's and María's laughter in lines 35 and 36.

With lines 31 to 46, Muñoz negatively evaluates the students' work based on her assessment that they are TELLING her a story and not SHOWING her a story, which is what she needs them to do in order to make a video. Through her interactional work, Muñoz has transformed the participant roles within this small group in a way that makes them similar to those that characterize more traditional classroom interaction, including the tripartite sequence Initiation-Response-Evaluation discussed above. Muñoz's utterance in line 46 *I want you to show me . . . where* is the first part of this sequence, and it initiates the interaction. Clarisa in line 47 responds with *well . . . we are writing first . . . what is going to happen,* and Miguel continues to respond with his utterance in line 48 *the house.* Clarisa chooses to use the pronoun *we* in her response, although it is not clear who the referents are (i.e., is Miguel included as part of this group?). Miguel begins to demonstrate his involvement in their joint construction of meaning (which has been all in English, a language that he supposedly does not speak or understand very well) with his utterance and his nonverbal indexing of the storyboard that he is drawing. Notice here that this is the first time that any of the students have begun to respond to Muñoz's request that the students SHOW her their story, although she does not take up Miguel's visual contribution at this point in the interaction.

Muñoz's utterances from lines 49 to 52 can be understood as the evaluation of Clarisa's (and Miguel's?) response to her initiation of this tripartite sequence. She begins by positively evaluating their responses with her utterance in line 49 *well yeah*. Although she has ratified their written text and maybe Miguel's drawing, Muñoz's use of the contrastive connective *but* after the pause begins to demonstrate her negative evaluation of this response. Muñoz interrupts herself and switches strategies. She again ratifies their work with her utterance ok. Then in lines 50-52, rather than repeat her request that students SHOW her what they are doing, Muñoz asks for clarification of their scene. Line 51 *what is your scene exactly* could look like a request for information. This on the one hand positions the students as experts who have information. Muñoz's earlier negative evaluation of their work, however, restricts the possibility that this request for information will be taken up as an effort to position them as experts. Given that Muñoz continues to ask the students *what is your scene exactly* (line 51) and *what is it that you're supposed to be writing* (line 52), we can see that she has negatively evaluated what the students have written so far.

Muñoz's interactional move, however, does function to begin to construct a shared understanding of their work. Clarisa hesitates in her response in line 53, **el bochinche**, and she utters this response in a very soft voice and into her hand. Her change of voice and body posture is not due to her not knowing the answer because she does. Her change in stance suggests her awareness of the evaluative force of all of Muñoz's utterances as either right or wrong. In line 54 Muñoz repeats Clarisa's response **el bochinche** and thus ratifies this response as a correct answer. Muñoz continues in line 54 with a humorous contribution *see that's the juicy part*, which invites the students to again become involved in their work, which will enable them to get the help that they need to complete their scene. They laugh (again we see that Miguel is involved in this English-only exchange and clearly aligned with Clarisa and María) and Muñoz continues in line 58 *yeah this should be fun*.

This interactional work seems to be Muñoz's attempt to change the participation framework back to a collaborative we. She is trying to position herself as a facilitator of this process and not as an evaluator of their work, which is what had been happening. Further evidence of this involvement strategy can be seen in Muñoz's change of pronoun from *you* in line 59 *ok how are you going to make this* **bochinche** *happen* to *we* in line 60 *exactly how are we going to*. She continues to try to involve the students with a series of information questions (*what are they going to say*, line 61, and *what is he going to say*, line 62) and then confirmation checks (*you know what I mean?* line 64) and then a near repetition of her earlier question in line 65 *how are they going to accomplish this* **bochinche**. Note, however, that Muñoz has chosen the pronoun *they* here which refers to the characters in their scene. With this pronoun choice, she has placed the responsibility for "accomplishing the bochinche" not on the students and not on the teacher, but on the characters, which is much less face-threatening to the students.

Evaluating the teacher's response

Clarisa's interactional work in the next excerpt (lines 66-77) changes the participation framework of this activity dramatically. Recall that María initiated the interaction with Muñoz to request help (lines 27-30), and that Muñoz has been trying to respond to that request ever since (lines 31-65). Line 66 marks the beginning of Clarisa's negative evaluation of Muñoz's response, which she refuses because it positions the students as not having done their work well. Notice how Clarisa assumes the role of leader in this speech activity, and through her interactional work reconstructs the discourse. Miguel provides important supportive work in this exchange, and both María and Eduardo are silent. Once the students have reconstructed the discourse in a way that positions them as doing a good job but in need of help, they are in a position to negotiate the nature of the help that they needed.

66	Clarisa:	but I'm I'm doing it like this right
67		I write the means part and then in there I write what they're saying
68	Muñoz:	aaaah
69	Clarisa:	you understand what I'm trying to say
70	Muñoz:	oooh I understand yes I do
71	Clarisa:	because in the other part **tambien** (also) I wrote the same thing
72		now when he finishes I'll write in what they're saying
73	Muñoz:	oooh
74	Miguel:	(shows storyboard) miss the close up **verdad?** (true)
75	Clarisa:	you understand what I mean
76	Muñoz:	oh ok ok all right all right
77		then you guys are doing fine

Since the preferred response to a question is an answer, we would expect Clarisa or one of the students to have answered Muñoz's question *how are they going to accomplish this **bochinche*** (line 65). Because dispreferred responses are potentially face-threatening, they are generally accompanied by some kind of face-saving politeness strategies (e.g., an explanation for why the preferred response was not provided; see Brown and Levinson 1987, for discussion of politeness strategies), which tends to make dispreferred responses longer than preferred responses. Line 66 is not an answer to Muñoz's question. Instead, Clarisa begins her utterance with an explanation of how she is doing the job *but I'm I'm doing it like this right* (line 66) and *I write the means part and then in there I write what they're saying* (line 67). Clarisa's utterance positions the teacher not as the expert, nor as the facilitator, but as someone who does not understand how Clarisa is doing the job.

Clarisa's interactional move has now positioned Clarisa and not Muñoz (or María) as the leader in this activity. Muñoz now follows Clarisa; her supportive backchanneling *aaaah* (line 68) and her minimal responses *oooh I understand yes I do* (line 70) to Clarisa's confirmation check *you understand what I'm trying to say* (line 69) demonstrate the teacher's alignment with this new construction of how the students are doing their work. In addition, Muñoz's minimal responses do not give her the floor. Clarisa continues to hold the floor in line 71 as she provides further explanation of how the students are working together to write their scene. In line 72, *now when he finishes I'll write in what they're saying* we see Clarisa's first reference to Miguel. Again we see Miguel's clear involvement in this all-English interaction. That he has been paying attention and understanding the exchange between Muñoz and Clarisa is evidenced through his support of Clarisa's proposition in line 74. That is, just as Clarisa makes reference to what he is doing, Miguel directs Muñoz's attention to the storyboard he is drawing with his utterance in line 74 *miss the close up **verdad***. His use of English clearly aligns him with the group and demonstrates his involvement. For the first time, we see that Miguel's participation is considered legitimate, this time by Clarisa, who is now taking on the leadership role in the interaction.

Again in line 75 Clarisa checks Muñoz's comprehension with her utterance *you understand what I mean*. It is interesting that the student is checking the teacher's comprehension because in more traditional teacher-fronted classrooms, it is the teacher and not the student who checks comprehension. In this activity, there is some sharing of the responsibility to check comprehension. Muñoz affirms in line 76 that she comprehends what the group is doing with her utterances *oh ok ok all right all right*. Her repetition demonstrates her involvement in what Clarisa is saying. Since Muñoz is the teacher, and her comments have considerable evaluatory force (especially given her earlier negative evaluation of the group's work), this utterance also functions as a positive evaluation of the group's work. She makes this positive evaluation explicit with line 77 *then you guys are doing fine*.

Negotiating what the students need

In the following excerpt (lines 78–91), Muñoz initiates the interaction, but the frame for this negotiation is very different (see Tannen 1993 for discussion of framing in discourse). The group has negotiated an understanding that the students are doing a good job but are stuck and need some help. Now they can negotiate the exact nature of that help.

78	Muñoz:	where are you stuck
79	Clarisa:	right there
80		we don't know what's going to happen next
81		like we don't know
82	Muñoz:	what has happened so far
83		according to your scene what has already happened
84	Clarisa:	**pues** (well)
85	Muñoz:	what am I going to see
86		tell me
87		what am I seeing
88	Clarisa:	**pues** (well) Cristina and Mateo are trying to break up
89	Muñoz:	no no no
90		tell me what I'm going to see
91		tell me what I'm going to see

Given that María had called Muñoz over to the group and had requested her help, and given that she had said in line 30 *we don't know what to do now*, Muñoz can assume that they are not simply doing fine. In line 78 Muñoz asks the students directly *where are you stuck*. Clarisa responds directly to Muñoz's question in line 79 *right there* and explains the group's problem in lines 80 and 81 *we don't know what's going to happen next like we don't know*.

In her role as facilitator, and not evaluator, Muñoz ideally builds on her students' strengths, and she ideally can assess their needs so she can help them reach their academic goals, in this case to finish writing their scene. Muñoz changes strategies here. Rather than asking the students what comes next to make the **bochinche** happen (as she had done in lines 59-65), she focuses on what the students have already done. In lines 82 and 83, she asks the students *what has happened so far according to your scene what has already happened*. Given that the students have written their scene, they must know the answer to this question. In this way, Muñoz positions the students as the experts on their work. Clarisa begins to answer in line 84 with her utterance **pues**. Muñoz quickly interrupts and repeats her earlier question, *what am I going to see tell me what am I seeing* (lines 85-87). She has successfully refused the position as evaluator and taken up the position as facilitator through her involvement strategies. Just as Clarisa begins to TELL Muñoz what is happening in the story **pues** *Cristina and Mateo are trying to break up* (line 88), Muñoz repeats her negative evaluation no no no (line 89) again asks the students to SHOW her not TELL her in lines 90 and 91 *tell me what I'm going to see . . . . tell me what I'm going to see.*

Legitimating Miguel, legitimating Spanish

The next excerpt (lines 92-118) is initiated by Miguel, and it marks a radical change in participation framework as the students and teacher work through Spanish and use the storyboard that Miguel has been drawing (rather than the written text that they had been using) to arrive at an understanding of what the students are to do next. Although I do not analyze this rather lengthy excerpt in detail, I present it in its entirety so that I do not break up the continuity of this classroom activity.

92	Miguel:	**ellos están hablando** (they are talking)
93	Clarisa:	**sí** (yes)
94	Muñoz:	**quiénes están hablando** (who is talking)
95	Clarisa:	**Cristina y su hermano** (Cristina and her brother)
96	Muñoz:	**cómo se llama él** (what is his name)
97	Clarisa:	**Mateo** (Mateo)
98	Muñoz:	**Mateo** (Mateo)
99		**Cristina y Mateo están hablando** (Cristina and Mateo are talking)
100		**están hablando en en en una una sala** (they are talking in in in a a living room)
101	Miguel:	yeah
102	Muñoz:	**es una sala aparentemente ok** (it's a living room apparently)
103		**están hablando** (they are talking)
104		**de que están hablando** (what are they talking about)

105		**que tienen que destruir a alguien y dadadadada** (that they have to destroy someone and dadadadada)
106	Clarisa:	**uhhuh**
107	Muñoz:	**ok y esto lo vas a escribir despues verdad?** (ok and you're going to write this later, true?)
108	Clarisa:	**uhhum**
109	Muñoz:	**(?) ahora voy para allá dáme un minuto** (now I'll go there give me a minute-to students who called to her from across the class)
110		**um y despues que ellos hablan de como va a suce** (um `and after they talk about how it is going to happ)
111		**de lo que van a** (about how they are going to)
112		**que es lo que ellos están diciendo** (what is it that they are saying)
113	Clarisa:	**pues despues de eso** (well after that)
114		**tú vas a ver a uno por un lado y la otra por otro lado** (you are going to see one on one side and the other on the other side)
115	Muñoz:	**ok porque ahora se van a poner su plan en efectivo** (ok because now they are going to put their plan into action)
116	Clarisa:	**sí** (yes) **sí** (yes)
117		**uno va para la casa de Cristina y la otra** (one is going to Cristina's house and the other)
118	Muñoz:	**eso es ok ok ok** (that's it ok ok)

With his utterance in line 92 ***ellos están hablando*** *(they are talking)*, Miguel begins a new speech activity. His utterance, in Spanish (his dominant language) is an answer to Muñoz's question, *tell me what I'm going to see.* Prior to this exchange, Miguel had only provided one or two verbal contributions to their talk. Here Miguel positions himself as a legitimate participant in the activity who is actively involved in writing their scene. He evidences this participation in a variety of ways. First, he chooses to use Spanish, his dominant language, to make his contribution. That Spanish is a legitimate language for instructional purposes is demonstrated because Clarisa and Muñoz both continue in Spanish. As mentioned above, this pattern of language use, where interlocutors switch languages and follow each other's lead, is prevalent throughout the school and community. Clarisa ratifies Miguel's contribution with her utterance ***sí*** in line 93. Muñoz asks a clarification question in line 94 ***quiénes están hablando*** *(who is talking)*, and Clarisa, not Miguel, answers.

Notice that Clarisa continues to negotiate meaning with Muñoz throughout the rest of the activity in Spanish and not English. Recall that at the beginning of the year, Clarisa described herself as monolingual in English, and she had told me that she could understand some Spanish because her family sometimes spoke Spanish at home but that she only spoke English. We see through this activity a concrete example of how the TWI program gives English-dominant students the opportunity to acquire Spanish. The fact that the languages are not entirely separated for instructional purposes, but that students are free to draw on either Spanish or English or both to accomplish their academic goals, seems to contribute to this outcome.

As we can see, the students and teacher draw on the wide range of expertise in spoken and written Spanish and English in a variety of ways, depending on students' strengths, interests, and needs. In this case, Miguel uses his stronger language, Spanish, to help all of the students construct a collective understanding of what they need to do next in their scene. Clarisa uses her stronger language, English, to negotiate with María about the scene they are writing. Both use English for writing because their writing is stronger in English than in Spanish. In this way, the stronger language provides a foundation for the development of expertise in other areas (in this case development of video literacy for all of them, writing in Spanish for María and Clarisa, speaking in Spanish for Clarisa and speaking and writing in English for Miguel).

It is important to emphasize that Miguel has directed Muñoz's attention away from the written text that Clarisa (and María) had been writing and to his storyboard where he is SHOWING not TELLING what is happening in their scene. That Muñoz is drawing on information from the storyboard is apparent in her utterance in line 102 **es una sala aparentemente** *(it's a living room apparently)*, which Miguel ratifies. Miguel is able to use his drawing to demonstrate his active involvement in their scene, and this visual storyboard provides an important link to the group's development of video literacy.

In lines 113 and 114 ***pues despues de eso tú vas a ver a uno por un lado y la otra por otro lado*** *(well after that you are going to see on one side and the other on the other side)*, Clarisa provides an answer to Muñoz's request that the students SHOW her, not TELL her, what happens next in their scene. We have seen Muñoz repeatedly ask for this information, beginning in lines 39 and 40 *how're we going to show that, how're we going to show that on video*, then in line 46 *I want you to show me . . . where*, again in lines 85-87 *what am I going to see, tell me, what am I seeing*, and in lines 90 and 91, *tell me what I'm going to see, tell me what I'm going to see*. Muñoz and the students have done a considerable amount of interactional work in order to negotiate what the audience will see next in their scene.

This analysis has demonstrated how Muñoz positions the students to position themselves as agents who are responsible for their own learning, both as individuals and as a collective. Muñoz has drawn on her students' strengths, for example on their knowledge of the telenovela genre as well as on their interest in this genre. She has organized the students into heterogeneous working groups in which individual students can draw on their strengths in spoken and written Spanish and/or English, as well as on their artistic talents, as a means of facilitating their development of video literacy, which is one of the academic goals of the TV/Communications Team. When the students asked for help, the teacher did not tell them exactly what to do, nor did she do their work for them. Rather, she struggled to understand the exact nature of their problem, and she worked with them so that they could provide themselves the help that they needed so they could move forward in their work without her.

We have seen also how this activity helps the teacher reach the goals of the TWI program. That is, students are working with each other through two languages to achieve academically through both languages. Although the literature on TWI suggests that languages be kept separate for content-area instruction, we have seen how the teacher and students use both languages strategically to draw on their strengths in both languages as they work toward their academic goals. This example provides a close look at how the teacher manages some of the linguistic diversity she finds in her classes as a resource in her efforts to reach her goals.

Finally, we have seen how the interactional order that the students and teacher create in this classroom becomes a space at school in which Spanish and Spanish speakers are seen as legitimate. Although what is more typical at this school is language prejudice against Spanish and Spanish speakers, the telenovela project, as well as other projects like it that promote the use of oral and written Spanish across a wider range of genres, offers encouragement that educators can construct alternative discourses that provide more equitable educational opportunities to Spanish speakers than have been traditionally available to them in U.S. public schools.

A need for appropriate policies and programs

Although the two-way immersion (TWI) policy and bilingual educators at PS 17 had begun to make ideological space for bilingualism and biliteracy development for their English-speaking and Spanish-speaking students, there was little room for implementation. In order for TWI programs to realize their goals for their target populations, they must last at least five years, and they are most effective when they begin in the early elementary grades (Cloud, Genesee and Hamayan 2000; Lindholm 1990; Lindholm-Leary 2001). The PS 17 TWI program began when students were in 6th grade, and it only lasted for three years while students were in middle school. If the student had participated in a bilingual elementary school program that promoted bilingualism and biliteracy development, and that provided content-area instruction through Spanish at each grade level, the student could be expected to have acquired the language and literacies they needed to read and write to learn in Spanish. However, if the student had been educated through the all-English academic mainstream during their elementary school years, they would not have had the opportunity to develop the expertise in academic Spanish that they would need to participate and achieve in content-area instruction through Spanish. For this reason, the PS 17 educators decided to target only English language learners and English-speaking Latino students who had expertise in Spanish and motivation to continue to learn through Spanish, and their program became a one-way developmental bilingual program for middle school Spanish-speaking students.

The example of how the PS 17 educators struggled to interpret and implement the dual language policy that was handed down to them from above highlights several important points. First, it is critical for policymakers and program developers to look closely at their school and sociolinguistic context to determine if a particular type of language education is appropriate for that context. In the PS 17 case, it simply is not pedagogically sound for monolingual English speakers to begin a TWI program in middle school that only lasts for three years. Second, this chapter suggests the need to involve the teachers and administrators who are responsible for implementing a new bilingual program in the development of that program. The teachers and administrators who work together every day at school create their educational context through their programs and practices, and they have the potential to change that context. If teachers and administrators cannot be involved in planning the program, at the very least they need to be involved in intensive professional development prior to and throughout implementation to ensure that they have a coherent understanding of the goals of the program and the means to achieve those goals. Both of these points are taken up in detail in Part IV.

Part IV

Dual language planning for social change on the local level

Part IV of this book draws on our understanding of how individual teachers in individual classrooms translate language education policies and programs into practices that build on community bilingualism, and here we move into the larger school and school district contexts. Our focus in these chapters is on the School District of Philadelphia (SDP), which is the fifth largest school district in the United States. The SDP has a linguistically, culturally, and socioeconomically diverse student population, and the English language learners (ELLs) and heritage language speakers who live in Philadelphia bring a tremendous amount of linguistic and cultural expertise with them to school. Furthermore, the multilingual communities in which these students live are rich in linguistic and cultural resources that educators can readily build on.

The chapters in this concluding part of the book describe how networks of educators, from across the levels of institutional authority in the SDP and representing the dominant language groups of the multilingual communities throughout the city, are working to promote bilingualism in ways that make sense on the local school and community levels. These educators reject the assumption that ELLs should assimilate to monolingualism in English, and they reject the assumption that English speakers have no need for languages other than English. The programs and policies that are described in this part of the book provide evidence of dual language planning for social change on the local level.

The five chapters in this part of the book pull together the ideas developed in the preceding chapters, and they describe concrete programs and policies that promote bilingualism to the greatest degree possible for the target populations. These initiatives are funded largely through a five-year Title VII bilingual education systemwide grant known as the

Bilingual Education Enhancement in Philadelphia Project that the SDP was awarded in November 2000, and they are at an early stage of development at the time of this writing. A centerpiece of the Title VII grant is the development of dual language programs in elementary schools that serve the major multilingual communities in the city, and I was hired as the lead consultant for the dual language initiative. This introduction to Part IV begins by identifying the students and communities that the dual language initiative targets. Then I discuss important aspects of the larger SDP context that influence the dual language initiative, including the kinds of educational restructuring that the SDP has experienced throughout the Title VII grant period as well as the state of bilingual and English as a second language (ESL) education in the SDP over time. Finally, I review the main ideas that have been forwarded throughout the book and preview each of the chapters in Part IV.

Recall from chapter 3 that dual language programs provide content-area instruction through two languages, and they promote bilingualism, biliteracy development, and academic achievement in both languages for their target populations. But who are the target populations in the SDP? According to SDP data for the academic year that the Title VII grant was written (1999-2000), there were approximately 203,000 students who attended SDP schools. Sixty-three percent of the SDP students were African American, 20 percent were Caucasian, 12 percent were Latino, and 5 percent were Asian. Approximately 10 percent of the SDP students did not speak English as their first language, and more than seventy languages were represented throughout the district. In 2000 over 10,000 SDP students were receiving English for speakers of other languages (ESOL) instruction and/or bilingual program support services, and according to educators who work in the SDP today, this number is growing dramatically. While almost 50 percent of these ELLs are Spanish speaking, the SDP also serves large populations of Khmer, Vietnamese, Chinese, and Russian speakers and increasing numbers of students from Sudan, Somalia, and other African countries.

Until the spring of 2003, the Office of Language Equity Issues (OLEI) was the office that had the primary responsibility for ensuring that all ELLs in the SDP have access to equal educational opportunities, and OLEI staff members wrote and have directed the Title VII grant. The Office of Language Equity Issues chose the elementary schools that were to begin dual language programs based on the demographics in the SDP, and the ten target schools are located in the major multilingual communities in Philadelphia. Six of the original target schools are located in the predominantly Puerto Rican community in North Philadelphia that was the focus of Parts II and III of this book, and these dual language programs use

Spanish and English for instructional purposes. The Title VII grant also supports the development of a Russian program in a school in Northeast Philadelphia, a Mandarin program in a school in one neighborhood in South Philadelphia, a Khmer program in a school in another neighborhood in South Philadelphia, and a Vietnamese program in a school in Southeast Philadelphia. The target language that was chosen for each of these elementary school programs is the language spoken by the majority of the ELLs at the target school, and it is the dominant language other than English used in the local community.

It is important to emphasize that educational initiatives do not function in isolation, and the larger contexts in the SDP influence the dual language initiative in important ways. Like many school districts in the United States today, the SDP has been the focus of numerous educational restructuring and reform initiatives over the last decade. For example, in 1994 the SDP embarked on the *Children Achieving* reform agenda, and one part of that reform involved the restructuring of the school district into one central administration, which is called "downtown" by insiders, and twenty-two intermediate levels of school district administration that were called "clusters." A cluster was organized around the feeder patterns in the neighborhood and was defined as one high school and its feeder elementary and middle schools. Each cluster was led by a "cluster leader" who directed this regional level of institutional authority. This intermediate level was to mediate between the central administration's educational policies and mandates on the one hand and the local needs of students, teachers, school-based administrators, and community-based organizations on the other.

The Title VII grant that the SDP was awarded in November 2000 was a cluster-based initiative that was intended to promote the development of at least one dual language program in each cluster throughout the district, and I began my work on the cluster level. However, in the spring of 2001 the cluster system was dismantled and the SDP was reconfigured as eight "academic areas." In most cases, two to three clusters were brought together to form one academic area, and each academic area had an "academic area officer" that oversaw this level of the organizational bureaucracy. In the fall of 2002, the academic area offices became "regional offices" that were led by "regional superintendents." These structural changes on the intermediate level of institutional authority have been accompanied by dramatic changes in personnel, apprehension about the new direction that each new leader and his/her support staff would take, and the need for continual professional development to ensure that the regional leader and his/her administration understand, support, and promote the dual language initiative in the target schools.

In the fall of 2001 the SDP was taken over by the Commonwealth of Pennsylvania, the existing Board of Education was eliminated, and a School Reform Commission (SRC) was appointed by the governor of Pennsylvania and the mayor of Philadelphia to oversee educational reform in the SDP. At the time of this writing, the SRC had opted for a "diverse provider model" in which the forty lowest performing schools were taken over by a range of outside "providers," including universities, for-profit companies, and community-based organizations, and each provider brought their own leaders and organizational structures. Three of the target schools in North Philadelphia were on the list of forty, and the two schools that were taken over by a for-profit company no longer participate in the dual language initiative. The SRC hired a new chief executive officer in the summer of 2002, and every SDP position, process, and product has been under intense scrutiny since that time.

Throughout this turbulent period of educational restructuring, we have seen an ongoing effort to align instructional programs and practices, provide sustained professional development of educators, and account for student performance. As we saw in chapter 9, literacy education has been the focus of a systemwide reform that began in the mid-1990s, and we see increasing efforts to institutionalize a more or less standardized literacy framework and means of assessment. The No Child Left Behind Act of 2001 mandates that all schools and school districts be held accountable for the English language development and academic performance of every ELL, and the SDP is addressing this mandate as part of its ongoing educational restructuring and reform initiatives. What was formerly called the Office of Language Equity Issues (OLEI) is now called the Office of Language and Culture Education (OLCE), and this office is now responsible for the language and culture education of all learners in the SDP, including ELLs; heritage language speakers, and English speakers.

The dual language initiative is also influenced by the larger context of bilingual education and ESL within and across schools throughout the district. The SDP has a long and varied history of bilingual education, and we can find a wide range of bilingual and/or ESL programs and practices across schools that are intended to meet the needs of the linguistically and culturally diverse student population that the SDP serves. The first Spanish-English bilingual program was initiated over thirty years ago in North Philadelphia, and today we can find transitional, one-way developmental bilingual, and two-way immersion programs, as well as sheltered English programs and pull-out ESL classes for ELLs. We can also find confusion and controversy about what bilingual education means, who bilingual programs serve, what the goals of bilingual programs are for their target populations, how bilingual programs are structured, and whether bilingual programs are effective. This confusion and controversy on the local level reflects the confusion and controversy that we see on the state and federal levels in the United States today.

While a few of the district's bilingual education and ESL programs are pedagogically sound and well-implemented, the SDP struggles to provide all of its ELLs with access to equal educational opportunities as mandated by law. The SDP was the target of a class action suit that was brought on behalf of a Cambodian student in 1985 (Y.S. v the School District of Philadelphia), and in 1988 a Remedial Plan was developed that "set forth a proposed program of services and instruction for Asian language minority students of limited English proficiency." The Remedial Plan is also known as the Y.S. Stipulations, and it provides for the following:

1. a new address to the assessment and placement of LEP students in programs of ESOL instruction, regular education, vocational education and special education

2. the development, piloting and use of new organizational models for programs of instruction to LEP students in age appropriate settings

3. the development of criteria for entry, progress through and exit from various levels of ESOL

4. the articulation and definition of the concept of sheltered classes for content area instruction

5. the identification of various program options for students at the secondary school level

6. the design of new measures of program monitoring of attendance and academic progress

7. the description of a newly restructured ESOL standardized curriculum

8. the description of a plan for an instructional support program for LEP students

9. the establishment of procedures, services, and products for improved bilingual communication with students, parents, and community groups

10. the establishment of a comprehensive program of staff training for all levels of personnel who interact with LEP students

11. the restructuring of counseling services for LEP students

12. the review of current personnel practices for recruitment, employment, deployment, and professional development of bilingual staff who are fluent in Asian languages and proposed practices for increasing the number of Asian and/or bilingual instructional and support staff in the School District

13. the development of a plan for systematic research and evaluation of programs of services to LEP students, and

14. the dissemination of the remedial plan to all levels of administration and instruction within the School District of Philadelphia and to interested community persons, organizations, and agencies (Remedial Plan 1988; 1-2)

According to OLCE coordinators, the Y.S. Stipulations have been a driving force in the SDP since 1988, and many programs and practices have been developed to ensure that ELLs have access to equal educational opportunities. However, the OLCE staff members also recognize that, to date, the SDP has not complied with the Remedial Plan to the extent that was originally mandated. The OLCE directors, coordinators, and staff emphasize the need for ongoing monitoring and evaluation of programs and practices for ELLs as a means of informing program and professional development throughout the district. I return to this important point in chapter 11.

Although we see a wide range of bilingual education and ESL programs and practices implemented in schools across the SDP, the directors and coordinators that I have worked with at OLEI and OLCE emphasize their language-as-resource ideological orientation. The director of OLEI expressed this orientation in her response to Linda Chavez's 2001 article in the Philadelphia Inquirer (discussed in chapter 2). She writes,

> Bilingual education, as with any other educational program, is only as effective as its implementation. Strong programs require appropriate resources, such as qualified bilingual teachers, community support, diverse materials, advocacy and expertise. Both English and the home language should be emphasized in instruction.
>
> Bilingualism (or multilingualism) is an asset. Chavez must realize that it is up to the educational communities and their constituencies to make sure the positive potential of this goal is fulfilled by providing and ensuring high quality bilingual programs (Philadelphia Inquirer, July 9 2001).

The language ideology is clear. Languages other than English are resources to be developed. The real challenge lies in the design and implementation of programs and practices that can meet the needs of students and the local communities. The chapters in this part of the book show how particular groups of educators have taken up this challenge in their schools and communities.

The former OLEI director mentions the importance of qualified teachers. We saw in chapter 2 that until the No Child Left Behind Act of 2001 mandated that all teachers who work with ELLs be professionally trained to meet these students' needs, the Commonwealth of Pennsylvania did not require ESL teachers to be certified in TESOL (Teaching English to Speakers of Other Languages), and it did not require bilingual educators to have bilingual certification or endorsement. This has left individual teachers, schools, and the SDP to determine the professional development needs of the educators who work with ELLs, and until recently the SDP alone was responsible for determining ESL and bilingual teachers' credentials. In practice, this has meant that SDP teachers who work with ELLs have a wide range of expertise. While some teachers and schools have embraced the opportunity to pursue professional development, many lack the knowledge and skills they need to promote their students' language and literacy development.

Professional development has been a major focus of what was OLEI and is now OLCE. The Office of Language Equity Issues regularly obtained funding from Title VII for professional development of bilingual and ESL teachers and administrators, and OLCE now obtains additional funding from Title III for all teachers and administrators who work with ELLs. Most of this funding is directed toward long-term sustained professional development of educators rather than one-time or short-term workshops. Throughout the course of my work with the SDP, OLEI/OLCE has participated in joint initiatives with the University of Pennsylvania, LaSalle University, and Temple University. Professors from these universities and/or school district personnel who teach courses on a part-time basis at these universities offer a variety of courses in bilingual education, content-based second-language instruction, materials and methods in ESL, Spanish literacy development, and balanced literacy for ESL and bilingual teachers. I refer to these initiatives in the relevant chapters throughout the book.

As we see throughout the chapters in Part IV, this larger context of educational restructuring in general and of bilingual education in particular interacts with the dual language initiative in a variety of important ways. The programs and practices that the dual language initiative has stimulated are described in detail in these chapters, and they build on the major ideas developed in the preceding chapters. Let's briefly review some of those ideas as a preview to the chapters in this part of the book.

Part I of the book argues that schools and school districts that serve students who live in multilingual communities have a responsibility to promote bilingualism to the greatest degree possible for the target popula-tions. Chapter 1 highlights the importance of challenging the assimilation strategy that has been dominant in the United States since the beginning of the 20th century and emphasizes that English speakers and English lan-guage learners, their families and communities, and the nation overall ben-efit from programs that encourage the development of bilingualism and biliteracy. Chapter 2 reviews federal and local mandates surrounding the education of language learners and maintains that there is space in school districts and schools today for policies and programs that comply with all federal, state, and local mandates and accountability requirements AND that support the maintenance and development of languages other than English. Chapter 3 provides an overview of the types of bilingual, ESL, and world language programs that we find in U.S. schools today and summa-rizes what research tells us about each of these program types. Chapter 4 offers a series of guiding questions that school-based language planning teams can use to examine their local school and sociolinguistic contexts, make decisions about the type(s) of language education that are appropri-ate for that context, and address the challenges that they face as they develop and implement their programs.

A major premise of this book is that schools have the potential to challenge and transform their programs and practices in ways that provide many more opportunities for ELLs, heritage language speakers, and English speakers than have been traditionally available to them in U.S. schools. Educators can choose to work together to develop policies, pro-grams, and practices that build on community bilingualism and that pro-mote educational and social change on the local level. In order for schools to realize this potential, educators must abandon the language-as-problem orientation that has been dominant in U.S. schools over the last century, and they must value the linguistic and cultural expertise that students bring with them to school as resources upon which they can build. Schools that are working to develop a language-as-resource orientation that pro-motes bilingualism and biliteracy development for all students must understand local beliefs about languages and about language teaching and learning so that they can support ideologies that promote bilingualism while they challenge English-only currents. Moreover, schools that reject English-only approaches in favor of dual language programs must provide evidence to stakeholders that well-implemented dual language programs enable ELLs to develop the English language they need and to close the achievement gap.

Part II of this book takes us into the predominantly Puerto Rican community in North Philadelphia to investigate and document the ways that spoken and written Spanish and English are used and evaluated by students at home, school, and in other key contexts in their lives. The ethnographic portrait that I present in chapters 5, 6, and 7 describes and interprets the language ideologies that we hear in conversations, read in site documents, and observe in everyday practices, and explains how these ideologies structure the kinds of opportunities that students, their families, and community members have available to them locally and in the larger society. Moreover, the chapters in Part II provide evidence of the kinds of rich linguistic and cultural resources that we can find in what many simply see as a low-income neighborhood that is filled with poorly performing schools.

Part III of the book illustrates how particular teachers who work in particular schools in North Philadelphia build on the linguistic and cultural expertise that their students bring with them to school as they organize their classroom practices. The three classrooms that are featured in chapters 8, 9, and 10 are in many ways atypical of classrooms that serve ELLs in the SDP because of their clear language-as-resource orientations. While the three case studies were located in different types of bilingual and ESL programs, and the teachers were concerned with translating different language and literacy policies into practice, they all highlight the critical role of teachers in the educational project. However, these teachers are working in isolation and on the margins of the academic mainstream in each of their schools.

The chapters in Part IV demonstrate how educators across the levels of institutional authority in the SDP are working to bring language education from the margins into the academic mainstream in schools that are located in multilingual communities. Chapter 11 describes the recursive nature of language planning, implementation, and policy formulation in the SDP that the Title VII grant stimulated. While chapters 12 and 13 describe dual language planning and implementation projects in schools that serve the predominantly Puerto Rican community in North Philadelphia, chapter 14 highlights community language programs that move beyond the Spanish speaking population to address the language education needs of students living in communities with large numbers of Khmer, Mandarin, Russian, or Vietnamese students. Educational researchers, program developers, policy makers, and practitioners working in other multilingual contexts are encouraged to draw on the insider's descriptive account of language planning, implementation, and policy development that I share in this part of the book to stimulate creative thinking and action in other contexts.

The concluding chapter summarizes the main ideas that school-based language planners working in other multilingual contexts can consider as they plan programs that they believe are appropriate for their students, school, and community, and it highlights the kinds of challenges that language planners, program developers, and practitioners are likely to encounter as they work their way through the dynamic process of language planning and implementation on the local school and/or school district level. The particular programs that educators are developing in target elementary schools in the SDP are not meant to be uncritically reproduced in other schools. Instead, these detailed examples are meant to stimulate ideas about how educators in other contexts can work together to develop pedagogically sound programs and practices, and to formulate coherent policies, that promote bilingualism, biliteracy development, and improved cultural understanding and intergroup relations in ways that make sense in those contexts.

This part of the book clearly illustrates that school districts and schools have choices in the ways they address national, regional, and local mandates, and the choices that educators make have implications for the kinds of students schools produce, and for the kinds of communities and society they envision. Educators working in the target schools featured in this part of the book have chosen to work together to promote bilingualism and biliteracy development to the greatest degree possible for their target populations. School-based dual language planning and policy development initiatives like those that have begun in the SDP can move language education from the margins to the academic mainstream. In this way, language planning can promote educational and social change from the bottom up.

11

Language planning and policy making in the School District of Philadelphia

This chapter illustrates the recursive nature of language planning and policy formulation that is taking place in the School District of Philadelphia (SDP) during a period of extensive educational restructuring and reform. As mentioned in the introduction to Part IV, the SDP was awarded a five-year Title VII bilingual education systemwide grant in November 2000 that supports the development of dual language programs in target elementary schools that are located in the major multilingual communities in Philadelphia, and I was hired as lead consultant for the dual language initiative. Then in the fall of 2002, the newly appointed chief executive officer of the SDP invited the Philadelphia Association of Hispanic School Administrators (PAHSA) to develop a language policy for the SDP, and I was asked to facilitate the language policy formulation process. This chapter is based on my work on these language planning and policy making projects. Although both of these movements are in the early stages of development at the time of this writing, together they provide an excellent context to explore the dynamic, ideological, multidirectional processes involved in language planning and policy making in a large and linguistically, culturally, and socioeconomically diverse urban school district in the United States.

I have divided this chapter into four parts. First, I describe how I worked with target elementary schools throughout the school district to encourage the formation of language planning teams who would embrace the top-down dual language initiative, take ownership of the language planning processes on the local level, and develop language plans that the teams believed were appropriate for their school and community contexts. Then I review the types of language education programs that the different language planning teams are beginning to develop in the target schools. The third part of the chapter describes the language policy formulation process that is currently underway in the SDP to illustrate how it institutionalizes the language education programs that have emerged to date through the dual language initiative, and how it is intended to promote the development of other such programs in the future. I conclude the chapter by explaining how language planning and policy making on the school and school district levels can promote local educational and social change. Perhaps more importantly, I argue that the development of pedagogically sound, well-implemented dual language programs, and coherent language policies that promote bilingualism, can challenge the English-only currents that exist throughout the United States today and contribute to the development of an educational discourse that promotes bilingualism more broadly in this country.

Complementing top-down initiatives with bottom-up planning

The Title VII bilingual education systemwide grant that the School District of Philadelphia (SDP) was awarded in November 2000 is in many ways an example of top-down language planning. In March 2000, then Secretary of Education Richard W. Riley highlighted the effectiveness of two-way immersion (TWI) programs, and he challenged educators in the United States to increase the number of TWI programs to at least one thousand over the following five years. Title VII had been aggressively funding the development of TWI programs in schools and school districts across the country since 1994, and it continued to do so after Secretary Riley's speech. In November 2000 the federal government awarded the SDP a five-year grant to support the development of ten dual language programs in target schools in the major multilingual communities in the city, and the SDP provided financial incentives (e.g., compensation for planning time, materials, professional development of teachers) to those schools. As lead consultant on the dual language initiative, I wanted to complement this top-down language planning initiative with language planning on the local school and community levels. As I emphasized in chapter 4, my work is based on the assumption that the teachers, principal, and community members who work together every day on the local level create their educational context, and these constituents have the potential to collaborate and change that context. This first part of the chapter provides an insider's account of how I worked to promote language planning from the bottom up in the target schools.

The Title VII grant originally targeted ten elementary schools that had large numbers of students from the same language background, and these schools were to develop dual language programs that would use

English and the dominant community language for instructional purposes. The first year of the grant (November 2000–September 2001) was designated as a planning year, and target schools throughout the school district were to begin phasing in their dual language programs over the next four years of the grant period. Dual language programs in the target schools were to begin in kindergarten and grow one grade level per year as the students who began as kindergartners progress through the grades. Six of the original target schools are located in North Philadelphia, and these schools are to use Spanish and English for instructional purposes. Three of the original target schools are located in South Philadelphia, and one is to use Chinese and English, one is to use Khmer and English, and another is to use Vietnamese and English. Another of the original target schools is in Northeast Philadelphia, and that school is to use Russian and English. Although not all of the schools that were originally targeted have initiated dual language programs, additional schools have taken their place, expanding this systemwide initiative in ways that the grant coordinator and I believe to be consistent with the spirit of the grant. I elaborate on this point below.

One of my primary goals as lead consultant for the dual language initiative has been to encourage school-based language planning teams in each school to take ownership of the planning and implementation of their programs and to hold themselves accountable for their students' performance. To accomplish this, I needed to work directly with the target schools. However, negotiating the multiple levels of institutional authority in order to initiate and sustain school-based language planning within the changing educational context in the SDP has been, at times, challenging and uncertain. As I mentioned in the introduction to Part IV, the SDP has been in the process of extensive restructuring and far-reaching reform initiatives for the entire period that I have worked with them. This turbulence influences language planning within and across the target schools in important ways. For example, two of the six schools that were targeted to begin dual language programs in North Philadelphia were taken over by a for-profit corporation, and they have since dropped out of the dual language initiative.

No part of the central, regional, or school administration has been untouched throughout this period of restructuring, and staff members from what was the Office of Language Equity Issues (OLEI) and is now the Office of Language and Cultural Education (OLCE) and I have had to work through the intermediate level of organizational structure that is in place at any given time (i.e., the "clusters" when the Title VII grant began in November 2000, the "academic areas" in the late spring of 2001, and the "regional offices" since the fall of 2002) in order to work with the target schools. There has been considerable turnover in personnel at every level. In fact, many of the principals of the target schools were either new or not aware that their school had been targeted to begin a dual language program when I first met them, and one of the principals that began a dual language program retired and was replaced by a new principal.

This context of uncertainty and change has increased the importance of school-based language planning teams that embrace the opportunity to direct the language planning processes from the bottom up. In every case, the OLEI/OLCE staff member and the regional coordinator that I was working with at the time encouraged the schools to form language planning teams that would have, or be willing to develop, the range of expertise they needed to develop a dual language plan that they believed would be appropriate for their school and community context and that would be aligned with the interests of the relevant constituents (parents, educators, community members) as they worked through the language planning processes outlined in chapter 4.

Language planning is a complex process, and language planners who are working to promote educational and social change on the local level need to look for openings where they find them, and to build on the strengths and resources they identify and develop over time. I decided to begin my work as consultant to the dual language initiative in North Philadelphia in February 2002 because it was the most obvious place for me to start, given my experience in schools in this community and the foundation for dual language education already in place there. Since the Title VII grant did not fund personnel, and since the schools in Spanish speaking North Philadelphia had many more bilingual educators than any of the other multilingual school community contexts, it was much easier to develop school-based language planning teams there that could begin to plan programs for their schools.

I also began to make contacts with SDP educators who work in and/or are from the other target schools and multilingual communities in Philadelphia in the spring of 2002. Two of these educators, one a native speaker of Chinese and the other a native speaker of Khmer, have been integral parts of the dual language planning project in the less commonly taught languages (LCTLs) from the start. Although their titles and positions within the SDP have changed throughout the restructuring process, their passion for promoting bilingualism and biliteracy development for students who speak one of the LCTLs as their first or heritage language, their commitment to developing pedagogically sound programs for the schools that serve these students, and their connections to the different Asian communities in the SDP, have been driving forces of the dual language initiative outside of the Latino community.

Although it did not always work out according to the ideal, the regional coordinators with whom I was working in the different communities and/or I invited key administrators, language and content teachers, and community liaisons from each of the target schools to be members of the language planning teams. We asked each team to commit to the idea of designing and implementing a dual language program that would realize the goals of the Title VII grant, and we structured regular opportunities to work together throughout the language planning process. Many of the teams did include representatives from all of the relevant interest groups who worked together from the beginning, and others were made up of much smaller groups who had been given authority by the principal to proceed in their work. Although we have had a core group at each of the schools that have successfully launched programs (and not all of the target schools have), and these individuals have been integrally involved in all aspects of the planning and implementation from the start, we have also seen tremendous turnover of staff on the local school level. This turnover is a serious challenge to the dual language initiative in particular and to teaching and learning more generally throughout the SDP.

The dual language initiative in the SDP has benefited tremendously from the expertise of native speakers of the target languages, who in many cases are integral parts of the local community. Although many of these educators initially lacked the credentials or the professional development to implement the types of language education programs that we began to envision, they had the linguistic and cultural expertise, the connections to the community, and the passion for promoting bilingualism for ELLs, heritage language speakers, and English speakers necessary to move the dual language initiative forward in ways that made sense on the local level. While the Latino community had relatively large numbers of bilingual educators working in the school system (although quite a few of these teachers were working on emergency certifications), we found few educators who had experience teaching the LCTLs in the public schools. Fortunately, the Mandarin, Vietnamese, and Russian teachers had experience teaching the target language in a heritage language school in the local community, and several of the Asian educators had dedicated their professional careers to changing educational institutions so that they better meet the needs of students from other backgrounds. Finding creative ways to connect the school and the community is a critical area that the educators from all of the schools need to continually address, and as we see later in the chapter, it is an area that is strongly endorsed by the language policy that the SDP is developing.

Although the Title VII grant originally only targeted one school each in the Khmer, Chinese, Russian, and Vietnamese communities, the dual language initiative has actually spread to include more schools that use these languages. In one of those cases, the same Khmer teacher was assigned to teach Khmer part-time in one school and part-time in another school in South Philadelphia, so both schools decided to develop Khmer programs in their elementary schools. In another case, the Russian teacher from the original target school involved her friend, a Russian teacher who taught ESL in another school in the neighborhood, in her efforts to plan the target school's Russian program. The second Russian teacher introduced her school to the dual language initiative, and that school has begun to plan a Russian program for their elementary school students. In another case, the principal of an under-enrolled school in South Philadelphia was looking for ways to increase his student population and strengthen his school, so he wanted to develop a Chinese program in his school that would attract Chinese-speaking children that were beginning to move into this part of the city.

This kind of grass roots spreading of the dual language initiative is consistent with the spirit of the Title VII grant. The grant was intended to target specific schools and develop strong dual language programs and practices that would serve as prototypes for other schools in the district to emulate. In this way the Title VII grant would stimulate the development of programs that promote bilingualism, biliteracy development, academic achievement, cultural understanding, and positive intergroup relations systemwide. At the time of this writing, several additional schools in North Philadelphia are considering developing either TWI programs or world/heritage language programs in Spanish. If the language policy and implementation plan that is being developed in the SDP is ratified by the School Reform Commission, and if the Office of Language and Cultural Education develops a strategic plan that offers resources to other schools in the district, the dual language initiative promises to continue beyond the duration of the Title VII grant and spread well beyond the initial target schools (see below for further discussion).

Developing context-responsive language plans for the target schools

According to the Title VII grant, all of the target elementary schools were to develop dual language programs in their schools, and dual language programs were implicitly defined by the Title VII grant as two-way immersion (TWI) programs. As we see in this section, some of the language planning teams from the target schools in North Philadelphia did develop TWI plans, others chose to improve the one-way developmental bilingual programs that they had in place, and other schools dropped out of the dual language initiative altogether. However, language planning teams from the target schools that were to use either Khmer, Mandarin, Russian, or Vietnamese determined that TWI was not an appropriate type of language education for their school, at least at this point in time. The teams from these schools decided to begin to address their language planning goals by developing what we call "modified dual language programs." This section reviews the processes that led the language planning teams to make these decisions and highlights the need for schools to think critically about their resources and constraints relative to the critical features of any type of language education program. In this way, schools can set realistic goals for their target populations, and they can develop pedagogically sound programs and practices that promote bilingualism to the greatest degree possible for their students and communities.

Let's start by reviewing the critical features of TWI programs. Recall that TWI programs target English speakers and speakers of another language, and they provide content-area instruction through two languages to these students, who learn together in integrated classes. Although we find a tremendous amount of variation within and across programs, all TWI programs are aligned with the standards of the all-English academic mainstream, and they all provide at least 50 percent of the content-area instruction through the non-English language. Ideally, all TWI programs enable English speakers and speakers of another language to develop oral and written expertise in two languages, achieve academically through both languages, and develop positive intergroup understanding and relations.

Now let's review the questions that each of the language planning teams used to guide their efforts to determine (a) whether TWI was an appropriate type of language education program for their school and if not (b) what type of language education program would be appropriate. As I discussed in chapter 4, these questions are:

1. Who are the target populations?

2. What are the goals for the target populations?

3. How is the school currently addressing the language education needs of the target populations?

Team members were encouraged to consider how their target populations were performing relative to their goals. They were also asked to reflect on how satisfied they were with their goals and to consider whether their existing program(s) needed to be improved and/or changed in any way. As they considered potential changes in their program goals and/or structures, they were encouraged to think carefully about their resources and constraints and to identify challenges they would need to address as they proceeded in their efforts to develop their programs.

Although these three seemingly simple questions are written here in a linear order, it is important to reiterate that teams do not proceed in their efforts to answer these questions in a neat, orderly fashion. As the different members of the language planning teams looked more closely at the strengths and needs of their target populations, and as they considered the varied and at time competing interests of the relevant constituents (e.g., parents; bilingual, ESL, and mainstream teachers; counselors; administrators; community members), and as they looked more critically at what was happening at their school relative to what they were learning about in the literature, some team members readily clarified their goals, others became confused, and some teams ran into conflicts about the best ways to proceed. As I discuss in chapter 4 and illustrate in chapters 12, 13, and 14, language planning is an ideological, recursive process, and it takes time and effort for all of the constituents to develop a coherent understanding of their goals for the target populations, and of an appropriate program structure to reach those goals.

What did the language planning teams from the six target schools in North Philadelphia decide? These schools were to use Spanish and English for instructional purposes and, as we see in chapter 12, three of those schools decided to replace their transitional bilingual education or English-only programs with TWI programs. Each of these schools have large numbers of students who come from Spanish-dominant homes and large numbers of students who come from English-dominant homes, bilingual educators, access to curricular materials that are aligned with the content-area standards in the academic mainstream in Spanish and English, and local support for learning through two languages. Members of the language planning teams from these schools began to reject the assumption that ELLs had to transition to English as quickly as possible in order to participate and achieve at school, and these schools are now phasing out their transitional bilingual and English-only programs because they lead to subtractive bilingualism. Language planning teams from these schools embraced TWI as a means of promoting additive bilingualism for their ELLs, heritage Spanish speakers, and monolingual English speakers.

The other target schools in North Philadelphia had one-way developmental bilingual education (DBE) programs in place for their ELLs. Since research demonstrates that these dual language programs, when they are well-implemented, can enable ELLs to reach parity with English speakers in five to seven years, the language planning teams from these schools decided to concentrate their efforts on improving their one-way DBE programs. One of the schools that had a one-way DBE program for their ELLs also wanted to promote Spanish for the heritage language speakers and monolingual English speakers enrolled in the all-English academic mainstream. This group decided to teach Spanish as a subject area (i.e., as a world language) for students who were enrolled in the all-English academic mainstream and to make Spanish an integral part of the whole school community. The Spanish language program is aligned with the language programs that are being developed in the other community languages, which are discussed briefly below and in detail in chapter 14.

What did the language planning teams from the target schools that were located in the other multilingual communities decide? According to the Title VII grant, one school was to begin a Khmer program, one was to begin a Mandarin program, one was to begin a Russian program, and another was to begin a Vietnamese program. Unlike schools in North Philadelphia—which had a long history of bilingual education, sufficient numbers of bilingual educators, and access to curricular materials in the target language (Spanish) that were aligned with the regular all-English curriculum—the schools serving communities that use these less commonly taught languages face additional challenges. For example, they lack curricular materials that are aligned with the all-English content-area instruction in the target languages, they lack sufficient numbers of qualified teachers, and some lack sufficient numbers of students who speak the target language as their primary language. In addition to the numerous practical challenges these teams need to address, it is much more difficult to find ideological support for providing content-area instruction through these languages.

Members of the Khmer, Mandarin, Russian, and Vietnamese language planning teams and I decided that it was impossible, at least in the short term, to develop TWI programs that use these languages at the target schools. We also decided that it is definitely possible to promote bilingualism, biliteracy development, academic achievement, and positive intergroup understanding and relations in other ways. We searched the web, read the literature, attended academic conferences, and visited language education programs in other parts of the country to stimulate our thinking about creative, pedagogically sound alternatives for their schools and communities. We also revisited our guiding questions.

The first question was *Who are the target populations?* Each of the language planning teams identified the following (potential) target populations in their schools (see chapter 14 for more details about the specific demographics at each of the target schools):

1. ELLs who are native speakers of the target language (Khmer, Mandarin, Russian, or Vietnamese)

2. Heritage language speakers who have a wide range of expertise in the heritage language (Khmer, Mandarin, Russian, or Vietnamese)

3. Heritage language learners who have no expertise in the target language but who have a heritage relation to that language

4. Monolingual English speakers who have no expertise in the target language and no heritage relation to the target language

5. ELLs who speak a language other than the target language (e.g., Spanish in the target school in Northeast Philadelphia where the target language is Russian)

Team members talked about the range of expertise they could expect to find among their heritage language speakers, and they read the literature to determine the kinds of outcomes they could realistically expect for these target populations from different types of language education programs.

As the language planning teams looked more closely at the language and education backgrounds of their diverse student populations and at their ideological and practical resources and constraints, they began to reconsider their goals. Although specific teams and particular educators have additional objectives for their students and programs, the teams collectively agreed on the following goals:

1. To promote the development of academic English for all ELLs

2. To broaden the linguistic repertoires of heritage language speakers so that they can use their spoken and written heritage language to communicate across a wider range of topics for both formal and informal purposes, and to focus on the standard variety of the target language and on literacy development

3. To enable English speakers to develop expertise in the dominant community language

4. To improve intergroup understanding and relations on the local level

Because the language planning team members recognize the power of English over other languages, team members emphasized the need to organize their programs and practices in ways that would elevate the status of the target languages and speakers of those languages at school. By creating an environment that values languages other than English for all students, and that provides ELLs and heritage language speakers with opportunities to maintain and develop their home languages beginning at kindergarten and continuing throughout their educational experience, members of the language planning teams hope that their work will help reverse the trend toward monolingualism in English that has been dominant in their community, and in most immigrant communities in the United States, since the beginning of the twentieth century.

Our search led us to the "modified bilingual programs" in Chinese and in Korean in Cambridge, Massachusetts. The goals of these programs are aligned with the goals of TWI programs (i.e., they promote bilingualism, biliteracy development, and positive intergroup understanding and relations), but the programs are considered modified because they do not provide at least 50 percent of the students' content-area instruction in the non-English language. Following the lead of the Cambridge educators, the Khmer, Mandarin, Russian, and Vietnamese language planning teams and I decided to develop what we are calling "modified dual language programs" to reach the goals that team members had articulated for their target populations. The modified dual language programs have three components:

1. Content-based ESL instruction for ELLs

2. Target language instruction for all students (Russian, Khmer, Mandarin, or Vietnamese)

3. L1 literacy instruction for ELLs and heritage language speakers

These three components of the modified dual language programs work together to build on the existing resources that team members identified at each of the target schools as they address the goals that the team members articulated for their target populations within the constraints of their school and community contexts at this point in time. I briefly review each of these components in turn.

The first component of the modified dual language programs is content-based ESL instruction for ELLs. Consistent with existing mandates in the SDP and across the United States, all public schools must provide opportunities for ELLs to develop the English they need to participate and achieve in the all-English academic mainstream (see chapter 2 for discussion), and all of the target schools were providing some form of ESL instruction to their ELLs when we began our language planning work. Since that time, some of the team members have focused some of their professional development on improving the ESL services that ELLs are provided at their schools so that these students develop the academic language and literacies they need within and across content areas. This is an area that each school, like other schools in the SDP, across the state, and throughout the United States, is continuing to address.

The second component of the modified dual language programs is target language instruction for all students. As I discuss in detail in chapter

14, each of the target schools decided to teach the dominant community language as a subject area (i.e., as a world language) to all of the kindergartners in their schools beginning in the fall of 2002, and the Khmer, Mandarin, Russian, and Vietnamese programs will grow one grade level per year as the kindergartners progress through the grades in each of the target schools. The students in the language classes at each of the schools include ELLs who speak the target language as their first language, heritage language speakers of that language, and monolingual English speakers. In some cases, we also find ELLs or heritage language speakers who have expertise in a language other than the target language in the class. These language programs are inspired by the prototypical FLES (foreign language in the elementary school) program structure discussed in chapter 3, and by the K–8 Ni Hao program for English speakers and Chinese speakers that we visited in Cambridge, Massachusetts. Like FLES programs that we find across the country, these language classes meet three to five times per week for thirty to forty-five minutes per class.

This component of the modified dual language programs addresses the program goals that I listed above in several interrelated ways. First, like any FLES program, well-articulated, long-sequence language classes beginning in kindergarten and continuing throughout the students' academic experience at school provide English speakers with opportunities to develop oral expertise in the target language in the early elementary grades and to build a foundation for subsequent language and literacy development through continued language classes in the middle and high school levels. Furthermore, since English speakers and speakers of the target language are integrated for the target language class, these students are provided with opportunities to develop improved cultural understanding and intergroup relations. The Ni Hao educators said that this was one of the major benefits of their program for English speakers and Chinese speakers. Finally, since all students in the school are learning the target language, the status of that language and of speakers of that language are ideally elevated at school. By making the home language of ELLs and heritage language speakers a visible, integral part of the academic mainstream, language planning team members hope that their ELLs and heritage speakers will choose to maintain and develop their home languages in addition to English instead of rejecting them in favor of English.

Although ELLs and heritage language speakers participate in regularly scheduled classes that use their native or heritage language, the limited amount of time that schools have for this component of the modified dual language program means that ELLs and heritage language speakers really do not have the opportunity to seriously broaden their linguistic repertoires and focus on literacy development in the target language. For this, the target schools are beginning to develop the third component of their modified dual language programs, which is L1 literacy instruction for ELLs and heritage language speakers. During this part of the program, ELLs who are native speakers of the target language and heritage language speakers of the target language who have a strong foundation in the heritage language are segregated from English speakers for literacy instruction in their first or heritage language. The Ni Hao educators emphasize the importance of this component of their program. Although they highlight the benefits of integrating English speakers and Chinese speakers for Chinese class, they also stress the need to provide more opportunities for the Chinese students to broaden their linguistic repertoire in Chinese and acquire literacies in Chinese.

There are many different ways that schools can structure an L1 literacy program into their modified dual language program. For example, in the Ni Hao program in Cambridge Massachusetts, math is taught through Chinese for four hours per week, and literacy instruction in Chinese is an important part of this class. The Ni Hao educators decided to teach math through Chinese after consulting with the Chinese parents at their school. According to the Ni Hao educators that we talked with, the Chinese parents expressed concern about the low standards of the math curriculum that was being used in English in U.S. schools, and these parents believed that their children could learn more advanced math through Chinese. We also learned that there was a heated debate going on within the school at the time of our visit (spring 2002) about whether to use the simplified characters that are used in Mainland China or the traditional characters that are used in Taiwan. Although I do not know the outcome of the debate, the educators that we talked with said that they were meeting with the parents and the teachers to consider the pros and cons of each approach for their students and school

The Russian, Khmer, Mandarin, and Vietnamese language planning teams in the SDP recognize the importance of L1 literacy development, and we see variation across the target schools in the ways they have embraced the opportunity to develop this component of their program. The Russian team at one school, for example, decided to model their program after the Ni Hao program, and they teach math through Russian for the Russian-speaking ELLs and heritage Russian speakers beginning in fourth grade. This team decided to begin this component of their L1 literacy program in fourth grade because of their concern for what many call "the 4th grade slump." This group of educators hopes to support students' reading comprehension (in English and Russian) by focusing on their literacy development in their home language. The language planning team at this school consulted with the Russian parents, who agreed to enroll their children in this class.

The Russian teacher at the other elementary school in Northeast Philadelphia is an itinerant teacher who also works in the feeder middle school in the neighborhood. She had administered a survey to all of the Russian parents at the middle school asking whether they would like to see a Russian class at the school that provided literacy instruction in Russian. Although there is "no time" in the regularly scheduled day for this voluntary program, heritage Russian speakers whose parents chose to have their children participate are pulled out of their Physical Education or Health class for two periods a week (they must make up the work on their own time in ways that are agreeable to the teacher). During their Russian class, these students read and respond to authentic Russian literature. For their culminating activity in the spring of 2003, approximately 30 middle school heritage Russian speakers performed excerpts from what they had read throughout the year, including "The telephone" by Kornei Chukovski (a contemporary of Dr. Seuss) and "The fox and the bird," which is a traditional Russian fairy tale. The students invited their parents, the principal and other teachers at the school, the 4th and 5th grade Russian students who were participating in the Russian math program in the elementary school and who would be coming to this middle school in the future, and other interested parties to their performance. They began the performance with a translation or summary of what they would perform in English for those of us who do not understand Russian, and then they acted out the piece using elaborate props that they had created to ensure that everyone could understand the story line. They concluded the performance by introducing themselves and by answering questions about their project. We learned, for example, that although all of the students spoke Russian at home, some had never read anything in Russian prior to their participation in this class. The students, their parents, and the school administration seemed genuinely proud of their accomplishment and committed to continuing the L1 literacy program on a voluntary basis in future years.

The Khmer team decided to start an after-school Khmer literacy program at a community center in the neighborhood for Khmer students in the spring of 2003. This program was stimulated by the KEEP program that members of the Khmer language planning team learned about at the National Association for Bilingual Education (NABE) conference in Philadelphia during the spring of 2002 and visited in Fresno, California, later that spring. Since there is more than one school that offers Khmer in South Philadelphia, and another relatively large Khmer community in

North Philadelphia, the Khmer language planning team decided to pool their resources into one magnet after-school program for any interested Khmer students. According to the coordinator of this program, to date it has attracted only a few students, but he expects the interest to grow over time as parents, students, and other community members learn about its existence and goals.

The Mandarin team in one of the schools is currently considering how to develop a TWI program for English-speaking and Chinese-speaking students at their school, and some see the Mandarin program that has begun in the kindergarten as a first step in this process. This school is located near Chinatown and currently has a one-way developmental bilingual middle school program that feeds into a one-way developmental bilingual high school program for the large numbers of Chinese students who come to that school beginning in the middle school years. According to some of the educators at this school, a TWI program that begins in kindergarten and that continues throughout the grade levels would help unite the different programs in the school.

The Vietnamese team members are considering different ways to promote L1 literacy development for their students. For example, they have begun to talk about the pros and cons of an after-school program or a program that is part of the regular school day. What makes an after-school program attractive is that it does not take time away from an already crowded school day. However, making the L1 literacy component a voluntary after-school program does not demonstrate a strong school commitment to this part of the program for all students. Vietnamese team members, like members of the other language planning teams, continue to assess their strengths and resources relative to their constraints to determine the best way to proceed in developing the L1 literacy component of their modified dual language program so that it becomes an integral part of the students' academic experience.

As this brief discussion of possible approaches to developing the L1 literacy component of the modified dual language program makes clear, there are many different ways to structure in this part of the program. The language planning team members continue to assess the strengths and needs of their target populations and consider local resources and constraints as they explore possibilities. Ongoing action-oriented research and practice will determine the outcomes of these efforts.

The educators who are developing TWI programs in Spanish and English in North Philadelphia, and who are developing the modified dual language programs in Khmer, Mandarin, Russian, and Vietnamese in other parts of the city, face numerous ideological and practical challenges as they open spaces to promote bilingualism in their schools. As I discuss in chapters 13 and 14, I meet with the members of the TWI teams as one group, and with the members of the modified dual language teams as another group, for monthly professional development meetings throughout the school year and for intensive professional development in the summer. During these meetings, these networks of educators reflect on their programs and practices and together develop strategies to address the immediate, short-term, and long-term challenges that arise so that they can deliver on the promises they have made to their students, parents, and communities.

This part of the chapter has described how and why the language planning teams from the different target schools determined what type of a dual language program would be appropriate for their school and community context in the short and longer term. This discussion emphasizes the need for language planning teams to think carefully about the critical features of the types of language education program that they are considering for their schools and to carefully assess their local resources and constraints relative to those critical features. When schools determine that they do not have what it takes to implement one type of language education program (e.g., two-way immersion), they are encouraged to consider other program types that are realistic for their school and community context.

The next part of the chapter describes the language policy formulation project that is underway in the SDP at the time of this writing. If the SDP approves a language policy and implementation plan that promotes bilingualism to the greatest degree possible for students throughout the district, the programs described in this section will become an institutionalized part of the SDP. Furthermore, we may see the development of pedagogically sound, well-implemented K–12 programs that promote bilingualism, biliteracy development, academic achievement for all students, and improved cultural understanding and intergroup relations in magnet schools in multilingual communities throughout the city. Considerable research and action are needed to make this possibility a reality.

Formulating a language policy that promotes bilingualism

When I began my work on the dual language initiative, the School District of Philadelphia (SDP) did not have one coherent language policy that explicitly promoted bilingualism. However, as I describe in the opening section of Part IV, the SDP has been the focus of numerous educational restructuring and reform initiatives over the past decade, which culminated with a state takeover of the school district in the spring of 2002. In the summer of 2002, the School Reform Commission (SRC) appointed a new chief executive officer (CEO) of the SDP, and in the fall of 2002, he challenged the Philadelphia Association of Hispanic School Administrators (PAHSA) to give him a language policy that they endorsed. Members of PAHSA are key players at all levels of SDP administration, including the former Office of Language Equity Issues (OLEI)/current Office of Language and Cultural Education (OLCE) that oversees all issues related to language education throughout the school district and the Central East Regional Office (CERO) in North Philadelphia that oversees the majority of the bilingual programs in the predominantly Puerto Rican part of the city. Early in the process, I was asked by a group of PAHSA members to facilitate efforts to develop the SDP language policy. This section provides a brief description of the language policy formulation process in the SDP, which is underway at the time of this writing.

It is important to emphasize that the SDP was not without language policies when the newly appointed CEO made his request to PAHSA. Some of these language policies had been explicitly articulated and are written down. For example, according to the coordinators of the Office of Language and Cultural Education (OLCE) that I have talked with, the Y.S. Stipulations of 1988 have guided most of the school districts' efforts to provide equal access to educational opportunities for English language learners (ELLs) over the last fifteen years (see introduction to Part IV for discussion). However, many educators who work on the central, regional, and school levels are not aware of or familiar with the policies that were developed as part of that remedial plan. Other policies can be found in Title VII grant proposals that OLEI/OLCE has written over time to support the development of a range of programs and practices for ELLs. Others have been explicitly formulated on the regional or school levels to address particular issues on those levels. Still others have not been explicitly articulated but are implicit in programs and practices within and/or across schools in the city. While most of the language policies that have come from OLEI/OLCE promote the maintenance and development of the native language of ELLs, not all of the policies guiding practice within and across regions and schools share this language-as-resource orientation.

Early in the language policy formulation process, members of PAHSA and OLCE emphasized the need to ensure that the SDP language policy would address the language and cultural education needs of all students in the school district and not only those living in the Latino neighborhood in North Philadelphia. Leaders from the Association of Asian American Educators (AAE) were invited by OLCE to participate in developing the language policy, because these educators have been closely involved with addressing the language education needs of Asian students in the Chinese,

Khmer, and Vietnamese communities in Philadelphia. Members of AAE are also key players at many levels of SDP administration, although there are not as many Asians in high-profile positions in the SDP as there are Latinos at this point in time. According to the presidents of PAHSA and AAE, this is the first time that these two organizations have worked together to develop district-wide policy.

The language policy planning group now consisted of members of PAHSA, AAE, and OLCE, and we agreed that the school district language policy needed to be a coherent policy guiding language and cultural education, broadly defined. It needed to align and build on all of the existing language policies, those explicitly written as well as those implicit in practice, and it needed to promote bilingualism to the greatest degree possible for all SDP students (see chapter 2 for discussion of what a school language policy should include). The planning group decided to organize a two-day retreat that would bring together educators who collectively had experience with all of the issues relevant to language policy and implementation in the SDP. They decided to write a draft of their mission statement in preparation for the language policy retreat and to have the presidents of PAHSA and AAE present that draft at the retreat. That mission statement would guide work on the language policy and implementation plan that would be done at the retreat. The outcome of the retreat would provide a foundation for formulating the language policy that the CEO had requested and for developing the implementation plan that would ensure the policy would be realized in practice throughout the district.

Prior to the retreat, we collected all of the written policies and procedures that we could find concerning bilingual education, ESL, world languages, cultural education, and equity issues from the SDP Offices of Language and Cultural Education, Assessment, Compliance, and Human Resources. The language policy planning group invited educators from the SDP who collectively had a breadth and depth of experience relative to the charge, including representatives from the dominant language groups in the district and those with experience as elementary and/or secondary teachers, principals, regional administrators, and/or central administrators. Using the *Pennsylvania Guidebook for Planning Programs* and literature in the field as a guide, the language policy planning group organized the invitees into five working groups: (1) bilingual education, (2) ESL, (3) world languages and cultural education, (4) SDP supports, and (5) language issues, broadly defined. The planning group developed concrete tasks that each working group was to address during the retreat. Although each group had its specific charge outlined for it in the form of guiding questions or issues to consider, our objective at the retreat was for each group to first identify all of the existing explicit and implicit central, regional, and school policies relative to their charge, align those policies, and identify any gaps. Once each working group completed this task to the best of their abilities at the retreat, they began to address the policy gaps that they had identified.

The retreat was attended by approximately forty people, who enthusiastically rose to the occasion. After a large group discussion of the mission statement that the presidents of PAHSA and AAE presented, the working groups began to address their charges. They engaged in critical discussions about, for example, the policies and procedures regarding home language surveys and the choice of languages to be used in bilingual and/or world language programs. Groups discussed defining criteria of different models of bilingual education, ESL, and world language education, and they considered the SDP policies and procedures governing the identification, assessment, placement, movement, promotion, and graduation of students within and across different types of bilingual and ESL programs. In addition to identifying existing policies and gaps, the working groups also identified what they called "thorny issues," or issues that were surrounded by confusion, conflict, and/or controversy that needed to be clarified by a coherent, well-articulated policy. Many highlighted the need for trained educators who could implement the kinds of programs they envisioned, and they looked critically at policies and procedures guiding the recruitment, retention, and professional development of teachers, administrators, and staff who work with language learners at their schools.

Everyone emphasized the need for policies and procedures that govern all aspects of program implementation, monitoring, and evaluation, and they maintained that these policies and procedures need to be widely circulated, reviewed, and revised as necessary so that everyone in the district would have a coherent understanding of what the language policy was working toward and how it was to be translated into action within and across classrooms in schools in communities. These educators highlighted the need to move language education from the margins to the mainstream, and they discussed strategies for involving parents in the decision-making process at schools and for working more closely with community-based organizations and higher education. Perhaps most importantly, they articulated the need for a strategic plan and resources that would enable the SDP to develop standards-based programs and practices that would (1) enable ELLs to achieve academically in English while they maintain and develop their native language, (2) enable heritage language speakers to broaden their linguistic range at school, (3) enable English speakers to develop expertise in a language other than English, and (4) enable all students to develop improved cultural understanding and intergroup relations. At the time of this writing, members of the language policy planning team are actively involved in developing the language policy and implementation plan for the SDP.

This section has briefly described the process that members of PAHSA, AAE, and OLCE and I are engaged in to formulate a language policy and develop an implementation plan that promotes bilingualism to the greatest degree possible for the target populations. The actual policy that emerges as well as the implications of this policy for program development, implementation, and student outcomes remains to be seen. Ideally, the language policy will be a coherent statement that is aligned with local, state, and federal mandates, standards and accountability requirements, and ideally the implementation plan will provide the guidance that schools need to address their language and cultural education goals for all of their students, based on their local assessment of school and community resources and needs. Ideally this policy and plan will guide future program development, implementation, and evaluation efforts in ways that challenge English-only discourses with evidence about the benefits of alternative English-plus programs and practices.

Language planning and policy making for educational and social change

Educational language planning in the United States, like other educational change projects, can be initiated at the top with federal, state, or school district level policies and/or funding. Educational language planning can also be initiated on the local level by teachers, administrators, parents, and/or other community members. According to Fullan's (2001) review of the educational change literature, it is not clear whether the source of the change matters. However, it is clear that everyone on the local level must develop a coherent understanding of the goals of the educational plan as well as the means to reach those goals if the program is to be effective. Ultimately, a combination of top-down and bottom-up educational planning may be necessary for any far-reaching change.

In my experience working with particular schools in the School District of Philadelphia (SDP), one of the greatest challenges facing the school-based language planning teams has been creating a coherent vision of what a school's program will look like in practice. As research on educational change emphasizes, coherence does not just happen automatically (Fullan 2000). Challenging existing school and community norms that lead to subtractive bilingualism takes time and energy. Creating alternate visions of schooling that see bilingualism, biliteracy, academic achievement in two languages, and positive intergroup understanding and relations as real possibilities take time and energy. And ensuring that everyone at that school (students, teachers, parents, administrators, community members) develops a shared understanding of the target populations' strengths and needs, goals of the program, program structure, and expected program outcomes also takes time and energy. Chapters 12, 13, and 14 illustrate ways that I work with educators at the target schools to support their efforts to develop coherent visions of where they want to go as a school, and to develop coherent plans to get there.

The schools that have planned and begun to implement innovative programs that promote bilingualism provide examples of ways that language planning teams can work together to assess their target populations' strengths and needs, consider their local resources and constraints, and develop pedagogically sound programs that build on community bilingualism in context-responsive ways. The particular program plans described in these chapters are not intended to be uncritically reproduced in other school or community contexts. Instead, the detailed descriptions that I provide are intended to stimulate educators' thinking about how they can develop context-responsive language education programs and practices in their schools. More importantly, these chapters are intended to stimulate action.

Language planning and policy development in the SDP provides an excellent example of how top-down and bottom-up planning work together to promote educational and social change on the local level. The top-down process initiated by the federal government in the form of a Title VII systemwide grant was supported by bottom-up planning on the local school level. As schools develop programs that promote bilingualism for their target populations, the educators work to challenge language ideologies at school and in their communities that run counter to their emerging language-as-resource orientation. The educators from the target schools and I work to ensure that there is ideological space for the continuing development of these programs in the context of confusion and controversy about bilingualism and education on the district, state, and federal levels.

Now the bottom-up efforts of schools that are developing dual language and world language programs in the dominant community languages are being institutionalized by the development of a coherent language policy that promotes bilingualism at the top of the SDP. The central administration of the SDP has begun to work more aggressively with educators from across the levels of institutional authority (e.g., on the school, regional, and central administration levels) to move language and cultural education issues from the margins into the academic mainstream. The new language policy, if endorsed by the Board of Education, will mandate that all educators have a responsibility for the education of ELLs, and that all educational decisions made in the SDP (e.g., regarding curriculum, materials, assessment, promotion, graduation) must consider the needs of ELLs as an integral part of their decision making process and not as an afterthought, as has happened until now. The new language policy will ideally comply with all local, state, and federal mandates, and it will ideally promote bilingualism to the greatest degree possible for its linguistically and culturally diverse student population. Once this policy is formulated, it will ideally drive program development, implementation, monitoring, and evaluation on the local level. And ideally, more schools throughout the SDP will develop strong K–12 dual language, heritage language, and world language programs that will yield evidence of the effectiveness of these types of language education program for all language learners.

Many educators criticize the No Child Left Behind Act of 2001 for its exclusive emphasis on accountability in English, and for its exclusive reliance on standardized test scores that generally do not allow ELLs or low-income students to demonstrate their strengths. However, it is also possible to see this era of accountability as an opportunity for local schools and school districts to demonstrate the effectiveness of dual language programs for ELLs and English speakers. All schools are now required to assess every ELL's English language development, and all schools are required to assess every students' academic performance in English over time. The makers of standardized tests that states and school districts adopt must work to ensure that their tests are valid and reliable indicators of students' performance and development, and teachers must complement standardized tests with alternative forms of assessment to gather the formative data they need to guide instruction and inform program development. However, the enormous amount of data that the No Child Left Behind Act mandates means that educators and policy makers will be in a position to compare ELLs' English language development and all students' academic performance in English, within and across different types of ESL and bilingual education program. If dual language programs are as effective, as research to date suggests (e.g., Lindholm-Leary 2001; Thomas and Collier 2002), we will have concrete evidence to counter English-only currents across the country.

12

Initiating two-way immersion programs

This chapter explores how language planning teams from three schools in North Philadelphia worked together to initiate two-way immersion (TWI) programs in contexts that formerly had not promoted additive bilingualism or biliteracy development for their students. As discussed in chapter 3, TWI programs target balanced numbers of English speakers and speakers of another language, in this case Spanish. Two-way immersion programs aim for bilingualism, biliteracy development, academic achievement in Spanish and English, and positive intergroup understanding and relations for their target populations. The chapter is based on my work as the lead consultant for the dual language initiative that was the centerpiece of the Title VII bilingual education systemwide grant that the School District of Philadelphia (SDP) was awarded in November 2000, and it provides an insider's perspective on the first part of the dual language planning project.

I argue in this chapter that there is no one-size-fits-all TWI program that educators can just uncritically implement in their schools. Rather, educators make decisions about what is appropriate for their school and community contexts based on their understanding of the literature, evidence from what TWI programs look like in other contexts, and their own beliefs and experiences. The majority of the chapter describes how three of the schools targeted by the Title VII grant worked through this decision-making process. Then I share the TWI plans that the three schools developed in May 2001, and I highlight some of the challenges these plans present to the educators who are responsible for implementing the programs at school. Together, the parts of this chapter emphasize the importance of teachers as agents of educational and social change.

Decisions, decisions, decisions

As mentioned in chapter 11, the Title VII bilingual education systemwide grant is an example of a top-down language planning project that the Office of Language Equity Issues (OLEI) of the School District of

Philadelphia (SDP) initiated, and that I believed the target schools needed to embrace and direct from the bottom up. Since it was a cluster-based initiative, OLEI and one of the three cluster offices that served the predominantly Puerto Rican community in North Philadelphia organized a dual language planning seminar/workshop to launch the dual language initiative in that cluster in the beginning of February 2001. The cluster office invited key players from the three target schools that were to begin two-way immersion (TWI) programs the following fall, and I led the two-day meeting. Participating in that seminar/workshop were eleven teachers and one principal from PS 23, nine teachers and one principal from PS 31, five teachers and one principal from PS 29, the cluster leader, the cluster bilingual/ESOL coordinator, and the OLEI coordinator of the Title VII grant. This part of the chapter explores how these groups decided first, that TWI was an appropriate type of language education program for their schools and then, how the TWI program should be structured at each of the schools.

Is TWI an appropriate type of program for the target schools

The first decision that these three schools needed to make was whether TWI was an appropriate type of program for their schools. At the first dual-language planning meeting, educators from each school described their target populations, articulated their short-term and long-term goals for those populations, examined the schools' existing bilingual and ESL (English as a second language) programs with attention to student performance and reviewed the critical features of TWI programs. Each of the schools had large numbers of Spanish-speaking English language learners (ELLs) who needed more effective bilingual or ESL services than were offered at the school at that time, and they all had sufficient numbers of English speakers who would likely be interested in broadening their linguistic range in Spanish. Many of the educators lamented the fact that most of their ELLs quickly transitioned to English, and they expressed their interest in developing bilingual programs that would provide students with opportunities to maintain and develop their Spanish while promoting academic language and literacy development in English. The schools also had enough bilingual personnel to initiate TWI programs in one or two classes in either kindergarten or kindergarten and 1st grade the following year, and the educators expressed their commitment to finding more trained bilingual educators to grow their programs over time.

Together we agreed that PS 31, PS 23, and PS 29 were each appropriate contexts for TWI programs. However, these educators needed to do much more work to make space for TWI at their schools. This section describes this part of the language planning process.

Although the educators that I met at this dual language planning meeting were open to the idea of developing TWI programs as strands within their schools, many initially assumed that I was hired to tell them what type of TWI program they were expected to implement and then teach them how to implement that program. My goal as lead consultant of this dual language initiative, however, was to actively involve these educators in the dual language planning process so that they would take ownership of their TWI programs and assume responsibility for program outcomes. Although I have no evidence to support this assertion, I fully believe that this ownership helped teachers sustain their programs in the context of the dramatic restructuring in the SDP during the early years of implementation.

At the end of the first planning meeting, educators from each of these schools and I negotiated goals and a structure for our language planning work. Each group of educators agreed to the following:

- to work together as a team that was responsible for developing a TWI plan that they believed would be responsive to the needs of their students and community

- to consider the interests of a wide range of constituents, including students, parents, educators at their school, community members, the SDP, and the Commonwealth of Pennsylvania

- to learn about different types of language education programs, theories of second language acquisition, biliteracy development, and content-based second language instruction

- to explore what TWI programs looked like in practice in other contexts

- to share their work-in-progress (challenges, strategies) with the other school-based teams at monthly strategic planning meetings throughout the spring

- to present their TWI plan to the other school-based language planning teams in May 2001

- to participate in dual language professional development in the summer of 2001 to prepare for implementation

- to launch their TWI program in the fall of 2001

I agreed to visit each school between meetings in order to learn more about their particular school contexts, and I offered to facilitate their language planning processes in whatever ways the teams requested. We also agreed to work together throughout the Title VII grant period to monitor and evaluate their programs, address challenges, and ensure that each program was well-implemented over time.

To support their work, each educator was given a copy of the books *Dual Language Instruction: A Handbook for Enriched Education* by Cloud, Genesee and Hamayan (2000), *Biliteracy for a Global Society: An Idea Book on Dual-Language Education* by Lindholm-Leary (2000), and the Spanish and English versions of *If your child learns in two languages* (2000) that the National Clearinghouse for Bilingual Education (NCBE) produced for parents. I also introduced the seminar participants to the TWI Directory that is posted on the Center for Applied Linguistics (CAL) webpage (www.cal.org) and showed the video *Learning Together: Two-Way Bilingual Immersion Programs* that CAL produced.

Throughout the spring semester, the school-based language planning teams looked critically at their own and each others' TWI plans to determine whether they were pedagogically sound. They also shared strategies that they used to gain the support of parents and other educators at their school. Although I presented the same challenge to each of the language planning teams, the individual schools took up the opportunity to develop their TWI programs in different ways. These different language planning approaches reflected the educators' assumptions about how to promote educational change at their school, which were based on their experiences working together over time.

PS 31 began with the outside constituents. The principal (a monolingual English speaker) and the bilingual coordinator (an upper grade teacher with nearly 30 years of experience) led the effort to involve parents, community members, and other educators at the school in the language planning process from the start. They organized trips for parents and teachers to other TWI schools, and they held community meetings to share information, answer questions, and address concerns as they arose. The PS 31 team was convinced that TWI was a better approach than the transitional bilingual program they had been implementing. They expected all of the constituents to be interested in learning about effective programs and practices for ELLs, and they wanted to ensure that the parents would really understand how TWI could work at their school. They surveyed incoming parents and generated considerable support and enthusiasm for their innovative approach to bilingual education. Whenever there was tension (an inevitable part of any educational change project), the PS 31 team took on the conflict directly. The leadership style and approach of the principal and the bilingual coordinator, I believe, enabled this group to resolve their problems and generate wide support for their program.

The PS 23 team began on the inside by thinking critically about what type of TWI program would be appropriate for their student population. These educators were convinced that dual language education was a better model of bilingual education than the transitional bilingual program that they had been implementing. In fact, this school had initiated a TWI program in the early elementary grades in September 2000. However, according to the TWI teachers, they were not prepared for the job they were asked to do because they had not received the professional development they needed. Many of these teachers read voraciously to find answers to their questions, and they argued the pros and cons of various approaches to TWI. Some attended the National Association for Bilingual Education conference in Arizona in the spring of 2001, and others visited TWI programs locally. The PS 23 team focused on their TWI instructional plan, and by the end of the spring this small group of language planners seemed to have developed a coherent understanding of how they would change their TWI program so that they could effectively reach their goals.

In contrast to PS 31 and PS 23, PS 29 did not have a bilingual education program in place. Instead, they had what they called "ELL-friendly" classes, which meant that all of the ELLs were put together in classes with teachers who were supposedly sensitive to the language learning needs of these students. The PS 29 team addressed the challenge to garner support for TWI at their school from a variety of directions, and they pursued the ideological openings that they found. First they introduced the idea of TWI to the PS 29 staff, and they encountered resistance from some of the monolingual English-speaking staff who were worried about their jobs. The principal assured the staff that none of the existing teachers would lose their jobs (changes in personnel would take place gradually over time as the student population changed and as faculty turned over naturally), and the PS 29 team turned their attention to the incoming kindergarten parents. They organized numerous meetings with parents to educate them about the benefits of TWI for their children, and they convinced many to enroll their child in this innovative program. The parents' enthusiasm gave the PS 29 team the support they needed to develop their TWI program, and parental support continues to be an importance force in the acceptance of this program by the larger school community.

Although the language planning teams encountered resistance that they needed to address inside of their schools, they found strong support for TWI programs outside of the SDP. Despite the conflicts and controversies surrounding bilingual education in the United States, we have seen increasing numbers of TWI programs nationally (at the time of this writing there are nearly 250 listed on the TWI Directory, and there are likely more than that in practice). As we saw in chapter 3, educators can turn to a solid research base that documents the effectiveness of well-implemented dual language programs across the country to inform their TWI program development and to advocate for their programs.

Educational change requires changing beliefs and practices, and changing beliefs and practices about bilingual education is not simple or straightforward. Teachers are critical agents of change in this complex process. Through ongoing observation, reflection, and conversations about TWI practices, the TWI teachers from each of the schools helped each other, other educators at their schools, parents, and community members develop a coherent understanding of what TWI would mean at their schools. The monthly planning meetings that we held throughout the spring offered an important structure for teachers' efforts to develop as a community of reflective practitioners who can and do turn to each other for help in solving problems as they arise (see also Fullan 2000; Wenger 1998). The language planning teams shared their work in progress at these meetings, discussed challenges that they faced, and brainstormed strategies to address those challenges. They worked together to think critically about literature on second language acquisition, biliteracy development, bilingual education program types, and organizational dynamics and change. They challenged each other to clearly articulate their short-term and long-term goals and objectives for their target populations, and they used each other as an important scaffold in their efforts to plan TWI programs that would address the interests and concerns of constituents as they encountered them.

However, as Fullan (2000) reminds us, beliefs do not change overnight. Real change, if it were to come at all, would come throughout the implementation stage as people observed how the TWI programs functioned on the local level over time. I return to this point in chapter 13, where we discuss the challenges of implementation.

With this general understanding of how the language planning teams developed their TWI plans, I turn now to critical questions that all TWI planners must consider. First I describe prototypical TWI programs, and we review the research on the effectiveness of each of these program types. Then I describe the different approaches to literacy instruction that we find in the early elementary grades, and I consider the pros and cons of each approach. The parts of this section illustrate how the school-based language planning teams looked to the literature, consulted with other TWI programs in the United States, and considered their own and each others' experiences to guide their decision-making processes.

How should the TWI program be structured

As the language planning teams were working to open space for two-way immersion (TWI) at their schools, they also needed to decide how they should structure their TWI program so they could address the needs and interests of their target populations and constituents while they built on the resources that they found within their contexts. This section distinguishes the two major variants of TWI that we see across the United States, which are referred to as the 90:10 and 50:50 programs. After I describe these prototypes, I review some of the variation that we see in practice. The language planning teams from each of the schools were encouraged to look critically at these prototypes and at this variation in order to develop an appropriate program for their school and community context.

According to the prototypical 90:10 program, at the kindergarten and 1st grade levels 90 percent of the instructional day is devoted to content-area instruction in Spanish and 10 percent in English. While specials like physical education, music, and/or art might be taught in either language depending on the resources and needs of the specific school, program designers need to ensure that 90 percent of the students' total instructional time is in Spanish. Reading instruction begins in Spanish for all students (including monolingual English speakers), who learn together in integrated classes. At the 2nd and 3rd grade levels, students spend 80 percent of their day in Spanish and 20 percent in English. Students may be exposed to English print and English literature from the beginning of the program, but they do not begin formal English reading instruction until 2nd or 3rd grade. By 4th, 5th, and 6th grades students spend half of their time in Spanish and half of their time in English. At these upper elementary grade levels, all students receive formal language arts in both languages, and content instruction is divided equally between the two languages (Lindholm-Leary 2000).

According to the prototypical 50:50 program, all students receive half of their instruction in English and the other half in Spanish throughout all of the elementary years. Within prototypical 50:50 programs, we see two major variants that can be distinguished by their approach to initial literacy instruction. One approach provides all students with initial literacy instruction in both languages beginning in kindergarten, primarily or exclusively in integrated classes. The other approach segregates English-dominant and Spanish-dominant students for formal literacy instruction in the student's dominant language during the early elementary years. In this second approach, students are introduced to formal literacy instruction in their second language (either Spanish or English) beginning around 3rd grade.

When we look at how 90:10 and 50:50 programs are implemented in practice, we see a tremendous range of variation. In addition to the differences between program types discussed above, programs vary in terms of how they allocate languages for instructional purposes. For example, some schools separate languages by teacher, with one teacher speaking one language (e.g., Spanish) and the other teacher speaking the other language (e.g., English). Some schools separate languages by time, with one language used in the morning and the other in the afternoon, or by switching languages on a daily or weekly basis. Some schools separate languages by content area, with one language used for certain content areas (e.g., math, science) and the other language for other content areas (e.g., language arts, social studies). Schools determine the specific allocation of languages for instructional purposes for their schools based on their assessment of local needs, resources and constraints.

To help the dual language planning teams consider what type of program would be appropriate for their school, we considered what types of TWI programs were being implemented in other school contexts. First, we searched the TWI directory that the CAL has on its webpage (www.cal.org). At the time of the first dual language planning seminar, there were 188 elementary schools listed on the directory. Out of those schools, 103 reported that they implemented a MINORITY LANGUAGE DOMINANT program (i.e. the 90:10 program type), and 80 elementary schools reported that they implemented a BALANCED program (i.e., the 50:50 program type). Five elementary schools reported that they implemented a DIFFERENTIATED program, with English speakers and Spanish speakers receiving different amounts of Spanish relative to English. For example, in differentiated programs English speakers may get 50 percent of their instruction in Spanish and 50 percent in English while Spanish speakers get 90 percent in Spanish and 10 percent in English in the first years of the program. Our search also showed that most TWI programs are strands within a school and not whole-school programs. Only 31 of the reporting schools provided TWI for all of their students.

As the language planning teams designed their TWI programs, their questions became more focused on the details of program structure. In order to push their thinking about possibilities for their own designs, I encouraged the teams to look at concrete examples of other programs and talk to other TWI educators about the ways that they interpret and implement their programs. Because I was familiar with the well-implemented TWI program at Oyster Bilingual School in Washington D.C., I encouraged team members to visit that school. Another group organized a trip to visit a TWI program in Englewood, New Jersey, and many had opportunities to visit TWI programs when they went to the meeting of the National Association for Bilingual Education in Phoenix in the Spring of 2001. I also encouraged the language planners to use CAL's TWI Directory to find concrete examples of schools with profiles similar to what they were thinking about, and to make contact with those programs to address their questions.

As these educators learned about the 90:10 and 50:50 types of TWI and about the range of possibilities they needed to consider as they make decisions about their program, they often asked which model was "best." I turn now to the research on 90:10 programs relative to 50:50 programs to help address this question. Then I consider the critical question of biliteracy development in TWI programs.

Research on student outcomes in 90:10 and 50:50 programs

Lindholm-Leary has been doing longitudinal research on student outcomes in TWI programs since 1986, and she reports the findings from this research in her (2001) book entitled *Dual Language Education.* Lindholm-Leary's data was collected in over 20 schools with TWI programs in different stages of implementation in which the students come from diverse cultural, socioeconomic, and language backgrounds. Her analysis of student outcomes is based on 4,900 students in TWI programs collected over a period of 4 to 8 years. She evaluated student outcomes relative to four goals of TWI programs:

1. oral language proficiency in Spanish and English

2. biliteracy development

3. academic achievement in two languages

4. student, parent, and teacher attitudes toward the dual language program.

Lindholm-Leary (2001) based her analysis of student outcomes on teacher ratings of student proficiencies, oral proficiency tests, standardized tests, and reading rubrics developed as part of a language arts portfolio. Then she examined these outcomes according to program type (90:10 or 50:50), school demographic characteristics (number of Spanish speakers relative to English speakers in the program), and student background characteristics (socioeconomic class, parents' education level). Where possible, she compared data from TWI programs to outcomes in transitional bilingual education or English-only programs. I have organized my review of Lindholm-Leary's (2001) research in this section around her discussion of language proficiency and academic achievement, two of the primary goals of dual language programs. Literacy is considered here under language proficiency.

English language learners language proficiency in English and Spanish. When Lindholm-Leary (2001) examined Spanish-dominant ELLs' proficiency in English and in Spanish in 90:10 and 50:50 programs, she found no significant program differences associated with these students' English proficiency. Although this finding runs counter to what some people initially assume, the fact is that receiving more Spanish than English in the curriculum in the early elementary grades does not negatively affect ELLs' acquisition of English over time. Lindholm-Leary (2001) did find, however, that there were significant differences associated with Spanish-dominant students' development of Spanish across programs. Spanish-dominant students in 90:10 programs received higher ratings in Spanish than Spanish-dominant students in 50:50 programs did, demonstrating that Spanish speakers acquired more Spanish when they had more instructional time in Spanish

Lindholm-Leary's (2001) findings that additional instruction in Spanish is associated with higher levels of proficiency in Spanish and with no loss to English proficiency are consistent with research on ELLs' performance in other types of bilingual education programs in the United States. Research continually demonstrates that ELLs in one-way developmental bilingual programs and in late-exit transitional bilingual programs acquire higher levels of proficiency in English than ELLs do in early-exit transitional bilingual programs (August and Hakuta 1997; Thomas and Collier 2002; Escamilla and Medina 1993; Medina and Escamilla 1992; Padilla et al. 1991; Ramirez et al. 1991; Willig 1985). This research indicates that ELLs who develop a strong language and literacy foundation in their native language ultimately develop higher levels of proficiency in English.

English-dominant students' proficiency in English and Spanish. When Lindholm-Leary (2001) compared English-dominant students' language proficiency in English across program types, she found that there were no significant program differences associated with English language development in 90:10 or 50:50 programs. Students receiving as little as 10 or 20 percent of their instructional time in English in the early elementary grades scored as well as students spending half their instructional day in English, and both of these TWI participants were rated as high as monolingual English speakers in English-only programs. However, Lindholm-Leary (2001) did find significant program differences associated with Spanish proficiency, with English-dominant students in 90:10 programs outscoring those in 50:50 programs in Spanish. Most English speakers were classified as medium bilinguals when they completed the program, with one-half of 90:10 students classified as high bilinguals.

These findings for English-dominant students' development of proficiency in Spanish and English in TWI programs in the United States are similar to findings from immersion research in Canada (see, for example, Genesee 1987; Swain and Lapkin 1982). That research clearly demonstrates that English speakers develop high levels of proficiency in their first language (English) regardless of whether they participate in a partial immersion program (approximately 50 percent of their instructional time in French) or full-immersion program (100 percent of their instructional time in French). Furthermore, English-dominant students develop high levels of proficiency in the target language (French) in both partial and full immersion programs (Campbell et al. 1985; Genesee 1987), though their proficiency is higher in full-immersion programs (Campbell et al. 1985). English-dominant students enrolled in these programs do not, however, generally develop native-like proficiency in their second language (see Lindholm-Leary 2001 for extended discussion of this point).

Lindholm-Leary's (2001) longitudinal research uses a wide range of formative and summative assessment measures, and it provides empirical evidence of English-speaking and Spanish-speaking students' language proficiency in English and in Spanish. Her research clearly demonstrates that English-speaking students and ELLs develop high levels of proficiency in English in both 90:10 and 50:50 programs. Whether Spanish-dominant or English-dominant students spend 10 to 20 percent or 50 percent of their instructional day in the early elementary grades in English, students were equally proficient in English when they completed the program. English speakers in TWI programs were rated as high as monolingual English speakers in English-only programs, and ELLs developed higher levels of proficiency in English in TWI programs than ELLs in other types of bilingual programs (see also Murphy 2002, for similar findings of the superior performance of ELLs in TWI programs over transitional bilingual education (TBE) programs in the Evanston/Skokie School District in Illinois).

While we see no significant difference between the 90:10 and 50:50 program types for English speakers or Spanish speakers when we look at English proficiency, we do see a significant difference between program types when we look at Spanish proficiency. English-dominant and Spanish-dominant students were both more likely to develop high levels of proficiency in Spanish and bilingual proficiency in 90:10 programs than in 50:50 programs. If high levels of proficiency in Spanish are an important goal of a TWI program, a 90:10 program is clearly the better choice.

Academic performance of Spanish-dominant and English-dominant students. When Lindholm-Leary (2001) analyzed Spanish-dominant

TWI students' academic performance across program types, she found that Spanish-dominant students in both 90:10 and 50:50 programs scored at grade level and at least as high as their peers across the state of California in Spanish reading and math. She contrasts this with Spanish-dominant students in transitional bilingual education and English-only programs who scored below average in Spanish reading and math on standardized test scores. At 6th grade, she found that Spanish-dominant students in 90:10 and 50:50 programs scored comparably in English reading and math. This is commendable given the low performance that we often see among Latinos in U.S. public schools overall (see chapter 1).

When she looked at English-dominant TWI students performance on academic tests, Lindholm-Leary (2001) found that English-speaking students scored average and at least as high as the California statewide norms for English speakers instructed only in English in both English reading and math in both 90:10 and 50:50 programs. Lindholm-Leary was unable to find much data on Spanish reading and math achievement by English speakers in 50:50 programs. However, she did find that in 90:10 programs English speakers scored average to above average in Spanish reading and math.

Lindholm-Leary's (2001) data clearly indicate that TWI students can function at least at grade level in two languages in the content areas. Their scores are on par with their peers across the state in California, even when the peers are English monolinguals in English-only classrooms. Furthermore, the lack of differences between students in 90:10 and 50:50 programs in English reading and math at upper grade levels demonstrates that English speakers and Spanish speakers in 90:10 programs are not at any disadvantage because of the additional Spanish and consequently less English in their instruction. This research demonstrates that (a) students learn content regardless of which language they learn it through; (b) students learn English regardless of whether they are in a 90:10 or 50:50 program; and (c) students learn more Spanish in 90:10 programs than in 50:50 programs.

Although the research finds clear advantages to the 90:10 program type, it is common to find ideological opposition to this approach from both English speakers and Spanish speakers. According to Lindholm-Leary (2001) we now see 80:20 programs (a variation of the 90:10 program type) that are intended to address these fears. In 80:20 programs, kindergarten students begin with 80 percent of their instructional time in Spanish and 20 percent in English instead of starting with 90 percent in Spanish and ten percent in English. The major reason, Lindholm-Leary (2001) argues, lies in parental and administrative fear that there will not be enough English instruction. Fear also promotes the other major design variation, which is the language of initial literacy instruction. While most 90:10 programs begin with initial literacy instruction in Spanish, some begin with initial literacy instruction in the students' native language and segregate language learners during this time of the day.

Since literacy instruction in the early elementary grades has been a primary focus of curricular reform and professional development in the SDP for the last several years, and since elementary schools are being held increasingly accountable for students' literacy development, the teachers from PS 23, PS 31, and PS 29 focused their attention on this aspect of TWI programs. I turn now to a discussion of different approaches to biliteracy development that we find in theory and in practice.

Questioning biliteracy development in two-way immersion programs

Bilingual teachers, mainstream teachers, administrators, parents-everyone has many questions about and opinions on literacy instruction. This section begins with a brief overview of research that the language planning teams drew on as they made decisions about their programs. Then it describes how TWI programs across the country address the question of which language(s) for initial literacy instruction. I conclude this section by considering how the larger political context surrounding the education of English language learners (ELLs) influences local beliefs about initial literacy instruction in each of the schools.

What does the research say about approaches to literacy instruction

We saw in chapter 3 that the greatest indicator of academic literacy development in a second language is strong first language (L1) literacy development, and that strong L1 literacy is associated with strong academic performance in both the first and second language. All sound TWI programs in the United States provide ELLs with opportunities to develop a strong foundation in their native language and to build on that foundation with initial literacy instruction in their L1. However, questions remain about literacy instruction in TWI programs in particular and about biliteracy development in general. For example, when should ELLs begin literacy instruction in English (simultaneously or sequentially)? What language(s) should they use for literacy instruction with English speakers? As we see in this section, scholars agree that there is no one "best" approach, and schools must make decisions based on their assessment of what is appropriate for their local school context.

Nancy Hornberger is a leading international scholar on biliteracy development, and she has synthesized research on biliteracy development from around the world. Her recent book *The Continua of Biliteracy* (2003) provides an important perspective on the sequential vs. simultaneous literacy debate. She writes,

> The findings that a stronger L1 leads to a stronger L2 do not
> necessarily imply that the L1 must be fully developed before
> the L2 is introduced. Rather, the L1 must not be abandoned
> before it is fully developed, whether the L2 is introduced simul-
> taneously or successively, early or later, in that process.

We often find that people who are raised in contexts in which monolingualism is the norm (e.g., the United States) believe that simultaneous literacy instruction will somehow confuse the child. We see this belief reflected in school district policies that discourage literacy development in a second language until 2nd or 3rd grade, and we saw it reflected in Claudia's story about language use in her household (see chapter 5). There is, however, no evidence to support the belief that simultaneous biliteracy development is a problem. There is also some evidence that simultaneous literacy development in Spanish and English is not only possible but also beneficial to the students in many cases.

The following contribution to the debate on language(s) for initial literacy instruction is taken from Cloud, Genesee, and Hamayan's (2000) book entitled *Dual Language Instruction: A Handbook for Enriched Education.* These experts on dual language education recommend

> providing initial reading/writing instruction to both groups in
> the non-English language first. Alternatively, some dual lan-
> guage program organizers choose to provide formal literacy
> instruction to each group of students in their respective prima-
> ry languages to capitalize on their existing oral language skills,
> while emphasizing the non-English language for instruction in
> other content areas.

Here we see support for the approach to initial literacy instruction taken in 90:10 programs, with all students receiving initial literacy instruction in Spanish first. However, these authors also recognize the validity of other approaches.

What is not clear in the Cloud et al. (2000) recommendation, however, is whether program organizers provide formal literacy instruction to each group of students *exclusively* in their primary language (i.e., English literacy instruction for English speakers and Spanish literacy for Spanish speakers in the early elementary grades) or formal literacy instruction to each group of students in their primary language *in addition to their second language* (i.e., simultaneous literacy instruction in Spanish and English for all students). Perhaps this ambiguity is intentional.

Lindholm-Leary (2001) provides the clearest response to the question of which approach to biliteracy development is best. She writes,

> While most 90:10 models begin reading instruction in the target language (n = 70), parents and administrators at some sites have worried that English speaking students will fall behind in English reading. As a consequence, they use a 90:10 or 80:20 model with initial literacy instruction in the students' L1 (n = 19). Similarly, two major variations exist in the 50:50 model, with most sites (n = 56) beginning reading in the students' L1, and other sites (n = 19) beginning reading instruction in both languages. *Currently, no research exists to determine which is the best approach.* Such a comparison would be complicated by the cultural, social class, and linguistic diversity represented in the student populations at different school sites and in the different approaches used for literacy instruction (36-37; italics added for emphasis).

Since the research clearly demonstrates that there is no one-size-fits-all program type that educators can simply implement at their schools, we began to ask questions about how other TWI programs addressed this critical issue of biliteracy development.

How do TWI programs across the United States approach initial literacy instruction

The language planners from PS 31, PS 23, and PS 29 and I turned our attention to the Center for Applied Linguistics (CAL)'s TWI directory (www.cal.org) to answer this question. When I searched the directory and specified *language for emergent literacy instruction,* I found that there were 203 programs in 23 states. Of those programs, 88 offered initial literacy instruction to all students in the minority language; 60 offered all students initial literacy instruction in both languages, 53 offered initial literacy instruction to all students in their first language, and 2 offered initial literacy instruction to all students in English.

Nearly all of the students in North Philadelphia are low-income, and we hear strong ideological assumptions about what low-income students can and cannot do. We therefore searched for schools in which 76 percent or more of the student population (English speakers and minority language speakers) qualify for free or reduced lunch. Of the 54 schools with majority low-income English-speaking and Spanish-speaking student populations, 21 programs provide initial literacy instruction to all students in the minority language, 19 provide initial literacy instruction in both languages, 14 provide initial literacy instruction to all students in their first language, and none provides initial literacy instruction to all students in English.

Since many bilingual programs in the United States have a low-income minority language population and a middle-income English-speaking population, I also searched the directory using this criteria. I found 92 programs with low-income language minority population and an unspecified English-speaking population. Of those programs, 36 provided all students with initial literacy instruction in the minority language, 30 provided all students with initial literacy instruction in both languages, 25 provided all students with initial literacy instruction in their first language, and one program provided initial literacy instruction to all students in English.

As we talked to TWI educators across the country and read the research on literacy instruction and biliteracy development, we found that it is not the type of TWI program that matters the most. Any pedagogically sound well-implemented type of TWI program can reach its goals, and any pedagogically unsound poorly implemented type of program is likely to fall short of its goals. The key is a sound program design and strong implementation. Since educators' and parents' ideological beliefs influence the ways that they interpret and implement a program, we needed to look locally at language ideologies at school and in the community.

How does the larger context influence local beliefs

We saw in chapter 2 that there is confusion and controversy surrounding bilingual education in the United States, and we saw in Part II of the book that there are complex and contradictory ideologies about spoken and written Spanish and English in the everyday lives of people in this predominantly Puerto Rican community. These larger ideological debates inform local opinions about bilingualism, biliteracy development, academic achievement, and intergroup relations. As we saw earlier in this chapter, the school-based language planning teams were encouraged to explore the ideologies that various constituents had in order to determine (a) what type of program is appropriate for a particular school context and (b) what ideologies need to be addressed in order to make space for the new TWI program.

We also saw in Part II of this book that student performance in most schools in North Philadelphia is poor, and we saw in Part III of the book that the SDP has been working to address this challenge in the area of literacy instruction. Schools are being held increasingly accountable for student performance, and the lowest performing schools are being the most closely scrutinized. The No Child Left Behind Act requires all schools to provide evidence of every student's academic development as well as evidence of every ELL's English language development. Although there is no explicit anti–bilingual education legislation on the federal or state (Pennsylvania) level, we do see some   evidence of anti-bilingual, English-only sentiments as everyone focuses on test scores in English. This larger context influences local decisions about which type of bilingual education is appropriate and which language(s) for initial literacy instruction should be selected.

Educators in TWI programs need to address a range of language ideologies that stand in opposition to their vision. For example, some educators that I have talked with in North Philadelphia believe that TWI can work for middle-class English speakers who are not struggling to develop basic skills in English, but they emphasize that their students do not fit into that category. Some fear that English-speaking students, especially low-income monolingual English-speaking African-American students, will not be able to learn to read and write in two languages. Some educators strongly reject the idea of integrating Spanish speakers and English speakers for instruction through two languages because they believe it might harm their struggling English-speaking students' efforts to learn to read and write in English. Some educators believe that two-way immersion can work only if English speakers and Spanish speakers are segregated for initial literacy instruction in their dominant language. Others argue that low-performing schools in North Philadelphia need to focus on improving test scores in reading and in math in English, and some believe that spending any time in Spanish will take away time needed to develop proficiency in English. Educators in TWI programs need to listen to these competing beliefs about literacy development, and they need to counter those beliefs with the facts about TWI in ways that the various interest groups understand.

Although North Philadelphia is a low-income neighborhood that is plagued by many of the problems that challenge any low-income urban neighborhood, and although many of the schools are failing to meet the educational needs of the students and community they serve, North Philadelphia is a linguistically rich environment. As we saw in Part II of this book, most of the students who attend schools in this neighborhood are heritage Spanish speakers, and most of the parents and educators that I have talked with believe that Spanish is important resource for ELLs and heritage Spanish speakers to maintain and develop. Educators in TWI programs need to demonstrate that it is possible to organize their programs and practices in ways that enable ELLs and English speakers to develop expertise in spoken and written English AND Spanish. Chapter 12 describes how the TWI educators from PS 31, PS 23, and PS 29 are working to address this challenge.

Local educators' beliefs and practices about bilingualism and bilingual education are influenced by the complex and at times contradictory language ideologies that we see on the national, state, school district, community, and school levels of context. While it is clear that TWI educators need to challenge language ideologies that stand in opposition to TWI programs with evidence about the effectiveness of these programs, it is unclear exactly how to best accomplish this. Some people respond to research evidence, others respond to the beliefs of other influential people in the community, and for others, seeing is believing. The burden of responsibility is on the TWI educators as they implement their program to continue to address these language ideologies so that everyone involved develops a coherent understanding of the goals of the program, the program structure, and the expected outcomes. With this understanding of the dynamic processes of language planning in North Philadelphia in mind, let's turn now to the actual TWI plans that emerged.

Two-way immersion programs in North Philadelphia

This section presents the two-way immersion (TWI) plans that the language planning teams from the three target schools developed for their schools during the spring of 2001. As we see, PS 23 and PS 31 both decided that a 50:50 program was best for their schools, but the way that they organized the program differs based on their assessments of human and material resources and constraints at the school and on local beliefs about the development of bilingualism and biliteracy in the early elementary grades. PS 29 preferred a program that emphasized Spanish in the early years and chose to implement an 80:20 program. After I briefly review each of the school's TWI plans, I review some of the challenges that these plans present to the TWI educators.

Two-way immersion at PS 23

The PS 23 team decided on a 50:50 program that would begin in kindergarten and 1st grade in September 2001 and grow one year at a time as the

TWI students progress through elementary school. According to the PS 23 50:50 plan, each grade is divided into two groups (group A and group B) and the students are always integrated for instructional purposes. According to the teachers, each group includes balanced numbers of English language learners (ELLs) and English speakers. It is important to emphasize that the overwhelming majority of the English speakers (99 percent) at PS 23 are Latino. Most of those students are heritage Spanish speakers who come to school with some expertise in Spanish, although the degree and nature of that expertise vary tremendously. All students are provided simultaneous literacy instruction in Spanish and English, and they study all of their content-area subjects through both languages beginning in kindergarten and continuing throughout their educational experience at PS 23.

The PS 23 educators separate languages by time and by teacher. Group A and group B alternate teacher and language of instruction weekly so that group A is taught by the Spanish-dominant teacher who ideally speaks only in Spanish while group B is taught by the English-dominant teacher who ideally speaks only in English. The PS 23 educators are very concerned to ensure that 50 percent of students' educational experience is in Spanish and 50 percent is in English, and they have bilingual personnel in the school who teach all of the specials (e.g., physical education, art, music) through either or both languages. When the TWI students go to the specials, the TWI teachers have a common prep that they can use for program planning.

Two-way immersion at PS 31

The PS 31 team also decided on a 50:50 program that would begin in kindergarten and 1st grade in September 2001 and grow one grade per year over time. PS 31 has a smaller student population than PS 23 and could therefore only begin their TWI program with one class at each grade level. About one-third of the students in the first class were Spanish-speaking ELLs, and a few were monolingual English-speaking African-Americans. The rest of the students in this linguistically heterogeneous class were Latino, and most of them had some expertise in Spanish. According to the TWI plan that PS 31 developed in the spring of 2001, one bilingual teacher and one bilingual literacy intern are to be assigned to each grade level class, and those teachers alternate languages by time of day. In both the kindergarten and 1st grade, Spanish is the language of instruction in the morning and English is the language of instruction in the afternoon. Students are provided with literacy instruction in both Spanish and English everyday in the morning (in Spanish) and in the afternoon (in English). The schedule is organized so that the TWI teachers have a common prep in the middle of the day, and students return to their regular classroom after the prep (which was sometimes in Spanish and sometimes in English). This schedule gives the teachers a common time to plan together, and it gives TWI students a natural break from one language to another each day.

When the PS 31 teachers were asked why they chose to use Spanish every morning and English every afternoon, they explained that English has more status at school and all of the children were very motivated to learn and use English. Since it was a bit more of a challenge to encourage all of the students to use Spanish, the teachers use Spanish in the morning when the children are more alert and English in the afternoons when they were likely to be a bit more tired and potentially resistant. The TWI teachers drew on their assumptions about the sociolinguistic situation to inform the choices they made in program design.

Two-way immersion at PS 29

The PS 29 team decided on an 80:20 program that would begin in kindergarten in September 2001 and grow one year at a time. They had originally wanted to develop a prototypical 90:10 program, but their schedules and personnel dictated the 80:20 distribution of Spanish and English. PS 29 decided to begin their TWI program with only one class, and about one-third of those students were ELL, one-third were monolingual English speakers, and one-third were bilingual Latinos. According to the TWI plan that the PS 29 team presented in May 2001, the Spanish-dominant teacher teaches the kindergarten students 80 percent of the time in Spanish, and she is assisted by a bilingual literacy intern who also speaks only in Spanish during Spanish time. All of the PS 29 students begin formal literacy instruction in kindergarten exclusively in Spanish. In kindergarten, the English-dominant teacher comes into the class for 20 percent of the time, and she focuses on oral language development in English, primarily through social studies content. According to the program plan that the PS 29 educators developed in the spring of 2001, in 1st grade 70 percent of students' instruction will be in Spanish and 30 percent will be in English; in 2nd grade 60 percent will be in Spanish and 40 percent will be in English; and in 3rd, 4th, and 5th grade 50 percent of students' instruction will be in Spanish and 50 percent will be in English. While students are exposed to print in English from the beginning of the program in kindergarten, formal literacy instruction in English does not begin until 2nd or 3rd grade for any of the students (whether formal literacy instruction in English begins in 2nd or 3rd grade is being debated at the time of this writing; new Pennsylvania standardized testing requirements that begin in 3rd grade bear on this decision).

Challenges

The choices that the language planning teams made in terms of the types of programs they have planned have implications, and some lead to real challenges for the TWI educators who are working to implement these programs. Some of these challenges relate to classroom implementation, and others relate to language ideologies surrounding the programs. The TWI educators are developing an understanding of the nature of these challenges as they implement their programs at their schools. They work with each other within and across schools to develop strategies to address these challenges on the local level. I discuss this point in much more detail in chapter 13.

For example, the PS 23 educators chose to alternate languages by the week beginning in kindergarten, and some outsiders have questioned whether this is too much time for very young students (e.g., English speakers) to be immersed in their weaker language (i.e., Spanish) with no support from their stronger language (English). The PS 23 educators respond that they just need to ensure that they make the content comprehensible to second language learners. They argue that the intensive-week-on/week-off period of time actually facilitates this effort. The two teachers have also realized the need to plan their instruction very closely together so that they seamlessly build on what students have learned in each language across the content areas over time. The Spanish-dominant and English-dominant teacher work together to ensure that all students develop the knowledge and skills that they need in every content area in both languages, and each teacher is accountable for all of the students' performance and development in one or the other language.

The PS 31 educators chose to alternate languages in the middle of each day, and the same teacher offers formal literacy instruction in the morning in Spanish to her students and then in the afternoon in English to the same group of students. At first, the PS 31 educators were asked whether their students had any trouble addressing the same person in one language in the morning and another language in the afternoon, given the fact that this is a rather artificial way to distribute languages. The PS 31 educators respond that the children understand that morning is Spanish time and afternoon is English time, and they often monitor their teachers if they use the "wrong" language. The PS 31 educators have also been asked by outsiders to consider whether their intensive focus on formal literacy instruction takes away from time that they need to focus on content-area instruction, for example, in social studies, math, and science. To this, the PS 31 teachers respond that they just need to organize their instruction thematically so that formal literacy instruction is integrated with content-area instruction, and they need to ensure that they address all of the content-area standards within the context of their integrated approach.

The PS 29 educators were convinced by the research on two-way immersion programs that it was important to provide more time in Spanish during their program to counter the dominance of English in the larger school, community, and societal contexts. These educators therefore chose to provide 80 percent of their content-area instruction in Spanish and formal literacy instruction to all students in Spanish first. The PS 29 educators have been asked by outsiders to consider whether their English speakers can develop literacies in Spanish first. As we saw earlier in the chapter, there is a strong ideological assumption that low-income monolingual English speakers in this neighborhood will struggle to develop literacies in English. There is also a strong assumption that formal literacy instruction in Spanish could harm English speakers' literacy development in English. Although I know of no research to support this position, this ideological belief is reflected in questions that the PS 29 educators are asked to address on a regular basis.

The TWI educators also face some common challenges as they work to develop their programs. For example, each school chose to begin its program as a strand in the school, and each school only includes about 30 students per grade level in their TWI program. Although we discussed the possibility of attrition from the beginning, the schools believed that they could only enroll this number of students in their program given their assessment of local resources and constraints. Hopefully we will not see tremendous attrition over time, and each school will have the numbers of students it needs in the upper grade levels. We will also hopefully see more interest in the TWI programs as people see evidence of their effectiveness, and schools can offer more than one TWI class per grade level. This is a pattern that we have seen in other TWI programs that began as a strand in the school and grew to be a whole-school program over time.

These educators face many other common challenges that they work together to creatively address. For example, all of the schools are challenged to keep their long-term vision of two-way immersion clearly in mind as they work to develop their programs, which is a difficult challenge for a developing program in the best of worlds. However, this challenge is compounded in these schools because of the larger context of educational reform in the school district. In this context of dramatic turnover and change, TWI teachers are regularly required to explain what they are doing and why, and their programs and practices promise to be even more closely scrutinized in the future. It seems that this challenge actually brings the TWI teachers together in their struggle to develop programs that promote bilingualism. As the next chapter highlights, these teachers are well aware of this challenge. They want to be able to provide concrete evidence of the effectiveness of their programs to those who question their ideologies, programs, and practices.

Conclusion

This chapter has described the dynamic processes of dual language planning in three schools in North Philadelphia. We have seen how teachers and administrators from PS 31, PS 23, and PS 29 embraced the opportunity that Title VII, the School District of Philadelphia, the Office of Language Equity Issues, and the regional office offered them to design two-way immersion programs that they believed could meet the needs of their students and community. They embraced the professional development opportunities that they were offered to learn about second language acquisition, biliteracy development, content-based second language instruction, and different types of bilingual education programs. They embraced the opportunity to become advocates who educate parents, teachers, district officials, and other support personnel and community members about how their TWI program meets the needs of their target populations. And as we see in the next chapter, they embraced the opportunity to become reflective practitioners who look closely at their practice and at their capacity to implement their TWI program, coordinate the ongoing professional development they need, and collaborate with other educators in professional learning communities so that they can adapt their program and practices as necessary.

13

Addressing the challenges
of implementation

This chapter describes how two-way immersion (TWI) educators worked together to address the numerous ideological and practical challenges that arose as they began to implement TWI programs in the early elementary grades in their schools. It is based on my work as lead consultant on the dual language initiative of the Title VII bilingual education systemwide grant that the School District of Philadelphia (SDP) was awarded in November 2000, and it focuses on three target schools that are located in the predominantly Puerto Rican community in North Philadelphia. As we saw in chapter 12, language planning teams from PS 31, PS 23, and PS 29 worked throughout the spring of 2001 to open ideological spaces at their schools for TWI programs, and they developed TWI plans that they believed would be appropriate for the school and community contexts. They held themselves accountable for their students' performance, and they wanted to be prepared to address the questions and concerns that would inevitably arise. In the fall of 2001, we turned our attention to the challenges of implementation.

The first part of the chapter describes the professional development series that the TWI teachers and I developed to share TWI practices and support teacher learning about second language acquisition and biliteracy development. Then, in the context of the state takeover of the SDP, increasing English-only activity across the United States, and the accountability requirements of the No Child Left Behind Act of 2001, the urgent need to gather evidence of student performance became obvious (see chapter 2 and the introduction to Part IV for further discussions). The second part of this chapter provides an overview of the assessment plan that the TWI teachers and I developed to address this challenge. The data that are collected and analyzed through this assessment plan are intended to drive instruction, program development, and professional development on the local level and will ideally contribute to the growing database that documents the effectiveness of TWI programs in the United States (Thomas and Collier 2002; Lindholm-Leary 2001).

Dual language teachers talking

As I argued in Part III of the book, the effectiveness of any educational initiative depends on the teachers who implement the program. Part of my job as lead consultant on the dual language initiative was to ensure that teachers get the professional development that they need (e.g., in second language acquisition, biliteracy development, content-based second language instruction, intercultural communication, sociolinguistics) to effectively implement the two-way immersion (TWI) programs that they had planned for their schools during the spring of 2001 (see chapter 12 for detailed discussion of the language planning phase). More importantly, the TWI teachers requested ongoing professional development so that they could deliver on the promises that they had made about two-way immersion.

At the end of our three-week summer professional development on TWI programs and practices in the summer of 2001, the teachers asked for regular meetings throughout the 2001-2002 school year to support implementation. This section describes the professional development series that we developed to address challenges as they arise. I begin with a brief discussion of the theoretical orientation that informs this professional development series, and then I describe how the teachers work together within the context of these meetings to reflect on and improve their practices and programs. I conclude this part of the chapter with an overview of the action-oriented project that the TWI teachers and I have begun that will investigate and document how students develop literacies in Spanish and English through their participation in the TWI programs over time.

Developing as a community of practice

I call the professional development series "dual language teachers talking," a name that highlights the importance of dialogue. Following Little (1990) and Fullan (2000), my work with the teachers is informed by the assumption that school improvement occurs when

- teachers engage in frequent, continuous, and increasingly concrete talk about teaching practice,

- teachers and administrators frequently observe and provide feedback to each other, developing a shared language to describe their practices, and

- teachers and administrators plan, design, and evaluate teaching materials and practices together (see Fullan 2000, 84-85 for further discussion).

The professional development series is intended to provide a space for the TWI teachers to become a "community of practice" (Wenger 1998) and meet on a regular basis to reflect on their own and each others' practice, share successes, and collaborate in their efforts to address the challenges of implementation. Through ongoing conversations about their TWI practices and program development the TWI teachers deepen their understanding of how TWI programs function on the local level.

One of the TWI teachers' primary concerns during the first year of implementation was their students' bilingual and biliteracy development, which reflects the systemwide focus by the School District of Philadelphia (SDP) on early balanced literacy (EBL) in the early elementary grades (see chapter 9 for discussion of EBL in the SDP). In the first dual language teachers talking meeting (September 2001), the TWI teachers and I agreed to focus our attention during year 1 on the following questions:

1. How does your TWI program encourage English-speaking and Spanish-speaking students to become bilingual and to develop literacies in Spanish and English?

2. What evidence do you have of students' bilingual and biliteracy development over time?

The teachers embraced the opportunity to direct their own and each others' learning. They decided that each of our monthly meetings would be facilitated by a different TWI teacher who would share an aspect of her practice within the context of her classroom. As my discussion of the first year of the professional development series illustrates, we situate our discussion of theories of language teaching and learning within the context of the practices that the teachers share, and their questions about their practices and programs drive our professional development.

Talking about classroom practices

The dual language teachers talking meetings over the fall 2001 semester covered a range of topics that the teachers selected. One month, the 1st grade team from PS 23 shared how they use the SDP mandated K-3 assessments in both languages to guide literacy instruction within and across languages. Another month, the kindergarten and 2nd grade teachers from PS 23 shared how they use centers as contexts for second language acquisition, biliteracy development, and content area learning. Another month the kindergarten teacher from PS 31 shared how she reads big books in Spanish to her heterogeneous group of students in ways that involve the English speakers and challenge the Spanish speakers. Another month, the 1st grade teacher and the principal from PS 31 shared a video that the principal had made of a cooperative learning group of English speakers and Spanish speakers negotiating meaning through Spanish at a center. The teachers embraced the opportunity to look closely at their own and each others' practice, and they drew on each others' expertise and the literature to answer their questions and to help them make sense of their observations.

As mentioned in chapter 12, a common question that the TWI teachers and outside constituents had was whether the monolingual English-speaking non-Latino students in this neighborhood would be able to acquire Spanish and develop literacies in Spanish through their classes, especially given the fact that many of these students were struggling to develop literacies in their first language. Although their reading in the field and their visits to other TWI programs the year before had convinced the TWI teachers that it was possible for English speakers to learn through Spanish, these teachers still had many questions about whether and how this would happen in their classes. As the year progressed, teachers enthusiastically shared stories of their observations. Two examples of very different learners illustrate some of the variation that teachers noticed about how their English-speaking students were acquiring Spanish in their classes. Teachers' observations, reflections, and dialogue about examples like these were also helping everyone develop a more coherent understanding of what TWI actually means in practice at their schools.

Aisha was a monolingual English-speaking African-American girl in kindergarten at PS 31, and she was very verbal. At the beginning of the year she would utter nonsense words in response to the teacher during Spanish time. Her utterances began to sound more Spanish-like in their intonation over time, and she began to utter words in Spanish that made sense. Aisha's teacher provided lots of input, for example, in the form of teacher talk and read alouds, and she drew Aisha's attention to the contributions from other Spanish-speaking students in the class. She also gave Aisha many opportunities to negotiate meaning and extend that input. As the year progressed Aisha's talk in "Spanish" began to make more sense to Spanish speakers.

Bobby, in contrast, was a monolingual English-speaking European American at PS 29, and he was very quiet when he entered the program. At the beginning of the year he sat at the front of the rug while his teacher read stories or led activities with his attention clearly fixed on the teacher. Soon Bobby began to repeat formulaic utterances, for example, from the morning message or some other highly predictable activity. As time progressed, Bobby began to sing songs in Spanish enthusiastically with the other students, and he began to participate in conversations in Spanish with groups of boys in his class. The teachers were surprised one day when Bobby knew the answer to a question in Spanish that the Spanish speakers in the group did not know. The teachers could not understand at first how this was possible because the other children spoke Spanish and Bobby did not. Through reflection, the teachers realized that it was possible for Bobby to know the answer in Spanish that Spanish speakers did not know because he understood the concept and the others did not. The Spanish-speaking students could not talk about a concept if they did not know about it, no matter what language. For Bobby, who understood the concept, talking about it in simple terms was largely a question of vocabulary.

The teachers' observations were becoming more analytical as the fall semester progressed, and they were beginning to talk about their practice in ways that reflected their developing understanding of issues in the field of second language acquisition. Their questions, conversations, and practices demonstrated their focus on the crucial roles of input, interaction, and output, and their observations of how their students, especially their monolingual English speakers, were acquiring their second language answered many of their earlier questions and addressed many of their concerns. My job was to help the teachers realize that they were developing these understandings as they implemented their programs and reflected on their practices, and to continue to push them forward in their learning.

Thinking critically about biliteracy development

During the spring of 2002, the Office of Language Equity Issues (OLEI) offered a variety of professional development opportunities for bilingual and ESL teachers from across the SDP, and some of these opportunities led to critical thinking and action by TWI educators. This section describes how the teachers drew on what they were learning through these outside opportunities, first at the NABE conference of the National Association for Bilingual Education in Philadelphia and then in a graduate course on Spanish literacy development at Temple University, to inform their TWI professional development series. As this discussion makes clear, the TWI teachers incorporated *what* they were learning about biliteracy development as well as *how* they could analyze their students' biliteracy development into their dual language teachers talking network.

The National Association for Bilingual Education held its annual meeting that year (spring 2002) in Philadelphia, and OLEI sent many bilingual and ESL (English as a second language) teachers to the conference.

Many of the TWI teachers went to TWI sessions that broadened their thinking about some of the challenges that they faced. For example, many of the TWI teachers realized that although they had been more concerned with English speakers and English language development, the national level concern in the TWI field was with Spanish speakers and Spanish language development. Elizabeth Howard from the Center for Applied Linguistics (CAL) shared findings from the joint Center for Applied Linguistics/Center for Research on Education, Diversity, and Excellence (CAL/CREDE) longitudinal study on biliteracy development in TWI programs across the United States that highlighted this concern. Her analysis demonstrated that although English-speaking and Spanish-speaking students in TWI programs were consistently performing at or above grade level in Spanish and English, Spanish-speaking students' performance was generally lower than English-speaking students' performance on writing tasks in both Spanish and English. This finding echoed Valdéz' (1997) cautionary note about dual language education. Valdéz (1997) warned that if TWI educators do not provide high-quality Spanish programs and if they do not closely monitor their Spanish-speaking students' performance, TWI programs may actually end up perpetuating the kinds of inequities between Spanish speakers and English speakers that these programs are intended to address (see chapter 3 for further discussion).

The Office of Language Equity Issues funded a Temple University graduate course on Spanish literacy development for SDP teachers during the spring 2002 semester through one of their Title VII professional development grants, and this course also pushed the TWI educators' thinking about biliteracy development. Although I did not attend the course, the teachers told me that it was taught entirely in Spanish, the majority of the readings were in Spanish, all of the students' oral and written presentations were in Spanish, and the teachers looked critically at a range of approaches used to promote literacy development in Spanish. Unlike any of their earlier professional development experiences, this course did not see Spanish in relation to English or as subordinate to English. This course looked at Spanish literacy development as the primary focus. Many of the TWI teachers who took this class became concerned that the frameworks and assessment tools that the SDP uses are biased toward English. These teachers began to question whether these tools allow for an accurate assessment of literacy development in Spanish, and they began to demand the development of more valid assessments.

Consistent with my goal of using the teachers' questions and concerns to drive their professional development within the context of the dual language teachers talking network, I encouraged the teachers to use what they were learning about biliteracy development in general and about Spanish literacy development in particular to inform the content and structure of their summer 2002 professional development workshops. The teachers embraced the opportunity to use samples of their students' writing in Spanish and English to inform their thinking about biliteracy development as both Liz Howard from CAL and the Temple professor had recommended, and they embraced the opportunity to direct their own and each others' learning as they had been doing throughout the year. Before the school year was over, the teachers developed a reading and writing activity that each of the TWI teachers used in her classroom to generate comparable writing samples in Spanish and English within and across TWI programs in North Philadelphia. The teachers decided to make descriptive accounts of student writing a focal point of the summer workshop, and they decided to use the literature that they had been reading on literacy development in Spanish and English to guide their work.

Each day of the four-day summer biliteracy development workshop was structured to integrate theory and practice in the field and to guide teachers' efforts to look critically at the literature in relation to their students' writing. Day 1 was dedicated to Spanish literacy development, and in the morning TWI teachers who had attended the Temple University class led our discussion of selections from the literature that the class had read during the spring 2002 semester. These teachers highlighted features that we should look for in Spanish writing, and in the afternoon the teachers used what they had discussed in the morning to guide their descriptive accounts of Spanish writing. Day 2 was dedicated to English literacy development and Sonia Barinov, who co-taught the balanced literacy for ESOL and bilingual teachers course at the University of Pennsylvania that I mentioned in chapter 9, led our discussion about the literature on English literacy development. In the afternoon, the teachers worked together to relate what they knew about English literacy development to their descriptive accounts of student writing in English. On day 3, the teachers used the approach that Howard (2000) had developed to compare writing in Spanish and English on the CAL/CREDE longitudinal study of biliteracy development, and the teachers discussed what they noticed about the English writing and Spanish writing of their kindergarten and 1st grade students. On day 4, the TWI teachers generated ideas for an action-oriented research project that was aligned with the work that Howard had done for the CAL/CREDE project, and that would allow them to look closely at their own students' reading and writing development in Spanish and English over time. The next section discusses this project in more detail.

Initiating an action-oriented bilteracy development project

The TWI teachers revised the questions that had guided our work through the 2001-2002 school year, and the new research questions now focus more directly on literacy. These research questions were stimulated by the CAL/CREDE research questions that investigate the relationship between first and second language writing ability over time (Howard 2000). However, the questions that the TWI teachers in the SDP ask also consider how the data that they collect and analyze can inform instruction and program development in the short term. Our action-oriented research questions are:

1. How do students develop literacies in Spanish and English through their experiences in a TWI program?

2. How can we assess students' bilingual and biliteracy development?

3. How can we use the data that we collect and analyze to guide instruction and to provide evidence of biliteracy development over time?

Although the TWI teachers had decided to align their biliteracy development project with the CAL/CREDE study in terms of their data collection and analysis methods, they also wanted to use assessment tools that were required in the SDP. The TWI teachers therefore began by considering to what degree the local accountability requirements allowed them to assess their students' biliteracy development. When they identified gaps between what the SDP requires and what the TWI teachers needed, they looked to the national biliteracy development study for guidance.

Assessing reading development is already an integral part of the early balanced literacy program that is in place in the SDP, and some (not all) of the assessments are currently available in both Spanish and English. All K-3 teachers are required to determine their students' independent reading level in the language that is used for instructional purposes three times a year, and that reading level is recorded on the report card each report period. The SDP has also identified target reading levels for students at each report period, and these reading levels are used as promotion criteria. Students who are enrolled in English-only instruction have their reading levels assessed in English, and students who are enrolled in Spanish-only instruction have their reading levels assessed in Spanish.

The TWI teachers who are implementing 50:50 programs that provide initial literacy instruction in both languages decided that they needed to assess their students' reading levels in both languages. Since the SDP report card that is used today only has a place for one reading level, the TWI teachers decided to record their students' reading level in the students' dominant language on the report card, but keep track of their reading levels in both languages in their portfolio (see below for further discussion of this portfolio). The TWI teachers who are implementing the 80:20 program offer initial literacy instruction in Spanish, and they assess all students' reading levels in Spanish in the early elementary grades. They enter the students' reading level in Spanish each report period on the report card, and communicate carefully with the English-speaking parents so they understand the school's approach to literacy instruction in Spanish and English over time.

The teachers decided to replicate the methods that Howard had used to analyze writing development in the CAL/CREDE biliteracy development project (Howard 2000; personal communication) for their analysis of Spanish and English writing development in the TWI programs in the SDP. The CAL/CREDE methods involved collecting writing samples from the students in Spanish and English in response to open-ended tasks in a writers workshop format three times per year so that they could monitor their students' performance in both languages over time. By replicating the methods used in the CAL/CREDE project, the action-oriented research project on biliteracy development in North Philadelphia can contribute to larger conversation about biliteracy development in TWI programs nationally.

While one objective of the biliteracy project in North Philadelphia is to document the effectiveness of TWI in promoting students' development of literacies in Spanish and English, that is not the only objective. The TWI teachers want to use their ongoing analysis of student writing to guide their instruction and program development. One of the academic coaches from the regional office that serves the target schools in North Philadelphia had been participating in the TWI professional development from the beginning, and she had also taken the Spanish literacy course at Temple University. She agreed to help launch the biliteracy project by facilitating a discussion of writers workshops at the first dual language teachers talking meeting of the fall 2002. As part of this workshop, the teachers clarified their understanding of how they should organize instruction in their classes to collect their first writing samples in Spanish and English. At the end of this meeting, the teachers agreed to collect the first writing sample in Spanish and English by the November meeting. They also decided to schedule their data collection and analysis so that they could draw on their analysis for report cards and parent conferences (i.e., in November, March, and May).

The PS 31 teachers volunteered to lead our discussion of the first set of writing samples that the TWI teachers collected at our November 2002 meeting. As the teachers looked at the data that they had collected, they realized that they would need to revise their research methods a bit in order to collect writing samples from kindergarten and 1st grade students. Although the 3rd, 4th, and 5th grade students whose writing was the basis for the CAL/CREDE biliteracy study were able to write about the topic of their choice, the kindergarten and 1st grade teachers from PS 31, PS 29, and PS 23 who were at the meeting argued that they needed to structure their writing tasks in ways that would yield more writing. To address this challenge, the teachers decided that they would select a story at the beginning of the week in the language of the writing sample they wanted to collect that week (one week in Spanish, the next week in English). The story would be part of their regular literacy instruction, and the teacher would immerse the students in the kinds of activities that they normally did in the context of literacy instruction (e.g., read alouds, using puppets to dramatize the story, bringing a guest to read the story, asking students to act out the story; see chapter 9 for detailed discussion of balanced literacy framework used in the SDP). The writing generated for the action-research project was not to be an additional burden on the teachers; rather it was to be an integral part of their regular instruction. At the end of the week, the teacher gave the students a writing prompt to stimulate their narrative writing that was in some way related to the literacy instruction that week. The teachers agreed that they did not want to use the same book in Spanish one week and in English the next. They recommended that teachers choose different books, but those books could be related thematically.

Consistent with the CAL/CREDE study, the TWI teachers have begun to collect samples of their student narrative writing in Spanish and in English three times per year, and they have begun to record their students reading and writing levels in Spanish and English three times per year. The teachers use the data that they collect and analyze to guide instruction in the short term, and this data will provide evidence of how students are developing literacies in Spanish and English through their participation in the TWI programs over time. Teachers can share this data with parents at parent conferences so that they can see firsthand how their children are learning in the TWI program. The database that the TWI teachers are beginning to compile will also allow for some comparison of biliteracy development over time within and across program types (an 80:20 program and two 50:50 programs) among students from similar backgrounds in schools that use a similar approach to literacy instruction in public elementary schools in North Philadelphia.

This first part of the chapter has described how the TWI teachers took ownership of the development of their TWI programs and of their own professional development. The TWI teachers' reflections on practice throughout year 1 of TWI program implementation in North Philadelphia culminated in a summer professional development workshop on biliteracy development that in turn stimulated both a deeper understanding of research and practice in the field as well as many more questions about biliteracy development that the teachers wanted to continue to address. That work led to an action-oriented biliteracy development project that is intended to yield the data that the TWI teachers need to demonstrate how their students develop their expertise in spoken and written Spanish and English over time. This kind of data will allow them to address the questions that they hear and to challenge the misconceptions they encounter. Changing conditions on the federal, state, and local levels, however, required us to broaden the scope of our project. The next section describes the assessment plan that the TWI teachers and I developed to address these changing conditions.

Assessing two-way immersion students, practices, and programs

In the spring of 2002, the US Congress passed the No Child Left Behind Act (NCLB), which requires that schools provide evidence of English language learners' (ELLs') English language development on an annual basis, and evidence of all students academic achievement over time. In the fall of 2002, the TWI educators and I broadened our original biliteracy development project to address the new challenge that the NCLB presents. This part of the chapter describes the assessment plan that the TWI educators and I have developed, a plan which is inspired by the TWI assessment plan used in the Community Consolidated School District 54 in Schaumburg, Illinois, in general and by ongoing discussions with Margo Gottlieb, the Director of Assessment and Evaluation at the Illinois Resource Center in Des Plaines, Illinois, and Ngoc-Diep Nguyen, the Director of Bilingual and Multicultural Programs at Schaumburg School District #54 in Schaumberg, Illinois (Gottlieb and Nguyen 2002) in particular. First I outline the objectives of the School District of Philadelphia (SDP) assessment plan, and then I discuss the components of that plan. In addition to providing evidence of student performance that can be used to address local, state, and federal accountability requirements, the teachers will also be able to use the data that they collect and analyze as part of this assessment plan to inform instruction and to develop their TWI programs in ways that can meet the language education needs of their students and community.

Objectives of the assessment plan

As Gottlieb and Nguyen (2002) emphasized, the purpose of any assessment plan is to answer questions about students, teaching, learning, and program design. Two kinds of assessment data are required. Formative assessment data enable us to understand teaching and learning within the context of classroom practice, which can and should be used to drive instruction. Summative assessment data allows schools to respond to external accountability requirements on the district, state, and federal levels. Together, formative and summative data analysis give a comprehensive view of what students, teachers, and a program can do. Formative and summative data from TWI programs can and should be used by educators to target instruction, determine professional development needs, and direct program restructuring efforts in ways that address changing circumstances at school and in the community.

The objectives of the TWI assessment plan are based on the goals of TWI programs and the external accountability requirements that all SDP schools must address. Let us start with the external accountability requirements. Title III of the NCLB requires states, school districts, and charter schools to define objectives that are aligned with the standards and that are observable, measurable, and attainable; articulate means of assessing performance and development relative to those objectives with research-based tools; show evidence of all English language learners' annual English language development and academic growth; and demonstrate that they are closing the achievement gap between ELLs and English speakers and between low-performing English speakers and target levels. Two-way immersion programs have additional goals. Not only do all TWI programs aim for expertise in oral and written English and academic achievement in English, they also aim for expertise in oral and written Spanish (or other target language) and academic achievement in that target language. The components of any TWI assessment plan must provide formative and summative evidence of students' bilingual and biliteracy development, and of their academic performance and development in two languages.

As we discussed earlier in the chapter, formative data on teaching and learning in the classroom can and should be used to guide instruction and inform program development. Summative data provide empirical evidence that responds to the federal, state, and local mandates and accountability requirements. The summative analysis of data gathered through the TWI assessment plan will demonstrate how TWI students perform relative to

- students in the all-English academic program in the same schools
- ELLs and English speakers in other schools in the school district
- ELLs and English speakers on state and national standardized tests

Ideally, the TWI assessment plan will yield data that contributes to the growing body of evidence that demonstrates the effectiveness of well-implemented TWI programs in the United States (Thomas and Collier 2002; Lindholm-Leary, 2001)

Components of Student Assessment Plan

There are three components to the student assessment plan, and these components address the primary goals and objectives of all TWI programs. First I introduce the plan to assess oral language development in Spanish and English. Then I review the plan to assess biliteracy development. I conclude this discussion with the plan for assessing academic performance in Spanish and English. Before I proceed, however, it is important to emphasize that this plan is in the early stages of development. Just as Gottlieb and Nguyen's (2002) work has inspired the work of TWI educators in the SDP, this presentation of work in progress is intended to inspire other TWI educators' efforts to assess their English-speaking and Spanish-speaking students' performance relative to the goals of TWI programs in ways that respond to local, state, and federal accountability requirements.

Language development. First, TWI programs need to gather evidence of English language development to meet state and federal accountability requirements. Because there are ELLs in the TWI programs, the TWI teachers must administer the test that Pennsylvania mandates to test English language development. At the time of this writing, it is unclear which test of English language development the state will choose. What is clear, however, is that this test must be administered one time per year at the time that the state mandates. The data generated from this test will allow for comparison of the English language development of ELLs in TWI programs with the English language development of ELLs in other kinds of programs in the SDP. This data will also allow for comparison of the English language development of ELLs in TWI programs in the SDP with the English language development of ELLs in TWI programs and other types of programs across the state and country.

TWI educators also need evidence of students' bilingual development. If the state-mandated test in available in Spanish and English (e.g., the LAS), then the TWI educators can also administer the Spanish portion of the test to assess their English-speaking students' development of Spanish over time. If, however, the state-mandated test is not available in both of the languages used for instructional purposes, the TWI program needs to find a test that is available in both languages. This is the case that TWI educators in Schaumberg, Illinois, face, and they use the Idea Proficiency Test (IPT) to assess second language proficiency development. English speakers are tested in Spanish, and Spanish speakers are in English one time per year. The data generated from this test enables the TWI teachers to compare second language development of English speakers and Spanish speakers within and across programs over time.

Biliteracy development. All schools in the SDP must provide evidence of students' reading and writing development in English unless the student is Spanish dominant and enrolled in a bilingual program that provides initial literacy instruction in Spanish. In this latter case, schools need to provide evidence of students' reading and writing development in Spanish. The SDP teachers are currently required to administer the K–3 Assessments in either English or Spanish, depending on the language used for literacy instruction, to determine students' reading levels at different points in time, and to determine whether a student meets the promotion criteria for reading in their dominant language. They are also required to use the developmental writing continuum to determine students' writing level in English or Spanish, again depending on the language used for literacy instruction.

Since the TWI teachers who are implementing 50:50 programs are providing initial literacy instruction to all students in two languages, they need evidence of English-speaking and Spanish-speaking students' development of literacies not only in their first language but also in their second language. To this end, teachers in the 50:50 programs administer the K–3 assessments to all students in both languages before each report period and they assess students' writing levels in both languages. Since PS 29 provides initial literacy instruction to all students in Spanish until 2nd grade, PS 29 K–2 students are assessed using the K-3 assessments in Spanish. Educators can use these assessments of their students' reading and writing development to inform instruction, and they can compare their TWI students' literacy development in both languages to students' literacy development in other ESL (English as a second language), bilingual, and mainstream programs in the SDP and to national standards.

As discussed earlier in the chapter, TWI teachers had already decided to do their action-research project analyzing writing development in Spanish and English. Each teacher collects a sample of each TWI student's writing in both Spanish and English three times per year throughout the course of the student's time in the TWI program. Currently the TWI teachers use the developmental writing rubrics that the SDP has developed to assess writing development in Spanish and English. However, several of the teachers have expressed concern about the validity of the Spanish assessment tools that are used in the district. Time will tell whether the TWI teachers, or another group in the SDP, will take up the challenge to develop more appropriate assessment tools for Spanish.

The data collected and analyzed through the biliteracy development aspect of the project promise to yield a wealth of information that can guide instruction and program development. For example, TWI teachers will be able to provide evidence of transfer across languages to demonstrate how students draw on the range of languages in their linguistic repertoire to solve language-related problems (like learning to read and write in any language). As teachers analyze particular student's writing over time, and/as they see trends in the kinds of errors that students make, teachers will be able to provide the input that students need to continue their development in either or both languages. And like the CAL/CREDE study, the summative analysis of students' writing development will allow for comparison of English-speaking and Spanish-speaking students' writing development in Spanish and English over time, as well as for comparison of SDP TWI students' writing development in both languages with the Spanish and English writing development of TWI students in other contexts in the United States.

Academic achievement in two languages. Local, state, and federal mandates require students to be tested academically on a regular basis and require school districts to provide evidence of performance and development relative to national standards and norms. To meet this accountability requirement, the SDP mandates that schools assess students' academic performance at the beginning and end of each academic year throughout each students' academic career, and they currently require the Terra Nova to assess the academic performance of all students who are enrolled in all-English programs, and the Supera (the Spanish counterpart of the Terra Nova) to asses the academic performance of Spanish-speaking students who are receiving instruction through Spanish. Pennsylvania also requires all students to take the Pennsylvania System of School Assessments (PSSAs), currently beginning in 3rd grade, and the PSSAs are currently only administered in English. The TWI educators agreed to administer either the Terra Nova or the Supera, depending on the students' dominant language at the grade levels that the SDP requires. And of course, the TWI educators will also administer the PSSAs as required. This assessment data will enable comparisons of the TWI students with students in other ESL, bilingual, and mainstream program in the SDP and to national standards.

Consistent with the assessment plan used in Consolidated Community School District 54 in Schaumburg, Illinois, the teachers agreed that they should make a portfolio for each student, and that this portfolio should follow the student throughout their time in the TWI program. This portfolio would enable TWI teachers across grade levels to look back at samples of student work in English and Spanish to see evidence of their biliteracy development over time. The teachers agreed that each folder should have information about the student (e.g., home language use, language dominance at the beginning of the program). They also agreed that this portfolio was not to be the same as the student's regular portfolio, because the purpose of this portfolio was different from the portfolio that the SDP required them to keep. They could, however, use some of the same work for each portfolio.

While the teachers keep a portfolio for each of their students, and while the schools keep track of how each student is performing relative to their local and state accountability requirements, I also wanted the teachers to be able to use the data that they collected to address some of the larger ideologies that we have seen surrounding these programs. For example, many that I have spoken with in North Philadelphia are convinced by their experiences in bilingual education, either as students or teachers, and by their reading in the field, that ELLs can and should maintain and develop literacies in Spanish while they acquire English. Many educators and parents believe that Latinos who may be English dominant but who have some expertise in Spanish can benefit from participation in a TWI program. Some express concern that simultaneous literacy development is confusing to the students, and some believe that English speakers can not develop literacies in Spanish before they develop literacies in English. Many fear that low-income monolingual English-speaking students will not be able to develop literacies in two languages when they struggle to develop basic skills in English (see Part II for further discussion). I have asked the teachers to do case studies of selected students from their classes so that we can analyze data on students' biliteracy development within and across programs to address these beliefs. An important objective of this case study approach is take the portfolios that the teachers have collected and look across that data to provide evidence of how monolingual English-speaking non-Latino students, heritage Spanish speakers who are to varying degrees bilingual in Spanish and English, and monolingual Spanish speakers develop literacies in Spanish and English within and across TWI programs over time.

This section has presented the TWI assessment plan that the TWI teachers and I are developing to assess student performance relative to TWI program goals and objectives. My discussion illustrates how TWI educators begin with the federal, state, and local mandates and accountability requirements that they must address as teachers who work in the U.S. public school system. Then, TWI educators determine whether the assessment tools required by the district provide evidence of students' performance relative to the goals and objectives of the TWI programs. When the educators identify gaps, for example, in assessing English-speaking students' oral and written Spanish language development and academic achievement in Spanish, TWI educators need to take action to address those gaps. The assessment plan presented here is intended to support TWI educators' efforts to hold themselves accountable for their students' performance and development relative to their program goals within the context of the SDP today. As local, state, and federal account-ability requirements change, TWI educators need to revise their assess-ment plans.

Conclusion

This chapter provides an insider's view on local efforts to address the chal-lenges of implementing TWI programs in North Philadelphia. I began with a description of the dual language teachers talking professional develop-ment series that the teachers and I organized. The monthly meetings revolve around concrete practices that teachers share and provide a forum for them to ask questions, brainstorm solutions to problems, and look crit-ically at theories of language teaching and learning. The teachers have tak-en ownership of their programs and practices, and they have taken owner-ship of their professional development.

The TWI teachers also hold themselves accountable for their stu-dents' performance relative to the goals of TWI programs. Although this requires the teachers to do even more assessment than what is already required of them, they believe that they must assess students' perfor-mance and development in both languages. They recognize that in this era of accountability, what is not tested often slips through the cracks. The goals of TWI programs motivate them, and they are willing to do the extra work involved to support implementation. They use the data they collect on student performance to guide instruction, their ongoing professional development, and the development of their TWI programs.

Although the TWI teachers are not responsible for analyzing all of the summative data that they collect through this assessment plan, we are hoping for outside research support. Currently, several graduate students have signed on to the project, and ideally their qualitative and quantitative analysis of student performance in these TWI programs will contribute to the increasing database on the "astounding effectiveness of TWI programs (Thomas and Collier 2002).

14

Promoting community languages at school

This chapter describes school-based initiatives to develop world language programs that use the dominant community language for students who live in multilingual communities and participate in the all-English academic mainstream. This chapter is based on my work as consultant with the language planning teams in schools that support the maintenance and development of Khmer, Mandarin, Russian, Spanish, and Vietnamese. The community language programs that are the focus of this chapter are one component of the modified dual language programs that I described in chapter 11, and they are motivated by the teams' recognition that there are different ways that schools can draw on the linguistic and cultural resources that they find in the local community as they work to promote bilingualism to the greatest degree possible for their target populations. This language planning project is part of the dual language initiative that the Title VII bilingual education systemwide grant has supported in the School District of Philadelphia (SDP) since November 2000.

Although we see national, state, and local initiatives to build U.S. capacity in languages other than English, monolingualism in English is still the norm for most Americans. And although an increasing number of school-aged children live in households in which a language other than English is spoken, assimilation to monolingualism in English is still the dominant trend for immigrants in the United States. Heritage language speakers who live in multilingual communities bring a tremendous range of expertise in their home languages to school, but most schools fail to build on this community bilingualism. Individual students and their families, local communities and the United States more broadly all suffer because of our unwillingness and/or inability to preserve and develop these linguistic and cultural resources. This chapter works to address this gap.

This chapter provides an insider's account of an innovative language planning project that is currently underway in the SDP, and it divided into four parts. First I introduce the target populations at each of the schools. Next I outline the goals that the language planning teams have for their target populations and consider the kinds of outcomes that can be expected of the English speakers and heritage language speakers who participate in these programs. The third part of the chapter describes in general terms how the programs ideally look in practice. Finally, I discuss the kinds of challenges, both ideological and practical, that the target schools face in the early years of program implementation and development, and I outline strategies that we are using to address these challenges. Together the parts of this chapter are intended to inspire educators who are looking for creative ways to promote additive bilingualism in other school and community contexts.

Introducing the target populations

This section reviews data on the general demographics that the language planning teams collected about the target populations at their schools, and it identifies the target language at each of the schools. This information is not nearly as detailed as the ethnographic portrait that I provided about the predominantly Puerto Rican community in North Philadelphia in Part II of this book, which was based on several years of ethnographic research in schools, homes, and other key contexts in this community. However, each of the language planning teams in the target schools in different multilingual communities included at least one native speaker of the target language and at least one representative who knew the local community relatively well. The language planning teams continue to gather more information about their target populations using a variety of strategies, some of which I discuss in more detail in the introduction to my discussion of the goals of the programs in the next section.

The data presented in this section on target populations was collected by a variety of people. Two educators who work for the SDP, one a native speaker of Chinese and the other a native speaker of Khmer, have been integral parts of the language planning processes for the schools using the less commonly taught languages (LCTLs), and they collected data for the Mandarin and Khmer programs in South Philadelphia and for the Vietnamese program in Southwest Philadelphia. I collected data for the Spanish program in North Philadelphia, and the Russian teacher collected the data for the Russian program in Northeast Philadelphia. The following summary was presented by Chin, Ky, and Freeman (2002) at the 2nd Annual Heritage Languages Conference in Arlington, Virginia.

Target school (K–8) in South Philadelphia: Target language is Mandarin

- Thirty-five percent of the students are Chinese and live in Chinatown. Most of the Chinese-speaking students are designated English language learners (ELLs), but some are heritage Chinese speakers (American-born Chinese) who are proficient in English. Some of the Chinese students speak Mandarin, and some speak other varieties of Chinese. Most of these students are considered low-income.

- Sixty percent of the students are monolingual English speakers. Most of English-speaking students in the lower elementary grades are middle-income Caucasian, and most of the English speaking students in the upper elementary grades are low-income African American.

- Five percent of the students speak other languages, with no language group dominating.

Target school (K–5) in South Philadelphia: Target language is Khmer

- Thirty-five percent of the students are Khmer (Cambodian). Approximately half of the Khmer students are designated ELLs. Most Khmer students speak and/or understand some Khmer, although their expertise varies.

- Sixty percent of the students are monolingual English speakers. Most of these students are either African American or Caucasian.

- Five to 30 percent of these students speak other languages, either as their primary language or as an additional home language. The most common languages other than Khmer are Spanish, Vietnamese, and Chinese.

- Ninety-nine percent of these students are considered low-income.

Target school (K–5) in Southwest Philadelphia: Target language is Vietnamese

- Thirty percent of the students are Vietnamese. Most of the Vietnamese students were born in the United States, and few are

ELLs. Most are heritage language speakers who understand some Vietnamese. The Vietnamese community is not experiencing large numbers of new arrivals at this time.

- Sixty-five percent of these students are monolingual English speakers, and most of these English speakers are African American.
- Five percent of the students speak other languages, and some of these students are ELLs. The major languages spoken within this group are Chinese and Khmer.
- Ninety-nine percent of these students are considered low-income.

Target school (K–8) in North Philadelphia: Target language is Spanish

- Eighty-five percent of the students in the all-English academic mainstream are Latino. These heritage Spanish speakers have a wide range of expertise in Spanish (see Part II of this book for extensive discussion of these students).
- Fifteen percent of these students are monolingual English speakers, the majority of whom are African American.
- Ninety-nine percent of these students are considered low-income.

Target school in Northeast Philadelphia: Target language is Russian

- Twenty-five percent of the students are Russian. Some, but not all of these students are ELLs. The heritage language speakers generally speak Russian at home, but many are also proficient in English.
- Fifty-one percent of the students are monolingual English speakers. Forty-five percent of these students are Caucasian and 6 percent are African American.
- Twenty-four percent of the students speak a language other than Russian or English at home. Eleven percent of these students are Indian and speak Malaylam at home. Eleven percent are Asian and speak Korean or Chinese at home. Two percent are Latino and speak Spanish at home.
- Ten percent of the students are ELLs. The majority of these students are Russian.
- There are few low-income students at this school.

As this summary makes clear, each of the target schools has large numbers of heritage language speakers who speak the same community language. In every case, the Title VII grant chose the dominant community language as the target language. This choice was made based on the Office of Language Equity Issues (OLEI) data on student demographics throughout the SDP.

We also see from the demographic review that the circumstances surrounding that community language are different from school to school. For example, in the Spanish case we see few students enrolled at the target school who speak languages other than Spanish or English at home. Choosing Spanish for this target school has been unquestioned on the local school level. In contrast, in the Russian case we see increasing numbers of ELLs who speak languages other than Russian or English at home, and in the Khmer case we see increasing numbers of Chinese and Vietnamese students who speak languages other than Khmer or English at home. Although Russian and Khmer are the dominant languages in their respective communities, a few parents and teachers have questioned whether other languages could also be offered at those schools in the future. This kind of language choice question is an important one for the language planning teams at the target schools to address in the short and longer terms.

This demographic profile gives a preliminary idea of who the target populations are. However, as I argued in chapter 4 and illustrated in Part II of the book, educators who are working to build on community bilingualism need to understand in greater detail the ways that students use and evaluate the spoken and written languages in their linguistic repertoires. To stimulate this kind of local sociolinguistic inquiry, I gave each of the teams a list of guiding questions to help them consider the ways that their target populations use spoken and/or written English, the target language, and any other languages in their everyday lives at school, home, and in other key contexts. Teams also were asked to consider local language ideologies, or common-sense assumptions about the target language and speakers of the target language, and to think about how those ideologies structure interactions and opportunities at school and throughout the community, in the short and longer term (see chapter 4 for further discussion of ways that language planning teams can gather information about language attitudes and use in the community). Although details about the sociolinguistic situation surrounding each of the target schools are not included in this chapter, the language planning teams continue to gather this information to inform their program development.

As I have emphasized throughout this book, experience leads to expertise. Although the demographic information presented in this section does not give us an idea of the kinds of expertise that individual students bring with them to school, we can get a general idea about the range of expertise that language planning teams need to prepare for in their programs. In general terms, we can identify ELLs who are proficient in the target language, heritage language speakers of the target language who have a wide range of expertise in that language, and monolingual English speakers who have no expertise in the target language. In some cases, we also find speakers of languages other than the target language. With this general understanding of the target populations in mind, let us turn now to a discussion of the goals that the language planning teams articulated for their students, school, and community.

Clarifying goals and anticipating outcomes

As the language planning teams described their target populations in terms of their expertise in and affiliation with the target language, they began to articulate their goals and anticipated outcomes for each of those populations. This part of the chapter begins by reviewing the process the teams used to set their goals, and I outline those goals. Then I review research on the kinds of outcomes that educators can expect from English-speaking students in world language programs over time. Since there is no research on outcomes for heritage language speakers in world language programs that use students' heritage language, I conclude this part of the chapter by considering some of the exciting possibilities for this diverse population.

Developing clearly articulated goals

The teams clarified their understanding of their goals in different ways. As I discussed in chapter 11, each of the language planning teams included native speakers of the target language who were closely involved in some way or another with the target language community as well as educators (speakers of the target language and monolingual English speakers) who had worked with this community over time. Each of the teams drew on their insider knowledge and community connections to develop their understanding of the strengths and needs of their target populations.

Teams encouraged parents to talk with them about the strengths and needs of their children, and they asked them to share their language education goals in informal conversations and in more formal gatherings. The Russian team also enlisted the support of a doctoral student from Bryn Mawr College, and they developed and administered a language attitude and choice survey to all of the parents at that school. Members of the language planning teams read the literature on student outcomes in different kinds of language education programs, and they revised their goals to ensure that they were realistic and attainable given the resources and constraints of their schools. The language planning teams also considered the School District of Philadelphia (SDP) world language standards, the American Council for Teachers of Foreign Languages (ACTFL) standards, and the standards in other content areas.

Students living in multilingual communities have short-term and long-term social, academic, and professional language learning needs. The language planning teams determined that socially, their English speakers and heritage language speakers need to develop expertise in the community languages so that they are able to interact with monolingual speakers of the target language (Khmer, Mandarin, Spanish, Russian, Vietnamese) in their neighborhood and in other contexts. Heritage language speakers also need to maintain and develop expertise in their heritage language to keep them connected to their monolingual family members and to their heritage community, because strong family and community connections are necessary for healthy homes and communities. Academically, all students in the SDP, as in an increasing number of school districts and states in the United States, need to study a world language in order to meet graduation requirements, and the community language offers a natural resource to build on to address this requirement. Finally, although the professional need for expertise in languages other than English may not be readily apparent to all Americans, it is clear that students who have developed expertise in more than one language have access to an increasing number of jobs that are open to bilingual individuals, especially in bilingual communities like those in which the target schools are located (see chapter 1 for further discussion).

The goals for the target populations and for the language programs that serve them follow from this needs assessment, and they are aligned with the goals of the two-way immersion (TWI) programs that the Title VII grant endorsed (see chapter 11 for further discussion). Each of the schools that was developing a community language program agreed on the following goals for their target populations:

- To enable heritage language speakers to broaden their linguistic repertoires so that they can use their spoken and written heritage language to communicate across a wider range of topics for both formal and informal purposes

- To enable English speakers to develop expertise in the community language

- To enable all students to develop improved intergroup understanding and relations on the local level

Although these goals are clearly aligned with the goals of TWI programs, members of the language planning teams recognized the limitations of the programs they were developing. Since the community language programs do not provide at least 50 percent of the content-area instruction through the target language, their target populations cannot be expected to develop the same range of expertise as students who are enrolled in TWI programs. I return to this important point in my discussion of the kinds of outcomes we can expect from students below.

Since promoting bilingualism at school in the United States has an ideological dimension, the language planning teams also articulated ideological goals. As we saw in Part II, Spanish—especially Puerto Rican Spanish—is often stigmatized by students, parents, and other educators in North Philadelphia, and Spanish-speaking students often reject Spanish in favor of English. Although I have not developed an understanding of the particulars of the sociolinguistic situations surrounding each of the target schools in the other communities described in this chapter, members of the language planning teams from the other schools describe similar language ideologies. Generally speaking, English has much more prestige than the target language in each of the schools, and many educators and some parents see other languages as problems that speakers of those languages need to overcome in order to learn English and achieve in the all-English academic mainstream. The language planning teams in the target schools in the SDP strongly reject this language-as-problem orientation.

An important goal of each of the community language programs is to challenge this ideological orientation. Members of the language planning teams work in important symbolic and practical ways to elevate the status of heritage languages and of speakers of those languages at school and to make the community language an integral part of the academic mainstream that is visible and valued by all. Ideally, if all students, parents, and educators come to see community languages as important resources to develop, the programs will begin to reverse the trend toward monolingualism in English that dominates in the community. I return to this point at the end of the chapter.

Anticipating outcomes

As we saw in chapter 3, effective programs are aligned with national standards and they have realistic expectations for their target populations.

What kinds of outcomes can we expect from students who are enrolled in elementary school world language programs that target the dominant community language? Outside factors influence the kinds of outcomes we can expect for English speakers and heritage language speakers in that target language. Since English speakers and heritage language speakers (a) bring different kinds of expertise in the target language with them to school, (b) have different opportunities to use the target language outside of school, (c) have different motivations for using and learning that language, we must expect different outcomes for these target populations. This section considers the research on the kinds of performance that educators can expect from English speakers who are enrolled in standards-based world language programs over time, and it considers the expanded possibilities for the heritage language speakers that are enrolled in their programs.

We can turn to the *American Council for Teachers of Foreign Languages Performance Guidelines for K–12* (ACTFL 1999) to understand the developmental path that second language learning takes for monolingual English speakers when it occurs in a school setting. The performance guidelines are intended to describe realistic language performance for these students at various benchmarks along the instructional sequence. The guidelines are organized to facilitate educators' and learners' recognition of language performance across levels of proficiency (novice, intermediate, pre-advanced), modes of communication (interpersonal, interpretive, presentational), and criteria for accuracy (comprehensibility, comprehension, language control, vocabulary, cultural awareness, communication strategies). The K–12 performance guidelines provide educators, parents, and students with sets of descriptors that are based on information gathered from foreign language professionals representing a variety of program models and articulation sequences, and they are appropriate for languages more commonly taught in the United States (e.g., Spanish, French, German). The descriptors assume a sustained sequence of standards-based language instruction.

As mentioned in chapter 3, it may take longer for English speakers to reach the same performance levels in the less commonly taught languages (LCTLs) because the target language is considerably different from the native language. It is therefore more important for schools to begin instruction in the LCTLs in the early elementary grades if they want students to develop expertise in those languages. When English speakers are enrolled in well-articulated, long-sequence, standards-based world language programs that target the LCTLs, they can be expected to develop a wide range of expertise in the target language over time.

Exactly what kinds of performances can we expect from English speakers over time? According to the ACTFL K–12 performance guidelines,

English speakers who complete a well-articulated K–4 world language program can be expected to reach the mid-novice range. Mid-novice learners communicate minimally and with difficulty using a number of isolated words and memorized phrases about familiar topics (e.g., numbers, colors, days, months, date, time, weather, family, basic objects, clothing). When they respond to direct questions, they may utter only two or three words or an occasional formulaic answer. Mid-novice learners pause frequently as they search for simple vocabulary or attempt to recycle their own and others' words. When they are asked to present on unfamiliar topics, they may show evidence of false starts, prolonged and unexpectedly placed pauses, and they may switch to their native language. Because of hesitations, lack of vocabulary, inaccuracy, or failure to respond appropriately, it may be difficult for mid-novice learners to make themselves understood.

English speakers who complete a K–8 sequence can be expected to reach the low-intermediate range. Low-intermediate learners are able to handle a limited number of uncomplicated communicative tasks. They can create novel utterances about familiar topics in straightforward social situations, and they can participate in concrete and predictable conversational exchanges that would be necessary for survival in the target language country (e.g., information about self and family, daily activities and personal preferences, ordering food, seeking lodging, getting transportation, asking directions, making simple purchases). Learners at this level are still primarily reactive to direct questions or requests for information, and they can ask a few appropriate questions. Low-intermediate learners express meaning by combining and recombining language that they know into short statements. Their utterances are often filled with hesitancy and inaccuracies as they search for appropriate linguistic forms and vocabulary while attempting to communicate. Low-intermediate learners do use past and future tense in their utterances, but they primarily rely on present tense to express their thoughts. Although their vocabulary and syntax are strongly influenced by their first language, with repetition and rephrasing low-intermediate learners can make themselves understood by those who are accustomed to dealing with language learners.

When English speakers continue their world language study until the 12th grade, we can expect them to move into the pre-advanced learner range. Pre-advanced learners are able to sustain interactions with native speakers on a range of topics of personal, school, and community interest. They can use language confidently and with ease, although there may still be linguistic inaccuracies and the interactional partner may occasionally need to make a special effort to understand the pre-advanced learner's message. They can narrate and describe using connected sentences and paragraphs orally and in writing, and they can comprehend a wide range of vocabulary and discourse about concrete and abstract meanings. Pre-advanced learners can successfully communicate new meanings orally and in writing by applying familiar structures to new situations and less familiar topics (see ACTFL 1999; Omaggio Hadley 2001 for further discussions).

Although it is not generally considered fair to hold students from diverse language backgrounds to different standards for academic achievement, the community language programs that the language planning teams are developing in the SDP do hold monolingual English speakers and heritage language speakers to different standards in the target language. Because heritage language speakers come to school with such a wide range of expertise in their heritage language, and because they have very different motivations and opportunities to use that language in their everyday lives outside of school, we can and should expect more from these students than we can from monolingual English speakers.

What standards should drive language instruction for heritage language speakers? Educators from the target schools in the SDP decided to address the (English) language arts standards for their heritage language speakers. These standards require students to use the spoken and written language for a wider range of social and academic purposes. A serious challenge facing these community language programs, however, is developing language arts standards in the target languages that are not simple translations of the English language arts standards. As I mention later in the chapter, the language arts standards that are developed for each of the target languages need to address language-specific forms and functions on the sentence and discourse levels.

There are no guidelines available to help educators determine what kinds of performances we can expect from heritage language speakers who are enrolled in world language programs that use students' heritage language as the target language. Furthermore, given the fact that heritage language speakers come to school with such a wide range of expertise in spoken and written varieties in their heritage language, combined with the fact that heritage language speakers have different motivations and opportunities to use their heritage language outside of school, educators can and should expect tremendous variation in the kinds of expertise that heritage language speakers in the same program develop relative to the language arts standards. The goal in every case is to find ways to assess the nature of an individual student's specific linguistic and cultural expertise and to provide opportunities for that student to broaden his/her linguistic range. Heritage language speakers have the potential to develop a wide range of expertise in the spoken and written target language, and to develop a deep cultural understanding of the English-speaking and heritage language–speaking worlds in which they move.

This section has reviewed the goals that the language planning teams articulated for their English speakers and heritage language speakers. It also has suggested the kinds of outcomes that can be expected from these students through an elementary school community language program. With these goals and anticipated outcomes in mind, let's turn to a discussion of the actual programs and practices.

Planning the language programs and practices

This part of the chapter focuses on the language plans that the teams developed for their schools, and it highlights the kinds of decisions that members of the language planning teams made throughout the language planning process. The first section provides an overview of the general characteristics of all of the community language programs, and the second section provides a concrete example of a content-related language curriculum that is being developed for a grade 1–4 Spanish program. I conclude this part of the chapter by explicitly reviewing the principles of language, literacy, and learning that underlie the community language programs and practices that are being developed in the School District of Philadelphia (SDP) today.

General characteristics of the language programs in the SDP

The language planning teams had many decisions to make as they developed their language plans. For example, they needed to decide how to address the language learning needs of students who had such a wide range of expertise in the target language, and they needed to determine how much time to allocate to language instruction on a daily, weekly, and yearly basis. They needed to define the language teacher's role relative to the regular classroom teacher, and they needed to find ways to make the language program an integral part of an enriched mainstream academic program. As this section illustrates, language planning teams reviewed the literature and visited schools to stimulate their thinking about creative ways to address each of these areas.

First, how could they address the diverse language learning needs of English speakers and heritage language speakers? One of the critical features of two-way immersion (TWI) programs is that English speakers and speakers of another language are integrated for instructional purposes, and one of the goals of these programs is that English speakers and speakers of other languages develop positive intergroup understanding and relations. Like TWI programs nationally and the modified bilingual programs that we visited in Cambridge, Massachusetts, the language planning teams from the target schools in the SDP decided that integration of English speakers and speakers of the target language would be a defining feature. Beginning in kindergarten and continuing throughout their academic career, all students who participate in the all-English academic mainstream in the target schools are to gain experience interacting with each other through English and through the community language every day. Members of the language planning teams and I believe that when English speakers study the community language as an integral part of the academic mainstream, the status of that language is elevated. When the status of the language is elevated, heritage language students are more likely to want to maintain and develop their expertise that language.

A quick anecdote from the Khmer program illustrates this point. One of the members of the Khmer language planning team is a native speaker of Khmer who immigrated from Cambodia to the United States when he was a teenager. Now he has a son who is in the kindergarten Khmer program at the target school in South Philadelphia. According to this individual, when he spoke Khmer at home last year, his son would sometimes say, "Dad, stop speaking that Buddha-temple language." This utterance reflects the child's sociolinguistic awareness of which domains are used for which languages (Khmer is to be used at the temple and English is to be used elsewhere), and it also reflects the symbolic domination of English over Khmer. The father said that this year his son enthusiastically shares what he is learning at school in Khmer with his family at home and expresses his pride that the other children in his class want to learn Khmer from him.

While there are many benefits associated with integrating English speakers and heritage language speakers, there are also drawbacks. One is that heritage language speakers may not get the enriched language and literacy education that they need in their heritage language to expand their linguistic repertoire to the greatest degree possible. In an effort to address the language learning needs of the English speakers in the class, language teachers may not provide sufficient learning opportunities to push their heritage language speakers' linguistic and cultural development. As I mentioned in chapter 11 the Ni Hao program in Cambridge, Massachusetts, addresses this challenge by offering an L1 (first language) literacy class to all of their English language learners and heritage language speakers who have developed a strong oral foundation in their heritage language, and the target schools in the SDP are exploring a variety of ways to develop the L1 literacy component of their modified dual language programs.

How much time should be allocated to language instruction? The community language programs that are being developed in Khmer,

Mandarin, Russian, Spanish, and Vietnamese in the target schools are structured into the academic day like prototypical FLES (foreign language in the elementary school) programs. As we discussed in chapter 3, well-articulated, long-sequence FLES programs ideally begin in kindergarten, and students continue their study of the target language throughout their elementary, middle, and high school years. According to Curtain and Pesola (1994) and Gilzow and Branaman (2000), elementary school students should have a 30- to 45-minute language class three to five times per week for a minimum of 90 minutes total per week. The target schools in the SDP vary in terms of how much time they allocate for language instruction based on their local assessment of school resources and constraints. While all of the schools offer language instruction at least three times a week for at least 30 minutes per class, some of the schools offer language instruction five days a week for up to 45 minutes per class. The language teachers emphasize the importance of honoring the time allocated for language class on a regular basis and not allowing other requirements to take away from language time. This regular scheduling of language class contributes to the notion that language education is an integral part of every students' academic experience.

Schools also have choices in how they organize the language teacher's role relative to the mainstream classroom teacher's role. As discussed in chapter 3, the elementary school language teacher can either travel to the regular classroom for language class, or the students can travel to the language teacher for language class. And there are, of course, pros and cons to each of these choices. For example, in the case of the Khmer, Mandarin, Russian, and Spanish programs the language teacher travels to the regular classroom. Some of the kindergarten teachers participate enthusiastically in language class, which demonstrates the regular teacher's commitment to languages other than English. This arrangement can contribute in important ways to the effort to make language instruction an integral part of the whole school. In the Vietnamese case, the language teacher has her own classroom. This situation is much easier on the Vietnamese teacher who does not have to carry her things all throughout the school, and it allows her to create a large Vietnamese space within the school where Vietnamese is the dominant language of communication. However, this solution may not as clearly demonstrate the symbolic importance of Vietnamese within the academic mainstream. The school therefore addresses this challenge in other ways, like morning greetings in Vietnamese and examples of Vietnamese print throughout the school.

How should teachers organize instruction in the elementary school language programs? As I discussed in chapter 3, language is best learned through content and any content area can provide the basis for the language program. The language teachers in each of the community language programs in the SDP work in different ways to relate their language instruction to the regular classroom content (e.g., in math, social studies, science, language arts) and to align their curriculum with the ACTFL standards. Let us look more closely at an example of an instructional unit in Spanish that the Spanish teacher and I developed to illustrate how we translated a content-related Spanish program into practice. The language teachers from the Khmer, Mandarin, Russian, and Vietnamese programs have used this example to inform their work developing their content-related language curricula, demonstrating that the approach taken for this unit can readily be adapted to develop community language curricula for other multilingual contexts.

Developing units for the content-related language curriculum

The content area chosen for the unit described in this section is based on the social studies curriculum frameworks that are used in the SDP. First I motivate the choice of this content area as the basis of the language curriculum, and then I explain how the content-related language curriculum functions within and across grade levels. I conclude by discussing the ways that language educators can use performance-based assessments to guide instruction and to provide evidence of students' development, relative to the standards, in the target language over time.

Why choose social studies content to drive the language curriculum? First, social studies content is language rich. A wide range of topics is discussed in this content area, which means a wide range of language (i.e., vocabulary, grammar, genres, registers) can be used. Social studies also provides a lens for looking at the culture(s) of the speakers of the target languages and the communities in which they live and for comparing those cultures and communities with the culture(s) and communities of the student populations. In this way the social studies–related program not only addresses the local school district standards in social studies, world language, and language arts standards, it also provides students with opportunities to develop what the SDP calls "multicultural cross-cutting competencies." Another increasingly important reason to use social studies content for the language curriculum is that schools have been paying significantly less attention to social studies than to reading, writing, and math. Since there are currently no high-stakes tests in social studies, and educators have begun to pay extraordinary amounts of attention to testing, social studies often gets overlooked. The unit in Spanish described in this section is intended to address this gap.

Like all content-based or content-related curricula (see chapter 3 for discussion of this distinction), the language teacher starts planning the unit with the content-area curriculum and considers what s/he expects the students to know and/or be able to do at the end of the unit. The SDP social studies curriculum frameworks encourage the study of social studies themes in the context of students' expanding environment. This approach makes developmental sense to elementary school children. In kindergarten, students are encouraged to look at and learn about themselves, and in 1st grade students look beyond themselves to the level of their family. In 2nd grade students begin to look beyond their family into their surrounding neighborhood. By third grade, as students develop more of a sense of abstract time and space, students are encouraged to look at their larger community and consider its history. In 4th grade, students are encouraged to focus on the state level, which in this case is Pennsylvania. In 5th grade students broaden their scope to look at the United States.

Curtain and Pesola (1994) offer a framework for curriculum development for FLES programs that informed the development of this unit. This framework begins with a thematic center and relates subject content, language in use, and culture to that thematic center. The content-related language curriculum is then spiraled over time within and across grade levels. This means that the language forms and functions that are introduced within the context of a particular theme in kindergarten are reviewed and built on within the context of thematic units that are studied at a later time during kindergarten. These language forms and functions are also reviewed and built on when students revisit the theme in 1st grade, and again in 2nd grade, and so on throughout the duration of the language program. The theme provides a vehicle for making connections within and across content areas and languages at each grade level, and across grade levels over time.

The thematic center of this sample unit in Spanish is *Home*, and each year students explore a broader dimension of where they live (i.e., their expanding environment). Grade 1 students learn about their family/household. Grade 2 students begin to explore the neighborhood, and they focus on Puerto Ricans in North Philadelphia. Grade 3 students move their social studies inquiry to the community, and their social studies unit focuses on the Puerto Ricans and other Latinos in Philadelphia historically and today. Grade 4 students focus on Pennsylvania, so they broaden their study to look at Latinos and other immigrants throughout the state. Grade 5 students learn about Latinos and other immigrants on the national level.

The thematic unit on *Home* is organized around a series of guiding research questions that students can explore using quantitative and/or qualitative research methods. At each grade level, students ask the following question:

1. Who lives there?
   - Grade 1 in the household
   - Grade 2 in the neighborhood
   - Grade 3 in the community
   - Grade 4 in the state
   - Grade 5 in the country
2. Where do they live?
3. What do they do?
4. When did they come?
5. Why did they come?
6. What languages do they use?

Students learn how to conduct interviews and to administer surveys to collect data. They also do library research, read the newspapers, listen to the radio, search the web, go on field trips, and observe everyday interactions to collect and analyze data that helps them answer their research questions. Students do a wide range of culminating projects that enable them to demonstrate what they have learned. For example, students can make books, music, dramas, videos, graphs, charts, timelines, and maps. These projects provide students with opportunities to address the content-area standards in social studies, math, language arts, and world languages and to learn big ideas about people in society.

Let us look a bit more closely at how these instructional units can provide a vehicle for content and second language learning. Teachers should have both content and language learning objectives for their students in each unit. For example, students in 2nd grade are studying about their neighborhood in their social studies class. Some of the content objectives that the teacher may have come directly from the social studies standards, so students are to identify people, places, and events in the neighborhood. Since teachers encourage students to read and write across the curriculum, students may be reading books about neighborhoods in their dominant language. They may go on field trips to different places around the neighborhood, and they may make a street map or a model of the barrio. English-speaking students develop the concepts and academic language during social studies class in English, their dominant language. Then during Spanish class, Spanish teachers build on the content area knowledge and skills that students have developed in English, and introduce the language (vocabulary, expressions, grammar, genres) needed to communicate about those topics in Spanish. The Spanish teacher needs to determine what content-obligatory and content-compatible language students need to know to be able to accomplish the assigned tasks in the target language, and the teacher needs to organize activities that give students opportunities to acquire those language forms and functions (Snow et al. 1992).

How can teachers assess students' performance? Teachers can use performance-based assessments that are tied to the objectives of the instructional unit, because these assessments provide information about what students can actually do with language (Duncan 2001). For example, the 2nd grade students may be asked to make a book in Spanish about the different kinds of people they find in the neighborhood. English speakers could be expected to recognize the target vocabulary and language forms and functions, and they could be expected to produce limited and relatively formulaic language about the topic of the neighborhood. More proficient heritage Spanish speakers could be encouraged to talk more creatively about the people and places and events in their neighborhood, and they could be encouraged to write about those topics in Spanish. Teachers can develop rubrics that enable them to provide an indication of the quality of the student's performance on a particular task, and they can use this information to guide their instruction.

Teachers can also require students to develop their own language portfolios, and these portfolios can provide snapshots of students' language development through their participation in the elementary school language program over time (Stefanakis 2002). Since the instruction in the language program is aligned with the world language and language arts standards, these portfolios should include representative samples of students' spoken and written, informal and formal language production across a range of genres and modes of communication within and across grade levels. Teachers can assess where particular students are in their language development by comparing student performance on specific tasks with the descriptors outlined by the ACTFL K–12 performance guidelines.

Underlying principles of language, literacy, and learning

Although the unit described above uses social studies to drive the Spanish curriculum, the same principles about language, literacy, and learning would apply to any content area (e.g., science, music) and any language (e.g., Khmer, Russian). Furthermore, the principles that underlie content-related language programs for English speakers and heritage language speakers like those described in this chapter are the same as those that underlie the bilingual and ESL programs for ELLs that we explored in Part

III of this book. This section makes those principles of language, literacy, and learning explicit.

Let's start with content-area knowledge. We know that students learn by making connections between new knowledge and/or skills and knowledge and/or skills that students have previously learned. Teachers in content-based and/or content-related second language programs encourage language learners to activate their prior knowledge about the focus of study in their dominant language, and they provide students with opportunities to build on that knowledge and those skills to develop new knowledge and skills. When the students understand a concept in their dominant language, teachers can encourage students to communicate orally and/or through reading and writing about that topic in their second language, which in this case is Spanish. In this way language learners can connect new language forms and functions to known concepts, which helps make second language input comprehensible. And we know that comprehensible input is a necessary condition for second language acquisition.

What else do we know about second language acquisition? We know that second language acquisition is enhanced when students have (a) considerable comprehensible oral and written input, (b) opportunities to negotiate meaning to make incomprehensible input comprehensible, (c) opportunities to provide oral and written output in the target language, and (d) focused attention on form. The content areas (math, science, social studies, music, art) provide outstanding sources of input and ideas for classroom activities that use the target language. For example, students can use math concepts and skills to learn about social studies. They can learn to survey people in their neighborhood to determine how many people use Spanish, how many use English, and how many use both at home and at work. They can be encouraged to make charts and graphs, and they can read and write and talk about issues of language choice in the neighborhood through both Spanish and English.

Language teachers need to think carefully about the ways that they structure classroom interaction so that they can address the diverse language and learning needs of their English speakers and heritage language speakers. They need to find creative ways to differentiate instruction, for example by organizing cooperative learning groups of students who have a wide range of expertise in oral and written Spanish, and by requiring different kinds of participation and products from students with different kinds of language expertise. Language teachers can organize tasks that give students opportunities to negotiate the meaning of the target language that is not immediately comprehensible to them, and this negotiation of meaning enhances second language acquisition. Teachers can also structure opportunities for students to provide output in the target language.

Of course, language teachers need to consider the kinds of output or performances they can reasonably expect from individual students based on their assessment of that student's expertise in the target language. We know that teachers cannot expect the same kinds of performances from English speakers in the elementary grades as they can from heritage language speakers. To know what kinds of output teachers can reasonably expect from individual language learners, they need to have an idea of student's expertise relative to the kind of output that is expected. As I discuss in the next section, assessing the expertise of heritage language speakers and determining what kinds of language we can expect these students to produce is a challenge facing heritage language programs today.

We do know, however, that language educators can use students' errors to help guide the kinds of instruction they need. When teachers provide students with opportunities to produce oral and written output in the target language, they can analyze the nature of student output and determine ways that they can focus their instruction. Although students in the early elementary grades probably will not benefit from explicit grammatical explanations, they can be immersed in input that features language forms and functions that the students are struggling with. As students are immersed in rich oral and written comprehensible input, they can be expected to continue to acquire the target language. As students reach the middle to upper elementary grades, they may start to analyze the ways in which language forms function, and they may benefit from an explicit instructional focus on form. The point to highlight here is that teachers need to listen to and/or read the kinds of language that students produce, and then they can use student errors to guide instruction.

This part of the chapter has outlined what a content-related Spanish program could look like in an elementary school in North Philadelphia that has a large number of heritage Spanish speakers, and it suggests what a content-related language program could look like in any elementary school that is located in a multilingual community. In the example presented here, social studies themes drive the curriculum, and this integrated program addresses the standards in world languages (i.e., communication, cultures, content, comparisons, and communities) and in language arts more broadly. This program also enriches a more traditional social studies program because of the strong cultural content and perspective. Students are encouraged to build on what they learn in social studies within and across grade levels to develop expertise in Spanish. Monolingual English speakers are expected to demonstrate an understanding of Spanish about the topics addressed in the program, and they can be expected to express simple ideas in relatively formulaic language about these topics. Heritage Spanish speakers are expected to build on the linguistic and cultural expertise that they bring with them to school. Heritage Spanish speakers who come to school with a strong foundation in oral nonstandard Spanish should be expected to broaden their linguistic range and develop literacies in Spanish.

This type of a content-related Spanish program allows students to make connections between what they are learning in their Spanish class and other areas of their lives. For example, it encourages students to make connections across content areas. Social studies content provides the foundation for the language curriculum, and math and language arts are integrated into the instruction. Students use reading and writing and math to learn social studies concepts, and they draw on those concepts and skills as a foundation for their development of spoken and written Spanish. This approach also encourages students to make connections across languages. Students who are learning cognate languages, for example, can be encouraged to make connections across the vocabulary used in one language and the other. Students who are learning any other language can be encouraged to make connections at a more abstract level, for example to compare discursive structures or genres across languages. The program also encourages students to make connections across social groups. The structure of this program, which integrates students from English-speaking and heritage language–speaking backgrounds, encourages students to make connections across what are sometimes seen as linguistic and cultural borders and to discover similarities across groups as well as differences within groups. Heritage language speakers are encouraged to maintain and develop their heritage languages, which helps maintain connections across the generations and communities in which they move and live. English speakers are encouraged to connect with the monolingual speakers of the target language in their communities and to consider ways in which they can connect with a wider range of communities that use that target language in the world.

Addressing ideological and practical challenges

With the exception of the Spanish program, the community language programs described in this chapter were planned from the spring of 2001 until the summer of 2002, and they were launched in the fall of 2002 in the kindergarten classes. The Spanish program was never formally launched because the original target school that was developing the program was taken over by a for-profit corporation in the spring of 2002, and that school dropped out of the dual language initiative. Each of the schools that initiated programs in the fall of 2002 face numerous challenges as they implement those programs. As I discuss in this concluding part of the chapter, these challenges are both ideological and practical, and the specific nature of the challenges varies from community to community, school to school, and across grade levels. Here I provide a general discussion of the kinds of ideological and practical challenges facing the target schools throughout the School District of Philadelphia (SDP), and I review how we are working to address those challenges at the time of this writing.

Ideological challenges

As mentioned earlier in the chapter, the language planning teams were successful in their efforts to open ideological space to develop their language programs in the kindergarten. The ideological challenges that they face, however, are not over once they launch their programs. Members of the language planning teams need to identify the nature of the ideological challenge(s) at their school, and they need to develop strategies to address each specific challenge.

For example, each of the schools describes evidence of English-only currents and racism against the target language and speakers of that language on the local school level, although the nature and degree of this ideological orientation varies. Some schools see evidence of a language-as-problem orientation in educators' and parents' questions about whether English language learners (ELLs) who need to learn English to participate and achieve academically in the all-English academic mainstream have enough time in their school day to maintain and develop expertise in their home language. Some question whether an ELLs' continued use of their first language slows down their acquisition of English. Others question whether English speakers have enough time in their schedule to fit in a world language class, especially given the increasing concern for student performance on standardized tests in English. Some believe that a world language program is an important part of an enriched elementary school education, but question the choice of "that language." Some say that promoting "that language" at school will simply discourage "them" from learning English, which they need to do if they live in the United States.

As I argued in chapter 1, educators need to listen to the specific questions and concerns that parents and other constituents have about language education, and we need to respond with the facts about the benefits of bilingualism in ways that are understood by the people who have the questions and express the concerns. In some cases, the language planning teams organize educational meetings with parents and/or other constituents in forums that encourage dialogue about their concrete questions and concerns. Some schools have made brochures that not only describe their programs but that also include answers to frequently asked questions. Most of the language teachers open their classes to parents so they can observe how the class fits into the school day and so they can answer those parents' questions and concerns in the context of concrete discussions about practice. When teachers identify parents or mainstream educators who are enthusiastic about the program, especially those who were originally skeptical, some of the schools encourage those "converts" to talk to parents and other constituents that continue to have questions and concerns. Advocacy is an important part of promoting language education at school, and some of the educators turn to the Center for Applied Linguistics (www.cal.org) to identify and link to useful organizations and resource centers (see Appendix for a list of some of these resources). Language planning team members from the target schools in the SDP draw on different strategies at different times, depending on the nature of the questions or concern.

For many, seeing is believing. While trips to other schools that have elementary school language programs in the target language or for similar target populations can certainly address some questions and concerns, many concerns can only be addressed by seeing how the language program actually functions on the local school and classroom level over time. This takes us to discussion of the practical challenges facing the target schools that are developing these programs.

Practical challenges

Schools that are developing community language programs that can address the diverse language learning needs of English speakers and heritage language learners face numerous practical challenges. For example, in order for these programs to be effective, they must have trained teachers, a language curriculum, sufficient materials, time, and opportunities to coordinate instruction with the mainstream teachers within the same grade level, opportunities to articulate the language program across grade levels, and support from the parents and the whole school. This concluding section provides a brief discussion of each of these areas.

The community language programs that are described in this chapter require trained teachers who are native speakers of the target language or who have developed a wide range of expertise in that language as well as a sophisticated understanding of the target culture(s). These individuals need to understand theories of second language acquisition as well as the likely developmental sequences of the monolingual English-speaking students and of the heritage language–speaking students who are enrolled in their classes. They need to know how to assess the wide range of spoken and written expertise that their students have relative to the target language, and they need to be able to differentiate instruction in ways that enable each student to broaden his/her linguistic range. Since the program is a content-related world language program, these teachers need to understand the world language standards and they need to be familiar with the mainstream content-area curriculum. These teachers also need to be advocates for their programs who, as discussed above, listen to the views and concerns of the relevant constituents and take active measures to address those concerns. This is a tall order for any individual, and it is difficult to find people who have all of these qualifications.

At this point in time, educators who work with and in the community language programs in the SDP are taking an informal network approach to addressing this challenge. In each case, the native speakers of the target languages (i.e., the community language teachers and some of the coordinators from the regional offices and the Office of Language and Cultural Education) work through their networks to find other native speakers of the target language who are currently teaching either English as a second language (ESL) or in the mainstream classroom. When they cannot find such people, they look for native speakers of the language who are interested in positions teaching in their programs in the future. Most of these teachers work on an emergency certification, and they attend graduate courses in the evenings and summers to complete their requirements for certification. While the central administration has begun to develop policies to enhance the recruitment and retention of qualified teachers, the community language programs need teachers now. For this reason, the local educators continue to address this challenge as the programs grow. The current teachers and the new teachers need ongoing professional development, which we address in the context of our monthly meetings and intensive summer workshops. These meetings and workshops focus on curriculum and materials development, theories of language acquisition, and teaching methods. I elaborate this point below.

There is no curriculum currently on the market that has been developed for these programs, and it is unlikely that such a curriculum will ever be developed and marketed that can address the specific needs of these content-related community language programs. This means that the teachers must develop their own curriculum, and look for and/or develop materials as they develop the program. The Ni Hao program referred to above generously loaned the SDP teachers the K–8 thematic units that they had developed for their Chinese program, which have served as a model for the community language teachers in the SDP. The K–4 social studies unit that the Spanish teacher and I developed has also served as a model. During our intensive summer workshop in 2002, before the community language programs were launched, the target language teachers worked with content-area teachers and ESL teachers from their schools to develop an outline of the curriculum that they imagined they would need during the first year. This curricular framework was based on their reading in the field, observations of other world language programs and practices, and ongoing discussions. They also developed a range of materials and activities in the target language (songs, games, storybooks) that they would use in their classes.

Throughout the academic year, the teachers have begun to explicitly articulate their language curriculum, and during the summer of 2003 they will map out that curriculum, work together to look critically at the strengths and future possibilities for the different language programs they are developing, and project what the curriculum will look like for the fall 2003–spring 2004 academic year. We plan to use the English language arts and Spanish language arts curriculum frameworks as a guide but attend to the language-specific forms and functions and culture-specific content and perspectives that the teachers highlight. We plan to continue this articulation process throughout the years of the Title VII grant, a process that will ideally become institutionalized in the target schools and in other schools that develop community language programs in the future.

All of this requires ongoing professional development. In addition to the language curriculum development project, the teachers work together to look critically at their own and each others' practices. Just as the TWI teachers have developed a dual language teachers talking network to support their program and professional development (see chapter 13 for discussion), the Khmer, Mandarin, Russian, and Vietnamese teachers meet for regular monthly meetings throughout the school year. As we discuss the strengths and possibilities of their programs, one or more burning issues inevitably arise. For example, one of these teachers' earliest concerns was how they could use the target language all or nearly all of the time in their classes when the English speakers did not understand any of the target language. Furthermore, the teachers argued, since the children were so young, they would get restless when they did not understand what the teacher was saying and discipline problems would inevitably arise. Many of these teachers originally drew on their own experiences in traditional foreign language classes in their home countries and in the United States in which the target language is the focus of instruction but not the medium of instruction, and where teacher talk—not student activity—dominates the classroom discourse.

The coordinators that I have been working with to develop these programs and I recognized that this was a critical issue that needed to be addressed immediately. Since the teachers only have 30 to 45 minutes per day three to five days per work for language class, they need to use the target language all or most of the time if the students are expected to develop the kinds of expertise discussed earlier in the chapter. To counter the assumption that English speakers need to use English to learn a foreign language, the Chinese coordinator of our group organized a mini-lesson each day in Chinese to teach all of the teachers who were participating in the summer professional development how to count to ten in Chinese. She used big books, concrete referents, experiential activities, discovery learning techniques, games, songs, and participants who had some expertise in the target language to involve all of us in her instruction. After she modeled the first series of activities on day 1 of the summer workshop, each of the teachers of the other target languages was asked to organize a series of activities to teach something in their language (Russian, Vietnamese, Khmer, or Mandarin) to the group on one of the days of our workshops. The teachers chose to teach vocabulary related to colors or fruits or numbers or animals, and they experimented with the types of activities that the Chinese teacher modeled for them each day. Throughout this experience, all of participants were able to count to ten in Chinese and everyone had learned a few other words or songs in the other target languages. More importantly, they began to realize that it is possible to make content comprehensible to someone in a language that they do not understand, especially when the content is so concrete. They also gained experience designing a range of hands-on activities that they could use throughout the year.

We continued to work on the challenge of using the target language in the classroom for all or nearly all of the contact time throughout the year. At one of our early meetings, one of the Mandarin teachers volunteered to make a videotape of how she used Chinese in her classroom, which we watched and discussed at the next monthly meeting. The other teachers were amazed at what the English-speaking children could do after so little time in Chinese class—they could count to twenty when they worked as a whole group with the teacher using concrete referents and songs. The other teachers requested the opportunity to visit this classroom during one of their observation days (SDP teachers are encouraged to use one or two days per year to observe other teachers' practices), and they began to incorporate what they had learned into their own practice. We continued this pattern throughout the first year of our monthly meetings. First, an issue would arise in our discussions of practice, and all of the teachers would agree to focus on this issue. One of the teachers would agree to videotape her class to explore how she/he addressed this in the context of her practice, and we looked at the video together and made observations and asked questions about practice at the next meeting. Throughout this process, we discussed theories of second language acquisition and language teaching and learning within the context of their concrete questions, concerns, and practices. Although I have no evidence to support this claim, I believe that the teachers' observations, comments, and conversations have become increasingly sophisticated over time, reflecting their developing understanding of theory and practice in the field.

All of this program and professional development takes time, and it depends on the commitment and collaboration of dedicated language teachers, mainstream classroom teachers, ESL teachers, and school administrators. The monthly meetings and summer professional development are open to everyone who wants to come, and we have the rotating participation of some of the administrators from the target schools as well as some of the ESL and mainstream teachers. The community language teachers also work to involve the parents in the program in an ongoing basis. For example, at a recent monthly meeting in the spring of 2003, the teachers generated a short survey that they plan to administer to all of the parents to learn more about language use in the target language at home and about parental attitudes about the program to date. The language teachers also go to great lengths to showcase their program and practices to their parents and teachers on the local level as well as to educators and community members more broadly. The children in each of the schools are also integral parts of all of the school performances, and the Khmer and Mandarin children recently performed for the annual banquet of the Asian American Educators, which was attended by more than 300 educators and community members from throughout the SDP and the city.

Conclusion

This chapter has explored the language programs that are being developed in target schools in the major multilingual communities throughout the linguistically and culturally diverse School District of Philadelphia. Reflecting the demographics in the city, schools have begun programs in Khmer, Mandarin, Russian, and Vietnamese, and Spanish programs are in the planning stages. These programs aim to elevate the status of the community languages that their heritage language speakers use outside of school by making them an integral part of the whole school curriculum. Although these programs are only in the very early stages of development, they suggest possibilities for promoting a wider range of languages for a broader group of students in the SDP over time.

This chapter has described the target populations and program goals and structure of the community language programs. It has also identified some of the ideological and practical challenges that particular teachers, target schools, and the SDP overall face as they work to promote bilingualism to the greatest degree possible for their target populations. Although it is difficult to find time to fit languages other than English into an already overloaded curriculum, these educators believe that ELLs and heritage language speakers have the right to maintain and develop their home languages and that individual English speakers and U.S. society overall benefit when the citizenry knows more than one language and culture. These educators also believe that it is the school's responsibility to help address the challenge of promoting bilingualism in a society that often sees bilingualism as divisive and threatening. Perhaps more importantly, these educators are willing to do the hard work to open ideological space for these innovative programs at their schools and to continue to work to ensure that they can deliver on the promises that they have made.

15

Developing enriched language education programs in other contexts

Schools in the United States are required, by law, to provide services that enable their English language learners (ELLs) to develop the academic English that they need to participate and achieve in U.S. public schools. This book has argued that in multilingual communities, educators can build on the linguistic and cultural resources that students bring with them to school and/or that are available in the local community to address students' language education needs. Additive bilingual programs enable students (ELLs, heritage language speakers, and English speakers) to develop oral and written expertise in two languages, achieve academically, and develop improved intergroup understanding and relations. Well-implemented, enriched language education programs address ELLs' needs for academic English. At the same time, they offer additional short-term and long-term benefits to students, their families, local communities, and the nation overall.

This chapter synthesizes the major ideas forwarded throughout the book to consider how schools can organize their language education programs and practices to build on community bilingualism in other contexts. The chapter begins with a brief review of the theoretical orientation that informs the approach advocated in this book. The majority of the chapter is organized around the questions that I presented in chapter 4, which are the same questions that have structured my work with each of the schools described in Part IV of the book. These questions are:

1. Who are the language planners and how should they work together?

2. Who are the target populations and what are the goals for those populations?

3. How is the school currently addressing the language education needs of the target populations?

4. What type(s) of language education is/are appropriate for the school and community?

My discussion of each of these questions draws on examples from the case studies of bilingualism and education in Philadelphia presented throughout this book, and it reviews issues that educators should consider as they design, implement, monitor, and evaluate language education programs and practices in other contexts. The chapter concludes with a call for action.

Context is key here. This chapter asks educators not to uncritically embrace any particular type of language education program for their school as THE answer. Instead, I emphasize the need for educators to begin with their target populations' strengths and needs and to set realistic goals based on a clear understanding of their local school and sociolinguistic context on the one hand and of the research on language education on the other. Educators are asked to develop their language education programs and practices in ways that make sense given what they know/learn about (second) language acquisition, (bi)literacy development, (language) learning and teaching, and their school and community contexts.

Competing discourses about the education of English language learners

As I discussed in chapter 4, my work is aligned with earlier work in the ethnography of communication in schools (e.g., Heath 1983; Philips 1983) and with more recent work in sociolinguistics (e.g., Fairclough 1989, 1993; Gal 1995; Rampton 1995) and the new literacy studies (e.g., Gee 1990; Street 1995, 1998, 2000) that see language and literacy as social practices that are reflected and negotiated in what people say and do in their everyday lives. The focus of my research and practice since the mid-1980s has been in public schools that are located in multilingual communities. I see schools as major socializing agents that can either reflect and reproduce the dominant social order or challenge and potentially transform that order. When we review some of the research that has investigated English language learners (ELLs) in public schools in the United States, we see competing discourses about languages, speakers of languages, and language teaching and learning. These discourses influence the ways that educators organize their policies, programs, and practices, and they have major implications for students, schools, communities, and society.

On the one hand, there is a considerable body of research that documents how mainstream U.S. schools reflect and reproduce the dominant social order. According to this line of work, the dominant social order is characterized by a language-as-problem orientation (Ruiz 1984), which is reflected in transitional bilingual education and English-only policies, programs, and practices. Under this ideological orientation, ELLs are expected to reject their home languages in favor of English and assimilate to monolingualism in English so that they can participate and achieve in the English-only academic mainstream. Unfortunately, large numbers of ELLs in transitional bilingual and English-only programs do not develop academic English and the literacies in English that they need for academic success in mainstream classrooms, and we see a disproportionate drop-out rate among these students. On the other hand, there is an increasing body of research that documents how schools can organize their policies, programs, and practices in ways that reject this dominant ideology in favor of a language-as-resource or English-plus orientation. My work at the Oyster Bilingual School (Freeman 1998) provides evidence of such an alternative educational discourse. We also find an increasing number of dual language programs in the United States that offer many more exciting examples of schools that promote bilingualism and biliteracy development as they enable all language learners to achieve academically in English and other languages (see www.cal.org for a directory of two-way immersion programs in the United States).

My research and practice in North Philadelphia, throughout the School District of Philadelphia (SDP), and in other contexts in the United States and internationally suggests that many schools and communities are constituted by competing discourses about languages, speakers of languages, and language teaching and learning. The challenge for educators who are working to promote bilingualism on the school and school district levels is to find ways to work through these conflicts and controversies so that they can open ideological space for programs and practices that promote the maintenance and development of expertise in English AND in other languages. There is no easy recipe that language planners can follow, and the particular concerns and interests that they encounter in one school and community are unlikely to be exactly the same as those encountered in other schools and communities. The preceding chapters are filled with examples of ways that educators in the predominantly Puerto Rican community in North Philadelphia, and in the Khmer, Chinese, Russian, and Vietnamese communities in other parts of the city, are working through the competing discourses that they have encountered at their schools. The remainder of this chapter provides a brief review of the approach advocated in this book as a guide for school-based language planning projects in other contexts.

Who are the language planners
and how should they work together

As we have seen in this book, school-based language planning is a complex process that requires a considerable range of expertise, time, and energy. As Corson (1999) suggests and I emphasize throughout the preceding chapters, language planners need to have or develop an understanding of

- the theoretical and practical base in the field of language education with attention to language acquisition, language teaching and learning, language education program types, and research on program effectiveness,

- the local sociolinguistic situation with attention to the ways that students, parents, and other community members use and evaluate the spoken and written languages in their linguistic repertoires in the key contexts in their lives, and

- the school context with attention to the local resources and constraints as well as local, state and federal policies, mandates, and accountability requirements.

In addition, language planners need to understand how to work their ways through local parent and community networks, as well as through the multiple levels of institutional authority at the school and throughout the school district, in order to make space for a new language education program. Because this range of expertise is more than one person generally has or can develop within the time the school has available to plan their program, and because of the turnover that we often see on the local school and school district level, I advocate that target schools organize language planning teams who collectively have and/or are willing to develop the expertise necessary to develop a program that addresses all local, state, and federal mandates, is aligned with all of the constituents' interests, and is pedagogically sound and well-implemented. There is also strength in numbers, and the language planning initiative is more likely to be able to sustain dramatic turnover and change if a team that shares a common goal is involved in the planning process.

The language planning team needs to take responsibility for two major areas. They need to work with parents and the larger school community to determine the type of language education program that is appropriate for the target populations, and they need to determine how their school program should be structured so that it builds on the resources that are available in the school and community while acknowledging the constraints that limit what is possible in that context. These two areas involve very different kinds of tasks, and both areas should be addressed from the beginning of the language planning process. As mentioned in the preceding chapters, language planning teams from the different target schools in the School District of Philadelphia (SDP) approached these areas in different ways, depending on the concerns and interests of the constituents and on the existing beliefs and practices about languages, speakers of languages, and language teaching and learning that they found in their school and community contexts. In every case, team members looked for openings and built on the resources they found as they worked to develop understanding and support for the dual and world language education programs they advocated. They also made themselves aware of the challenges that they needed to face and the obstacles they needed to overcome as they worked to counter English-only ideologies.

The language planning team needs to help all of the relevant constituents (parents, teachers, administrators, community members) develop a coherent understanding of the language education program that they are developing for the school, including an understanding of the strengths and needs of the target populations, the goals of the proposed program, the program structure, and the anticipated outcomes. However, as Fullan (2000) argues and I have emphasized throughout the preceding chapters, coherence does not happen automatically. Let's review the guiding questions and main ideas that language planning teams can use to work through the dynamic, ideological processes involved in school-based language planning. My goal is to contribute to the development of many more coherent, pedagogically sound, well-implemented programs that promote bilingualism, and to stimulate efforts to document their effectiveness.

Who are the target populations and what are the goals for these populations

Educators need to begin planning their language education programs by considering the strengths and needs of their target populations and by clarifying their goals for those students. As we saw in chapter 2, since the late 1960s all U.S. public schools have had a legal obligation to organize their programs and practices so that English language learners (ELLs) have access to equal educational opportunities, and as of 2002 all schools are being held accountable for the English language development and academic achievement of these students. I argue in this book that schools that serve students who live in multilingual communities have the additional responsibility to organize their programs and practices in ways that build on the linguistic and cultural expertise that heritage language speakers bring with them to school and that are readily available in the local community as they work to promote bilingualism, biliteracy development, and positive cultural understanding and intergroup relations. This section briefly revisits the students that educators who work in multilingual communities can expect to find in their classes, and reviews in very general terms the kinds of expertise they may find among those students. Then I summarize how language ideologies structure the ways that students tend to use and evaluate the languages in their linguistic repertoire, and I reiterate the goals that I advocate for public schools in the United States today.

Educators who are working to build on community bilingualism need to understand the kinds of expertise their students are likely to bring with them to school. As we discussed in chapter 1 and have seen throughout the book, these educators can expect to find four broad categories of students in their schools: ELLs, heritage language speakers, heritage language learners, and monolingual English speakers. We can situate these categories of students on a continuum that represents the kinds of linguistic expertise they have relative to the target language, with ELLs on one end and monolingual English speakers on the other.

Generally speaking, ELLs have developed the most expertise in the target language because they use that language for most or all of their everyday interactions. However, educators should also expect to find variation in their ELLs' expertise in the target language because of the variation in the ways that these students use the spoken and written target language in their everyday lives, and their home language use influences the ways that they continue to develop that language at school. Next we find heritage language speakers who have a wide range of expertise in and attitudes toward the target language and speakers of that language. Educators must understand that this variation influences these students' future development of expertise in their heritage language. Some of these students may use both English and their heritage language effortlessly because they live in bilingual homes and/or are in continual contact with speakers of their heritage language. These heritage language speakers can be expected to readily develop literacies in their heritage language. Others may be English-dominant, but they may only understand, for example, their grandmother when she talks to them about familiar topics (even if they respond in English or minimally in their heritage language). Since these students do not have the same opportunities to use their heritage language outside of the classroom, we can not expect them to develop the same range of expertise through their experiences at school. As we move along the continuum we find heritage language learners who have no expertise in the target language but do have a heritage relation to the target language group. This category of students might include third- or fourth-generation immigrants who do not have any linguistic expertise to build on in the target language. However, these students may have some allegiance to the target language (because of the heritage relation) that may enhance their language learning. At the other end of the continuum we find monolingual English speakers who have no heritage relation to the target language and no expertise in that language. This last group includes the students that we have traditionally found in foreign language classes.

One of the main ideas of this book is that experience leads to expertise. As I argue in chapter 4, educators who work in schools that are located in multilingual communities need to investigate how their students use languages in their everyday lives in order to understand the nature of this expertise. For example, we saw that some students living in the predominantly Puerto Rican community in North Philadelphia had developed strong simultaneous translation skills as they move between oral and/or written Spanish and or English. We also saw a sophisticated understanding of some genres (e.g., the novela), a passionate interest in language issues, and a variety of home/community literacy practices (e.g., playing school, reading the Bible, letter writing). Some of the educators that are featured in the chapters in Part III of the book were aware of these kinds of expertise, and they organized their classroom practices around them. Other educators happened upon cultural funds of knowledge accidentally in the course of their practice and decided to build on this foundation. Some educators organized projects around inquiry and encouraged students to explore how they use and evaluate languages in their everyday lives as part of the official curriculum. The point to highlight is that educators who understand and/or are willing to explore the kinds of linguistic and cultural expertise that their students bring with them to school are in a strong position to build on that foundation as they work toward their short-term and long-term goals in the heritage language AND in English.

Another main idea of this book is that language ideologies influence the ways that students use and evaluate languages at school and in other contexts in their lives. As we saw in Part II, some students in North Philadelphia resist using Spanish because it is socially stigmatized, especially as they move into the upper elementary and middle school grades. Some parents resist using Spanish with their children because they believe it can hurt their English language development. Some educators resist requiring English speakers to learn Spanish because they worry that two languages are too much for students who are struggling to develop basic skills in English, their first language. Ideologies like these leave little space for additive bilingualism because students, families, and educators do not understand or believe in the benefits of bilingualism. Language planners need to pay attention to these beliefs and counter them with facts about bilingualism.

However, we also saw that many students in North Philadelphia embrace the opportunities to use and develop Spanish because there are exciting possibilities for bilingual individuals in the short and longer terms. Many families may want to see their children maintain and develop their home/heritage language so they continue to be connected to each other, their local community, and their heritage. Many educators embrace the opportunity to develop programs in which all of their students (English speakers, heritage Spanish speakers, and ELLs) develop expertise in spoken and written Spanish as well as English because of the cognitive, academic, social, personal, and professional benefits that are associated with bilingualism. Language planners need to build on these kinds of ideologies as they work to promote dual language and/or world language education at school.

Since my experience working with schools that serve the Vietnamese, Chinese, Russian, and Khmer students and communities is very limited, and since I do not speak or understand any of those languages, I do not personally understand the nature of language ideologies in these schools and communities. However, I encourage members of the school-based language planning teams to pay attention to the ideologies they encounter through their language planning efforts. As we have seen throughout this book, when educators understand the ways that people use and evaluate the spoken and written languages of their community, they are in a position to challenge ideologies that do not promote bilingualism, biliteracy, and positive cultural understanding and relations, and to build on those that do. Although the particulars are likely to vary tremendously across school and community contexts, the underlying principle remains the same.

Language planning teams must have or develop a clear vision of their goals for their target populations, and those goals must be meaningful to the students, parents, teachers, administrators, policy makers, community members and any others who have an interest in the program. Some of those goals may be in response to policies, mandates, and/or requirements that are handed down to schools from the top, and these goals are incontrovertible. For example, all public schools in the U.S. today must have the English language development and academic achievement of all ELLs as a goal of their language education program because of federal, state, and local mandates. Some states or school districts have additional mandates in the area of bilingual education (either for or against, or for a certain type of bilingual education that is structured in a certain way), and school districts and schools must orient to those state and local mandates as they articulate their goals. Other states and school districts have no additional mandates or requirements about language education, but particular individuals or groups may have additional goals that they lobby for or against, and some of these goals may be controversial or in conflict with each other. This is the case in the School District of Philadelphia (SDP), where we see conflict and controversy on the local school level about English-only education, transitional bilingual education, and dual language education but no additional mandates from the Commonwealth of Pennsylvania. The important point for school district and school level language planners and policy makers who are working to promote bilingualism through schooling is that they work through this conflict and controversy, find ideological and implementation space for enriched bilingual programs, and clearly articulate goals for the target populations that everyone from the top-down and bottom-up ultimately understands and supports.

We saw in chapter 11 that the SDP has been working through this process, and is currently formulating a language policy and implementation plan that promotes bilingualism to the greatest degree possible for its target populations. The language learning goals of this policy can be stated as follows for ELLs, heritage language speakers, and English speakers:

- ELLs acquire the English language and literacies they need to participate and achieve in the all-English academic mainstream (as mandated by the No Child Left Behind Act; Pennsylvania Department of Education *Guidebook for Planning Programs for English Language Learners;* Y. S. stipulations).

- Students who come from homes in which languages other than English are spoken (including ELLs and heritage language speakers) maintain and develop expertise in their home or heritage language, with an emphasis on adding literacies in the standard variety of that language.

- English speakers develop expertise in a language other than English.

- All students develop an understanding of and appreciation for other cultural groups in particular and linguistic and cultural diversity more generally.

The policy and implementation plan that the SDP is developing will specify how the different levels of institutional authority (central, regional, school, program administration) should work together to ensure that ELLs, heritage language speakers, and English speakers have opportunities to reach these goals through their K–12 educational experience in the school district.

Since language planning is always about "much more than language" (Freeman 1998), language planners need to have additional goals. As I have argued throughout this book, the dominance of English in the United States leads to the social stigmatization of languages other than English and to the subordination of speakers of those languages. Schools must include in their goals efforts to elevate the status of languages other than English and to position speakers of those languages as legitimate members of the school community so that ELLs and heritage language speakers maintain and develop their expertise in these languages and resist the assimilationist trend that dominates in this country. To this end, U.S. public school educators need to make language education an integral part of the academic mainstream for all students, and U.S. citizens need to expect all students to develop expertise in languages other than English through their participation in well-implemented programs at school.

How is the school currently addressing students' language education needs

As the language planning teams begin to look closely at the strengths and needs of their target populations, and as they begin to articulate their short-term and long-term language education goals for those target populations, I ask the team members to work together and think critically about the ways in which they are currently addressing their students' language education needs. More importantly, I ask team members what evidence they have of their target populations' performance and development relative to their goals. This approach is consistent with the recent emphasis on data-driven decision-making that schools are asked to adopt, and it often gives educators a concrete opportunity (a) to think critically about what counts as evidence of student performance and development and (b) to see discrepancies between the goals that they have begun to articulate, the way that their existing language education program is structured, and student outcomes relative to each of the goals. Educators' discussions about the discrepancies that they identify often lead to action.

In some cases, educators realize that the type of language education program that they have in place does not allow them to realize the goals that they have articulated for their target populations. This is what we saw in the majority of the target schools that I have worked with in the School District of Philadelphia (SDP). Three of the target schools in North Philadelphia that were to use Spanish and English for instructional purposes began to look critically at the transitional bilingual and English-only programs that they had in place, and they began to reject the notion that their ELLs give up their Spanish in order to learn English. All of the target schools in the other multilingual communities had English-only programs in the elementary schools, and with the exception of the Chinese bilingual program that was in place in the middle school in one of the target schools, none of these schools promoted the development of the first or heritage languages of their students. Language planning team members from all of these schools realized that they needed to plan new programs for their schools if they were to realize their language education goals.

In other cases, educators realize that the type of language education program that they had in place could allow them to reach their goals if it were well-implemented. This is the case that I found in the target schools in North Philadelphia that had one-way developmental bilingual (DBE) programs. These schools wanted to promote the maintenance and development of Spanish for ELLs while they acquire the English they need to participate and achieve in the academic mainstream, and they were convinced by the research (e.g., Thomas and Collier 2002) that DBE programs could enable their ELLs to reach these goals. These schools focused their attention on improving the existing DBE program and practices in their school in ways that are aligned with all of the other reform efforts in the SDP.

In still other cases, educators wanted their English-speaking students to have opportunities to develop expertise in a language other than English. As discussed above, some of the English speakers who are enrolled in the all-English academic mainstream are monolingual English speakers. However, schools that are located in multilingual communities are likely to have students enrolled in the all-English academic mainstream who are heritage language speakers and who speak languages other than English at home and/or in other parts of their lives. A few of the schools in North Philadelphia have Spanish programs for students enrolled in the academic mainstream, but none that I have seen is a well-articulated, long-sequence program that builds on the expertise that heritage language speakers bring with them to school and/or on the linguistic and cultural resources that are readily available right outside of the school in many of the students' homes and throughout the local community. As we saw in chapter 14, several schools have begun to develop world language programs that target the dominant community language for their monolingual English speakers and their heritage language speakers who are enrolled in the all-English mainstream.

My experience working with language planning teams in the SDP and in other contexts in the United States and internationally demonstrates that when educators look closely at their target populations, program goals, program structure, and program outcomes, and when they are given the opportunity to consider alternative programs structures that could enable them to reach their goals in ways that they believe are appropriate for their school and community context, many times teams embrace the opportunity. Then, when team members make a commitment to themselves, each other, their students, and their community to develop pedagogically sound programs and practices, they become motivated to read the literature and visit other programs in order to realize this possibility for their students.

What type of program
is appropriate for the school and community

I argue throughout this book that there is no one-size-fits-all type of language education program that educators can uncritically implement in their schools. Not all types of language education programs are appropriate for all schools. As we saw in chapter 11, not all schools have the human or material resources, including students, teachers, curriculum, materials, assessment tools, or ideological support for every type of program. Language planning teams must look closely at their target populations, goals, resources, and constraints to determine if a one-way developmental bilingual program, or a two-way immersion program, or a modified dual language program, or a heritage language program, or a world language program is appropriate for their school and community context.

Table 1 (see p. 338) provides a summary of the types of language education programs that we can find in schools today, including bilingual education, content-based ESL, world language, and heritage language programs. Each type of program is categorized according to the students it targets, the goals for those students, the prototypical program structure, the length of the program, and the anticipated outcomes for the target populations. This table is intended to facilitate language planners' efforts to compare and contrast the range of options they can consider as they work to develop a program for their school. Chapter 3 provides detailed discussions of each of these types of programs.

In order to determine which types of language education programs might be appropriate for a particular school and community context, language planners need to identify how many students they have in each of the following categories: (1) ELLs that speak the dominant community language, (2) heritage language speakers of the same language, (3) heritage language learners of that language, (4) English speakers who are interested in learning the dominant community language, and (5) ELLs who speak other languages and who are interested in learning the dominant community language (and English). As we saw in chapter 3, one of the defining criteria of different program types is target population. Two-way immersion (TWI) programs, for example, target balanced numbers of English speakers and ELLs, and heritage language programs exclusively target heritage language speakers. As we saw in chapter 11, if schools do not have sufficient numbers of students at their school who speak the target language as their dominant language, then TWI is not an option. We also saw that if schools have large numbers of students in the all-English academic mainstream who are heritage speakers of the same language but the school does not have the materials or teachers or support for a TWI program, a heritage language program that promotes literacy development in that language may be an option. In addition to knowing the relative numbers of students in each of these categories, language planners also need to know whether their demographics are relatively stable or in the process of change. For example, if the sociopolitical or economic context has changed in ways that have led to a rapid increase in the immigration of one group into the community, or the sudden decrease in immigration of another group to that community, the school must be prepared to respond appropriately.

It is important to emphasize that schools can, and in many cases should, have more than one language education program as they organize the whole school to promote additive bilingualism to the greatest degree possible for their ELLs, heritage language speakers, and English speakers. We saw in chapter 11 that seven of the target schools in the SDP are developing what we call "modified dual language programs" that are made up of three different types of language education programs that work together to realize the school's goals for all of their students (see Context 2, below). We also saw that one school that had a one-way developmental bilingual (DBE) program in place for its Spanish-speaking ELLs also was beginning to plan a Spanish program for students enrolled in the all-English academic mainstream (see Context 1, below). Here I consider these and other possible configurations for schools that serve a range of target populations in different types of communities.

Context 1

An elementary school that is in a bilingual community that has access to curricular materials in the non-English language, bilingual educators, and community support for a bilingual program (e.g., in the Puerto Rican community in North Philadelphia, and/or in the Chinese community in Central/South Philadelphia) may have

(text continues on page 340)

Table 1. Types of language education programs

	Students	Goals	Structure	Length	Outcomes
Transitional Model of Bilingual Education (TBE)					
Early-exit TBE program	ELLs	Academic English	Segregate ELLs Provide content-area instruction in L1 and ESL	One to three years	Do not generally reach parity with English-speaking counterparts
Late-exit TBE program	ELLs	L1 literacy Academic English		Four to five years	May reach parity with English-speaking counterparts
Dual Language Model of Bilingual Education					
Immersion program	English speakers	Bilingualism Biliteracy development	Segregate students by language background	At least five to seven years	Develop high levels of oral and written expertise in two languages
One-way developmental bilingual (DBE) program	ELLs	Academic achievement in two languages	Provide 50 to 90 percent of content-area instruction in TL	Preferably K–12	Achieve academically at or above grade level
Two-way immersion (TWI) program	English speakers and ELLs	Positive cultural understanding	Integrate students Provide 50 to 90 percent of content-area instruction in TL		Develop positive cultural understanding

Other Types of Language Education Programs

Program	Target students	Goals	Program type	Program length	Outcomes
Content-based ESL program	ELLs	English language development Academic achievement in English	Pull-out ESL classes Sheltered ESL programs	Program length varies depending on local exit criteria	Wide range of outcomes reflects diversity in student backgrounds and program structures Do not generally reach parity with English-speaking counterparts
World language program	English speakers	Oral and written expertise in world language Cultural understanding	As a school subject Content-related Well-articulated	Preferably K–12	Develop intermediate to advanced levels of expertise after 12 years
Heritage language program	Heritage language speakers	Broad linguistic repertoire Expertise in standard variety of language and literacies in that language	As a school subject Content-related Well-articulated	Preferably K–12	No data available on the effectiveness of these programs Expect students to exceed expertise of English speakers in world language programs

ELL = English language learners   L1 = First language
ESL = English as a second language   TL = Target language

EITHER
- a two-way immersion (TWI) program as one strand in the school for English speakers and speakers of the other language

AND
- a heritage/world language program that promotes the community language for students enrolled in the all-English mainstream

OR
- a one-way developmental bilingual (DBE) program for ELLs

AND
- a heritage/world language program that promotes the community language for students enrolled in the all-English mainstream

Context 2

An elementary school that is in a bilingual community but that does not have the necessary conditions for a dual language program (e.g., not enough materials, personnel, or community support) may have a "modified dual language program" that includes three components

- a content-based ESL program for ELLs

AND
- an L1 literacy program for ELLs

AND
- a world/heritage language program that promotes the community language for students enrolled in the all English mainstream

Context 3

An elementary school that is in a bilingual community and that has the necessary resources for a bilingual program, but that only allows transitional bilingual education (because of local or state mandates or ideologies) for a maximum of three years may have

- a transitional bilingual program for ELLs

- a heritage language program for ELLs who have exited the transitional program and who are enrolled in the all-English academic mainstream to support their continuing development of their heritage language and literacies in that language, and for other heritage language speakers in the academic mainstream

- a world language program for monolingual English speakers

Context 4

An elementary school that has a large number of ELLs from a wide number of language backgrounds may have

- a sheltered ESL program for ELLs

AND

- an extensive library of materials in the languages of the ELLs and creative ways for those students to build on their L1

AND

- a world language program for all students in the language that the school chooses

As have seen throughout this book, language planning teams have choices not only in the types of language education programs that they develop for their schools, but also in the ways that they structure those programs to reach their goals. The chapters in Part IV provide examples of ways that educators in different schools in the SDP worked through the decision making process in order to develop programs that they believed respond to their school and community context.

I have also argued throughout this book that a language education program is only as good as its implementation. The chapters in Part III of the book examined how three teachers working in different types of ESL and bilingual programs translated their interpretation of the policies and programs that they were to implement into practice by mediating between their understanding of that policy or program, relevant theories of language, literacy, and learning, the school and community context, and their ongoing assessment of their students' strengths and needs relative to the goals of the program or policy. Table 2 (see p. 342) synthesizes the major theories of language, literacy, learning, and assessment that inform my work throughout the book and outlines implications of these theories for practice. More detailed discussion of these theories and references, as well as examples of most of these practices, are provided in the school-based chapters in Part III of the book.

A call for action

This concluding section emphasizes the dynamic nature of language planning and policy making on the local school and school district levels and suggests how bottom-up efforts to promote bilingualism through schooling can challenge top-down English-only discourses. Title III of the No Child Left Behind Act requires all schools to hold themselves accountable for all

(text continues page 344)

Table 2. Translating theories into practice

Theoretical assumption	Implication for practice
About learning	
• Teacher has high expectations for all students.	• Have equally high standards for all.
• Learning is a constructive, social process in which the learner uses spoken and written language to make meaning in communities of learners.	• Organize students into groups to work together to solve meaningful problems (e.g., cooperative learning, shared reading, buddy journals, peer review).
• Students learn by connecting new information to what they already know.	• Activate students' prior knowledge (e.g., prereading and prewriting activities) and scaffold instruction to build on that knowledge.
• Students have a wide range of background knowledge.	• Use a wide variety of groups and activities (e.g., teacher-fronted, small group, pair, individual) to accommodate learner needs/wants.
• Students have a variety of ways of learning.	
• Students should be encouraged to take on more and more responsibility for their own learning.	• Give students choices about topics and genres they read and write; involve students in their assessment.
• Students need to learn language/content as well as how to learn language/content.	• Use predictable learning structures (e.g., cycles, centers); teach strategies.
About language	
• Second language acquisition is enhanced when students have comprehensible input, opportunities to negotiate meaning, and to produce meaningful output.	• Immerse students in comprehensible content; use experiential, cooperative and/or project-based learning, have students use language for a wide range of purposes.
• Reading, writing, listening, and speaking are interrelated processes; each is enhanced by the use of the others.	• Integrate reading, writing, listening, and speaking activities in theme-based instruction.
• Immersion alone does not enable all learners to develop the ability to use spoken and written language correctly and appropriately.	• Focus on form within the context of meaningful content.
• Errors provide evidence of growth.	• Use errors to signal areas to target for instruction.

Theoretical assumption	Implication for practice
About literacy	
• Literacy is a form of social practice that cannot be separated from its social context.	• Connect students (actually or virtually) with communities in which they need to use spoken and written language; have students transact with texts.
• People participate in a wide range of literacy practices; they use reading and writing for different purposes.	• Expose students to genres that they need to use and give them opportunities to read and write in those genres across contexts.
• Literacy practices and conventions vary cross-culturally.	• Direct students' attention to differences in contexts, rhetorical styles, and organizational structures.
• L1 literacy development enhances L2 literacy development.	• Encourage students to maintain and develop L1 literacy, and to compare L1 and L2 oral and written practices.
• Writing is a process, and writing instruction includes five interrelated phases: prewriting, drafting, revising, editing, and publishing.	• Use writing workshops, writers' journals, peer review, conferences. • Balance attention to process and product in writing instruction.
About assessment	
• Assessment is ongoing and should guide practice.	• In student-centered, learning-centered classrooms, teachers should listen and observe students closely to identify their strengths and needs relative to their goals. Teachers should direct instruction toward specific student needs as they arise.
• Testing influences teaching.	• An integrated approach to teaching, learning and assessment means that testing both reflects and informs teaching; tests should provide summative and formative information that guides teaching.

English language learners' (ELLs) English language development and academic achievement in English. Educators who work in existing dual language programs, and educators who are developing new dual language programs, are encouraged to work together to ensure that their programs are pedagogically sound and well-implemented, and to provide evidence of the effectiveness of these programs in ways that are considered valid and reliable by policy makers on the local, state, and federal levels. Action-oriented researchers are encouraged to combine quantitative and qualitative research methods that look closely at how teachers translate dual language programs into practice, and that provide evidence of how students are performing and developing as measured by the state mandated standardized tests AND by alternative assessments that can supplement and inform each other. The approach called for in this section reviews and synthesizes many of the main ideas forwarded throughout this book for dual language educators and action-oriented researchers working in other contexts.

Diagram 1 represents the multidirectional and recursive nature of language planning and policy making that has been described in this book, and it is intended to show that regardless of whether the language policy is generated at the top (i.e., on the state, school district, or school level) or on the bottom (i.e., by the teachers and/or parents of the language learners at school), ultimately a combination of top-down and bottom-up efforts are likely to be necessary to ensure that the program is well-implemented and sustainable over time. In the School District of Philadelphia (SDP), for example, we see a combination of top-down and bottom-up initiatives as educators in particular schools, schools in particular regions, schools across regions, and the central administration continue to develop an understanding of the kinds of bilingual education, ESL, world language, and heritage language programs that educators and parents believe are appropriate for their ELLs, heritage language speakers, and English speakers. Let us briefly consider how this diagram represents a few of the different language planning and policymaking projects that have been described in this book.

Let us begin with the development of the two-way immersion programs in the predominantly Puerto Rican community in North Philadelphia, which is represented by the cycle on the lower part of the diagram. As we saw in chapter 12, when the dual language initiative began, I went to the target schools to stimulate language planning from the bottom-up. Individual language planning teams from three schools in the same academic region prepared for program development by identifying students who would participate in their programs and by developing two-way immersion (TWI) plans during the spring of 2001. Dual language teachers from these three

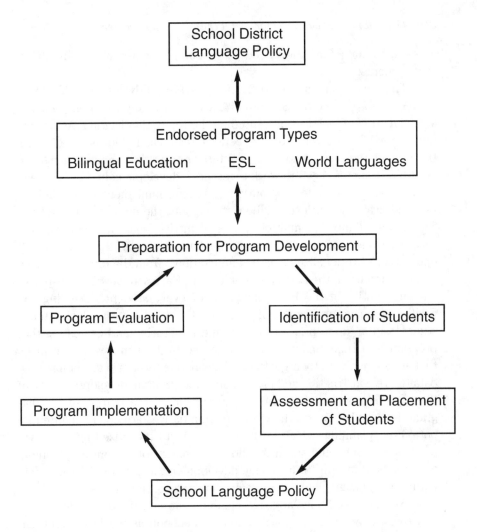

Diagram 1: The recursive nature of language policy planning and program development on the local level.

schools continued to prepare for program development through their three-week intensive summer professional development, and their efforts were guided and supported by the central and regional levels of SDP administration. These three schools began to implement their programs in the fall of 2001, which is when they began to assess their students. As we saw in chapter 13, TWI teachers continued to develop their assessment plan over the first two years of program implementation to ensure that it will provide the formative assessment data that they need to guide instruction and professional and program development, as well as the summative assessment data that they need to respond to external accountability requirements.

Then in the summer of 2002 a new chief executive officer (CEO) was appointed to oversee the SDP, and he asked for a language policy for the school district, which is represented on the top of the diagram. As we saw in chapter 11, educators from the central, regional, and local school levels throughout the district and representatives from the dominant language groups in the city began to work together to develop a coherent language policy that would guide program development, implementation, monitoring, and evaluation in every school throughout the district in the future. This is an example of multiple levels of institutional authority working together to develop the policy and implementation plan that, once developed and institutionalized, will be handed down from the top for language planning teams on the bottom to implement. Each school will be responsible for identifying the home language of every student, assessing the English language proficiency of all ELLs on a regular basis, placing those students in an appropriate program, and monitoring and evaluating that program over time. Schools will be required to develop assessment plans that are aligned with their goals and that provide formative and summative data to drive instruction and professional and program development. All of these processes are represented by the cycle on the bottom of the diagram. In the SDP, we see how top-down initiatives are complemented by bottom-up planning, which leads to and is institutionalized by top-down policies, which should stimulate the development of bottom-up planning, which should inform future policy development, and so on. The dynamic nature of language planning and policy making continues.

We have seen how language planning can contribute to educational and social change on the local school and school district levels. But can language planning on the local level stimulate educational and social change on the state and federal levels? Future research and practice will determine if this is in fact possible, but here I suggest an approach that dual language educators and action-oriented researchers can pursue as they work toward this end.

First, we need to look closely at the accountability data that is collected over the next several years under Title III. If schools, school districts, and states use the federally mandated accountability data that they are required to collect to do a comparative analysis of ELLs and English speaking students' performance and development within and across program types, we should generate an enormous database for research that the federal government considers "scientific" and "rigorous." If schools, school districts, and states compare the performance and development of ELLs who are enrolled in different types of bilingual and ESL programs, and if the future findings on the effectiveness of dual language programs support the longitudinal data that has been collected to date (e.g., Thomas and Collier 2002; Lindholm-Leary 2001), we should have compelling evidence that can be used to counter English-only ideologies. And if dual language programs within and across schools, school districts, and states compare the performance and development of English speakers who learn through two languages with their English-speaking counterparts who only learn through English, we should have compelling evidence that English speakers (across the socioeconomic spectrum) can learn through two languages AND achieve academically in English, and this evidence can be used to promote the development of two-way immersion programs in the future. Perhaps federal funding for dual language programs will follow from this kind of "scientific evidence" that demonstrates the effectiveness of these programs.

As I have emphasized repeatedly throughout the book, implementation is key. Qualitative research is desperately needed that documents how teachers translate their interpretation of policies and programs into practices for ELLs and English speakers, and this qualitative research can inform our understanding of the quantitative data that the No Child Left Behind Act requires. Detailed ethnographic and discourse analytic studies can demonstrate how teachers organize learning and teaching in their classrooms, which can provide an understanding of how students participate in those classroom practices. Researchers can compare standardized test scores of students' performance with alternative assessments of those students' performance and development and consider how our understanding of the classroom practices can inform our understanding of the qualitative and quantitative assessment data. Finally, researchers can explore how the standardized and alternative assessment data that are collected and analyzed can inform our understanding of the actual performance and development of students over time. This approach should yield an understanding of the strengths and needs of language learners and the programs that are intended to serve them. It should also allow us to think critically about the validity and reliability of the standardized tests that have become such an important part of schooling in the United States today.

Conclusion

This chapter synthesizes the major ideas that have been put forward throughout the book. I begin with the theoretical orientation that informs my work to emphasize that educators have choices in the ways that they organize their programs and practices. Moreover, the choices that educators make have important implications for individual students and their families, schools and communities, and society overall. I strongly believe that schools located in multilingual communities have a responsibility to build programs that encourage ELLs and heritage language speakers to maintain and develop their native and/or heritage languages, and that this work can begin to challenge the assimilation strategy that has been dominant in the United States over the last century. I also strongly believe that English speakers living in our global society need to develop expertise in languages other than English, and I advocate for public school programs and policies that work to this end.

The majority of the chapter reviews the approach to school-based language planning that informs the language planning projects described in Part IV of the book. Drawing on examples of how individual educators and school-based teams from the predominantly Puerto Rican community, and to a lesser degree from educators and teams from other multilingual communities in Philadelphia, I present an approach that is intended to guide school-based language planning teams as they work their way through the dynamic, ideological processes involved in language planning for educational and social change.

The last section of this chapter is a call for action. In this increasingly English-only era of accountability, many find it difficult to develop and sustain dual language programs that take seriously the goal of bilingualism, biliteracy development, academic achievement in two languages, and positive intergroup understanding and relations. Like many others in the field, I encourage dual language educators to ensure that their programs are pedagogically sound, well-implemented, and strongly supported on the local level. I also encourage educators and researchers across the country to work together to collect the data that we need to seriously challenge English-only discourses from the bottom up.

Glossary

additive bilingualism: is a situation in which the acquisition of a second language is added to an individual or group's linguistic repertoires without the loss or displacement of the first language (contrast this with *subtractive bilingualism*).

bilingual education: a model and/or type of language education that uses two languages for instructional purposes. There are different models of bilingual education that have different ideological orientations and goals, and different types of bilingual programs that have different target populations, goals, program structures, and anticipated outcomes (see *transitional bilingual education, dual language education, immersion education, one-way developmental bilingual education, two-way immersion education*).

content-based second language instruction: a type of language education and/or an approach to teaching a second language that is designed to promote the acquisition of the second language using non-language (e.g., academic, professional) content as the basis for teaching. Under this approach, language teachers use instructional materials and activities from academic content areas (science, social studies, mathematics) as the vehicle for developing second language, content, cognitive, and study skills. Content-based second language instructional approaches can be used in ESL, bilingual education, or world language programs (see also *sheltered instruction*).

dual language education: a model and/or type of enriched bilingual education that promotes bilingualism, biliteracy development, and academic achievement through two languages for its target populations and that uses a minority language for at least 50 percent of the content area instruction (see *immersion education, one-way developmental bilingual education, two-way immersion education*).

early-exit bilingual education: a type of *transitional bilingual education* program that uses the primary language of ELLs for no more than one to three years, and that encourages ELLs to exit the bilingual program and enter the all-English academic mainstream as quickly as possible (i.e., transition to English). These programs aim for the development of academic English, they provide no support for native language maintenance or development, and they often lead to *subtractive bilingualism*.

English as a second language (ESL): English as a second language programs or classes target students who are learning English as a second or additional language in contexts in which English is used as the language of wider communication (e.g., in the United States, Australia, United Kingdom).

English immersion: This term is increasingly used by English-only advocates to describe programs for ELLs that exclusively use English for instructional purposes. There is no generally accepted definition or set of criteria for these programs, and they are regularly critiqued by language educators for the lack of attention to the special needs of language learners. Critics of this approach often use the term *submersion* to refer to these "sink or swim" programs for ELLs.

English language learner (ELL): a term used increasingly in the United States to refer to someone who does not speak English as their first language and who is learning English. This term is increasingly used instead of the term *limited English proficient* (LEP), which has been criticized because it defines students who are learning English in terms of what they lack.

foreign language: foreign or *world language* programs teach the target language as a subject area for students who do not live in contexts (homes, communities, societies) that use that language as a medium of communication (Spanish as a foreign or world language program for monolingual English speakers in the United States; English as a foreign language for Koreans who study English at school in Korea). The term *world language* is increasingly used in the United States.

heritage language: a home language (indigenous, immigrant, colonial) that is not the dominant societal language and that is part of an individual's linguistic repertoire.

heritage language programs: heritage language programs promote the maintenance and the development of the *heritage language for heritage language speakers* (e.g., Spanish for Spanish speakers, Russian for Russian speakers).

heritage language speaker: an individual who has some expertise in his/her *heritage language*. We find a wide range of variation in the kinds of spoken and written expertise that heritage language speakers have developed in their heritage languages, with some heritage language speakers demonstrating considerable expertise in spoken and written varieties of the heritage language and other heritage language speakers simply understanding the variety of the heritage language used at home to talk about familiar topics. An individual student's expertise in his/her heritage language depends largely on opportunities to use the heritage language (e.g., at home, church, other key contexts in the community, with different family or community members).

immersion education: a type of dual language education that exclusively targets language majority students (e.g., English speakers in the United States or Canada, Italian speakers in Italy) and promotes bilingualism, biliteracy development, and academic achievement in two languages for these students. Second or foreign language immersion programs provide at least 50 percent and up to 100 percent of students' content-area instruction through their second language during the elementary and secondary grades. The programs vary with respect to the amount of the second language that is used for instruction and the grade level during which immersion in the second language is offered (contrast this with *submersion programs* and *English immersion programs*).

language education: A broad term that includes *bilingual education, English as a second language education, world language education, and heritage language education* (see each of these terms for specific definitions).

language majority students: students who speak the dominant societal language (e.g., English speakers in the United States, Italian speakers in Italy).

language minority students: students who speak a language other than the dominant societal language (e.g., Spanish or Chinese speakers in the United States; English speakers in Italy).

late-exit bilingual education: a type of transitional bilingual education program that uses the primary language of ELLs for four to five years and that encourages ELLs to learn academic content and acquire literacies in their first language as a foundation for their transition to the all-English academic mainstream. These programs aim for the development of academic English and provide opportunities for ELLs to build a solid academic and linguistic foundation in their first language as a means to that end(contrast this with *early-exit bilingual education*).

one-way developmental bilingual education (DBE): a type of dual language education that exclusively targets language minority students (e.g., Spanish speakers in the United States or Canada) and that promotes bilingualism, biliteracy development, and academic achievement in two languages for these students. One-way developmental bilingual education programs provide at least 50 percent of the content-area instruction in the minority language, and content-based ESL is an integral part of these enriched bilingual programs.

sheltered program/instruction: A type of *content-based second language program* or an approach to teaching a second language. Sheltered ESL programs segregate ELLs from the academic mainstream and teach academic material using sheltered instructional strategies to ensure that the material is comprehensible to second language learners and that it promotes their second language and literacy development. All teachers who adjust the language demands of the lesson use sheltered instructional strategies (i.e., in any kind of content-based ESL program, in two-way immersion programs, in mainstream all-English classes that include ELLs).

submersion programs: This term is not an official term used to refer to a type of language education program but is an unofficial critique of what is commonly referred to as a "sink or swim" approach to the education of ELLs. In these programs, English is used as the exclusive language of instruction, and there may or may not be specialized support for ELLs (see also *English immersion*).

subtractive bilingualism: a situation in which the acquisition of a second language displaces the primary language. This occurs frequently in the case of language minority students who attend schools where no provision is made to maintain and develop their primary language (contrast this with *additive bilingualism*).

transitional bilingual education (TBE): a type of bilingual education that targets ELLs. Transitional bilingual programs use the students' primary language for some content-area instruction for a limited number of years (generally one to three years in *early-exit bilingual programs* and four to five years in *late-exit bilingual programs*), and they aim to promote the students' mastery of academic material while they are learning English as a second language.

two-way immersion programs (TWI): a type of dual language education that targets balanced numbers of language minority and language majority students (e.g., Spanish and English speakers in the United States) and integrates these students for content-area instruction in two languages for most or all of the time. Two-way immersion programs provide at least 50 percent (in 50:50 programs) and up to 90 percent (in 90:10 programs) of the content area instruction in the minority language, and they promote bilingualism, biliteracy development, academic achievement in two languages, and positive intergroup understanding and relations for language minority and language majority students.

world language: *foreign language* or world language programs teach the target language as a subject area for students who do not live in contexts (homes, communities, societies) that use that language as a medium of communication (Spanish as a foreign or world language program for monolingual English speakers in the United States; English as a foreign language for Koreans who study English at school in Korea)

Resources for language educators

American Council on the Teaching of Foreign Languages (ACTFL)
www.actfl.org

Center for Advanced Research on Language Acquisition (CARLA)
www.carla.acad.umn.edu

Center for Applied Linguistics (CAL)
www.cal.org

Center for Research on Education, Diversity, & Excellence (CREDE)
www.crede.ucsc.edu

ERIC Clearinghouse on Languages and Linguistics
www.cal.org/ericll

Illinois Resource Center (IRC)
www.thecenterweb.org

International Reading Association (IRA)
www.ira.org

Joint National Committee for Languages (JNCL) and the National Council
for Languages and International Studies (NCLIS)
www.languagepolicy.org

National Association for Bilingual Education (NABE)
www.nabe.org

National Clearinghouse for English Language Acquisition
www.ncela.gwu.edu

National Foreign Language Center (NFLC)
www.nflc.org

National Foreign Language Resource Center (NFLRC)
www.lll.hawaii.edu

National Network for Early Language Learning (NNELL)
www.cal.org/projects/NNELL.html

Teachers of English to Speakers of Other Languages (TESOL)
www.tesol.org

Bibliography

Alfaro, M., Letriz, L., Santos, M., Villanueva, M., and Freeman, R. 2001. Our world. In: J. Shultz and Cook-Sather, A. (eds.), *In our own words: Students' perspectives on school.* Boulder: Rowan and Littlefield, pp. 19–38.

American Council of Teachers of Foreign Languages. 1999. *ACTFL K–12 Performance Guidelines.* Yonkers: ACTFL.

Atwell, N. 1987. *In the middle: Writing, reading, and learning with adolescents.* Portsmouth: Heineman.

Au, K. 1980. Participation structures in a reading lesson with Hawaiian children. *Anthropology and Education Quarterly* 11:91–115.

August, D. and Hakuta, K. 1997. *Improving schooling for language minority children: A research agenda.* Washington, D.C.: National Academy Press.

Baker, C. and Jones, S.P. 1998. *Encyclopedia of bilingual education and bilingualism.* Clevedon: Multilingual Matters.

Bamgbose, A. 1989. Issues for a model of language planning. *Language Problems and Language Planning* 13 (2,): 24–34.

Bourdieu, P. 1991. *Language and symbolic power.* Cambridge: Polity Press.

Brecht, R.D. and Ingold, C.W. 1998. *Tapping a national resource: Heritage languages in the United States.* ERIC Digest. Washington, D.C.: ERIC Clearinghouse on Languages and Linguistics.

Brecht, R.D. and Rivers, W.P. 2000. *Language and national security in the 21st century: The role of Title VI/Fulbright-Hays in supporting national language capacity.* Dubuque: Kendall/Hunt.

Brinton, D.M., Snow, M.A., and Bingham Wesche, M. 1989. *Content-based second language instruction.* Boston: Heinle & Heinle.

Brown, P. and Levinson, S.C. 1987. *Politeness: Some universals in language usage.* New York: Cambridge University Press.

Calkins, L.M. 1986. *The art of teaching writing.* Portsmouth: Heineman.

Campbell, R.N., Gray, T.C., Rhodes, N.C., and Snow, M.A. 1985. Foreign language learning in the elementary school: A comparison of three programs. *Modern Language Journal* 69: 44–54.

Canale, M. and Swain, M. 1980. Theoretical bases of communicative approaches to second-language teaching and testing. *Applied Linguistics* 1(1): 1–47.

Carreira, M. and Armengol, R. 2001. Professional opportunities for heritage language speakers. In: J. Peyton, D. Ranard, and S. McGinnis (eds.), *Heritage languages in America: Preserving a national resource.* McHenry: Delta Systems Co., Inc. pp. 109–142.

Cazden, C.B. 1988. *Classroom discourse: The language of teaching and learning.* Portsmouth: Heinemann.

Center for Applied Linguistics. 1997. *National survey of foreign language instruction in elementary and secondary schools in the United States.* Washington, D.C.: Center for Applied Linguistics.

Chall, J.S., Jacobs, V., and Baldwin, L. 1990. *The reading crisis: Why poor children fall behind.* Cambridge: Harvard University Press.

Chamot, A. U. and O'Malley, J.M. 1994. *The CALLA handbook: Implementing the cognitive academic language learning approach.* Reading: Addison-Wesley.

Chin, M., Ky, C., and Freeman, R. 2002. *Promoting heritage language development in the School District of Philadelphia.* Poster presented at the 2nd National Heritage Languages Conference: Arlington, Virginia.

Christian, D. 1994. Two-way bilingual education: Students learning through two languages. In: *The National Center for Research on Cultural Diversity and Second Language Learning: Educational Practice Report 12.* Washington, D.C.: Center for Applied Linguistics.

Christian, D. 2002. Heritage language education policy: US elementary and secondary education. On panel *National policy statement on heritage language development: Toward an agenda for action.* Presented at the 2nd National Conference on Heritage Languages in the United States. Arlington, Virginia.

Cloud, N., Genesee, F. and Hamayan, E. 2000. *Dual language instruction: A handbook for enriched education.* Boston: Heinle & Heinle.

Colombi, M.C. and Alarcón, F.X. (eds.). 1997. *La enseñanza del español a hispanohablantes: Praxis y teoría.* Boston: Houghton Mifflin.

Community Consolidated School District 54. 2001. *Bilingual Education Resource Guide.* Schaumburg, Illinois.

Cooper, R.L. 1989. *Language Planning and Social Change.* Cambridge: Cambridge University Press.

Corson, D. 1999. *Language policy in schools: A resource for teachers and administrators.* Mahwah: Lawrence Erlbaum.

Cummins, J. 1987. Bilingualism, language proficiency, and metalinguistic development. In: P. Homel, M. Palij, and D. Aaronson (eds.) *Childhood bilingualism: Aspects of linguistic, cognitive and social development.* Hillsdale: Lawrence Erlbaum, pp. 57–73.

Cummins, J. 2001. *Negotiating identities: Education for empowerment in a diverse society.* Los Angeles: California Association for Bilingual Education.

Cummins, J. In press. *Reading and the ESL student.* Victoria: Orbit Press.

Curtain, H. and Pesola, C.A.B. 1994. *Languages and children: Making the match.* New York: Longman.

Davies, B. and Harré, R. 1990. Positioning: The discursive production of selves. *Journal for the Theory of Social Behavior* 20 (1): 43–63.

Duncan, G. 2001. Measuring up to the standards: Practical applications of the ACTFL Performance Guidelines for K–12 Learners. Presented at a pre-conference workshop at the American Council on the Teaching of Foreign Languages ACTFL annual meeting, Washington, D.C.

Durgunoglu, A.Y. and Verhoeven, L. 1998. *Literacy development in a multilingual context: Cross-cultural perspectives.* Mahwah: Lawrence Erlbaum.

Dutcher, N. 1995. *Overview of foreign language students in the United States.* National Clearinghouse for Bilingual Education. Resource Collection Series, 6. Washington, D.C.: Center for Applied Linguistics.

Echeverria, J., Vogt, M., and Short, D.J. 2000. *Making content comprehensible for English Language Learners: The SIOP model.* Boston: Allyn & Bacon.

Edelsky, C. 1989. *Writing in a bilingual program.* Norwood: Ablex.

Edwards, J. D. 2003. *National language policies and activities 2002. Learning languages: The journal for the National Network for Early Language Learning* 8 (1): 6.

Escamilla, K. and Medina, M. Jr. 1993. English and Spanish acquisition by limited-language-proficient Mexican Americans in a three-year maintenance bilingual program. *Hispanic Journal of Behavioral Sciences* 15: 108–20.

Fairclough, N. 1989. *Language and power.* New York: Longman.

Fairclough, N. 1993. *Discourse and social change.* Cambridge: Polity Press.

Fishman, J. 1972. The sociology of language. Rowley: Newbury House.

Fishman, J. 1974. Language modernization and planning in comparison with other types of national modernization and planning. In: J. A. Fishman (ed.), Advances in language planning. The Hague: Mouton, pp. 79–102.

Fishman, J. 2001. 300-plus years of heritage language education in the United States. In: J. Peyton, D. Ranard, and S. McGinnis, (eds.), *Heritage languages in America: Preserving a national resource.* McHenry: Delta Systems Co., Inc., pp. 81–97.

Fountas, I.C., and Pinnell,G. S. 1996. *Guided reading: Good first teaching for all children.* Portsmouth: Heinemann.

Freeman, R. D. 1998. *Bilingual education and social change.* Clevedon: Multilingual Matters.

Freeman, R. and McElhinny, B. 1996. Language and gender. In: S. McKay and N. Hornberger (eds.), *Sociolinguistics and language teaching.* Cambridge: Cambridge University Press, pp. 218–280.

Fullan, M. 2001. *The new meaning of educational change.* New York: Teachers College Press.

Gal, S. 1995. Language, gender, and power: An anthropological review. In: K. Hall and M. Bucholtz (eds.), *Gender articulated: Language and the socially constructed self.* New York: Routledge, pp. 169–182.

Gardiner, M. 1992. *The dialogics of critique: M M Bakhtin and the theory of ideology.* London: Routledge.

Gee, J.P. 1990. *Social linguistics and literacies: Ideology in discourses.* Bristol: Taylor & Francis.

Gee, J.P. 2003. Decontextualized language: A problem, not a solution. Paper presented at the 4th International Symposium on Bilingualism. Arizona State University, Phoenix, Arizona.

Geertz, C. 1973. Thick description: Toward an interpretive theory of culture. In: *The Interpretation of Culture.* New York: Basic Books, pp. 3–30.

Genesee, F. 1985. Second language learning through immersion: A review of US programs. *Review of educational research* 55:541–561.

Genesee, F. 1987. *Learning through two languages:Studies of immersion and bilingual education.* Rowley: Newbury House.

Gilzow, D. F. and Branaman, L.E. 2000. *Lessons learned: Model early foreign language programs.* McHenry: Delta Systems Co., Inc.

Goffman, E. 1981. *Forms of talk.* Philadelphia: University of Pennsylvania Press.

Goode J. and Schneider, J. 1994. *Reshaping ethnic and racial relations in Philadelphia: Immigrants in a divided city.* Philadelphia: Temple University Press.

Gottlieb, M. and Nguyen, D. 2002. Evaluating the effectiveness of TWI programs in Schaumburg, IL. Paper presented at the Illinois State Bilingual Conference, Oakbrook, Illinois.

Graves, D.H. 1983. *Writing: Teachers and children at work.* Portsmouth: Heineman.

Gumperz, J. 1982. *Discourse strategies.* New York: Cambridge University Press.

Hamayan, E. 2003. National dual language standards. Draft presented at Desplaines, Illinois: Illinois Resource Center.

Heath, S.B. 1981. English in our language heritage. In: C.A. Ferguson, and S. B. Heath, (eds.), *Language in the USA.* Cambridge: Cambridge University Press, pp. 6–20.

Heath, S.B. 1983. *Ways with words: Language, life, and work in communities and classrooms.* Cambridge: Cambridge University Press.

Heller, M. 1994. *Crosswords: Language, education and ethnicity in French Ontario.* Berlin: Mouton de Gruyter.

Hernandez, T. 1999. Jíbaros, los puertorriqueños del campo. University of Pennsylvania: Unpublished paper.

Hornberger, N. H. 1991. Extending enrichment bilingual education: Revisiting typologies and redirecting policy. In: O. García (ed.), *Bilingual education Focusschrift in honor of Joshua A. Fishman, Vol. 1.* Philadelphia: John Benjamins, pp. 215–234.

Hornberger, N.H. 1997. Indigenous literacies in the Americas: Language planning from the bottom up. Berlin: Mouton de Gruyter, pp. 3–16.

Hornberger, N. H. and Skilton-Sylvester, E. 2000. Revisiting the continua of biliteracy: International and critical perspectives. *Language and Education: An International Journal* 14(2):96–122.

Hornberger, N.H. 2002. Multilingual language policies and the continua of biliteracy: An ecological approach. Language Policy 1(1):27–51.

Hornberger, N.H. (ed.). 2003. *The continua of biliteracy.* Clevedon: Multilingual Matters.

Howard, E. 2000. CAL/CREDE longitudinal study of biliteracy development. Presented at the 8th Annual National Two-Way Bilingual Immersion Summer Conference, California Association of Bilingual Education.

Hymes, D. 1966. Paper presented at the Research Planning Conference on Language Development among Disadvantaged Children. New York: Yeshiva University.

Hymes, D. 1974. *Foundations in sociolinguistics: An ethnographic approach.* Philadelphia: University of Pennsylvania Press.

Krashen, S. 1982. *Principles and practices in second language acquisition.* Oxford: Pergamon Press.

Krashen, S. 1996. *Under attack: The case against bilingual education.* Culver City: Language Education Associates.

International Reading Association. 2001. *Second language literacy instruction: A position statement of the International Reading Association.* Newark, Delaware: IRA.

Lambert. W.E. 1987. The effects of bilingual and bicultural experiences on children's attitudes and social perspectives. In: P. Homel, M. Palij, and D. Aaronson, (eds.), *Childhood bilingualism: Aspects of linguistic, cognitive, and social development.* Hillsdale: Lawrence Erlbaum, pp. 197–221.

Lambert, W.E. and Tucker, G.R. 1972. *The bilingual education of children: The St. Lambert experiment.* Rowley: Newbury House.

Lewelling, V.W., and Peyton, J. 1999. *Spanish for native speakers: Developing dual language proficiency. ERIC Digest.* Washington, D.C.: ERIC Clearinghouse on Languages and Linguistics.

Lindholm, K. 1990. Bilingual immersion education: Criteria for program development. In: A. Padilla, H.H. Fairchild, and C.M. Valdez (eds.), *Bilingual Education: Issues and Strategies.* Newbury Park: Corwin Press Inc., pp. 91–105.

Lindholm-Leary, K. 2000. *Biliteracy for a global society: An idea book on dual language education.* Washington, D.C.: National Clearinghouse for Bilingual Education.

Lindholm-Leary, K. 2001. *Dual language education.* Clevedon: Multilingual Matters.

Little, J.W. 1990. The "mentor" phenomenon and the social organization of teaching. In Cazden, C. (ed.), *Review of research in education 16.* Washington, D.C.: American Educational Research Association, pp. 297–351.

Long, M.H. 2001. Focus on form. In: C.N. Candlin, and N. Mercer, (eds.), *English language teaching in its social context.* New York: Routledge.

Marcos, K. 1998. *Are we wasting our nation's language resources?: Heritage languages in America.* Washington, D.C.: ERIC Clearinghouse on Languages and Linguistics.

Martin-Jones, M. and Jones, K. (eds.), 2000. *Multilingual literacies.* Philadelphia: John Benjamins.

McGroarty, M. 1992. The societal context of bilingual education. *Educational Researcher* 21 (2): 7–9.

McGroarty, M. 1997. Language policy in the US: National values, local loyalties, pragmatic pressures. In: W. Eggington, and H. Wren (eds.), *Language policy: Dominant English and pluralist challenge.* Canberra: Language Australia and Amsterdam: John Benjamins, pp. 67–90.

Medina, M., Jr. and Escamilla, K. 1992. English acquisition by fluent and limited Spanish proficient Mexican Americans in a three-year maintenance bilingual program. *Hispanic Journal of Behavioral Sciences* 14: 252–67.

Merino, B.J., Trueba, H.T., and Santiago, F.A. (eds.). 1993. *Language and culture in learning: Teaching Spanish to native speakers of Spanish.* London: Falmer Press.

Michaels, S. 1986. Narrative presentations: An oral preparation for literacy with first graders. In J. Cook-Gumperz (ed.), *The Social Construction of Literacy.* New York: Cambridge University Press, pp. 94–116.

Mohatt, G. & Erickson, F. 1981. Cultural differences in teaching styles in an Odawa school: A sociolinguistic approach. In: H. Trueba, P. Guthrie, and K. Au (eds.), *Culture and the bilingual classroom: Studies in classroom ethnography.* New York: Newbury House, pp. 105–119

Moll, L. 1992. Bilingual classrooms and community analysis: Some recent trends. *Educational Researcher* 21(2):20–24.

Moll, L. 1995. Bilingual classroom studies and community analysis. In: O. García and C. Baker (eds.), *Policy and practice in bilingual education.* Clevedon: Multilingual Matters, pp. 273–280.

Morales Carrión, A. 1983. *Puerto Rico: A political and cultural history.* New York: W.W. Norton & Co.

Murphy, H. 2002. TWI evaluation and bilingual committee report. Presented to the Evanston/Skokie School District 65 Board of Education Meeting. Evanstan/Skokie, Illinois: unpublished.

National Center for Research on Cultural Diversity and Second Language Learning. 1996. *Learning together: Two-way bilingual immersion programs.* Santa Cruz: The University of California, Santa Cruz.

National Clearinghouse for Bilingual Education. 2000. *If your child learns in two languages.* Washington D.C.: NCBE.

National Clearinghouse for Bilingual Education. 2000. *Si su niño aprende en dos idiomas.* Washington D.C.: George Washington University.

National Foreign Language Center. 1995. *Heritage languages in the national interest.* Washington D.C.: NFLC.

National Study of School Evaluation. 2002. *Program Evaluation: English as a second language.* Indicators of Schools of Quality Program Evaluation Series. Schaumburg, Illinois: NSSE.

Ochs, E. 1988. *Culture and language development: Language acquisition and language socialization in a Samoan village.* New York: Cambridge University Press.

Olsen, L., Bhattacharya, J., Chow, M., Jaramillo, A., Tobiassen, D.P., and Solorio, J. 2001. *And still we speak: Stories of communities sustaining and reclaiming language and culture.* Oakland: California Tomorrow.

Omaggio Hadley, A. 2000. *Teaching language in context.* Boston: Heinle & Heinle.

Padilla, A.M., Lindholm, K.J., Chen, A., Duran, R., Hakuta, K., Lambert, W.E., and Tucker, G.R. 1991. The English-only movements: Myths, reality, and implications for psychology. American Psychologist 46: 120–130.

Pennsylvania Department of Education. 2002. *A guidebook for planning programs for English language learners.* Harrisburg: PDE.

Peregoy, S. and Boyle, O. 1997. *Reading, writing, and learning in ESL: A resource book for K–8 teachers.* New York: Longman.

Perez, B., McCarty, T., Watahomigie, L., Torres-Guzman, M., Dien, T., Chang, J., Smith, H and Dávila de Silva, A. 1998. *Sociocultural contexts of language and literacy.* Mahwah: Lawrence Erlbaum.

Peyton, J., Ranard, D. and McGinnis, S. 2001. Charting a new course: Heritage language education in the United States. In: Peyton, J., D. Ranard, and S. McGinnis (eds.), *Heritage languages in America: Preserving a national resource.* McHenry: Delta Systems Co., Inc, pp. 3–26.

Philips, S.U. 1983. *The invisible culture: Communication in the classroom and community on the Warm Springs Indian Reservation.* New York: Longman.

Pica, T., Young, R. and Doughty, C. 1987. The impact of interaction on comprehension. *TESOL Quarterly* 21(4): 737–58.

Ramirez, J.D., Yuen, S.D., and Ramey, D.R. 1991. *Executive summary final report: Longitudinal study of structures English immersion strategy, early-exit and late-exit transitional bilingual education programs for language minority children.* San Mateo: Aguirre International.

Rampton, B. 1995. *Crossing language and ethnicity among adolescents.* New York: Longman.

Rand Reading Study Group. 2002. *Reading for understanding: Toward an R&D program in reading comprehension.* Report prepared for the Office of Educational Research and Improvement. Santa Monica: RAND.

Romaine, S. 1989. *Bilingualism.* Oxford: Basil Blackwell.

Rubin, J. 1977. Bilingual education and language planning. In: B. Spolsky and R.L. Cooper, R.L. (eds.), *Frontiers of bilingual education.* Rowley: Newbury House, pp. 282–294.

Ruíz, R. 1984. Orientations in language planning. *NABE Journal* 8(2): 15–34.

Ruíz, R. 1990. Official languages and language planning. In: K. Adams, and D. Brink, (eds.), *Perspectives on Official English*, pp. 11–24.

Sacks, H., Schegloff, E., and Jefferson, G. 1974. A simplest systematics for the organization of turn-taking in conversation. *Language* 50: 696–735.

Saville-Troike, M. 1996. The ethnography of communication. In: S. McKay, and N. Hornberger, (eds.), *Sociolinguistics and language teaching.* New York: Cambridge University Press, pp. 351–382.

Schieffelin, B. and Ochs, E. (eds.). 1990. *Language socialization across cultures.* Cambridge: Cambridge University Press.

Schieffelin, B., Woolard K., and Kroskrity, P.V. (eds.). 1998. *Language ideologies: Practice and theory.* New York: Oxford University Press.

Schiffrin, D. 1994. *Approaches to discourse.* Cambridge: Basil Blackwell.

Schlicher, R. 2003. Practical applications to implementing English language proficiency standards. Presented at Washington D.C.: TESOL Academy.

Scollon, R. and Scollon, S.B.K. 1981. *Narrative, literacy, and face in interethnic communication.* Norwood: Ablex.

Shultz, J. and Cook-Sather, A. (eds.), 2000. *In our own words: Students' perspectives on school.* Boulder: Rowan & Littlefield.

Snow, C.E., Burns, M.S., and Griffin, P. 1998. *Preventing reading difficulties in young children.* Washington, D.C.: National Academy Press.

Snow, C.E., Met, M. and Genesee, F. 1992. A conceptual framework for the integration of language and content instruction. In: P.A. Richard-Amato, and M.A. Snow, (eds.), *The multicultural classroom: Readings for content-area teachers.* New York: Longman.

Standards for foreign language learning: Preparing for the 21st century. 1999. Yonkers: National Standards in Foreign Language Education Project.

Stefanakis, E.H. 2002. *Multiple intelligences and portfolios: A window into the learner's mind.* Portsmouth: Heinemann.

Street, B.V. 1993. *Cross-cultural approaches to literacy.* New York: Cambridge.

Street, B.V. 1995. *Social literacies: Critical approaches to literacy in development, ethnography, and education.* New York: Longman.

Street, B.V. 2000. Literacy events and literacy practices: Theory and practice in the new literacy studies. In: M. Martin-Jones, and K. Jones (eds.), *Multilingual literacies.* Philadelphia: John Benjamins.

Swain, M. and Lapkin, S. 1982. *Evaluating bilingual education: A Canadian case study.* Clevedon: Multilingual Matters.

Swain, M. 1985. Communicative competence: Some roles of comprehensible input and comprehensible output in its development. In: S.M. Gass and C.G. Madden (eds.), *Input in second language acquisition.* Rowley: Newbury House, pp. 235–253.

Tannen, D. 1993. What's in a frame: Surface evidence for underlying expectations. In: Tannen, D. (ed.), *Framing in discourse.* New York: Oxford University Press, pp. 14–56.

Teachers of English to Speakers of Other Languages. 1997. *ESL standards for pre-K–12 students.* Alexandria: TESOL.

Thomas, W. and Collier, V. 2002. *A National study of school effectiveness for language minority students' long term academic achievement.* Santa Cruz: Center for Research, Education, Diversity and Excellence, University of CA, Santa Cruz.

Tucker, G. R. 1999. A global perspective on bilingualism and bilingual education. *ERIC Digest.* Washington, D.C.: ERIC Clearinghouse on Languages and Linguistics.